DATE DUE

P9-APJ-171

THE SOVIET UNION
a half-century of communism

PUBLISHED IN CO-OPERATION WITH
THE INSTITUTE FOR SINO-SOVIET STUDIES
THE GEORGE WASHINGTON UNIVERSITY

International Conference on World Politics, 6th, Berlin, 1967
[1]

THE SOVIET UNION
a half-century of communism

edited by Kurt London

THE JOHNS HOPKINS PRESS
Baltimore, Maryland

Manufactured in the United States of America
Library of Congress Catalog Card Number 68–28874

Originally published, 1968

Johns Hopkins Paperbacks edition, 1968

TABLE OF CONTENTS

CONTRIBUTORS

JOHN A. ARMSTRONG
Professor of Political Science, University of Wisconsin, Madison, Wisconsin

FREDERICK C. BARGHOORN
Professor of Political Science, Yale University, New Haven, Connecticut

ROBERT A. FELDMESSER
Associate Professor of Sociology, Dartmouth College, Hanover, New Hampshire

ANDREW GYORGY
Professor of International Affairs, Institute for Sino-Soviet Studies, The George Washington University, Washington, D.C.

JOHN P. HARDT
Professorial Lecturer in Economics, Institute for Sino-Soviet Studies, The George Washington University, Washington, D.C., and Head of the Strategic Studies Department, Research Analysis Corporation, McLean, Virginia

DAN N. JACOBS
Professor of Russian Government, Miami University, Oxford, Ohio

HARISH KAPUR
Professor of International Relations, The Graduate Institute of International Studies, Geneva, Switzerland

ROMAN KOLKOWICZ
Senior Staff Member, Institute for Defense Analyses, Arlington, Virginia, and Visiting Professor of Foreign Affairs at the University of Virginia

KURT LONDON
Professor of International Affairs and Director, Institute for Sino-Soviet Studies, The George Washington University, Washington, D.C.

KLAUS MEHNERT
Professor of Political Science and Director, Institute of Political Science, Technical University, Aachen, Germany, and editor of *Osteuropa*

BORIS MEISSNER
Member of the Directorate of the Federal Institute for Research in East European and International Studies, Cologne, and Professor of Law and Director, Institute of East European Law, University of Cologne, West Germany

CARL MODIG
Staff member of the Research Analysis Corporation and graduate student at The George Washington University, Washington, D.C.

OTTO SCHILLER
Professor of Comparative Agrarian Policy and Rural Sociology at the South Asia Institute, University of Heidelberg, West Germany, and Director of the Research Centre for Agrarian Structure and Rural Cooperatives, Heidelberg

H. GORDON SKILLING
Professor of Political Science, University of Toronto, Toronto, Canada, and Director, Centre for Russian and East European Studies

ROBERT C. TUCKER
Professor of Politics and Director, Program in Russian Studies, Princeton University, Princeton, New Jersey

THOMAS W. WOLFE
Senior Staff Member of the RAND Corporation, Washington, D.C.

EDITOR'S INTRODUCTION

I

Celebrations of political or military jubilees have been popular since man invented the calendar. They serve as occasions for parades, memorials, and political reminders. Such magic anniversaries as 25, 50, 75, or 100 years have become milestones on the road to life's relentless denouement—and windfalls for mass communication media.

For the masters of propaganda and the henchmen of totalitarian isms, commemorative numbers games have always played singularly important roles. They were used as pegs on which to hang political campaigns. The higher the number, the more impressive the celebration. Thus the fiftieth anniversary of the Bolshevik Revolution set in motion mammoth ceremonies in the Soviet Union and aroused considerable attention elsewhere. Even in our fast-paced era, half a century is a long time for humans; surely it is enough to gain sufficient distance for a relatively detached analysis and a preliminary summing up of the event.

There can be no doubt that this anniversary was an occasion of considerable significance, for the Revolution had an extraordinary impact on world affairs and social relations. It is therefore fitting that scholars studying Soviet affairs should meet and exchange views with their colleagues in an atmosphere conducive to free discussion. Such a meeting took place from September 4 to 8, 1967, in West Berlin. Within the framework of the Sixth International Conference on World Politics, it set itself the task of reviewing and evaluating the most important aspects of fifty years of Soviet rule. This book contains a selection of the papers presented at that conference.

II

The evolution of this series of international conferences has been described in the introductions to previous anthologies.* In all, thirty-four participants attended from eleven countries in North America, Europe, Africa, Asia, and Australia; some fifty observers came from fourteen countries.

As in the five previous conferences, the consensus of the participants and the Steering Committee was that scholars from communist-ruled countries should be excluded. It was taken for granted that they would have felt constrained to transmit the official line of their parties or governments with which the participants were familiar. In any event, it was deemed unlikely that communist scholars would have been permitted to attend a meeting in West Berlin, the locus chosen for the conference because it was the headquarters of the sponsoring organizations.

In selecting the papers to appear in this book, the editor and the publisher's review board were guided by two main considerations: substance and economics. The conference agenda was so full that the focus of this volume had to be narrowed; it was not intended that we publish a quasi-encyclopedic work. In addition, publishing costs had to be taken into account. Since the quality of the papers was generally high, I regret that not all of them could be included.

As was to be expected, there was no unanimity of opinion on the subjects discussed. Most scholars expressed individual

* Kurt London, ed., *Unity and Contradiction: Major Aspects of Sino-Soviet Relations* (New York: Praeger, 1962); *New Nations in a Divided World: International Relations of the Non-Aligned Afro-Asian Countries* (New York: Praeger, 1964); and *Eastern Europe in Transition* (Baltimore: The Johns Hopkins Press, 1966).

interpretations of events, and there was considerable disagreement over the character of the changes that have occurred in the Soviet Union since Khrushchev came to power. The absence of consensus, however, must be judged a positive, not a negative, result. The differing views and approaches were a measure of the liveliness of the interchange and the exploration of complex questions to which there are no sure or simple answers.

III

Soviet representatives had been most anxious to discover all they could concerning how the "imperialist" countries, especially the United States, would observe the fiftieth anniversary of the Bolshevik victory. This interest was conveyed to me repeatedly. I do not know what they expected. But their behavior toward the Berlin conference, which they began to attack two days before its opening, reflected what seemed an inordinate sensitivity.

Their attacks came against the background of a decree by the Soviet Communist Party Central Committee, published in *Pravda* on August 22, 1967, concerning "the measures to be taken to further develop the social sciences and to increase their role in building communism." Basically this decree is a pep talk to students of the social sciences which follows the line of the October, 1964, Plenum of the C.P.S.U. Central Committee and the Twenty-third C.P.S.U. Congress. The decree indicates a need for more indoctrination and ideological guidance in the field of philosophy, economics, history, law, and "scientific communism." Foremost attention in scientific research is to be devoted to Marxist-Leninist methodology and to the principles of the party's historical approach to social phenomena:

The most important aim of the social sciences is to conduct a systematic offensive struggle against anticommunism, thoroughly criticize contemporary bourgeois philosophy, sociology, historiography, law, and the economic theories of capitalist apologists; expose the falsifiers of Marxist-Leninist ideas, the history of the developing society, and the communist and workers' movement; and give a decisive rebuff to the displays of both "right" and "left" wing revisionism and national narrow-mindedness, both in their theory and policy.

In the spirit of this decree, a harsh attack against the conference was published by *Komsomolskaya Pravda* on September 2, 1967—two days before the conference opened. In an article entitled "The Specialists," signed by one Y. E. Kubichev, the conference was previewed as a well-planned "global attack" against Soviet ideas, society, and accomplishments. Aware that many meetings were to be held in the United States and elsewhere to observe the fiftieth anniversary of the Bolshevik Revolution in its various aspects, Kubichev chose to represent all such gatherings as little more than anti-Soviet provocations. What apparently irked him most, however, was the fact that the Sixth International Conference on World Politics was to take place in West Berlin:

> The fact that West Berlin had been especially selected as the place for the next regular anti-Soviet meeting makes one wonder at the flagrant political myopia of the present "town fathers" and West Berlin political figures who persistently strive to transform West Berlin into an all-European center for provocations and diversions now to include the ideological.

It is indeed a matter of regret that political myopia, to use Kubichev's term, should have prompted the automatic assumption that the choice of West Berlin was politically motivated. And it is regrettable that the label "anti-Soviet" should be attached almost by rote to every such conference. The international academic community is aware, of course, of the character and record of the two organizations that made this meeting possible. The Deutsche Osteuropa Gesellschaft, an institution almost as old as the Soviet Union itself, has enjoyed a fine reputation for decades for its scholarly research and publications; the East European Institute, a research and teaching organization not concerned primarily with contemporary affairs, has an equally fine reputation.

Given the Soviet public position on West Berlin, it is perhaps understandable that the Sixth International Conference on

World Politics would have occasioned a vocal reaction from Soviet propagandists while its predecessors did not. The sensitivities prompting it may be regarded as more emotional and propagandistic than rational. Even so, one can only wonder at the rancor of Kubichev's assault on the meeting as "a gathering of Hitler's remnants, hangmen, and spies." He lashed out at certain German scholars with charges of active collaboration with the Nazi regime and indicted one American scholar for membership in the Office of Strategic Services during World War II—at a time when the Soviet Union was allied with the West! Condemning the conference before the fact, the substance of the contributions and discussion yet to be heard, he attacked personalities. The depth of the xenophobic sensitivity reflected in his article is revealed particularly in the following passage:

This loathsome portrait gallery, using the respectable front of a "scientific" conference as its cover, could be continued but we think the nature of the gathering is clear enough. The "ears" of C.I.A. and Gehlen's intelligence operation are clearly evident behind the academic apparance of these hardened anti-Soviets. . . . Thousands of similar anti-Soviet gatherings have been held by our enemies during the fifty years of existence of the Soviet state. In the opinion of their initiators they were to become "bombs" in the global anti-communist campaign to "crush" communism.

Pravda on September 11, 1967, published an article entitled "Barking From Behind the Fence" in which the conference was again severely critized:

. . . By now even the most possessed anticommunists have learned that October has transformed our motherland into the greatest socialist country of the world. The enemies of communism can essentially only try to downgrade the world-shaking historical conquests of socialism in order to prevent newly-emerged nations from entering the same path. And they are straining themselves, utilizing every weapon in their secret arsenal, mobilizing all their reserves, in a feverish effort to scrape together a bit of mud and throw it into the shining edifice of victorious socialism. . . .

It seems to this writer that intellectual "bridge-building," at least between the United States and the Soviet Union, remains more a hope than an imminent reality. It is a matter of deep regret that the chasm between Western and Soviet concepts is so deep that every Western attempt at developing a broader understanding of the Soviet Union is regarded a priori as suspect by the Soviet authorities.

IV

As the editor of this volume, I should like to express my deepest appreciation to those organizations which made the conference possible. They are, as already mentioned, the Deutsche Osteuropa Gesellschaft and the East European Institute of the Free University of Berlin, as well as the Senate of the city of West Berlin. Thanks are also due to the Dutch Secretariat, created with the help of Major General Dr. M. W. J. M. Broekmeijer of The Hague, whose members came to Berlin to render invaluable service to the conference and to assist the representative of the Osteuropa Gesellschaft, Dr. Ernst von Eicke, in his difficult preparatory work. I am also grateful for the co-operative spirit of the contributors to this volume and of those authors whose papers could not be included.

I am greatly indebted to Mrs. Tybel Litwin for her invaluable and knowledgeable editorial assistance and to Miss Sally Jansen for preparing the manuscript.

Institute for Sino-Soviet Studies   KURT LONDON
The George Washington University
Washington, D.C.

THE HISTORIC FRAMEWORK

Paths of Communist Revolution, 1917–67

Robert C. Tucker

I

That the revolution of October, 1917, was of tremendous importance in the national history of Russia is a point that needs no arguing. With the advent of its fiftieth anniversary, it is natural that its impact upon various aspects of Russia's development should be scrutinized. The present essay addresses itself to a different but related task. It is concerned with the Russian Revolution as part of a larger historical process. In the fifty years since it occurred, there have been successful communist revolutions in thirteen other countries, which, together with Soviet Russia, comprise about a third of the globe's land surface and population. In these pages I want to consider Russia's October as one of fourteen communist revolutions in the twentieth century. The subject is the comparative politics of communist revolution.

Classical Marxism—the thought of Marx and Engels—projected the communist revolution as a universal phenomenon. The goal it foresaw for *Weltgeschichte* was a planetary communist society wherein man would realize his essential creative nature, having overcome by the socialization of private property the alienation endured in the course of history. Although the arenas of proletarian communist revolution would be national, the revolutionary movement would not and could not be confined to one or a few major nations but would overflow national boundaries, owing to the emergence of large-scale

3

machine industry and a world market linking all countries in the bourgeois period. Thus the *Communist Manifesto* spoke of the communist revolution as occurring initially in "the leading civilized countries at least." In a first draft of the document, Engels had written that "the communist revolution will not be national only but will take place simultaneously in all civilized countries, i.e., at any rate in Britain, America, France and Germany."[1] The communist revolution would be no less universal than its historical predecessor, the bourgeois revolution, for the world that the proletarians had to win was one that capitalism itself was fast transforming into a socioeconomic unit.

Not surprisingly, the theory of the world communist revolution underwent significant modification in the movement of thought from classical to communist Marxism, or Marxism according to Lenin. In 1915 Lenin laid down "uneven economic and political development" as an absolute law of capitalism and deduced from it that a communist revolution was possible in several capitalist countries or even in one such country taken singly. He added: "The victorious proletariat of that country, having expropriated the capitalists and organized its own socialist production, would stand up *against* the rest of the world, the capitalist world, attracting to its cause the oppressed classes of other countries, raising revolts in those countries against the capitalists, and in the event of necessity coming out even with armed force against the exploiting classes and their states."[2] In the wake of the Russian revolution of February, 1917, which overthrew the Tsar, Lenin's party attempted to enact this revolutionary scenario. After taking power in October, however, their efforts to raise revolts in other countries had little success, the revolutionary outbreaks in Hungary and Germany were abortive, and the venture in revolutionary war in Poland in 1920 ended in failure. A Communist International was brought into existence under Russian auspices to promote communist revolutions in other countries, but the latter showed few signs of materializing.

Despite this fact the Russian communist mind held tenaciously to the view that the October Revolution was no mere national event but represented the beginning of a world revolution. "This first victory *is not yet the final victory*," declared Lenin in an address on the fourth anniversary of October. "We have made a start. When, at what date and time, and the proletarians of which nation will complete this process is not a matter of importance. The important thing is that the ice has been broken; the road is open and the path has been blazed."[3] Even in his last essay, written in March, 1923, in the shadow of approaching death, Lenin optimistically maintained that "the whole world is now passing into a movement which must give rise to a world socialist revolution." Significantly, however, what then sustained his confidence in the final outcome was not the immediate prospect of a communist revolution in "the counter-revolutionary imperialist West" but developments in "the revolutionary and nationalist East." In the last analysis, he wrote, the upshot of the struggle would be determined by the fact that Russia, India, China, etc., accounted for the overwhelming majority of the population of the globe: "And it is precisely this majority that, during the past few years, has been drawn into the struggle for emancipation with extraordinary rapidity, so that in this respect there cannot be the slightest shadow of doubt what the final outcome of the world struggle will be. In this sense, the complete victory of socialism is fully and absolutely assured."[4]

The universalistic significance of the Russian Revolution remains a basic postulate of communist ideology at the present time. In the opening words of the new Program of the Communist Party of the Soviet Union, adopted in October, 1961, "the great October Socialist Revolution ushered in a new era in the history of mankind, the era of the downfall of capitalism and the establishment of communism." The communist revolutions in Asia and Europe following the Second World War are viewed as a continuation of a world revolutionary process initiated in Russia at the close of the First World War; and the process itself is depicted as one that is destined ultimately to embrace the entire world. The Soviet literature on the fiftieth anniversary of October stresses this theme heavily and is replete with denunciation of Western scholars for refusing to acknowledge the "world-historical" character of the Russian Revolution. Thus, the author of an editorial in the journal of party history dismisses as erroneous the opinion of the American historian Robert V. Daniels that "the Russian revolution was not a national instance of a presumed international trend toward proletarian revolution, but a distinctive national event" and that "with all its international trappings and designs, communism remains a specifically Russian movement, a product of Russian society, Russian ideas, the Russian revolution, and Russian power." The Soviet writer affirms, in opposition to such a notion, "the indisputable fact that the experience of the first victorious socialist revolution has universal significance, that certain features of the October Revolution reflect basic regularities of social development inherent in our epoch."[5] And the "Theses" of the C.P.S.U. Central Committee on the fiftieth anniversary state simply: "The October Revolution marked the beginning of the transition from capitalism to socialism throughout the world."[6]

These contentions raise a series of important theoretical questions that are still in need of clarification and solution. Was the October Revolution the Russian expression of a revolutionary process that is not specifically Russian even though it occurred first in Russia and has been heavily influenced by this fact? Was it the national Russian form of a wider communist revolution going on in the contemporary world? If so, is the communist revolution to be seen in universalistic terms, as a developing *world* revolution? On the basis of the fourteen communist revolutions that have occurred, what generalizations can be drawn concerning its nature? And, finally, is it possible to construct a typology of communist revolutions, with special reference to the manner in which communism comes, or has come, to power? Recognizing that a definitive treatment of these questions is beyond the scope of the present essay, I should like, nevertheless, to outline some answers and my reasons for offering them.

‖

Although it originated in Russia and bears a host of Russian birthmarks and influences, communism is not accurately described as a "specifically Russian movement." The familiar analogy with the history of religions remains relevant. A religion that arises in one nation and reflects its spirit can nevertheless spread and take root elsewhere; and it can do this even though it may initially spread through conquest and forcible conversion. Such is the case with communism as an ideological movement professing "Marxism-Leninism" as its credo. Russia's communist revolution was the first and in some ways the precondition of others still to come, and its leaders have striven incessantly to play a hegemonic role in communist revolution wherever it occurs. The spread of communist revolution beyond Soviet borders in the wake of the Second World War was assisted, and in numerous countries even engineered, by the Soviet Union. Yet the non-Russian communist revolutions cannot be satisfactorily explained as a mere cover for Soviet imperialism or Russian expansion. Communist revolutions enlist indigenous forces in the societies concerned and tend to develop—even when initially imposed from without, as in Rumania—an internal dynamic of their own. There is thus some truth in the Soviet thesis that Russia's communist revolution was only the beginning of a larger process of revolutionary change taking place in the twentieth century, that it was no mere national Russian phenomenon. This does not, however, imply that the communist revolution is destined to become world-wide. In order to pass judgment on that question, it may be of use to inquire into the character of communist revolutions.

It has often been noted—and remains notable—that communist revolutions have not occurred on the model projected by classical Marxism. For Marx and Engels the revolutionary overthrow of bourgeois society was something inherent in the very dynamics of capitalism as a mode of production based on wage labor and the drive to maximize profit. Their argument is complex and need not be repeated here in detail. Suffice it to

7

say that capitalist economic development, in Marx's view, necessarily brings a proletarianization of the masses of factory workers and a progressive worsening of their living and working conditions. Marx formulates it as the "absolute general law of capitalist accumulation" that "the accumulation of wealth at one pole of society involves a simultaneous accumulation of poverty, labor torment, slavery, ignorance, brutalization, and moral degradation at the opposite pole—where dwells the class that produces its own product in the form of capital."[7]   At the postulated point in this process where conditions become wholly intolerable, the masses of workers revolt and with the seizure and socialization of private property, the communist revolution occurs.   Thus, classical Marxism envisaged the communist revolution as a *revolution of capitalist breakdown* occurring in the most advanced stage of development of the capitalist system. This was the assumption underlying the expectation of Marx and Engels that communist revolutions would come first in the countries of Western Europe where capitalism was most highly developed.

History, however, has diverged in two fundamental ways from their theory. First, capitalist societies, instead of suffering self-destruction in a proletarian upheaval, have gone through a process of self-modification that Marx would not have thought possible and for which his theory, in any event, made no provision. In violation of the "absolute general law of capitalist accumulation," the industrial worker has won improved conditions and has become more and more integrated into the society rather than more alienated from it. Capitalist economies have evolved into post-capitalist, mixed economies with self-stabilizing tools of fiscal regulation and planning. Although significant communist movements still exist in some of these societies— Italy and France in particular—what prospects they may have of coming to power do not derive from the dynamics of capitalist development. No communist revolution has taken place on the classical Marxist model, and no such revolution seems likely. Indeed, societies that have experienced thorough-going capitalist development appear to be among the least likely prospects for communist revolution.

If classical Marxism erred in projecting the communist revolution in a form in which it would not occur, it likewise erred in failing to foresee the revolution in the form in which it *would* occur. The communist revolution has not come about as a revolution of capitalist breakdown; large-scale industrialization has been among its consequences rather than its causes. It does, however, show a certain general pattern. With but two exceptions (Czechoslovakia and East Germany), the typical habitat of communist revolution has been a country of precapitalist or, at most, semicapitalist economic formation, and one which shows a tendency to stagnate in its further economic development and modernization. It has been a country heavily populated with peasants and dependent upon agriculture although usually with at least a small industrial working class and some development of modern industrial economy; a socially and politically as well as economically backward country, with very sharp class divisions and political institutions of traditional authoritarian complexion. Finally, it has been a country with chronic social unrest and a radical intelligentsia ready to furnish the leadership of a mass-based revolutionary movement to overthrow the old order in the name of national renovation and development. Russia and China are both classic cases in all these respects.

The communist revolution—insofar as we can draw a generalization concerning its nature on the basis of these facts—is *a revolution of underdevelopment,* and is this in two senses: (1) it typically comes about in the setting of underdevelopment just described; and (2) it becomes, after the achievement of power by the communist movement, a long-term effort to overcome the country's underdevelopment, a revolution of modernization. The communist revolution is not the sole or necessary form of the revolution of underdevelopment. In some countries, particularly since the end of the Second World War, there have been attempts to carry through such a revolution under noncommunist nationalist leadership, which, however, usually borrows some aspects of communist experience and organizational technique. The most that communism might reasonably claim is to have been so far the most influential and in certain respects the most efficacious form of the revolution of underdevelopment. Its notable disadvantage lies in the peculiarly great difficulty that it experiences in coming to power. In the Arab Middle East, for example, the revolution of underdevelopment has proceeded—where it has proceeded at all—under nationalist rather than communist auspices, not because the nationalist political forces can carry it through most successfully but because no indigenous communist movement has been capable of competing with nationalist revolutionary groups in the contest for power.

A further general observation concerning communist revolution relates to international war as its chrysalis. If, in a flight of fantasy, we imagine the leading representatives of the capitalist countries coming together in secret conclave around the year 1910 to organize a long-range conspiracy for the prevention of communism, it is easy to see in retrospect what could have proved to be a simple but quite effective conspiratorial formula: no war. For, without the two world wars of our century, it is not at all certain that any communist movement anywhere would have come to power. The fabric of Russian government, economy, and society was so strained by the First World War that Bolshevism, under the inspired leadership of Lenin and Trotsky, was able to maneuver itself to power in the chaotic conditions that ensued with the deposition of the tsar. It is notable that when news of the February revolution reached Lenin in Switzerland, he immediately saw it as a revolution engendered by the war; and in one of the last of his writings, he still spoke of the Russian Revolution as "the revolution that broke out in connection with the first imperialist world war."[8] Moreover, if the initial communist revolution took place in Russia as a result of the First World War, communism came to Eastern and Central Europe, China, Korea, and Vietnam as a direct outgrowth of the Second World War. On the one hand, Soviet occupation of neighboring lands at the war's end created conditions in which communist regimes could come to power. On the other hand, the war so strained the fabric of some societies—most notably China's—that communist revolution could take place in the aftermath independently of Soviet help.

The organic connection between international war and the spread of communist revolution became an axiom of Soviet thought in the Stalinist era. Should a new war come, Stalin declared in his report to the Seventeenth Party Congress in 1934, it would be a most dangerous war for the bourgeoisie: "And let not Messieurs the bourgeoisie blame us if some of the governments near and dear to them, which today rule happily 'by the grace of God,' are missing on the morrow of such a war."[9] Still earlier, in a speech delivered to a closed session of the party Central Committee on January 19, 1925, Stalin had envisaged the policy that the Soviet Union should follow in the event of a new European war. He observed that conditions were maturing for such a war, and he urged that everthing be done to strengthen the Soviet army. Then he went on: "Our banner is still the banner of *peace*. But if war breaks out we shall not be able to sit with folded arms. We shall have to take action, but we shall be the last to do so. And we shall do so in order to throw the decisive weight in the scales, the *weight* that can turn the scales."[10] In the latter part of the 1930's, Stalin attempted to make events unfold according to this plan by seeking an agreement with Hitler. He knew that the Nazi-Soviet pact of August, 1939, would unleash war, but he calculated that it would be a long-drawn-out war between the Axis states and the western allies, a war in which the U.S.S.R. would remain free to "throw the decisive weight in the scales" at a time of its choosing. Stalin's error—an error made by many at the time—lay in overestimating the strength of France, whose swift defeat in 1940 laid Russia open to the invasion that duly followed.[11] But, despite this terribly costly miscarriage of Stalin's plans, Russia emerged victorious, and communist revolutions took place in numerous countries in the aftermath. The link between international war and the spread of communism was thus further strengthened in the Stalinist mind, and many

Soviet pronouncements in Stalin's last years warned that a third world war would witness the final collapse of the capitalist system. Furthermore, Stalin insisted in his final work, *Economic Problems of Socialism in the U.S.S.R.* (1952), that wars would remain inevitable, as Lenin had written, so long as "imperialism" continued to exist. "To liquidate the inevitability of war," he concluded, "it is necessary to eliminate imperialism."[12]

The notion that world communist revolution can continue in peaceful international conditions is a post-Stalinist innovation in Soviet party doctrine. At the Twentieth Party Congress in 1956, the Leninist-Stalinist thesis on the inseparability of imperialism and wars was finally revised, wars were declared to be avoidable calamities in the nuclear age, and the novel idea was put forward that international peace and coexistence might prove propitious for the further spread of communist revolution. "Socialist revolution is not necessarily connected with war," proclaims the new Soviet party program in this connection. "Although both world wars, which were started by the imperialists, culminated in socialist revolutions, revolutions are quite feasible without war." This proposition is accompanied by the thesis—also promulgated at the Twentieth Party Congress—that a communist revolution can, and if possible should, take place along a peaceful parliamentary path. Under favorable conditions, asserts the party program, the working class can "win a solid majority in parliament, transform it from a tool serving the class interests of the bourgeoisie into an instrument serving the working people, launch a broad mass struggle outside parliament, smash the resistance of the reactionary forces and provide the necessary conditions for a peaceful socialist revolution."[13] In various Soviet statements during the Khrushchevian era, the Hungarian revolution of 1918–19 and the communist conquest of power in Czechoslovakia in February, 1948, were cited as historical examples of communist revolution without civil war; and underdeveloped countries with parliamentary institutions were described as the most likely contemporary proving-grounds for communist revolution by the peaceful path. Since the fall of Khrushchev the doctrine of peaceful communist revolution has been de-emphasized in Soviet writings but not repudiated. It is noteworthy in this connection that the Central Committee's "Theses" for the fiftieth anniversary of the October Revolution reaffirm "the possibility of using, in the transition to socialism, diverse—peaceful and non-peaceful—forms of struggle, depending on the concrete relationship of class forces in this or that country. . . ."[14]

The new Soviet doctrine on the possibility of peaceful communist revolution proved highly controversial in the international communist movement and has been one of the central issues in the Sino-Soviet ideological dispute that began in the aftermath of the Twentieth Party Congress. The leader of the Chinese communist revolution, Mao Tse-tung, who had once written that "political power grows out of the barrel of a gun,"[15] and continued to believe it, undertook to defend Leninist-Stalinist orthodoxy on the methods of communist revolution against Khrushchevite "revisionism." During the conference of world communist leaders in Moscow in November, 1957, he took a stand on this issue against the effort of the Soviet party leadership to secure adoption of the Twentieth-Congress line as the general line of the world communist movement. In a then secret memorandum to the C.P.S.U. Central Committee outlining views on the question of peaceful transition, the Chinese delegation declared: "We must fully utilize the parliamentary form of struggle, but its role is limited." Using Lenin's line of argument in *The State and Revolution,* the Chinese memorandum stressed that a communist revolution necessitated the destruction of the old state machinery, for which purpose it would not be sufficient to gain a majority in Parliament. Hence the communist movement should be prepared to use armed force against the class enemy at the critical juncture of the revolution where power changes hands. In not a single country was the possibility of peaceful transition of any practical significance, and it would not be advisable to place much emphasis upon this possibility in a document published for the guidance of communist parties.[16]

When the controversy came into the open in the early 1960's, the tone was more acrid. The concept of the parliamentary road was now denounced by the Chinese leadership as "parliamentary cretinism." Violent revolution was said to be "a universal law of proletarian revolution." History, argued the Chinese, offered no precedent for peaceful transition to communism. Soviet claims that the October Revolution was "the most bloodless of all revolutions" were totally contrary to historical facts and a mockery of the martyrs who shed their blood to create the world's first communist state. The Hungarian revolution of 1918–19 was by no means a nonviolent affair or a model of peaceful transition, although, as Lenin himself had pointed out, the young Hungarian Communist party had committed the fatal error of not being sufficiently decisive in the use of force at the critical moment. Nor was the "February event" of 1948 in Prague describable as a "peaceful" conquest of power. And, contrary to the tales of the Arabian knights being spread by Khrushchev and his ilk, conditions were not now maturing for peaceful transitions to communism. To win a majority in Parliament or enter a coalition government owing to electoral success would only be an invitation to the kind of repression that overtook the Chilean Communist party in 1946. Acceptance of the revisionist line against armed struggle had cost the Algerian Communist party a position in its country's political life, and it had led the Iraqi Communist party to disaster in the anticommunist coup of 1958. In sum, "To realize socialism through the 'parliamentary road' is utterly impossible and is mere deceptive talk."[17]

Granted its revolutionary assumptions, the Chinese position is a strong one, just as Lenin's was in his debate with the Social Democrats a half-century ago. If the political essence of a communist revolution is the creation of a one-party state ruled by communists, it is hard to see how it could take place by peaceful parliamentary means. For the previously dominant noncommunist political forces could hardly be expected to submit peacefully not just to a temporary loss of power but to permanent exclusion from the possibility of regaining it by peaceful means. In order for nonviolent communist revolution to become a real possibility, it would be necessary to devise so insidious a technique of revolution by subversion that the forces being overthrown would hardly be aware of this fact before it was too late to resist. The fifty-year history of communist revolutions contains no instance that would exemplify such a pattern or point to its feasibility.

If peaceful parliamentary transition to communism is unlikely in the extreme, how are we to explain the Soviet espousal of the idea? It can be interpreted as a means by which a no longer radical and indeed post-revolutionary Soviet leadership tries to reconcile a continued *verbal* commitment to world communist revolution with a foreign policy whose real first objective is the peace and security of the Soviet Union.[18] Since the further spread of communist revolution would not, in this view, be a serious concern of the Soviet leadership, the unfeasibility of the peaceful parliamentary path would not stand in the way of its espousal in theory. Alternatively, it may be that some Soviet leaders are inclined to see peaceful transition to communism as a more than marginal possibility in historically unprecedented conditions now taking shape in certain parts of the world, such as the Arab Middle East. They may envisage the revolution of underdevelopment as eventually coming into communist receivership in certain countries where nationalist forces have begun it and where Soviet political influence has been built up through economic and military assistance, diplomacy, etc. Such a strategic conception may be implicit in a Soviet suggestion that "in present circumstances the question of the possibility of transition to socialism [i.e., to communism] *under conditions of a multi-party system* has topical significance for a number of countries."[19] The local communist party, in other words, would seek participation in a coalition government committed to carrying through the revolution of underdevelopment; and once it had achieved a foothold in power, it would strive—with judicious Soviet assistance on the side, or with Soviet protection— to maneuver its way to dominance, thereby bringing the revolution from the stage of so-called national democracy to that of people's democracy, i.e., to communism.

Such, in any event, is one construction that might reasonably be placed upon the Soviet writings in question. Whether the indicated tactics of revolution by political maneuver would have much chance of being applied successfully in practice is another matter. To form a reasoned opinion on this and related questions, it will be useful to examine the various paths that communist revolution has taken in the past.

IV

With respect to the manner of coming to power, the fourteen successful communist revolutions fall into three classes. Russia's communist revolution is in a class by itself. Those in Yugoslavia, Albania, China, Vietnam, and Cuba belong to the class of revolution by armed struggle; and those in Mongolia, North Korea, Poland, Bulgaria, Rumania, Hungary, East Germany, and Czechoslovakia fall into still a third class, that of the imposed revolution.

The October Revolution was a seizure of power by armed insurrection carried out in the capital and other main centers at a time of grave national crisis when the government lacked effective control, conditions were chaotic, and masses of people were in a revolutionary mood. The taking of power came at the climax of a period of intensive political preparation during which the Bolsheviks endeavored to stir up revolutionary sentiment with slogans like "land, peace, and bread," to cultivate mass support in the soviets and the country at large, and to isolate their left-wing competitors, the Socialist-Revolutionaries and Mensheviks. The revolutionary coup was thus the culminating event in a political process that involved mass agitation and propaganda, maneuvering for position in the soviets, and the organization of insurrection.

The relation of town and country, of worker and peasant, in the Bolshevik Revolution calls for special attention. In his final written comment on the revolution, Lenin spoke of certain "peculiar features" that distinguished it from earlier revolutions in Western Europe and foreshadowed the pattern the revolution would take in "passing to the Oriental countries." One was the fact that it combined the "peasant war" with the working-class movement under the special emergency conditions created by the world war.[20] The "peasant war" was the upheaval in the countryside during which peasants seized and divided the remaining landed estates. The Bolsheviks' encouragement of such action was one of the decisive factors in their revolutionary success, and the agrarian upheaval itself was undoubtedly an essential element of the October Revolution. Yet the countryside was, at least initially, the "rear" of the revolution; the major cities—above all, Petrograd and Moscow—were its "front." The revolutionary-minded industrial workers, although only a small minority of the Russian population, nevertheless constituted, along with elements of the armed forces, the spearhead of the Bolshevik movement's mass support, and the main urban centers were the strongholds of revolution. In this sense and to this extent the October Revolution was "proletarian," as it claimed to be. Without the "peasant war" as its companion piece, it probably would not have survived in power. But without the working-class support that it received in the major cities, it could hardly have taken place.

The events of 1917 represented, to a remarkable degree, the fulfillment of a vision of Russian revolution that Lenin had harbored since the turn of the century when he wrote his seminal work, *What Is To Be Done?* There he contended that socialist revolution would require long preparation and leadership by an elite party consisting primarily of professional revolutionaries, who would inculcate revolutionary ideas in the popular mind by propaganda and agitation. The party was thus conceived as the veritable lever of future revolution. But Lenin did not envisage this revolution in Blanquist terms as a conspiratorial coup d'état to be carried out, as it were, behind the backs of the people. The revolution itself, which would ensue after a series of revolutionary outbreaks alternating with periods of calm, would be a mass affair culminating in a national armed insurrection against the tsarist regime. It would draw its motivating force from large numbers of nonparty people—workers and others—who would engage in massive insurgency under the guidance and inspiration of the revolutionary party.

St. Petersburg's "Bloody Sunday" in January, 1905, touched

off a series of revolutionary outbreaks which did not subside until 1907. This revolution of 1905–07 was perhaps the most spontaneous large-scale insurrectionary movement to be seen in the twentieth century before the Hungarian uprising of 1956, and it influenced Leninist revolutionary thought profoundly. First, it revealed that the peasantry—which Russian Marxists previously had tended to view as a politically inert force and a support for tsarist despotism—actually possessed a far-reaching revolutionary potential. This in turn brought Lenin to his audacious conclusion that in a backward country like Russia, which had not yet experienced its "bourgeois revolution," it might be possible to create in the course of such a revolution a "revolutionary democratic dictatorship of the proletariat and peasantry." Here was a crucial component in the developing theory of communist revolution as a revolution of underdevelopment. Further, the 1905 revolution reinforced Lenin's assumption that the final assault upon the old order would come, if ever, at a time of mass revolutionary action and excitement. It confirmed his belief—expressed years later—that "revolutions are made at moments of particular upsurge and the exertion of all human capacities, by the class consciousness, will, passion and imagination of tens of millions, spurred on by a most acute struggle of classes."[21]

In the years between the first and the second Russian revolutions, Lenin elaborated this belief into a theory of the "revolutionary situation." For a Marxist, he wrote in 1915, it is beyond doubt that a revolution is impossible without a revolutionary situation, although such a situation can exist without necessarily giving rise to an actual revolution. There were three principal symptoms of a revolutionary situation: first, a crisis of the policy of the ruling class, creating a crack into which the discontent of the oppressed classes can penetrate; second, an aggravation of the sufferings of the oppressed classes beyond the ordinary level; third, a tendency of the latter, by virtue of the first two factors, to engage in mass revolutionary action. These views on revolution, added Lenin, "were confirmed particularly graphically for us Russians by the experience of 1905."[22] Nor did he ever abandon them. Indeed, in *Left-Wing*

Communism he formulated it as the fundamental law of revolution, which had been confirmed by all revolutions, including three Russian revolutions of the twentieth century, that "only when the *'lower classes'* do not want the old way and when the 'upper classes' *cannot carry on in the old way*—only then can revolution triumph. This truth may be expressed in other words: revolution is impossible without a nationwide crisis (affecting both the exploited and the exploiters)." Such a crisis, he went on, is characterized by the fact that at least a majority of the class-conscious, politically active workers fully understand that revolution is necessary and that the ruling classes are going through a government crisis which draws even the most backward masses into politics, weakens the government, and makes it possible for the revolutionaries to overthrow it rapidly.[23]

It was just such a situation that Lenin saw emerging in the spring of 1917, in large part because of the provisional government's unwillingness to take Russia out of a war that had become an intolerable burden for masses of the people. "Russia at present is seething," he wrote in early April, pointing out that "one of the chief symptoms of *every* real revolution is the unusually rapid, sudden and abrupt increase in the number of 'ordinary citizens' who begin to participate actively, independently and effectively in political life and in *the organization of the state*."[24] This is what led him to espouse a maximalist revolutionary policy of no support for the provisional government in the "April Theses" that he put out immediately upon his return from Switzerland to Petrograd. The dominant trend of on-the-spot opinion in the Bolshevik leadership was initially resistant, but it yielded to Lenin's forceful advocacy of the revolutionary slogan "All power to the soviets!" The further unfolding of events showed the soundness of his perception that Russia was in the midst of a true revolutionary situation, which, if properly taken advantage of by the Bolshevik party, could eventuate in a far more radical revolution than the one that had taken place in February.

In presenting the new doctrine of communist revolution by a peaceful parliamentary path, Khrushchev and others have pointed out that for a time in 1917 Lenin believed that the

Russian Revolution might take place peacefully in the framework of an assumption of state power by the revolutionary soviets. It is true that in his pamphlet "On Slogans," written in July, 1917, when the Bolsheviks were under severe harassment by the authorities, Lenin advocated abandonment of the slogan "All power to the soviets!" on the ground that it was a slogan for "a peaceful development of the revolution," which had been possible at first but which was so no longer.[25] But it is highly questionable whether Lenin ever seriously envisaged a revolutionary consummation without violence. Although revolution to his mind was essentially a process of *political* warfare against a form of society represented and upheld by the existing governmental regime, he appears to have taken it for granted that the final, decisive battle—the actual taking of power— would involve armed violence. Not even in a time of crisis, he wrote in the above-mentioned article of 1915, would the old government "fall" without being "dropped."[26] In *The State and Revolution,* on which he worked while in hiding in August and September of 1917, he corrected Marx's allowance for the possibility of a peaceful revolution in England and America by saying that conditions permitting such a development had changed in those countries since Marx's time; and he formulated it as a general principle that "the replacement of the bourgeois by the proletarian state is impossible without a violent revolution."[27]

Lenin's preferred title for the violent consummation of revolution at the point where power changes hands was "armed insurrection." In "Marxism and Insurrection," one of his series of secret letters to the party Central Committee in September and October of 1917 urging a coup without further delay, he laid the theoretical groundwork. Marxism was distinguished from Blanquism, he argued, not in its rejection of insurrection as a means of revolution, but rather in its insistence that successful insurrection must rely not simply upon conspiracy nor simply upon a party but upon a whole class, and, indeed, upon the rising revolutionary spirit of the people. Further, insurrection must be launched at the crucial moment in the history of the growing revolution, when revolutionary ferment in the popular ranks is at its height and vacillations in the ranks of the enemies and half-hearted friends of the revolution are strongest. Such a crucial moment was now at hand, he went on. Shortly afterward, in another communication to the same effect, he quoted Marx on the principal rules of insurrection as an art: (1) Never play with insurrection, but see it through to the end. (2) Concentrate a great superiority of forces at the decisive point at the decisive moment. (3) Once the insurrection has started, act with the greatest determination and take the offensive. (4) Try to take the enemy by surprise. (5) Strive for daily successes, even if small. The success of the Russian and world revolutions, Lenin concluded, would depend on two or three days of fighting.[28] Insofar as the Russian Revolution was concerned, events shortly afterward proved him right.

V

"The world-historic significance of the October Revolution," assert the Central Committee's "Theses" on its fiftieth anniversary, "lies in the fact that it pointed out the paths, uncovered the forms and methods of revolutionary transformation, which have acquired an international character."[29] This claim does not find support in the facts of the historical record. October was the classic example of communist seizure of power, but it was destined to be a lonely classic, the only successful case of its type in the half-century of communist revolutions which it inaugurated. This, of course, is not to deny that communist revolutions outside Russia have in many important ways profited from their Russian heritage, and from Leninist revolutionary theory in particular. Yet the paths taken by the communists of other countries in acquiring power have diverged greatly from that of the first communist revolution. Some of the serious setbacks of communism have occurred as a consequence of unsuccessful efforts to emulate the October pattern. And the other thirteen successful communist revolutions have in no instance replicated this pattern.

Of the reasons why the October pattern has not repeated itself in other countries, one merits particular attention. The fact is that a "revolutionary situation" in Lenin's sense is an exceedingly rare phenomenon in social history, especially in the highly complex "bourgeois" societies of the present age. Lenin saw revolution as an elemental movement involving millions, occurring at a time of "particular upsurge" when masses of aggrieved humanity were driven by unusually harsh adversity into an insurrectionary mood that could find an outlet in action because of a partially incapacitating crisis at the top of society and government. Such times of revolutionary crisis have occurred in modern societies, as they did in Russia in 1905 and 1917, but only as the result of an unusual combination of circumstances inevitably involving an element of fortuity. Lenin himself recognized this when in 1920 he wrote in *Left-Wing Communism* that no amount of propaganda and agitation alone could win over the broad masses to a position of support for the revolutionary "vanguard." "For this the masses must have their own political experience," he went on. "Such is the fundamental law of all great revolutions. . . ." The First World War had provided this "political experience" in the immediate past, but what would provide it in the future? Surveying the postwar scene, Lenin found social life in many countries "crammed full of inflammable material" needing only a spark to be kindled into revolutionary conflagration. Yet he admitted that no one could foretell "*what immediate cause* will most serve to rouse, kindle and impel into the struggle the very wide masses who are at present dormant."[30] Subsequent history suggests that he may have overestimated the inflammability of the masses in modern society; they have not proved, on the whole, so susceptible to large-scale revolutionary excitement. Ironically, one of the few genuine popular upheavals of the ensuing period occurred in 1956 in communist-ruled Hungary, where all the elements of a revolutionary situation in Lenin's special threefold sense of the term were present.[31]

Although it did not produce revolutionary situations like the one that came about in Russia in 1917, the Second World War created new opportunities for communist revolution. It might be said to have produced a new *kind* of revolutionary situation, characterized not by rebellious movements of urban masses but rather by the breakdown of indigenous established authority—particularly in rural areas—under conditions of enemy occupation. The Japanese invasion and occupation of large parts of China in the 1930's and subsequently of much of Southeast Asia, and the German invasion and occupation of Eastern Europe and the Balkans in the early 1940's provided the setting. Under these conditions it became possible for communist revolutionary movements to reconstitute themselves as *resistance movements* and to embark upon a piecemeal takeover of the country by military means, particularly guerrilla warfare. The classic case is, of course, China; Mao Tse-tung, who led Chinese communism to power, is the foremost theorist of communist revolution by armed struggle. With variations growing out of the peculiarities of their national settings, the war-born communist takeovers in Yugoslavia, Albania, and Vietnam also exemplify this pattern, and the Cuban case—although a special one in important respects—is closer to this category of communist revolution than to either of the other two.

A statement of Mao's in 1938 concerning the Chinese prospect forms the best starting-point for a comparison of the October pattern and revolutions of the Chinese Communist type: "Basically the task of the communist party here is not to go through a long period of legal struggles before launching an insurrection or war, nor to seize the big cities first and then occupy the countryside, but to take the other way round."[32] A difference of relation between town and country, and therefore between worker and peasant, is involved. Instead of a "peasant war" as a companion piece to the effort to take power in the major urban centers—with workers as the revolutionary shock force—we have here a pattern of communist revolution in which the countryside becomes the principal revolutionary arena in the early stages, and in which peasants therefore are the main social base of the revolution. Only in Mao's third strategic stage of revolutionary war, when the guerrilla warfare that predominated in the previous two stages of strategic defensive and strategic stalemate gives way to regular warfare in the strategic counteroffensive, do the large cities move to the center of the picture. Their capture is the "final objective of the revolution."[33]

In the earlier stages, the communist-led resistance movement seeks not simply to carry on warfare in the countryside in the manner of historical peasant wars of the roving insurgents type, but to establish so-called revolutionary base areas to function as the rear of the movement. This is obviously facilitated by the presence of extensive mountainous, forest, or jungle regions in the country concerned which are difficult to reach with regular troops, and it is notable that all five of the successful communist revolutions of this type have occurred in countries that possess such regions. In the Chinese case, the communist forces established a base area at Yenan after the Long March, and then, in the 1937–41 period, created large guerrilla bases in each of the provinces of north China. In Yugoslavia, Tito's partisan forces in the fall of 1941 established a base area in northwest Serbia which became known as the "Uzhice Republic." Later that year they retreated into the relatively primitive mountain areas of Bosnia. In Albania, the communist guerrillas under Enver Hoxha operated in the mountains that cover most of that small land.

In the October Revolution, the taking of power preceded the revolutionary transformation of the sociopolitical order in the country. In the type of communist revolution now under consideration, the revolutionary transformation takes place, or at any rate begins in the protracted process of conquering power and becomes one of the most important means by which power is extended. The sociopolitical revolution develops in the liberated base areas, where the communist movement seeks to build not only military strongholds but also enclaves of a new society and polity. Not only are new organs of public authority created, such as the "people's councils" that the Yugoslav communists set up in their base areas and the "democratic governments" that were formed in the north China guerrilla bases.

Schools, newspapers, and other social institutions are established under communist auspices. Self-defense corps and so-called mass organizations for peasants, youth, women, children, and other groups are founded as means of enlisting the people's participation in public life under communist guidance. All this serves the needs of "political mobilization," which Mao described as the promotion of anti-Japanese resistance by telling the people about the political objectives of the war, viz., the ousting of the Japanese and the building of a new China.[34] Thus, military operations go hand-in-hand with a piecemeal process of nation-building. Guerrilla warfare creates a territory for political mobilization of the populace, which in turn augments the communist resistance forces and makes possible the expansion of military operations into new areas. The results are most impressive in the Yugoslav and Chinese cases. By February, 1945, Tito's partisan army consisted of fifty-four divisions numbering 800,000 troops. By the time of Japan's capitulation in 1945, one-fifth of the population of China was living in the communist-controlled revolutionary base areas. When the communist government was officially proclaimed in China on October 1, 1949, this marked not the beginning of the communist revolution there but the climax of one that had been in progress for upwards of a decade.[35] The communist-Kuomintang civil war of 1947–49 had been no more than a last act in the drama, the completion of a revolutionary takeover that already had been largely accomplished in the period of anti-Japanese resistance and its aftermath.

As best shown in the Chinese case, communist resistance movements face a difficult problem with regard to agrarian policy in the revolutionary base areas. In December, 1939, Mao declared that, because the peasantry was the main force in the Chinese revolution, it must be given help in overthrowing the feudal landlord class. Distribution of the landlords' land among the peasants was one of the programmatic measures of the revolution in its ongoing "new-democratic" or presocialist phase. However, he also stipulated that private capitalist enterprises should be preserved and that "rich-peasant economy should not be eliminated."[36] The policy actually followed by the party during the period of the anti-Japanese war was a moderate one of reducing rents and interest owed by the peasants to their landlords. Radical measures of land redistribution were avoided for fear of alienating large segments of the very peasant population that the resistance movement looked to as its prime source of recruits and general support. As Chalmers Johnson puts it, the economic policies of the communists during the Sino-Japanese war were designed to create maximum unity for national defense.[37]

Chinese communism, like the other communist movements that have come to power by the road of wartime resistance, built its mass following among the peasants (and other strata) primarily on the basis of an appeal to nationalism—the patriotic desire to liberate the country from the foreign invader. The political mobilization of the Chinese peasants after 1937 proceeded mainly in terms of the anti-Japanese slogan "national salvation," while the partisans appealed to the Yugoslav peasants with patriotic antifascist slogans aimed primarily at the Germans. In both instances the communists took a more militant stance in the resistance than did their rivals (the Kuomintang and Mihailovic's Chetniks), engaging in bold operations that provoked from the foreign occupiers harsh reprisals, which in turn helped destroy the remaining fabric of the old society and made the peasants all the more amenable to patriotic mobilization. In wartime Albania the communist guerrillas used patriotic antifascist slogans similar to those of the Yugoslav partisans. After the defeat of Japan the Vietnamese communists espoused Vietnamese nationalism against the French, and more recently have done so against the Americans. The Castro movement is exceptional among the guerrilla movements that have won power, both in the fact that its communist alignment came afterward and in the circumstance that there was no foreign occupation against which to mobilize the population. There was, however, a history of American domination of the country and an oppressive Cuban regime which could be identified with American influence; and political mobilization of

the Cuban lower classes in the post-revolutionary pe.,
relied heavily upon the slogan of Cuban national independence
against "Yankee imperialism."

So far-reaching is communism's identification with nationalism in this pattern of revolution that an actual fusion has been
hypothesized. Noting that both Chinese and Yugoslav communism was legitimized by the nationalistic credentials established by the communist parties during the resistance, Chalmers
Johnson suggests that the resulting Chinese and Yugoslav governments are the "offspring of indigenous nationalism" and that
in both cases the communist ideology "serves as the theoretical
expression of these nationalisms."[38] Such an interpretation appears unnecessarily extreme and overlooks the alternative possibility that we are here concerned with movements of authentic
communist ideological affiliation which at the same time have
identified themselves with national goals in the process of winning power and subsequently have retained a strong nationalist
orientation. In this connection it must be pointed out that in the
Russian Revolution we see a very different relationship of the
communist movement to nationalism. Here communism came
to power on an antiwar platform. Far from identifying itself
with Russian national aims in time of war, the Bolshevik movement used the slogan of revolutionary internationalism. From
the outbreak of war in 1914, Lenin advocated revolutionary
defeatism, the transformation of the international "imperialist
war" into a series of revolutionary civil wars inside the warring
countries, his own included. *Defensism* became a Bolshevik
term of opprobrium for Russian socialists who supported the
national war effort. Only in the post-revolutionary period—and
particularly under Stalin—did Russian communism take on a
pronounced Russian nationalist orientation.

A final comparative observation has to do with the role of
armed force in communist revolution. Where the main form of
struggle is war and the main form of organization is the army,
as in China, the notion of revolution by armed struggle can
easily become an obsession. Whoever wants to seize the political power of the state and to maintain it must have a strong

army, declared Mao in 1938, and he went on: "Some people have ridiculed us as advocates of the 'omnipotence of war'; yes, we are, we are the advocates of the omnipotence of the revolutionary war, which is not bad at all, but is good and is Marxist." Observing further that everything in Yenan had been built up by means of the gun, he added: "Anything can grow out of the barrel of a gun. . . . With the help of guns the Russian communists brought about socialism. We are to bring about a democratic republic. Experience in the class struggle of the era of imperialism teaches us that the working class and the toiling masses cannot defeat the armed bourgeois and landlords except by the power of the gun; in this sense we can even say that the whole world can be remoulded only with the gun."[39]

It is difficult to picture Lenin recognizing this as an authentic voice of Marxism, or agreeing with the implied view of the Russian communist revolution. As noted earlier, armed insurrection is a vital ingredient in the Leninist theory and practice of communist revolution. For Lenin, however, the revolutionary process was fundamentally political, rather than military, in nature. It was the politics of taking power in a society brought by an unusual combination of stresses to a state of turmoil and incipient breakdown. In harmony with his essentially political vision of the revolution, Lenin saw the armed insurrection itself as "a *special* form of the political struggle."[40] It was the coup de grâce that the revolutionary movement would have to administer to the regime it sought to replace, an episode of planned violence at the conclusion of the political struggle. But what about the place of the civil war in the Russian Revolution? It is true that, shortly after the Bolshevik seizure of power, Russia became the scene of a bloody three-year civil war, in the course of which the Revolution took to arms, created its Red Army under Trotsky, and defeated the forces that took the field against it. If the Russian Revolution is viewed as a social epoch, the civil war of 1918–21 must be considered an integral part of it. However, the civil war, important as it was historically, was not an element in Lenin's strategy of revolution. It was forced upon the Bolshevik regime by the efforts of various forces in Russia (aided from abroad) to overthrow it. From a Leninist point of view, especially as shaped by the Russian experience, the need to wage a protracted armed struggle to preserve the power won by revolution is a contingency with which every communist movement must reckon. But such an armed struggle is not seen as either inevitable or desirable, and the gun barrel is not seen as the only significant source of revolutionary power. To this limited extent the post-Stalinist Soviet theory of a peaceful path can claim an authentically Leninist ancestry.

VI

In both patterns of communist revolution examined above, the revolution is basically an internal process in the country concerned. This is not to deny that the Soviet Union rendered significant assistance (along with some disservices) to the communist revolutions in countries like China and Yugoslavia. But the assistance was not decisive; at most it was supplementary, and the revolutions in question could have taken place without it. Like the Russian Revolution in its time, these revolutions fundamentally made their way on their own. In contrast, the communist regimes in Mongolia, North Korea, Bulgaria, Rumania, Hungary, Poland, East Germany, and Czechoslovakia did not come to power by means of basically indigenous revolutions. These communist revolutions were imposed from outside. In all instances but the first, they were engineered by the Soviet Union under conditions of military occupation or domination which followed the Soviet victory in World War II. One could, of course, add to the eight instances of imposed communist revolution just listed the cases of the three Baltic countries, on which communist revolution was imposed in 1940 during the period of the Stalin-Hitler pact. It is, perhaps, all the more important to mention these three instances, since the experience in the Baltic countries, as well as in the areas detached from Poland in 1939, was a forerunner of the process of imposed revolution as it developed in the aftermath of World War II throughout much of Eastern and Central Europe.

Although Marxism-Leninism has contemplated the revolutionary war across national boundaries as one possible form of just war (and the Soviet march into Poland in 1920 stands as an historic example of this form of action), the doctrine assumes that the country invaded would be in the throes of an internally generated revolution or "revolutionary situation" at the time. The forcible imposition of communist revolution upon a country from the outside not only lacks sanction in Soviet ideology but has many times been explicitly disavowed as an aim. According to Stalin's famous statement to Roy Howard in 1936, "the export of revolution is nonsense." Yet, without ever admitting it, the Soviet Union has *practiced* such "nonsense" on a large scale. Insofar as conditions in that primitive, nomadic country permitted, communist revolution was engineered in Outer Mongolia following the military conquest of the area by the Soviet Union in the early 1920's. In 1939–40, not long after Stalin's remarks to Roy Howard, the communist system was forcibly installed in Soviet-occupied eastern Poland and the three Baltic states. And in the aftermath of the Second World War, Soviet satellite regimes of "people's democracy" were established in North Korea and in Eastern and Central Europe, wherever Soviet power predominated.

The devastation and dislocation of war did much to destroy or greatly weaken the prewar sociopolitical order in Eastern Europe. Although revolutionary situations in the Leninist sense did not exist at the war's end, it was widely accepted among the peoples and political parties that restoration of the status quo ante bellum was out of the question and that social change was in order. Yet the communist movements in these countries had little chance of independently coming to power on the tide of change. It is true that communism had not been a negligible indigenous force in prewar Eastern Europe. Communist movements of varying strength had existed in spite of domestic repressions and the loss of many of their leaders in Stalin's purges of 1936–38, and they carried on underground activities during the war. The Polish Communist party, which had been dissolved formally in 1938 at the height of the Soviet purges, was reconstituted in 1942 and played a part, although a relatively minor one, in the Polish resistance movement. In Czechoslovakia, where communism had shown real strength in the democratic pre-Munich period, underground communists were active in the Free Slovakia resistance movement in 1944. But nowhere in Eastern Europe (outside of Yugoslavia and Albania) did local communists achieve a politically commanding position under war conditions. Only in Czechoslovakia, through a combination of favorable circumstances, did they emerge at the war's end in great strength. There the communists gained control of key posts, including the ministries of interior (police), agriculture, and information, and the communist leader Gottwald became premier after his party polled 38 per cent of the vote in the parliamentary elections of May, 1946, the first held after the war. Significantly, however, Czechoslovakia, from which the Soviet army was withdrawn in December, 1945, was the only country in the region not yet under total or near-total communist domination at the beginning of 1948.

In Poland, Bulgaria, Rumania, Hungary, and East Germany, where Moscow was in a controlling position because of the continued presence of its military forces, communist rule was imposed in a process which showed local variations but was everywhere the same in basic pattern. The communists sought to enlarge their popular support by taking charge of land reform or, as in Poland, by exploiting the large patronage opportunities inherent in the postwar resettlement of Poles in the western lands detached from Germany. Meanwhile, under Soviet direction and with Soviet assistance, they acquired strategic positions in the coalition governments initially formed, and drove for ascendancy. Unco-operative political forces, such as the peasant parties that enjoyed strong support in a number of these countries, were pressured, harassed, and simply terrorized in the process. Noncommunist leaders like Maniu in Rumania, Petkov in Bulgaria, and Mikolajczyk in Poland were imprisoned, executed, or hounded out of their countries. Social Democratic parties were deprived of their autonomy and were eliminated as possible rivals through forced mergers with the communists in communist-controlled united workers' parties. Public organizations were purged of leaders not amenable to communist direction. Gradually the coalition governments were transformed into pseudo-coalitions dominated by the communists, and then into opposition-free regimes on the Soviet model.[41] These communist revolutions from above were completed in all essentials by 1947–48.

Although not occupied by Soviet forces, Czechoslovakia was ringed by lands that were, and she had no access to effective assistance from the noncommunist world. The Soviet military presence on its frontiers, significantly activated at the time, formed the backdrop for the communist action of February, 1948, in Prague, and there is reason to believe that the action was taken under political pressure from Moscow. With the backing of Premier Gottwald, the communist Minister of Interior ignored an instruction from the majority of the cabinet that he stop packing the police with communists, whereupon ministers belonging to two of the government parties resigned in protest. In the ensuing cabinet crisis, the communists, acting by both constitutional and extra-constitutional means, sent armed detachments of workers into the streets and put pressure on President Eduard Benes (then an old and sick man) to form a new government of predominantly communist complexion. After he yielded on February 25, the communist takeover of all power in Czechoslovakia proceeded swiftly. As noted earlier, post-Stalinist Soviet writings have cited this as an example of communist revolution by the peaceful parliamentary path. It is true that no civil war occurred. But the *coup de Prague,* which bears a certain resemblance to the pattern of so-called legal revolution by which Hitler's National Socialist party took power in Germany in 1933, involved the ruthless application of political coercion and a scarcely veiled threat of armed violence. To call it a "peaceful" revolution would stretch unduly the meaning of that word, and to speak of its path as "parliamentary" should not obscure the fact that it led immediately to the suppression of parliamentary democracy in Czechoslovakia.

One other feature of the imposed communist revolution as it developed in Eastern Europe after World War II was the satellization of the communist regimes that arose. Stalin, then at the apogee of his dictatorship, demanded not only communist regimes but dependably subservient ones. Communist governments of relatively independent persuasion, pursuing their national paths of communist development, were no more acceptable to him, if not less so, than noncommunist governments. Accordingly, from the very outset the Soviet authorities made every effort to guarantee Soviet control over the emerging communist regimes. Thus, Soviet advisers were installed in key positions in the police, army, and other ministries of the governments, and the countries concerned were placed in relations of economic dependency upon the Soviet Union. To ensure cooperation by the local communist authorities in these and similar measures, political responsibility was entrusted as much as possible to thoroughly reliable communist cadres, typified by Matyas Rakosi and Walter Ulbricht, who had spent the war years in Moscow. Initially, however, these "Muscovites" shared positions of power with communist leaders who had worked in underground resistance movements in their own countries during the war, men like Gomulka in Poland, Kostov in Bulgaria, Rajk in Hungary, and Patrascanu in Rumania. Tendencies toward what later came to be called "national communism" were present to a greater degree in the latter group. Although not at all anti-Soviet, and no less serious and rigid in their communist ideological convictions than others in the movement, some communist leaders who had stayed in their countries were inclined—like Tito—to resent Soviet tutelage and dictation of their policies, to place a high priority upon the interests of communism in their own national context, and to adapt the Soviet communist pattern in various particulars to local conditions.

In the new phase of the East European revolution signaled by the creation of the Cominform and by Moscow's anti-Tito declaration of June, 1948, Soviet control over the newly established communist regimes was tightened. Stalin's move against Tito probably was intended not merely to provoke the overthrow of the Titoist leadership group in Yugoslavia but also to inaugurate a systematic campaign against national-communist tendencies in Eastern Europe. In the wake of the unexpected failure to force the change in Yugoslavia, the campaign developed into a general purge of "national communists" in other countries of the area. In Soviet-engineered purge trials, Kostov, Rajk, and others were condemned for alleged "nationalist deviationism." In a typical accusation, the Bulgarian communist leader George Dimitrov (a "Muscovite") attributed to Traicho Kostov the "shameful assumption" that Soviet interests might ever be opposed to Bulgarian interests. The purges of communists in 1948–52 consolidated the position of the "Muscovites" in the East European regimes and generally underscored Soviet dominance in the area. Even the fact that communist revolution had been made possible by the presence of the Soviet army was openly acknowledged and emphasized. Thus, the preamble of the new Polish constitution adopted in 1952 stated: "The historic victory of the U.S.S.R. over fascism liberated Polish soil, *enabled the Polish working people to gain power,* and made possible the rebirth of Poland within new just frontiers."[42]

Satellization of the regimes created by the communist revolution in its Soviet-imposed version would not appear to have been something necessarily inherent in this pattern of revolution. But owing to a number of factors—chief among which was the personality of the man directing the process, Stalin— revolution could not be exported after the Second World War without the newly established political enterprises being treated as Soviet property. Not only were communist regimes forcibly imposed upon countries where communism was not strong enough to come to power on its own; a whole system of measures was carried out to prevent these regimes from, so to speak, "nationalizing" themselves by developing policies that would reflect the special needs and circumstances of their countries. This went against the current of tendencies inevitably present within those regimes themselves, irrespective of the political fortunes of this or that leader of "national-communist" leaning.

It added to the stigma of foreign origin the onus of continued foreign dependency. Consequently, the post-Stalinist relaxation of Soviet dictatorship at home and abroad has been accompanied by an independence movement of varying strength in countries where communism was imposed at the war's end. Even without the Yugoslav example to inspire it, this movement would undoubtedly have emerged when conditions made it possible. The results so far have been mixed. In spite of that, they suggest the hypothesis that communism in power, regardless of how it acquires power, has a tendency to turn into national communism.

CONCLUSIONS

A priori schemes of world history aside, the future of communist revolution is no more scientifically predictable in the present state of knowledge than is the future of any other major political phenomenon of our time. However, the comparative study of communism and communist revolutions does suggest some tentative conclusions that bear upon future prospects:

1. The fact that communist revolution has spread to about a third of the world in its first fifty years does not imply that it will spread, in time, to the remaining two-thirds. There is no good reason to believe that something which could be called a "world communist revolution" is in progress.

2. Neither, on the other hand, would it be justified to assume that no more communist revolutions will take place anywhere. Communist movements of varying strength and vigor exist in more than eighty noncommunist countries. Depending upon internal and external circumstances, some may be or may become sufficiently strong to represent regimes of potential communist revolution. Yet, in no instance, with the possible exception of South Vietnam, does this now appear an inevitable or overwhelmingly probable eventuality.

3. The communist revolution is likely to preserve its character as a revolution of underdevelopment. Any future communist revolutions will probably occur not in developed industrial countries with advanced social and political institutions

but, as in the past, in underdeveloped countries where economic progress is slow or stagnant, where society is divided into a privileged minority and a disadvantaged peasant majority, and where authoritarian government prevails. There is no law stating that the revolution of underdevelopment must take place under communist auspices. Noncommunist leadership is possible, particularly with encouragement from influential noncommunist powers. However, the prospect for such leadership (and such encouragement) remains highly uncertain.

4. So far as communism's path to power is concerned, none of the three historical variants considered above can be automatically ruled out as a future possibility. But, for various reasons, neither the path of Russia's October nor the pattern of imposed revolution appears likely to furnish a model in the future. In underdeveloped countries the communist road to power through armed struggle and identification with nationalism may prove to be the highroad. Nor should communism's discovery of new roads to power be excluded, although reasons have been cited here for not expecting the "peaceful parliamentary path" to be one of them. A possible future path, which may have been foreshadowed in the Castro revolution in Cuba, is that of "communism by conversion," where a movement of predominantly nationalist and leftist complexion takes power and *subsequently* opts for Marxism-Leninism and communist political affiliations.

5. Owing in part to the tendency of communist movements and regimes to acquire a nationalist coloration, communism in power, contrary to the founding ideological prophecies, has not provide itself a cohesive force internationally. The spread of communist revolution beyond Russia has led to growing polycentrism and to diverse intercommunist divisions and discords, of which the Sino-Soviet conflict has been the most serious. The disintegration of international communism is in some sense a symptom of crisis. But it should not be assumed that this development is in all respects detrimental to communist movements not yet in power. On the contrary, it may be of assistance to some of them by compelling them to rely more upon their

own efforts and to chart their own paths, and by helping them to escape the onus of foreign inspiration and dependency. The prospects of communist revolution are not necessarily harmed by division in the communist world.

NOTES

1. Engels, "The Principles of Communism," in K. Marx and F. Engels, *Sochineniia* (Moscow, 1955), IV, 334.

2. Lenin, "The United States of Europe Slogan," *Selected Works* (Moscow, 1946–47), vol. 1, p. 632.

3. Lenin, "The Fourth Anniversary of the October Revolution," *ibid.*, vol. 2, p. 751.

4. Lenin, "Better Fewer, But Better," *ibid.*, p. 854.

5. T. T. Timofeyev, "Mezhdunarodnoe znachenie oktiabrskoi revoliutsii i sovremennaia ideologicheskaia bor'ba," *Voprosy istorii KPSS*, no. 6 (June, 1967), pp. 7, 9. For a typical example of the denunciation of Western "falsifiers" see the article by N. Mikeshin, "Pravda istorii i ideinaia nishcheta ee fal'sifikatorov," in *Politicheskoe samoobrazovanie*, no. 6, 1967.

6. *Pravda*, June 25, 1967.

7. Marx, *Capital* (London: J. M. Dent & Sons, 1933), p. 714.

8. "Our Revolution: Apropos of the Notes of N. Sukhanov," *Selected Works*, vol. 2, p. 837. For Lenin's reaction when the news of the first revolution reached him in Switzerland see his "Letters from Afar," *ibid.*, vol. 1, p. 751.

9. Stalin, *Works* (Moscow, 1955), vol. 13, p. 303.

10. *Ibid.*, vol. 7, p. 14. This speech was first published when vol. 13 of Stalin's *Sochineniia* came out in 1947.

11. For an examination of the evidence in support of this interpretation of Stalin's diplomacy in the 1930's see the Introduction to R. C. Tucker and S. F. Cohen, eds., *The Great Purge Trial* (New York: Grosset and Dunlap, 1965).

12. Stalin, *Economic Problems of Socialism in the U.S.S.R.* (New York: International Publishers, 1952), p. 30.

13. Arthur Mendel, ed., *Essential Works of Marxism* (New York: Bantam Books, 1961), p. 401.

14. *Pravda*, June 25, 1967. On the likelihood that the peaceful path would be more feasible in less developed countries, as distinguished from those where "capitalism is still strong," see N. Khrushchev, "For New Victories of the World Communist Movement," *Pravda*, January 25, 1961, p. 4.

15. Mao Tse-tung, "Problems of War and Strategy," *Selected Works* (New York: International Publishers, 1954), vol. 2, p. 272.

16. The Chinese memorandum was published in Peking in 1963 after the controversy had come into the open. The text of it appears in "The Origin and Development of the Differences between the Leadership of the C.P.S.U. and Ourselves" (Peking, 1963), pp. 58–62.

17. These quotations are taken from "The Proletarian Revolution and Khrushchev's Revisionism" (Peking, 1964), which contains the fullest systematic presentation of the Maoist position on the question of peaceful transition.

18. For an extended interpretation along these lines see the writer's "The Deradicalization of Marxist Movements," *American Political Science Review*, June, 1967.

19. P. N. Fedoseev, "Velikii rubezh v istorii chelovechestva," *Izvestiia*, April 30, 1967; italics added. Fedoseev, it should be mentioned, did not say or imply that the political regime of communist revolution would remain effectively "multiparty" following the transition. A façade of pseudomultipartyism could always, of course, be maintained, as it is now in certain communist-ruled countries, e.g., China. It is noteworthy in this connection that the C.P.S.U. Central Committee's "Theses" for the fiftieth anniversary of October explicitly reaffirm the doctrine that the regime born of communist revolution is a "proletarian dictatorship," which in Leninist language means communist-party dictatorship.

20. "Our Revolution: Apropos of the Notes of N. Sukhanov," p. 838.

21. *Left-Wing Communism: An Infantile Disorder, Selected Works*, vol. 2, p. 629. In *The State and Revolution* Lenin writes that the Russian revolution of 1905–7 was "undoubtedly a 'real people's' revolution, since the mass of the people, the majority, the 'lowest social ranks,' crushed by oppression and exploitation, rose independently and put on the entire course of the revolution the impress of *their* demands, of *their* attempts to build in their own way a new society in place of the old society that was being destroyed" (*Selected Works*, vol. 2, p. 167).

22. "Krakh II Internatsionala," *Polnoe sobranie sochinenii* (Moscow, 1961), pp. 218–19.

23. *Selected Works*, vol. 2, p. 621.

24. "The Tasks of the Proletariat in Our Revolution: Draft of a Platform for the Proletarian Party, *ibid.*, p. 28.

25. "On Slogans," *Selected Works*, vol. 2, p. 68. For an example of the post-Stalinist Soviet use of Lenin's references to a "peaceful development of the revolution'" to support the doctrine of peaceful transition see Khrushchev's speech at the Sixth Congress of the Socialist Unity Party of Germany, *Izvestia*, January 14, 1963.

26. "Krakh II Internatsionala," p. 219.

27. *Selected Works*, vol. 2, p. 155.

28. "Advice of an Onlooker," *ibid.*, pp. 133–34. "Marxism and Insurrection" appears in *ibid.*, pp. 120–24.

29. *Pravda*, June 25, 1967.

30. *Selected Works*, vol. 2, pp. 627, 630, 632.

31. This paragraph was written in July, 1967. In the light of subsequent social developments in various countries, and most notably the events of May-June, 1968, in France, I am now much less convinced of the relative non-inflammability of the masses in contemporary industrial society.

32. "Problems of War and Strategy," p. 267.

33. Mao Tse-tung, "The Chinese Revolution and the Chinese Communist Party," *Selected Works,* vol. 3, p. 86. On the three strategic stages, see *ibid.,* vol. 2, pp. 275, 278.

34. "On the Protracted War," *ibid.,* vol. 2, pp. 204–5.

35. Chalmers Johnson, *Peasant Nationalism and Communist Power* (Stanford, Calif.: Stanford University Press, 1962), p. 1.

36. Mao Tse-tung, "The Chinese Revolution and the Chinese Communist Party," *Selected Works,* vol. 3, pp. 87, 96–97. See also his subsequent statement in "On New Democracy" (*ibid.,* p. 122): "In the rural areas, rich-peasant economic activities will be tolerated." These statements presuppose a fourfold classification of the rural population into the landlord class, the rich peasants or rural bourgeoisie, the middle peasants, and the poor peasants (*ibid.,* pp. 88, 92–93).

37. *Peasant Nationalism,* p. 19.

38. *Ibid.,* p. 184. Elsewhere Johnson speaks of "the nationalistic basis of communism in the independent communist states (*ibid.,* p. 179) and states that "communism and nationalism were fused in wartime China and Yugoslavia as a result of the identification of the CCP and YCP, respectively, with the resistance movements of the two countries. . . ." (*ibid.,* p. 8).

39. Mao Tse-tung, "Problems of War and Strategy," pp. 272, 273.

40. "Advice of an Onlooker," p. 133.

41. For a detailed country-by-country description of the process see Hugh Seton-Watson, *The East European Revolution,* 3d ed. (New York: Praeger, 1956), esp. chap. 8.

42. *Ibid.,* p. 373; italics added.

PART I

SOVIET INTERNAL DEVELOPMENTS

SOVIET MILITARY DEVELOPMENTS

CHAPTER 1

The Party and the State

The Politburo in the First and Fifth
Decades of Soviet Power

Dan N. Jacobs

Prospects for Soviet Political Development:
Evolution, Decay, or Revolution?

Frederick C. Barghoorn

The Party, Opposition, and Interest Groups
in Communist Politics: Fifty Years of
Continuity and Change

H. Gordon Skilling

The Politburo in the First and Fifth Decades of Soviet Power

Dan N. Jacobs

There is a widely held misconception, adhered to even by some people usually regarded as quite sophisticated about the Soviet system, that the Politburo of the Central Committee of the Communist Party of the Soviet Union (C.P.S.U.) is, and has been since the inception of the Soviet state, the focus of Soviet power in all but unchanging fashion. Such is not the case; the Politburo has at times since its establishment been devoid of power, and it has infrequently, if ever, been the absolute instrument it is often pictured as being. Its control has changed as the Soviet Union and the quality and nature of power within it have changed. As the system and the society have developed and as the leading personnel have come and gone, the specifics of the role of the Politburo have undergone alteration. Situations make differences, and men make differences. One would not say that the American presidency has not been subject to wide-ranging changes in the past half-century nor that the quality of the carrying out of the presidential function has not been affected by the personality of the individual filling the role. Why, then, should it be thought that in a system where the flux of change has been much greater and where, power being less diffuse, the potential for the influence of personality would consequently be more abundantly present, the role of the guiding institution would remain largely static?

I

The first Politburo was established shortly before October, 1917, and was to provide the on-the-spot leadership for the Revolution. It never performed the role, however; the immediate direction of the Revolution, as history would have it, was carried out by the Military-Revolutionary Committee of the Petrograd Soviet.

In the following two years, most prominent Bolsheviks were scattered throughout Russia, fighting, arguing, organizing. Under the circumstances, Lenin, assisted by Sverdlov, made most decisions unilaterally or with the aid of ad hoc committees.[1] But in 1919 Sverdlov's death and Lenin's growing awareness of the need for a permanent body of advisers smaller than the Central Committee led to the creation of a new Politburo, the more or less direct lineal antecedent of the present body.

This re-establishment of the Politburo was seen by some party members, such as Obolensky,[2] as a bypassing of the Central Committee, a way point in the process anticipated by Trotsky almost two decades earlier whereby "the organization of the party takes the place of the party itself: the Central Committee takes the place of the organization; and finally the dictator takes the place of the Central Committee. . . ."[3] Lenin recognized the argument to the extent of making a few token obeisances in the direction of those who made it[4]—but the Politburo was established, and with it the Orgburo and the Secretariat.

Also in 1919, the apprehensions of those who feared that the authority of the Central Committee would be eroded began to be realized. Within three years the Orgburo had become "something like a subordinate Politburo."[5] By 1922 the Politburo and the Secretariat were the directing agents of the party and the government, and the Central Committee and the Orgburo were well embarked upon their increasingly token existence. Whatever the relation of forces between the Central Committee, the Secretariat, the Politburo, and the Orgburo, however, there was only one man in Russia in 1922 who was a member of all four: Joseph Vissarionovich Stalin. The story of Russia and of the Politburo during the following decades would largely be the story of Stalin, and even after his death the living out of the reaction to him.

This is not the place to retell in detail the manner in which Stalin gained control of the Politburo after Lenin's death,[6] but it is appropriate to indicate some of the tactics used by Stalin in the pursuit. Stalin did not control the Politburo in 1923 or 1924. His power base was in the Secretariat, which he had increased many-fold and honeycombed with his own appointments. Not being in control in the Politburo, he required allies among its members. While the game he was playing was politics, his allies were recruited to a considerable degree on the basis of policy. The issues were identified variously as "socialism in a single country," "collectivization," and so forth, and they were undeniably vital issues, of the greatest moment, encompassing the dreams of generations of revolutionaries, and setting the course for the entire system and ideology. But they were also—scarcely a matter of secondary concern—the vehicles through which the struggle for power was fought out.

In his personal demeanor, as in the positions he took, Stalin consistently pre-empted the "moderate" middle position for himself. Neither an advocate of the "right" nor a partisan of the "left," he was in a situation where allies were essential, closer to both than either was to each other. There were other Politburo members who were feared or despised by still other Politburo members more than Stalin was. Stalin was able consistently to divert antagonism from himself, to direct it or profit from its being directed at others more pre-eminent than himself who were in the process of mutual self-destruction, and at the same time to continue building his power elsewhere within the party. From the Secretariat Stalin gained control of the Central Committee, and from the Central Committee he gained control of the Politburo by replacing its disgraced and defeated members with his own appointees.

By 1927 Stalin had removed the "left" members of the Politburo and had gained a "majority." Two years later, the "right" was devastated as well. The Politburo was his; power had been attained. Now there arose the problem of keeping it.

The men whom Stalin had pushed to the top in his own ascent were not the groveling minions they are sometimes assumed to have been. They were "Stalin's men," but not forever. They joined with him for a variety of reasons—idealism, conviction, ambition, and so forth. But, if they were "loyal" to Stalin once, how could he be certain that he could count on their loyalty tomorrow, or the next day, or the day after that? Idealism, conviction, ambition, might lead elsewhere. It should be remembered that Stalin was no charismatic leader; he had not the authority of Lenin nor even the acquired authority of being the legally designated head of state. Despite his triumph after Lenin's death, he lacked self-assurance. His victories were at times like ashes in his mouth, for they lacked permanence. How to make them permanent? How to insure permanent loyalty? Seemingly, the answer that occurred was terror—and, while it was probably scarcely conceived of as such at first, it was inevitably a society-wide, permanent terror.

By the early 1930's Stalin personally was making the vital decisions in the Politburo; the other members acted as "advisers," albeit highly placed and privileged ones.[7] Nevertheless, on certain vital issues, such as the use of terror, individual Politburo members were prepared and able to oppose him, even, apparently, to plot to displace him,[8] which only confirmed Stalin's conviction that terror had to be used. If colleagues were not to be trusted, if the loyalty of one's wife could not be counted upon[9]—then what was left? Barbed wire and the machine pistol. These became Stalin's loyal and constant supporters.

Probably, at least at the later stages of his life, if Stalin could have so ordered it, the instruments of terror would have been his only accouterments. But he could not shoulder all the work of running the U.S.S.R. himself; he needed the assistance of others. Those who were co-opted into his service knew the risks and penalties of the roles they filled, as Khrushchev indicated in the "secret" speech and elsewhere.[10] The

Politburo member who lasted sensed what he dared tell Stalin and what he had best keep from him.[11] He was aware that any meeting with Stalin might be his last—meeting or day alive.[12] After the purges, Stalin might well have said "Le Politburo, c'est moi." And it was.

But terror itself was not sufficient, as Stalin saw it, to guarantee the permanence of his triumph and ascendency. Fear might cause some men to cower, but it could lead others to desperation, and desperation could lead to danger for Stalin. Throughout this society, which he manipulated from top to bottom, he was determined that there should not be a single organization that he did not control. And while he controlled them he was determined that, even should he lose control, no organization would be in a position to threaten him. In the case of the Politburo, although its members were thoroughly terrorized, Stalin still feared the potential threat to himself deriving from the mere existence of this body; yet he could not do without it or an analogous institution. What he could do was disperse its powers and rule through several vehicles, not just the Politburo. At his own discretion Stalin acted through the Politburo, the party, the government, the police—and his own personal secretariat.[13] Under Stalin, then, the Politburo was only one means of disseminating power, and in many ways and at many times not even the most important means.

During World War II the Politburo's activities were largely taken over by the State Defense Committee (GOKO), a streamlined Politburo which included the latter's most important members and ultimately almost all of them. In the midst of the war, poor communications, in particular, led to an enlargement of the possibilities for initiative on the part of individual Politburo members, to the opportunity for independent use of the power potentially residing within the Politburo. But the end of the war, and particularly the fears reawakened by the apprehension that "Titoism" would lead to—or reflected—the spread of "independence" throughout the now enlarged communist world, brought on a severe tightening up.[14] After 1949, when Politburo member Voznesensky and others accused of Tito-like activities were shot or imprisoned, the Politburo seldom met.[15] It still existed, but Stalin hardly ever called all of its members together at once, meeting rather with groups of them which, according to Khrushchev, were designated as "quintets," "sextets," "septets," and "novenaries."[16] Setting one group against another by never letting anyone see all the pieces of the puzzle, through guile and intrigue, and through terror, Stalin dominated Russia. The Politburo was one of his tools, but only one.

The position actually occupied by the Politburo in the power structure of the Soviet Union at the end of the Stalinist era is particularly interesting in light of the debate that raged in some Western circles in 1948 vis-à-vis the extent of Stalin's power. It was argued by many at that time that Stalin was a "prisoner" of the Politburo and could only do what it sanctioned. It may have been that by 1948 or shortly thereafter Stalin was in a sense a prisoner of the system that he had been so instrumental in developing, though scarcely of the Politburo itself. By the late 1940's Russia had reached the stage where the techniques that Stalin had utilized to embark upon large-scale industrialization, and to which success and age had given him a strong attachment, were no longer capable of very effectively utilizing the machine that had been created. The need for diversification, the growth of obsolescence, and, relatedly, the appearance of new techniques, the low productivity of slave and semislave labor, and the continued poor showing of agriculture are a sampling of the problems with which Soviet leadership had to deal. Solutions to these problems required what seemed at the time—and in some respects still seem from the inside—to be radical solutions. We see from subsequent statements of and about Politburo members[17] that there was discussion, apparently quite heated at times, of alternatives, at least in the case of some of the problems. But Stalin, regarding disagreement as disloyalty, must have seen any prospect for major change as a threat to his continued suzerainty.

Even though the Politburo as such was all but inactive[18] by this time, its members were still, next to Stalin, the senior leadership personnel of the U.S.S.R. Dominated by him, surviving because apparently they had neither the temperament nor the

position to threaten him, most of them had been on the Politburo for more than a decade. Molotov and Voroshilov had
served since 1926, Kaganovich since 1930, Andreev since 1932,
Mikoyan since 1935, and Khrushchev since 1939. It was during
the period from 1939 to 1952, when the Politburo was in most
ways at the weakest point in its history, that it had the greatest
membership stability.

However, in the last years of his reign, confronted by the unsatisfactory performance of the domestic industrial apparatus,
his suspicions aroused by the Titoist "heresy," aware of the lack
of foreign policy successes, increasingly concerned with the onslaught of age, and sensing that the world would not comply
with his demand that it stand still, Stalin suffered a full re-
awakening of his always partially exposed insecurities. He
moved to assuage them at the unexpected Nineteenth Party
Congress. Whatever the other reasons given for the enlargement of the Politburo—renamed the Presidium[19]—at that congress, it seems clearly to have been a move against the Politburo's senior members.[20] As earlier the power of the Central
Committee had been adumbrated by, among other things, increasing its membership and thereby reducing the influence of
each potentially hostile member, Stalin now reduced the status
of the senior members of the Politburo by more than doubling
their ranks. At the same time, however, he recognized the need
for a smaller body to continue to perform the advisory functions of the former "quintets," "sextets," etc.; and so, though
it was not known until 1955,[21] he created the Buro of the
Presidium.

But the new enlarged Presidium and its Buro were brought
down by the death of Stalin. Those members of the pre-1952
Politburo against whom the enlargement of that body and other
more physically threatening moves were directed in 1952 and
early 1953 took over the reins and quickly reduced the Presidium to more Politburo-like size. They were now in control—
and immediately the struggle to succeed Stalin began.

The emotional variety that must have assaulted the new "joint
leadership" can only be imagined: release, grief, consternation,
fear, hope, *ambition*—all combined in varying proportions ac-

cording to individual propensities. But, regardless of their emotional complexions, they were now engaged in the battle for—at the very least—their political survival.

Though it is easy enough to point out the differences between the situation which prevailed in Russia at Lenin's death in January, 1924, and that which existed in March, 1953,[22] nevertheless, the similarities in the manner in which the succession struggle worked its way out are striking.

As in the earlier episode, there was a unity against the front-runners—in the case of Beria, reinforced by the fear and hatred instilled by his control of the secret police, which had done such violence to the lives of countless individuals and which held tremendous potential for political interference. After Beria had been eliminated there was a turning against Stalin's perhaps chosen successor, Malenkov, and finally against his "closest disciples," Molotov and Kaganovich.

In this maneuvering the primary mover apparently was Khrushchev. Not strong enough to conquer alone—and perhaps not at first even designing to do so—it was he who formed and led the various victorious coalitions of the 1953–57 period. Again, while the political struggle was of major importance, policy issues were the vehicles through which the struggle was enacted. That the issues were important, though scarcely as fundamental as those of three decades earlier, there is no doubt; but that they were still, at least in the short run, secondary to the politics of *kto kogo*—of who was going to do what to whom —was indicated by the way in which Khrushchev alternately opposed and favored an identical position in order to gain political support.[23]

In all of his endeavors, and despite his personal flamboyance, Khrushchev took the middle position, attempting to pre-empt moderation for himself.[24] He invited support against first one extreme and then another. He sought to divert antagonism from himself. His style of operation would not allow him to stay out of the spotlight, yet the policy positions he advocated successfully deflected the glare away from himself—at least until the political opposition had been defeated and he emerged as the new *vozhd.* (One intriguing and obviously unanswerable question concerning Khrushchev's victorious course from 1953 to 1957 was whether—and, if so, to what extent—he recognized that he was following Stalin's guidelines to power. Of course, our knowledge that he was aware that the path he was traversing had been followed before or that he believed he charted it anew would be of little significance in determining whether the same path could, need be, or would be followed again.)

It is clear that from 1953 to 1957 the Politburo-Presidium had power such as it had not enjoyed since the mid-1920's. Certainly within it, collectively, vital decisions were being made, decisions that were long overdue and the need for which had in large measure created the problems of the last years of Stalin's life. But, at the same time, the succession struggle that was still unfolding limited the ability of the Politburo-Presidium to solve problems. In some instances irreconcilable conflicts apparently led to the repostponement of vitally needed decisions; in others, where the Politburo-Presidium could not reach a decision, the problems were referred to the Central Committee, as in the cases, for example, of the Virgin Soil Project of 1954, the proposed overtures of Tito in 1955, and the "antiparty" denouement of 1957.

But the ability of the Politburo-Presidium to make decisions was altered in still another and more significant way in the post-Stalinist period. While Stalin lived, the authority he had garnered over the years, augmented by the fear engendered by Beria's forces, enabled him to control society as few men have ever had the potential to control it. He manipulated the Soviet populace almost *in toto.* He ordered; others obeyed. Certainly he was aware of the existence of special-interest groups within society, for part of his manipulative technique was to set one group against the other. But, even so, essentially what Stalin had to have from these groups, as from the masses, was only their acquiescence, their continued "usability."

With Stalin's death, however, the situation changed, for what the leadership now required, for several reasons, was not only abject obedience, but positive support. From the very first spate of statements made by the drastically reduced Politburo-Presidium after March 5, 1953, its concern for popular support was apparent. Fearful of what might develop after the Man of Steel had breathed his last, aware of the early favor with which the German invaders of the Ukraine were met in 1941, and uncertain of how their successorship would be met specifically, they appealed again and again for "unity" and "solidarity," sometimes even emitting what seems to have been a note of alarm, until they felt safely ensconced.[25]

But, from the appeal of the Politburo-Presidium for support, there quickly developed the tactics of individual leaders seeking personal support in the struggle for power. Beria attempted to develop it in the few months before he was struck down.[26] Malenkov sought it, *inter alia,* with watches and bicycles.[27] Khrushchev went after it in as diffuse a manner as had been seen since Horace Greeley, with "goodies" for all. For the consumer, there was the promise of increased production (though Malenkov had earlier been berated by Khrushchev's man Shepilov for offering the same[28]); for the armed forces there was Zhukov; for industry there was Kosygin; for the women there was Furtseva; for the youth there was Polyansky. Khrushchev tried to touch all the bases.

Further augmenting the need for popular support was the dawning realization that the complex industrialized state created under Stalin could not reach its potential by depending on the public for its acquiescence alone. The positive co-operation of the masses had to be engaged if the economic goals of the system were to be realized. In short, popular support had to be engendered. Thus, for more than a single reason—conceivably, even for some idealistic ones—the operational attitude of the leadership toward the public changed in Russia, with effects that even now have to be sorted out fully.

It is obvious that the "appeal" to the public was not an acceptable technique to all the members of the post-Stalinist Politburo.[29] The public was to be controlled, not to control; so read that most basic of all Leninist concepts, *kto kogo,* which was now being most ignobly violated. The public was not only being solicited; it was being catered to. And with its cultivation the freedom of action of the Politburo-Presidium members was being curtailed.

Certainly all of the leaders of the mid-1950's and, indeed, those in power at this writing, must have had some regrets at this turn of events. In the old days, one gave commands and they were obeyed. There was no need to consider the masses, except largely as an afterthought. To rephrase a quotation attributed to Stalin, the masses would put up with anything they were told to do. Certainly there was no need to pander to special groups. The mounting sense of frustration experienced by Politburo-Presidium leaders at becoming arbitrators and reconcilers of interests has stronger verification than mere conjecture.[30] There are still men of power in the U.S.S.R. who more than long for the "good old days" when the same style locomotive was produced this decade as last, using the same techniques and the same personnel, handled in the same old command fashion.[31] The current recourse to "negotiation" has debilitated that system, they would say: compromise is for revisionists; a communist wants to command.

Regardless of the will to command, however—and it did not disappear with the ouster of the "antiparty group"—command tactics became less a part of the Soviet situation. This was so because of the insecurity and lack of status of the new leaders, because of their need for support as they sought to maneuver themselves into Stalin's old seat, and for other reasons as well. Certainly the personality of Khrushchev must be considered in this regard. He was never the somber introvert that Stalin appears to have been in his middle age, even less the paranoiac he was to become. What he might have grown into had he come to power in the mid-twenties is another matter. But given his character, his age, his established *modus operandi* developed in the Ukraine during the war, the circumstances of Russia in the mid-1950's, it was unlikely that Khrushchev would become a new Stalin; nor did his power, even as it grew after 1957, approach the Stalinist zenith. The situation was different, and the man was different. His ability to accommodate himself to that situation resulted in his triumph, but in triumphing he "acceded" to a lessening in his own power—and thus in the power of the Politburo-Presidium as well.

But there is yet a more fundamental and direct reason for the currently prevailing limitation of the Politburo-Presidium power potential, namely, the resolution thus far adhered to by all of Stalin's successors, except Beria, to minimize the use of terror in the struggle for succession and in the conduct of the day-to-day operations of the U.S.S.R. It has been noted earlier that terror was the method finally hit upon by Stalin to guarantee "loyalty." No matter how he had sought to tie others to him, it seemed that he could not rely upon them absolutely. At the critical moment, they would turn against him. Only total, personal, life-and-death power (and even that had its limitations) gave Stalin the feeling of security he craved and made the system and its men bend to his will. Khrushchev never had that power, nor do his successors, and in Stalinist terms of dominating Soviet society and guaranteeing the unassailability of their own positions they are the weaker for it.

Lacking terror, Stalin's successors have sought other ways of guaranteeing their control. That Khrushchev throughout his tenure was attempting to secure a power base there can be no doubt. For him it was a constant concern and presumably a constant frustration. He began by choosing to champion the party against the "government" interests that Stalin had fostered in the last years of his life. He packed the Secretariat and the Central Committee, and he established and packed the Buro of the Central Committee for the Russian Republic. He sought the "loyalty" that had also eluded Stain, by bringing in "friends" that he had known in the Ukraine and by promoting men quickly from the ranks. But, even had the pressures not been such as to force him to demote the incompetent and those unsuited in other ways for roles at the top, this would not have satisfied his goals. He promoted members of his family, thinking that at least one could depend on one's son-in-law. He established, against vigorous opposition, a new party-state control apparatus and put it in charge of an ex-KGB head who had done him yeoman service elsewhere. He sought to establish his own secretariat, as Stalin had done earlier. He went directly to the people, appealing to them, as it were, over the heads of the interests—party or otherwise—that seemingly stood against him.[32] But none of this was sufficient to bring Khrushchev the loyalty and absence of opposition that he sought. Apparently only terror, the awakening of the forces of the earlier Stalin era, could accomplish that, and, though Khrushchev came close at times to seeking that solution,[33] he would not or could not bring it off.

The opposition to Khrushchev sprang from a variety of sources. Ambition had never been throttled, even under Stalin. It was utilized and contained, but it was not eliminated. And in the Khrushchevian society's emphasis upon individual accomplishment and acquisition it was not to be played down. Where ambition is fostered, ambition for the top job can hardly be stilled, except by force. As for those who benefited personally from Khrushchev's favors, the question would speedily occur: And what have you done for me lately? Khrushchev had not been able, or had not deigned, to protect his incompetent favorites; therefore, the survivors must have concluded that they remained in office not because of Khrushchev but because of their ability. They had to watch out for themselves.

Thus, when failure came to Khrushchev and, at least by reflection, to his Politburo, its members apparently had less than immobilizing concern for his future or fear for the forces he could arrange against them. Where success is the *sine qua non,* the leader must also succeed—or be able to conceal his failures. In the early 1960's Khrushchev's economic and foreign policy failures came so fast that his identification with them was unavoidable. In trying to cope with his problems he had invoked the hostility of one group after another: the governmental bureaucracy, by his favoring of the party; the party, by the dual reform; the army, by his multilateral threat to its established priorities. The Party-State Control Committee aroused widespread fears,[34] for it aimed at establishing a new control device, both extraparty and extra-government. Particularly among those who were prone to find fault with him anyway, Khrushchev's style—shoe-banging, finger-shaking, headknocking—rankled. And there was the matter of his age; by 1964 Khrushchev was seventy. The impression of dynamism remained, but Khrushchev had become bogged down in his own mistakes. He was not able to handle the opposition as he had a decade earlier. He was now clearly the focus of attention—and the scapegoat. As Azrael has pointed out,[35] Khrushchev could not eliminate the opposition, and his own forces deserted him before he could. If he had had a Beria at his side, the unsuccessful secret meetings that took place in Bulganin's office in the first half of 1957[36] and the more successful ones that must have been held in some other Politburo-Presidium member's office, possibly Podgorny's in 1964, probably would not have occurred. But there was no police control tantamount to Stalin's; conditions were no longer so infinitely malleable. This was a different situation; it limited Khrushchev's power, it restricted his authority, and it would do the same to his successors, unless they could find another basis for stabilizing their power.

As for those successors, they have undone some of the mistakes to which their predecessor was committed, and in some ways they have carried out further revisions of the Stalinist model. In essence they have had to contend with the same problems that faced their predecessor; they operate in largely the same context and they are, because of the even greater weakness of their position (for they have even less authority than their predecessor), even less capable, and perhaps less willing, to make the radical resolutions that are called for. Furthermore, the route to power which both Stalin and Khrushchev followed is undoubtedly well understood, and the present array of Politburo candidates for the number one position, unimpressive though each Politburo member may be individually, appears determined to prevent any single member from assuming Khrushchev's mantle. Thus far they have so acted, but the power struggle has yet to unfold. In the past it has taken from four to six years for a victor to emerge, and at this writing less than two have passed.

The successor to Khrushchev's Politburo-Presidium continues to sit in on a retreat from an absolutist position. Party-oriented, it is beset by demands for recognition from the government bureaucracy, the industrial bureaucracy, the intelligentsia, the youth, the army, the consumer, and so forth. The claimants are not organized. They are still in many ways manipulable, but they cannot be disregarded, except at great costs, and their voices are not effectively being stilled. The Politburo leaders, collectively and individually, need support, and, like Khrushchev, they seek it through concessions. Each potential aspirant to the Khrushchevian role attempts to build a power base. Kosygin, seeking to build his image, played to the Soviet public during his trip to the United Nations. Shelepin has apparently wrapped himself in the mantle of youth and dynamism and a mixture of "liberal conservatism." Increasingly, as stated above, the Politburo has become a mediator of interests, a resolver of externally based demands. It retains the power of decision, but the alternatives open to it are narrow, and in most instances none of them are acceptable in the light of traditional Bolshevik values and behavioral patterns.

II

The evolution of the Politburo has been traced above through the five decades of its development—from aborted inception, to power, to gimcrack, and back to power, only to find its regained power in the process of erosion. By frequent statements asserting party power[37] and by such maneuvers as changing the name of their own grouping from "Presidium" back to the Stalinist "Politburo" and redesignating the First Secretary of the C.P.S.U. with the Stalinist title of General Secretary, the Politburo seeks to indicate that its power and determination to use that power remain undiminished. But titles do not instill power.

At this point, in order to assess in another way what the Politburo has become and perhaps to be better able to assess what it may become, let us take a look at some of the characteristics of the present Politburo members and some of the members of the past decade. And, in order to have a basis for comprehending the transition that has occurred, let us compare them with the Politburo members of 1927 and of the first decade of Soviet power. Certainly there are considerable difficulties in using these periods. The decision has been made arbitrarily to cover the period from November, 1917, to December, 1927, thus including the never-active first Politburo. Again, the December, 1927, cut-off date means that the ouster of the "leftists" will be included, but not that of the rightists. In 1957 the Politburo instituted by the Central Committee plenum of June 22–27 is taken as the starting point, thus omitting the older, ousted members of the anti-party "groups." Furthermore, by 1927 the power struggle of that era apparently had been more nearly resolved than has the struggle of the present period, and so on. There are difficulties also in comparing two decades in the life of an institution when three developmental decades separate the two extremes under consideration. At the very least the rate and flow of change cannot be properly gauged under such an arrangement, but a general comparison can be made.

It can be argued that it is not just the Politburo members who should be considered, but the alternates as well. Others would say that any consideration of the Politburo is meaningless without joint investigation of the Secretariat, the Central Committee, and, for the earlier period, the Orgburo; and in terms of the operation of the entire system, they would be correct. Nevertheless, it does seem apparent that, in the sense of the present consideration, the Politburo does have an existence uniquely its own. Despite all of the foregoing and perhaps other difficulties involved in making the kind of analysis proposed, the exercise seems worthwhile.

TOTAL NUMBER OF POLITBURO MEMBERS

1917–27[38]	*1957–67*
15	25

Dan N. Jacobs

SIZE VARIATION OF THE POLITBURO

1917–27	1957–67
5(1919-21)–9(1926-27)	11(1961, 1964, 1966-67)–16(1958)

The fact that the size of the Politburo in the fifth decade exceeds that in the first reflects, to a large degree, the expanded activity of the U.S.S.R. More men are required to direct that activity. In the 1960's the figure varies so slightly that it must be concluded that there has been a resolution setting the optimal figure at eleven or twelve. The Politburo apparently reaches a maximum size after the tide has begun to turn in favor of one candidate in a power struggle, or so it has happened in the past.

AVERAGE AGE OF POLITBURO MEMBERS

1927	1967
44	59

It is clear that the average Politburo member in 1967 is much older than was his counterpart in 1927. He is also, on the average, older than the members of the American or British Cabinets; in September, 1967, the average age of U.S. Cabinet members was fifty-one plus, and that of British Cabinet members occupying senior posts was a shade over fifty-five. Only one Politburo member is below fifty (he is forty-nine). Four are in their fifties, six are in their sixties. It is an old body. The semi-"antique" quality of the Politburo becomes even more noteworthy when it is seen that in the past decade such members of advanced years as Voroshilov (eighty-six, seventy-nine when ousted) and Kuusinen (eighty-three when he died, in 1964), and Shvernik (seventy-nine, seventy-eight when ousted) have left.

AGE AT WHICH MEMBERS JOINED PARTY

1917–27	1957–67	1967
20	21	22

The figure for 1917–27 is raised slightly because of Lenin, who was a decade older than most other Politburo members, a factor often overlooked in seeking the source of his "authority." Of all the Politburo members in both periods, he "joined" the party at the latest age. For 1957–67 the variation is from sixteen (Pelshe) to twenty-seven (Podgorny). Pelshe, the only member of the current Politburo to have joined the party before the Revolution, came into the Politburo only after Shvernik (who joined in 1905) and Mikoyan (who joined in 1915) were dropped in 1966; coming in without any previous tenure as a candidate member, he undoubtedly was chosen in large part for legitimizing purposes. With the exception of Pelshe and Suslov, all other members of the present Politburo joined in their twenties, two entering at twenty-five, one at twenty-six, and another at twenty-seven. Other than Pelshe, only Suslov (who joined in 1921) became a member in the pre-Stalinist period. The rest joined under Stalin's early command, one entering in 1927, another in 1928, one in 1930, and three in 1931. The year 1940 is the latest in which any current full member joined (Mukhitdinov, who was ousted in 1961, joined two years later). Thus all the present leaders are of pre–World War II vintage.

CLASS ORIGIN

1917–27		1957–67	
Lower class	6	Lower class	22
Middle class	9	Middle class	3

This information is as uncertain and arbitrary as any with with we are dealing. What does seem definite is that the middle-class origins which characterized the earlier leadership do not prevail at present.

Stalin's earlier prejudices against middle-class Politburo members (all of those who became ex-members before 1927 were of such origin) apparently were overcome by the 1940's, with Molotov, Beria, Malenkov, Voznesensky, and Bulganin all having non-working-class/peasant backgrounds. But by 1957 all of these except Bulganin, who was soon to go, were out. The current leadership is characterized by a strong made-it-the-hard-way background, and it indicates characteristics consonant with the syndrome.

HIGHER EDUCATION

1917–27	1927	1957–67	1967
8 out of 15	3 out of 8	15 out of 25	9 out of 11

Again, this is, particularly for the latter period, unsatisfactory in terms of exactness, not only from an informational point of view, but also because of the difficulty of determining what higher education is in general, and, in particular, what it is in the Soviet Union, and because of the difficulty in classifying the technical "institutes," especially those of the late 1920's and the 1930's. What is indicated is that as Stalin rid his early Politburo of its middle-class members he was obviously ousting its educated men as well. In the 1957–67 period a majority of the leadership again had "higher" educations. By 1967 only two had not achieved this level of education.

NATIONALITY (MOSTLY) ACCORDING TO BIRTHPLACE[39]

	1917–27	1927	1957–67	1967
Russian (R.S.F.S.R.)	9	5	14	5
Jewish	3	—	—	—
Ukrainian	1	1	6	4
Georgian	1	1	1	—
Latvian	1	1	1	1
Belorussian	—	—	1	1
Finnish	—	—	1	—
Uzbekistani	—	—	1	—

The above figures need considerable explanation. Each of the Politburo members, regardless of where he was born, had to be a Russian in terms of interests and affinities or he would not have been advanced. Simply because he was born in the Ukraine or in Georgia does not mean that he was selected particularly to represent the interests of that area. In practice, those coming from minority areas undoubtedly have bent over backward to indicate that they are, first and foremost, "Russians." Nevertheless, political capital has been made of the fact that a Ukrainian or a Central Asian has been promoted to a position of the first rank, and in at least one instance (Mukhitdinov) it would seem that an appointment was made at least in part because of nationality.

One difficulty with the table is that it conceals the information, for example, that Trotsky, a Jew, was born in the Ukraine, that Mikoyan, an Armenian, entered this world in Georgia, and that Kirilenko, who has an obviously Ukrainian name, was born in Voronezh (R.S.F.S.R.), etc.

But the table does make clear the degree to which Ukrainians lately have entered and remain in the Politburo. Brought in by Khrushchev, or at least raised to high position by him (though Shelest, one of his disciples, probably made the final jump to full membership because he supported the coup against Khrushchev in 1964), they are present in the Politburo in far greater numbers than the Ukrainian fraction of the total population would lead one to expect. As noted above, however, this in no wise indicates that they will seek to follow a more pro-Ukrainian policy. One would suspect that, because of the presence of Ukrainians in particular numbers in the Politburo, being connected with the Ukraine would at present be an impediment to promotion to the top.

Closely connected with region of birth is the matter of the size of the unit in which the Politburo member was born and presumably grew up—city, town, village. Here again there are some lacunae, but the indications are that only Kosygin, and possibly Pelshe, came from urban environments and that, at the most, two others were not village boys.

The biographies of the Politburo members do not lend themselves easily to this kind of analysis. All of the subjects, with the possible exception of Zhukov, have been heavily engaged in

PARTY VS. GOVERNMENT WORK EXPERIENCE

	1957–67	*1967*
Party	19	10
Government	4	1
Other	2	—

party work during their careers; otherwise they would not have been named to the Politburo. The principal distinction, therefore, must be between those who have had professional expertise (usually of a technical nature), which they have employed regularly, even when in the Politburo, and those who have been heavily, though not exclusively, involved with party administrative and ideological matters. Even so, it should be noted that many Politburo members designated as full-time party workers fill or have filled governmental roles. Moreover, almost all of the current Politburo leaders have technical specialties that they used early in their careers. For many of these and for others of the 1957–67 period the point of change-over to full-time party work was World War II.

The figures do seem to reinforce a widely held conclusion: that a stronger party background is now required for Politburo membership than was requisite earlier. As the party becomes weaker, the Politburo closes its gates.

AVERAGE NUMBER OF YEARS IN THE POLITBURO

1917–27 *(ousted)*	*1917–27* *(in power in 1927)*	*1957–67* *(ousted)*	*1957–67* *(in power in 1967)*
4	4	10	6

For the earlier period the average figure is relatively meaningless. In 1927, only Stalin had belonged to the Politburo continuously since 1917. But, of those who were in the Politburo just prior to the Fifth Party Congress in December, 1927—in addition to Stalin, who was to be a member for twenty-six years —Voroshilov was to serve for thirty-five years, Molotov for thirty-two years, and Kalinin for twenty. In the current Politburo only Suslov (twelve years) and Brezhnev have served for more than ten years, though Kosygin's two split terms total eleven years. Kosygin is the only member of the present Politburo to have served in Stalin's Politburo, all of the old regulars still around in 1957—Voroshilov, Mikoyan, Khrushchev—and others—having fallen by the wayside.

However, while none of the Politburo members have had more than a dozen years' service and two have belonged for only one year, and while their years of Politburo membership are few by Stalinist standards, it must not be assumed that they are neophytes to the top echelons of power. Kosygin was first named a candidate member in 1946; Kirilenko was a candidate for five years and Mazurov for nine years before each was named a full member. While the others were candidates for two years or less, or not at all, before being raised to full Politburo membership, no present member of the Politburo was a member of the Central Committee for less than six years prior to Politburo service, and the average number of years of membership was over fourteen. Kosygin entered the Central Committee in 1939, Suslov in 1941, three current Politburo members in 1952, four in 1956, and two—probably the weakest members—in 1961.

FATE OF FORMER POLITBURO MEMBERS

	1917–27	1927	1957–67
Natural death	3	2	2
Execution	7	3	—
Suicide	1	1	—
Death in prison	1	—	—
Still in Central Committee	1	1	5
Retirement (over 65)	2 (Bubnov, released from prison in 1956)	1	4
Obscurity (under 65)	—	—	3

The violent deaths of the members of the 1917–27 period have been noted so frequently as to require no further comment here. The two of the 1927 Politburo who were still alive in September, 1967, are Molotov and Voroshilov, the former living in retirement and the latter renamed a Central Committee member in 1966 after having been out of grace. Of the Politburo members in the 1957–67 period, none, apparently, have died violently. The three removed from the Politburo who have fallen from public view all left in 1961; Kirichenko had been named to the Politburo in 1955, Belyaev and Mukhitdinov in 1957. All three were identified with Khrushchev's rise and had proved useful to him politically. In the case of two, there were believable indications that inability to perform assigned duties satisfactorily was involved in their dismissals.

The fact that five ex-members of the Politburo continued in, or were renamed to, the Central Committee after their fall and that four ex-members continue in more-or-less graceful retirement indicates the prevalence of a situation far different from that which existed in and following the mid-1930's, when "retirement" and physical death were equated. Brzezinski suggests that there may now even be a special office to care for the needs of former Politburo members.[40]

FOREIGN TRAVEL

1917–27	1957–67
All	24 of 25 abroad
	19 of 25 beyond Iron Curtain

All the Politburo members in the 1917–27 period had grown up under the *ancien régime,* and most had spent many of their adult years in exile. But all had been abroad to attend congresses, conferences, etc. During the latter part of the Stalinist period, the complaint was often heard, as it is concerning China today, that Soviet leaders were isolated and consequently knew nothing of the outside world from personal experience. Whether or not the latter accusation was true then, it is clear that the most recent decade's leaders have been abroad, the majority of them beyond the Iron Curtain. This does not, of course, indicate that they have regarded what they have seen with open minds or that they have drawn the "proper" conclusions.

III

From the above it would seem that the "average" Politburo member today is in late middle age; that he has belonged to the party for more than thirty years; that he came from a provincial, working- or peasant-class background; that he is almost as likely to be Ukrainian as Great Russian, though probably it doesn't make much difference; that he has had a higher education, probably in some technological specialization at which he worked before he began devoting the greater part of his attention to party work; that his Politburo membership does not go back to the Stalinist period, and, indeed, that he has served in the Politburo for a shorter period than many of his predecessors but has had additional years of Central Committee membership which probably, at least in terms of relationships, stand him in good stead in his present position; and that he has some personal knowledge of the world outside the U.S.S.R.

What is likely to be the future of a Politburo made up of men of this type? We start with the fact that this is an old Politburo and we assume that its members exhibit the characteristics of older men. We add to this the understanding that comes from recognizing the Politburo as a group of self-made men who, beginning at very modest levels, have struggled long to reach the top and have only recently made it all the way. Most were in their fifties when chosen for Politburo membership. Most were promoted to the Politburo or to the higher echelons of party power by Khrushchev, though apparently this in no wise secured them to him permanently. These same men prepared the coup against him; a few seemingly helped boost their entrance into the Politburo by consenting to or even organizing his overthrow.[41]

It may be assumed that, being older, generally they are more "conservative," less "adventurous." Having recently come to power—after a long struggle and at a moderately advanced age —they are less likely to run the risks involved in attempting to take over the entire shooting match for themselves. They have savored top power, and it is good. It would be nice to have it all, but at sixty-five what are the chances? What power base do they have or can they build, upon which they can depend?

One suspects that at least among some of the members of the Politburo there has developed an old-guard feeling: we are the defenders of the party; we must guide it through the shoals of change (often seen as being embodied in youth) that threaten it; let us gird up our loins. One notes that the two most recent additions to the Politburo, Mazurov and Pelshe, are scarcely representative of the new generation. Mazurov, though only fifty-three, had been a candidate member for almost a decade. Pelshe's pre-revolutionary credentials have been noted previously. Neither could possibly be regarded as a serious contender for the top power. It seems plausible to regard both as team men, as defenders of the party "and its traditions."

There is the impression that, though this Politburo recognizes that societal change has occurred, is occurring, and cannot be stayed, its age and experiences make it want to go slow. It finds it hard to reconcile itself to a diminution of the power of the party—that party which nurtured them and in which they have risen to power. Collectively, the party is the foundation of their power, but, at the same time, in the struggle for power not one of them can command it. And so they must seek other sources of support, sometimes outside the party, though within it as well. These "groups" whose support must be solicited are at the same time the "groups" which are making the demands that absorb the attentions of the Politburo. As has been noted before, the Politburo seems increasingly to find itself under what it may regard as siege conditions. In such circumstances it would be psychologically justifiable to expect that older men—strong men, set in their ways, pushed and pulled, as it were, seeking to protect their own prerogatives and positions—will find good reason for binding together to man the barricades against the common foe.

Essentially, then, the present Politburo is defensive. It must defend against all those situations and developments which might erode the power of the party and the Politburo and, at the same time, against those who would take over personal power in the Politburo.

Certainly "youth" must be one of the Politburo's particular bogies, in its general aspect as the apotheosis of change and the continued demand for change, as well as in the power threat that it presents within the party. While it is true that the Politburo has become a stronghold of the aging, as has the Central Committee,[42] such is not the case in the republic central committees.[43] Sooner or later a push for power from those of the Shelepin-Polyansky generation is to be expected. Judging from what is known of the reaction to the Middle East war of June, 1967, such a development may already have gone through one storm, with the more youthful aspirants to power losing out.[44] According to one source, the development of an open fight for power was delayed only by the desire to maintain decorum for the celebration of the fiftieth anniversary, but after November 7 the lid was expected to come off—and it is likely that the battle that will flair will be between age and middle age, if not between age and youth.[45]

Obviously, in such a struggle, youth eventually will win out. Even as age in part made Khrushchev vulnerable, the same will happen to Brezhnev-Kosygin-Podgorny and company. In the meantime, this struggle is likely to add to the sense of besiegement experienced by the Politburo and to draw its leading members closer together.

As indicated above, it is also likely that by this time most of the older men in the Politburo are aware that power such as that enjoyed by Stalin or even by Khrushchev will not be theirs, even if they desire it. Circumstances and time have passed them by. Some members of the Politburo who have prestige because of long service in that body but who do not share the top power within it now and cannot realistically aspire to such power—

"senior advisers"—may hope that they will be included in any new Politburo; but aside from perhaps Suslov, there are no such Politburo members around anymore. Most of those at the top— men like Brezhnev, Kosygin, Podgorny, and perhaps most of the rest of their generation—must realize that this is the top for them, this is as high as they can go, and that a lateral move is unlikely. And so they defend themselves as best they can against all outside assaults on their power: from the youth, from the intelligentsia, from the industrial and government bureaucracy, from those who demand more change and those who would return to the past. In all probability, now aware of how Khrushchev (they were close witnesses), and Stalin before him, rose to personal power, they guard against those who would follow a similar path, against those who seek to find bases of support in Soviet society, whether it be in the secret police, in the Komsomol, in such institutions as the Party-State Control Committee, or in flooding the membership of the Central Committee or of the party. It is to be suspected that the present top Politburo members will settle for the power and positions they have now, and, if they can't have it all, neither will anyone else. Only desperation is likely to lead any present senior Politburo member to make a solitary run.

But, given the nature of ambition, given the continued moratorium on the use of terror, which makes an unsuccessful drive for the top politically though not physically fatal, and given the age of the current principal sharers of power, it is certain that new assaults will be made and that, sooner or later, in one form or another, one of these will succeed.

So much, then, for the current Politburo. But what about the future of the institution? As indicated in this paper, the development of the Politburo has been identified throughout the Soviet experience with the transfer of power, the succession problem.

In brief, if there were a regularization of the process, then the entire existence of the Politburo would be transformed. But to secure that regularization there would have to be a major alteration in the values of the system—an alteration that does not at present seem in the offing.

Institutionally, there is no reason why the Politburo cannot do a good job of running the Soviet Union through the various subagencies that it currently utilizes. What is lacking to enhance the effectiveness of the Politburo and the system for dealing with the circumstances of a highly industrialized society is the development of a "loyal opposition," which is implicit in any meaningful solution to the succession problem. But there is no significant development of the concept in the Soviet Union today. The mimeographed handouts of a Solzhenitsyn,[46] the smuggled-out ironies of a Voznesensky,[47] do not constitute a developed loyal opposition, nor do the increasingly open discussions in the Central Committee, even in its enlarged session. The concept of a "loyal opposition" is totally antithetic to the theory and practice of Soviet communism. Among other things the tentative gropings of the U.S.S.R. toward freedom of expression indicate the need for some such device in a modernized society, but the distance between "loyal opposition" and what the Soviet Union has is so great as to seem unbridgeable at this juncture. One does not anticipate the speedy legal development of a loyal opposition and the concomitant regularization of succession in the Soviet Union. It does not seem likely, but things almost as surprising have occurred in the U.S.S.R. within the past decade and a half. Barring such epochal change, it is likely that the Politburo will continue to be rocked by periodic struggles, rebellions, and coups of the type demonstrated in the past dozen years. The close relationship of policy and politics means that every policy crisis will present a political opportunity. Every failure or deprivation gives rise to hostility, real or potential. Repeated failure and/or deprivation solidifies opposition. Gigantic failure, or the prospect of new failures and deprivations, operationalizes opposition. But, while opposition may be widespread (short of revolution), without the intervention of terror or the army, only the Politburo, the Secretariat, and intermittently the Central Committe can act to unseat the incumbents. Change in leadership, therefore, is to continue to be not only irregular but mercurial.

It should also be noted that the continued relationship of policy and politics in the Politburo means that repeated or outstanding policy successes can build support, immobilize opposition, or prevent the opposition's genesis. Successful problem-solving, in which the leading role in a particularly critical situation is taken by a single individual, will lead at the very least to a tendency to defer to the judgment of that individual in other circumstances and thus to a strengthening of his position and power within the Politburo. It happens in every group.

However, the chances—still strongly present, and backed by centuries of precedent—of one man's emulating the role of Stalin and Khrushchev are attenuated, at least to some degree, by the absence of terror and by the knowledge shared by present leaders of how Stalin and Khrushchev came to power. But leaders die and circumstances change. Voluntary oaths—unenforced by legal and political institutions or by tradition—to abjure the use of terror where terror has been the rule are, to say the least, highly vulnerable to backsliding. Within the above-cited limitations, the fate of the Politburo is as much subject to accident as is that of any institution.

NOTES

1. L. Schapiro, *History of the Communist Party of the Soviet Union* (New York, 1960), p. 239.

2. L. Schapiro, *The Origin of the Communist Autocracy* (Cambridge, 1955), p. 262.

3. L. Trotskii, "Our Political Task," quoted in B. Wolfe, *Three Who Made A Revolution* (Boston, 1948), p. 253.

4. Schapiro, *Communist Party of the Soviet Union,* p. 240.

5. *Ibid.*

6. There are many such recountings. One of the best is in vol. II of I. Deutscher's Trotskii trilogy, *The Prophet Unarmed* (London, 1959).

7. R. C. Tucker, *The Soviet Political Mind* (New York, 1963), p. 156.

8. Schapiro, *Communist Party of the Soviet Union,* p. 391.

9. S. Alliluyeva, *Twenty Letters to a Friend* (New York, 1967), pp. 112–13.

10. N. S. Khrushchev, "Secret Speech," in *The New Communist Manifesto,* ed. D. N. Jacobs (New York, 1965), p. 163.

11. *Ibid.,* p. 145.

12. *Ibid.,* p. 163.

13. Tucker, *The Soviet Political Mind,* pp. 157–58.

14. Cf. J. A. Armstrong, *The Politics of Totalitarianism* (New York, 1961), pp. 214–15.

15. Khrushchev, "Secret Speech," p. 163.

16. *Ibid.*

17. L. F. Ilichev, *Pravda,* November 5, 1961.

18. B. E. Nicolayevskii, cited in Tucker, *The Soviet Political Mind,* p. 157.

19. As M. Fainsod has noted (*How Russia Is Ruled* [Cambridge, 1963], p. 323), no satisfactory reason was given by Soviet sources. The suggestion at the time, that it was done to broaden and unify the power base, is largely meaningless. Nor does it seem likely that even a disintegrated Stalin would have undertaken such a reorganization merely to get rid of a term that smacked of Trotskii and the Revolution, though this may have been involved to a degree.

20. Khrushchev, "Secret Speech," p. 164.

21. Schapiro, *Communist Party of the Soviet Union,* p. 519.

22. Cf. M. Fainsod, *How Russia Is Ruled,* p. 333, for example.

23. Cf. M. Rush, *Political Succession in the U.S.S.R.* (New York, 1965).

24. This was not a unique position from which to move to power. See Z. Brzezinski and S. P. Huntington, *Political Power: USA/USSR* (New York, 1965), p. 265.

25. D. N. Jacobs, "Slogans and Soviet Politics,"*The American Slavic and East European Review,* vol. XVI, no. 3 (October, 1957), p. 299.

26. *Pravda,* July 10, 1953.

27. *Pravda,* October 28, 1953.

28. *Pravda,* January 24, 1955.

29. *Partiinaia zhizn',* no. 20 (October, 1964) [see also *Current Digest of the Soviet Press,* vol. XVI, no. 42, p. 6 (hereafter cited as *CDSP*)].

30. *Partiinaia zhizn',* no. 20.

31. *Literaturnaia gazeta,* February 1, 1965 [*CDSP, vol.* XVIII, no. 5, p. 13].

32. H. W. Morton, in *Soviet Policy Making,* ed. P. H. Juviler and H. W. Morton (New York, 1967), p. 25.

33. As in the Party-State Control Committee (PSCC), activated in November, 1962.

34. G. Hodnett, in *Politics in the Soviet Union,* ed. A. Dallin and A. F. Westin (New York, 1966), p. 145.

35. J. R. Azrael, *Managerial Power and Soviet Politics* (Cambridge, 1966), p. 146.

36. *Pravda,* December 19, 1958.

37. For example, the party resolution on the fiftieth anniversary of the October Revolution, *Pravda,* January 8, 1967.

38. Data for the 1917–27 period were, in large part, derived from G. K. Schueller, *The Politburo* (Stanford, 1951).

39. For a valuable presentation of the role of nationality in the Central Committee see S. Bialer, "How Russians Rule Russia," *Problems of Communism,* vol. 13, no. 5 (September-October, 1964), pp. 45–52.

40. Z. Brzezinski, "The Soviet Political System: Transition or Degeneration," *Problems of Communism,* vol. 15, no. 1 (January-February, 1966), p. 7.

41. Shelepin, Shelest.

42. Eighty-three per cent of those elected to that body in 1961 were re-elected in 1966, while less than 50 per cent of those elected in 1956 were re-elected in 1961 (J. Hough, "The Soviet Elite," *Problems of Communism,* vol. 17, no. 2 [March-April, 1967], p. 19). In addition, the revolving membership rule of 1961 was terminated at the Twenty-third Party Congress; and the practice of *perestanovak* in the Soviet bureaucracy has been much restricted (*Pravda,* April 7, 1966, quoted in Hough, "The Soviet Elite").

43. Hough, "The Soviet Elite," p. 21.

44. The demotion of Moscow party chief N. G. Yegorychev and the relegation of Politburo member Shelepin to the limbo of trade union work following the June, 1967, plenum of the Central Committee is to be viewed in such a context. The subsequent announcement, little noted abroad, that Shelepin had been relieved of his work in the party Secretariat (*Pravda,* September 27, 1967) indicated that the hold of the "oldsters" was still strong. However, subsequently, Shelepin apparently was to attempt to convert the trade-union post into a power base.

45. Harrison Salisbury, *New York Times,* July 12, 1967, p. 21. While Mr. Salisbury's reputation has recently suffered—and understandably so wide circle of highly placed acquaintances, would seem to provide justification for quoting him in instances such as this.

46. For the text of his letter to the Soviet Union of Writers, see the *New York Times,* June 5, 1967, p. 36, and June 6, 1967, p. 4.

47. For the text of the letter *Pravda* refused to print, see the *New York Times,* August 11, 1967, p. 14.

Prospects for Soviet Political Development: Evolution, Decay, or Revolution?*

Frederick C. Barghoorn

DEFINITIONS AND ANALYTICAL FRAMEWORK

Political forecasting is a notoriously hazardous form of intellectual speculation. Its difficulties reflect not only our incomplete or defective understanding of the shape of things present and past but also the possibility that presently nonexistent factors may exert influence later. The modesty dictated by these sobering thoughts is reinforced by knowledge of the conspicuous failure of political analysts to predict major developments, especially in communist political systems, where our own biases and communist secrecy present peculiar problems. We have often been surprised by the timing, scope, and magnitude of such events as the ouster of Khrushchev, the course of de-Stalinization, or the intensity of Sino-Soviet rivalry. All too often we have assumed that communist leaderships could ignore internal pressures for reform. Most of us were unprepared for the Tito-Stalin break or the liberalization of Yugoslav communism that eventually followed it. Today, most of us are nonplused by the movement of Czechoslovakian communism in a pluralistic and democratic direction.

* The author wishes to thank the American Philosophical Society for a grant which helped make possible the research on which this paper is based. Thanks are also expressed to Yale University for assistance in connection with travel expenses and other support for this research.

We also wish to emphasize that, problematic as it is, the attempt to perceive the principal alternative lines of future Soviet political development can be useful. Even if our effort to identify emergent trends is not fully successful it may at least help us to understand the present, by forcing us to focus on the most essential elements that make for either preservation or disintegration of existing patterns. Refusal to engage in forecasting constitutes an abdication of intellectual responsibility. It can make us prone to violent and irrational overreactions to the unpleasant surprises, which could have been less shocking had we gotten into the habit of constantly weighing alternative probabilities.

The expectations incorporated in this paper are cautiously, and it is hoped realistically, positive, although the writer must admit that recent suppressive actions of the Soviet authorities against intellectual dissenters inspire in him a pessimism greater than he entertained when he began to work on this study in the spring of 1967. This paper argues that, at least for the next few years, adaptive evolution, rather than political decay or revolution, is the most likely outcome of the trends presently operating in Soviet political life. It is tentatively committed to the view that the beneficent trends now perceptible in the situation of the Soviet peoples will persist and increase their influence at least in the spheres of wealth and well-being, and probably also in the cultural and spiritual realms of life, provided that Soviet-Western relations remain relatively stable and that the Western democracies continue to prosper. *Adaptive evolution, political decay,* and *revolution,* as used herein, refer to separate, but not necessarily mutually exclusive, states of affairs. The dominance of one of these patterns at any particular time does not completely preclude some degree of coexistence with the others. In all societies and in all political systems elements of successful adaptation, or evolution, are usually commingled with patches of disintegration and decay. As for revolution, its latent spark is ever present. The interaction of many interdependent factors shaping a society's development, including its political culture and ideology, as well as technological and scientific innovation, generational differences, the rate of economic growth, the results of past wars and the threat of future wars, and the training, experience, courage, and skill of political leaders and their associates, must be taken carefully into account.

Political forecasting must follow a contingent strategy if confusion and oversimplification are to be minimized.[1] We hypothesize that an adaptive evolutionary path of political development in the U.S.S.R. is more likely to prevail than is either decay or revolution, and further—although this is peripheral to our main concern—that such an outcome is likely to foster Soviet policies that will be conducive to peace and welfare. It is further assumed that the outcome envisaged is heavily dependent upon a continued rise in the quantity and range of goods, services, and amenities available to the Soviet citizenry and wholly dependent upon the avoidance by the United States and the U.S.S.R. of nuclear conflict. The expectations underlying this paper are based on assumptions that might be regarded as too hopeful in some quarters. However, the paper also makes the negative assumption of a continued sharp political rivalry between the two superpowers, as well as a high degree of unrest and instability in the underdeveloped countries.[2]

The study of political development has both empirical and normative aspects. From an empirical, value-free point of view, it is concerned with the structures and activities by which a political system copes with the stresses and strains encountered in the internal and external environments, in transactions the outcome of which determines whether it flourishes, stagnates, or disintegrates. If a system disintegrates, it is either transformed —by internally generated forces—into a new system, more or less within the boundaries of its predecessor, or absorbed into those of formerly external systems. Political development thus involves, among other things, the successful surmounting of the major "crises" of identity, legitimacy, participation, distribution, and "penetration."[3] The ability of a political regime to deal creatively with these formative experiences both depends upon and determines such system "capabilities" as the "extractive," or coercive, the "regulative," the "distributive," the "symbolic," and the "responsive." These capabilities, in turn, are involved in the performance of the political "conversion" functions of interest articulation and interest aggregation by which a polity interacts with the society it guides, as well as by the functions of rule-making, rule application, and rule adjudication, and, finally, the system-maintenance and adaptation functions of political socialization and elite recruitment.[4]

Unlike the adherents of Marxism-Leninism, those who make use of the approaches referred to above strive consciously to avoid being culture bound.[5] Modern empirical political theory does not attempt to evaluate systems solely in terms of their approximation to particular institutional patterns. Thus, theoretical analysis can perhaps facilitate mutual understanding among members of systems with different traditions and different backgrounds of historical experience. It stresses what is common to political life but does not ignore differences that reflect diverse experiences.

Until recently a weakness of political systems and development theories has been their lack of attention to revolutionary movements, especially those led by communists, and in particular to the analysis of political orders established as a result of communist revolutions. However, in the opinion of this author, students of communist systems can make good use of the macroanalytical schemes developed by Almond, Pye, and others, provided, of course, that they do not uncritically transplant categories from noncommunist to Soviet-type systems. Particularly valuable for our purposes, perhaps, is the general approach to revolution developed by Chalmers Johnson.[6] According to Johnson, to maintain its equilibrium, and function effectively, any society must keep its established pattern of values and shared norms and expectations in a state of synchronization with the structures by which the division of political, economic, and social labor necessary to maintain it is, in its particular setting, effected. On this view, the synchronization between value patterns and the societal division of labor is constantly threatened by new ideas originating either within or outside the given society and also by environmental changes, which, by forcing adaptations of structure, can create discrepancies between established values and changing patterns of social action. If a society's political elite proves to be incapable of carrying out the adjustments and reforms needed to keep its values and the environment in balance, disequilibrium, or even revolution, may occur. In Johnson's definition, revolutions, as distinguished from less fundamental changes, such as rebellions, are social changes effected by violence directed against established authority. Johnson views revolution as endemic to society but as "always avoidable if only the creative potentialities of political organization can be realized."[7] Anticipating the subsequent argument a bit, we predict that the Soviet political elite will probably continue to display sufficient adaptiveness and cohesiveness to prevent either a revolutionary breakdown of the U.S.S.R. or the stagnation and "petrification" foreseen by some analysts. However, neither these possibilities nor a reformist coup d'état, perhaps led by military men, can be ruled out.

Relating development theory to the theory of revolution, we may say that development is most of the time evolutionary but that, when the "normal" pattern of evolutionary development breaks down, revolution results. Following the revolution, a new and painful effort, first of consolidation and then of reconstructive development, re-examination, and revision, occurs. A revolutionary regime usually must tackle simultaneously the difficult problems of establishing its legitimacy, creating a distinctive sense of identity, and organizing enough participation in the political process to generate adequate citizen support. With its attention focused on surmounting crises, it tends to overdevelop its coercive capabilities. As a result it may suffer a loss of voluntary support of the citizenry which partially offsets its advantage in ability to compel obedience to its commands. Its leaders, conscious of their own revolutionary political origins, are obsessed with fears of counterrevolution, which, in the case of communists, is perceived as the danger of the "restoration of capitalism." Revolutionaries' expectations of internal and external threats are usually high, and they seek to impress upon lieutenants, cadres, and citizens the need for "vigilance." However, a successful revolutionary regime eventually succeeds in establishing a new equilibrium based on a synthesis of its revolutionary ideology with the traditions of the political community it governs. If its program of economic development is successful, and if international pressures are not too difficult to cope with, a working synchronization of value patterns and the new division of labor is established. In other words, a successful revolutionary regime evolves and develops adaptively.

The above interpretation is based mainly on analysis of the experience of the U.S.S.R., although it is also relevant to the French Revolution of 1789 and perhaps to Chinese Communist experience. The characterization of Soviet political development as adaptive-evolutionary perhaps presents some difficulties. How, it may be asked, can Stalin's agricultural collectivization and de-kulakization measures or his great purges of 1936–38 be subsumed under the category "evolution"? Our difficulty in answering such questions forces us to admit that probably no existing set of system and development concepts, at least none known to this writer, is fully adequate. Perhaps the development of the Soviet system under Stalin should be characterized as both coercively evolutionary and revolutionary while the post-Stalinist Soviet system should be regarded as having assumed a more "responsive" and certainly a more rational line of development. The processes set in motion by social revolution may require generations for their completion, at least in some spheres, while in others, such as family and personal relations, conventional and universalistic patterns are quickly restored. It will be assumed that, since the consolidation of the Soviet system, and especially since the death of Stalin, development has been evolutionary. This judgment rests upon a definition of evolutionary development as development initiated and controlled by the established political authorities and compatible with established institutions and practices.

The pattern of change within continuity, in terms of which Soviet development is here viewed, poses many problems, most of which cannot be considered in this brief essay. However, it should be emphasized that in calling attention to continuity we are not seeking to create the impression that a restoration of the coercive Stalinist pattern is likely, although even it will not be entirely impossible so long as the Kremlin has at its disposal a police machine capable of preventing organized opposition. We envisage, rather, continued, gradually increasing responsiveness—carefully controlled by the political leaders—to such citizen aspirations as are regarded by the Kremlin as legitimate and reasonable. Increasing attention is likely to be paid to the gradually unfolding aspirations of the Soviet citizenry and, even more slowly, to the customs and norms of the international community. Positive developments in some fields may at times be accompanied by regression in others. Progress in wealth and welfare, which has already been significant, will probably continue to be more rapid than changes in political structure or ideology. The latter, in all probability, will be most difficult, for the C.P.S.U.'s claim that it has the right and capacity to rule Russia is still heavily dependent upon the justificatory and explanatory functions of the official political creed, Marxism-Leninism. However, Marxism-Leninism is a treasury of contradictions and fortunately can be interpreted in many and varied ways.

NEW INFLUENCES ON SOVIET POLITICAL LIFE

For purposes of compression it will be necessary to regard the entire post-Stalinist era more or less as a unit. However, this telescoping of what are increasingly seen as rather different periods, or subperiods, does not imply indifference to the changes involved in the replacement of Khrushchev's erratic behavior and his optimistic "populism" by the cautious realism of his business-like, professedly scientific, and, in their sober fashion, reformist successors.[8] Probably the two most important changes in the whole period since the death of Stalin have been, first, the substitution of rule by an oligarchy (utilizing but not depending mainly upon coercion) for tyranny (relying primarily on terror to survive), and, second, the attempt to reform the "command" economy by incorporating into its basically unaltered though frequently reorganized structure such features as increased use of monetary and "moral" incentives, greater responsibility and initiative for plant managers, and some gingerly borrowed techniques of the Western market economy. Other significant and well-known developments included a partial "secularization," if one may use that term, of Soviet intellectual life, tendencies toward the development of "interest-group" politics, and the stimulating, if somewhat destabilizing, reopening of Russia to Western ideas and culture. Apparently in self-defense against the latter, the authorities proclaimed a campaign against "ideological coexistence." In the new setting the creative elements of society, previously cowed by the party apparatus and the police, began, at first very timidly, to think independently and even, in effect, to claim for themselves the role of minority stockholders in a going concern to the success of which their contribution was vital. The new moral climate was the product not only of a tyrant's mortality but also of the steady maturing, and increasing confidence in the future, of a citizenry aware of the outstanding achievements of their country, not only in outer space, but in such diverse areas as education, public health, sports, and many others. The new stirrings in the public life of Russia were the product also of forces and situations even more significant, perhaps, for the future of Soviet society than any of the changes in leadership, policy, or organization referred to above. Indeed, these larger forces, which operate across organizational, institutional, and status boundaries, may be bringing, or may already have brought Soviet society into a state of at least partial disequilibrium. There is some significant evidence, particularly in the increasingly critical and independent attitudes of Soviet writers, that the major developmental crises (especially that of legitimacy) were not resolved as fully and finally as Stalin may have thought they were. Soviet history since Stalin—in particular, Khrushchev's efforts to create a "functional" Communist party, and much in his successors' criticism thereof, which does not mention Khrushchev by name, of course—indicates at least temporary confusion and perhaps waning confidence about the role and mission of the party in Soviet society. Perhaps more than ever before, the leadership of the C.P.S.U. considers it necessary to justify its status, roles, and functions before the Soviet public. Of course, the party's efforts to seek wider and deeper public support represent progress, from the point of view of the values of the Western "civic" political culture, but they also indicate an increasing lack of "fit" between old institutions and values, on the one hand, and new requirements, generated by a changing environment and by increasing contacts with the non-Soviet world, on the other.

Important in the setting and tone of Russian political life today are not only the saliency of new influences but the fortunate disappearance of old ones. For some years now Soviet life has been characterized by a slow reduction in tension and anxiety-producing pressures and deprivations, and by the gradual fading of traumatic memories. Although it would be a mistake to attribute the misery and degradation of Stalinism solely or mainly to the struggle of the Soviet Union for national security in an international environment of "capitalist encirclement," or to the hardships of rapid modernization of an underdeveloped economy, there is no doubt that these unfavorable factors in the international and domestic environments helped to blight the lives, darken the memories, and envenom the outlook of the Soviet people. The costs of modern technological development, national power, and international influence achieved through competition, the terms of which were defined (largely by Moscow) to rival those of the industrialized West, were higher and the consequences harsher for the peoples of the U.S.S.R. than the struggle for national greatness had been for those of the Russian empire.[9]

Of course, the beneficent impact of the current partial decompression on Soviet life should not be exaggerated. International instability, the Soviet-American arms race, the Sino-Soviet rivalry, and a Soviet economic policy that still emphasizes heavy industry and military production at the expense of a rapid rise in mass consumption persist and exert their painful pressures.

The massive and steady pressure of chauvinistic, anti-Western propaganda, as well as the vigilance and harshness of a still very powerful police machine, also inject special elements of tension and anxiety into the political life of Russia. Anti-Western propaganda is an important instrument of policy, but its most ominous aspect is the evidence it furnishes of the persistence of attitudes inappropriate to an era in which Soviet-Western co-operation is imperative if the cold war is truly to be ended.

Despite the persistence of ideological preconceptions, which to us in the West seem obsolete, there does seem to have been in recent years a perceptible dissolution of the Stalinist siege mentality. This waning of fears and obsessions, together with continued rapid economic development and increased access to foreign ideas, know-how, and patterns of conduct, fosters empirical and rational thinking at the expense of fanaticism and dogma. The new empiricism and cosmopolitanism both coexist with and infiltrate the still dominant Marxist-Leninist ideology. For example, at least a temporary *modus vivendi* has been achieved between, on the one hand, the official philosophy, and, on the other, empirical social science, which the party uses for its own purposes, but which is struggling, not entirely without success, to develop a life and sphere of competence all its own.

The more pragmatic, individualistic, and in some cases sophisticated attitudes referred to above, which seem to "bourgeois" Western observers to be signs of increasing normalcy but which to the "Maoist" faction in Chinese Communist leadership circles represent treasonable revisionist deviations, are, of course, most attractive to the younger, more highly educated, and most privileged strata of the Soviet population. We must be careful not to assume that the new sophistication has captivated the minds of all segments of either the Soviet intelligentsia or Soviet youth, even student youth, and we must also guard against attributing to Soviet intellectuals, including young Soviet intellectuals, anything approaching homogeneity of outlook.[10] Unfortunately, the relatively free-thinking young intellectuals of Moscow, Leningrad, perhaps of the "science city" of Novosibirsk, and of such other relatively Western-oriented centers as Odessa and Tbilisi, probably represent islands in an ocean of parochialism and chauvinism.

That there is a "conflict of generations" in the Soviet Union and that, from the official point of view, the state of mind of many youths leaves much to be desired is apparent from numerous statements at party and Young Communist League congresses and plenary-session meetings and from frequent articles in *Pravda, Kommunist,* and other major publications.[11] Concern over the moods of youth, including young party members, was indicated by inclusion in a resolution adopted by the Twenty-third Congress of the C.P.S.U. of a demand for "a serious improvement in the Marxist-Leninist education and the ideological tempering of party members, especially young communists." It is interesting that about three million, or almost one-fourth of the entire membership of the C.P.S.U., are either candidate probationary members or full party members of three years' standing or less.[12] An interesting aspect of the multifaceted problem of the attitudes expressed by the youth of the Soviet Union is the indication that the U.S.S.R. has not been spared the problems of discontent and disorientation among young people which can be a by-product of industrialization and urbanization. Brezhnev, in his report to the 1966 Party Congress expressed satisfaction that only 24.6 per cent of the Soviet population consisted of collective farmers, while the remaining 75.4 per cent were factory, office, and professional workers and their families.[13] However, other Soviet sources indicate that urbanization has created discontent, especially among rural youths, who, dissatisfied with the quality of life in the countryside, move to the small cities, there to become more discontented than ever or even to succumb to delinquency.[14]

It is prudent to assume, and the available evidence indicates, that Soviet youth is patriotic and basically loyal to the political system. However, it is clear that Soviet youth is also increasingly critical, and sometimes bored or restive. As Khrushchev pointed out in his speech to the Twenty-first Party Congress in 1959, contemporary Soviet youth, which, said Khrushchev, had not experienced the horrors of capitalism, grew up under conditions very different from those which shaped the outlook of their elders. Probably owing to propaganda efforts to keep alive memories of World War II and other wars in which Russians defended their homeland against foreign invaders and to the intensified glorification of "revolutionary traditions" in recent years, memories of World War II and perhaps even of the revolutionary years are more vivid in the minds of Soviet young people than is World War II or the Great Depression to American youngsters; but for the majority in both countries these events must seem ever more remote and shadowy. This fading of memories makes it increasingly difficult for the Kremlin to maintain "vigilance" among Soviet citizens, especially, of course, among those under thirty.

Conjecture about the probability of increasing difficulties for the Soviet political authorities in keeping political inputs and outputs synchronized is based not only on awareness of ferment among the "golden youth" of Moscow but also on evidence that even ordinary "toilers" throughout the vast Russian land, in their capacities both as producers and as consumers, are increasingly critical and demanding. The rebirth of public opinion among the "masses" is significant not only as a source of pressure to which the top political leadership apparently feels it should, and must, respond, but also for its potential as a "constituency" for oppositionist intellectuals, especially those writers and critics who advocate policies of "leveling up" to alleviate the lot of Russia's underprivileged masses.

Every few days, it seems, an article or editorial appears in a major Soviet newspaper or magazine which in some way reflects awareness of and concern about the rising expectations of workers or even of that most disadvantaged segment of Soviet society, the collective-farm villagers. Some of these items are caustically humorous. For example, one reads of a town with commercial air service—but with no surface transport from the airport and almost no dentists.[15] Other items express pride in progress achieved in correcting such deficiencies but admit that it is as yet woefully insufficient.[16] Related, but more specifically political, items criticize the failure of government officials to respond to citizens' letters or to criticism of the bureaucracy in the press.[17] Shortcomings in the actions of party executives, which aggravate political apathy, are ofteh criticized. According to a speech by an important Armenian party official, some party organizations in factories, farms, and scientific research institutes in Armenia hold only one or two meetings a year, and very few party members speak at the meetings that are held.[18] Very recently the need for regular public appearances by party leaders, to explain party policies and to give the citizenry an opportunity to put questions to their leaders, has been articulated.[19] Some recent political articles have stressed the value of the "personal touch" and the necessity that agitators and propagandists possess the skill and information needed to field tough questions.

Of course, such indications of increasing pressures from below and of concern about dealing with them do not mention factors even more troublesome than demands for more and better goods and services or for leadership efforts to implement "party democracy." In addition to evidence of such aspirations, there have been, in recent years, episodes revealing that some Soviet citizens, including workers, are bitterly alienated. There have been illegal strikes, demonstrations, and cases of flight and desertion. There even have been cases of the beating up of policemen by citizens outraged by police behavior toward alleged violators of public order.

The drama of Soviet political development is complex, and brevity forbids mention of all relevant factors. However, a number of influences that probably will play a significant role in future developments can be discussed briefly. Whether or not the Kosygin economic reform proves to be fully successful, it seems likely that the gross national product of the U.S.S.R. will continue to grow at a rate of at least 5 per cent a year. By 1980 Russia may enjoy something approaching a "Hoover" standard of living, and, fifteen or twenty years later, an "Eisenhower" standard. There is, of course, no certainty that the Soviet leadership and elite will increasingly follow welfare-state policies, but one does not have to be wildly optimistic to think that they will find it in their interest to move in this direction, provided, of course, that the necessary efficiency and productivity are forthcoming. Today, all of the peoples of the world are participants in a universal civilization characterized by ever-rising aspirations for material and intellectual satisfactions. In principle, the Soviet Union has always been committed to a welfare-state policy. Both the Khrushchevian and post-Khrushchevian leaderships reaffirmed this commitment, not only symbolically, but to a substantial degree in terms of organizational measures and allocation of resources. The Brezhnev-Kosygin leadership, in particular, inaugurated sensible policies, not only in the field of industrial reform, but also in agriculture, foreign trade, and technical and scientific exchange with the West, calculated not only to improve the international image of the U.S.S.R. but also to raise the standard of living of the Soviet people, beginning, of course, at the level of the most energetic, capable, and loyal elements. The aspects of this communist welfare-state policy which augur well for the constructive evolution of Soviet Russia include an unprecedented willingness on the part of the authorities not only to permit, but even to encourage, a relatively frank discussion of deficiencies in many fields of administration and performance, and an increasing eagerness to listen to and learn from "bourgeois specialists."[20] It appears that the most competent and enlightened elements in the Soviet intelligentsia, especially in scientific circles, are enthusiastically committed to policies of involvement in the international economic and cultural community, but such policies are also supported by powerful elements in the top political leadership. No doubt, of course, Soviet leaders committed to relative restraint in dealing with American policies—for example, in Vietnam—have to take account of opposition in high regime councils.[21]

A Soviet policy of "sharing the wealth" at home would not necessarily assure a policy of accommodation abroad. However, rising living standards have often been associated with liberal and reasonable domestic and foreign policies.[22] It seems reasonable to assume that, given increasing prosperity and a growing distributive capability and given, also, a tolerably favorable configuration of international affairs, the Soviet Union might move much more significantly than it already has toward increasing responsiveness and permissiveness in both domestic and foreign policies.

It would be beyond the proper scope of this essay to explore in detail the complexities of the international environment. However, it should be noted that the structure of international relations since World War II has provided a setting more propitious for the eventual working out of mutually advantageous relations between the Soviet Union and other great powers than did the far more anarchic pattern of the interwar period. At the very least, bipolarity in the essentials of the world power structure makes for a measure of stability of expectations which probably promotes moods of rationality and sobriety within the two superpowers.

The Damoclean sword of nuclear destruction hangs over our world, to be sure, but as Winston Churchill once predicted it would, consciousness of this sobering reality has produced, in the two major powers at least, a disposition to refrain from reckless or irresponsible behavior. On the whole, since the period of readjustment following, and resulting from, World War II, the West has succeeded in denying to the U.S.S.R. both victories and enemies.[23] On the Soviet side, there has in recent years been an increasing tendency to substitute, in analyses of world politics, the concept of the "world revolutionary process" for the more inflammatory and activist slogan of "world revolution."[24] However, as Moscow's role in the 1966 Tri-Continental Conference in Havana and its aftermath showed, the desire to exploit and, perhaps, a feeling of obligation toward the "national liberation" struggle of radical movements in underdeveloped countries, remain elements of Soviet foreign-policy ideology, and, at least formally, confidence in the ultimate collapse of "imperialism" persists. Khrushchev's successors, on balance, however, remain committed to a vision of struggle with "imperialism" mainly by means of economic and ideological competition. Significantly, *Pravda*'s sharp editorial attack on Washington, and pledge of support for Hanoi, on August 23, 1967, placed this policy explicitly in the framework of "peaceful coexistence of states with different social orders" and identified it with the decisions of the Twenty-third C.P.S.U. Congress.

There is an intimate connection between unrest in the underdeveloped lands and the survival of a "two world" psychology in Moscow, although the latter is not necessarily dependent on the former. Instability in the underdeveloped countries certainly does, however, provide temptations for the Kremlin. It fans the fires of Soviet chauvinism and messianism by furnishing apparent proof of the validity of major Leninist doctrines regarding the inevitable decline of "imperialism." Thereby it also strengthens the hand of orthodox elements in the party apparatus and even in the intelligentsia, some segments of which are by no means free of nationalist and even chauvinist moods. However, we can hope that the attractions of trade and cultural relations with the West and gradual realization of the frustrations involved in exploiting unrest in competition with Communist China, in what the Soviets call the "weakly developed" countries, will strengthen tendencies toward moderation and responsibility in Soviet relations with these areas.

In concluding this section a few words should be said about the role of political succession as a factor in Soviet political development.[25] Since the death of Stalin the succession problem, always a latent factor, has become an active, perhaps an increasingly important, one. The succession problem is always a difficult one—pregnant even with possibilities of political earthquakes—in any state that is neither a constitutional democracy nor a monarchy. It is protean in its complexity, pregnant not only with instability but with the opposite danger of inducing a caution approaching paralysis. In a dictatorship of revolutionary origin normal conflicts of interest may be compounded—especially in succession crises—by ideological passions. The relative stability of Soviet politics since the overthrow of Khrushchev may indicate the waning influence of ideology and also an impressive ability to cope with the perennial succession problem, but we cannot yet be sure. Even assuming that ideological disputes are no longer a serious divisive force in a bureaucratized Russia, conflicts of interest may continue to render succession crises—which are bound to recur as long as no legal and binding rules determining succession exist—embarrassing and dangerous to the political leadership elements and to the elite as a whole. However, from the point of view of advocates of interest-group and institutional autonomy, succession crises may be a boon. There is no doubt that the factional strife which they unleash weakens central controls and increases the maneuverability and bargaining power of reformist factions and of the latent, often *ad hoc* segmental groupings striving to wrest from the political authorities agreement on conditions and rules under which they can function in accordance with the standards and criteria of their professions and callings, as they, rather than the rulers, understand them.

Barring the rise of a new Stalin, the loosening up of the social and political system inherent in this situation can be expected not only to provide leeway for the kinds of group pressures and bargaining referred to but also to keep alive in some elite circles aspirations for fundamental constitutional reforms. In the latter connection it is not without interest that some Soviet diplomats, in the months after Khrushchev's ouster, told American colleagues that the "next time" a change of supreme leader occurred it would be handled "better," by which they may have meant that the process would bear less resemblance to a palace coup and would be conducted more openly and "legally."

TOWARD A MORE RESPONSIVE SOVIET POLITY?

The concept of responsiveness is used broadly here to denote the willingness and ability of the Soviet political authorities to pursue policies, particularly in the allocation of material resources, that, in their opinion, satisfy both the requirements of the citizenry and the long-term needs of the community. Because the Soviet leaders are not dependent upon popular elections for their tenure of office, they can afford to pay less attention to public opinion than can the leaders of constitutional democracies. Presumably the top-level decision-makers of a dictatorship, whether it be a tyranny or an oligarchy, will be heavily influenced by state, as against community, interests. To a considerable degree, in practice this means that they will be influenced by their own rather narrow interests as professional rulers rather than by the variegated and diffuse interests of the people as a whole. It is not surprising, then, that philosophical critics of dictatorship, and of elitism generally, are pessimistic about the future of the Soviet political system and about prospects for real improvement in political relations between the U.S.S.R. and the Western democracies.[26] It seems to this writer that it is possible to be prudently vigilant about Soviet intentions and capabilities and also straightforward in perceiving the moral and aesthetic defects of dictatorship, without abandoning hope for evolutionary development in Soviet Russia. This evolution could, conceivably, eventuate in some form of constitutional democracy. However, it is much more likely that, at least for the foreseeable future, it will fall far short of the parliamentary goal which this writer regards as desirable, but will produce behavior that conforms considerably more closely to Western standards than that of the U.S.S.R. does at present. This tentative prediction is based not only on evidence that men seek whenever possible to increase their freedom of choice but also upon consideration of the extensive reforms that have taken place in the Soviet Union since the death of Stalin. What began as tinkering with the Soviet system might, some generations hence, end in its fundamental transformation. The reforms achieved in Yugoslavia, for example, make such hopes seem far from wildly optimistic.

The impossible task of describing here in detail, or even of listing, the numerous and significant Khrushchevian and post-Khrushchevian reforms, which have affected virtually every sphere of Soviet life, will not be attempted. Instead, some general characteristics of these "outputs" of the political system will be identified, and an effort will be made to relate them to political "inputs" of demands upon and support for the political system. Excessively limited though they are in many ways, the reforms involved big enough efforts, dislocations, and risks to justify the assumption that Khrushchev, Kosygin, Brezhnev, and others who initiated or sponsored them, regarded them as necessary for the improvement, and perhaps the preservation, of the communist regime. The zigzag course of the reforms and the multiplicity of agonizing reappraisals that have accompanied them indicate that "conservative dogmatists" in the C.P.S.U. apparatus and in other crucial segments of society, and, to a lesser degree, even the top leaders who staked their personal lives and fortunes and the future of the communist cause on the success of the reforms had many misgivings about their potential unsettling and disintegrating consequences, particularly in the event that control of their execution should slip from the hands of the party leadership. In broad terms, the need for positive reforms of all kinds followed logically from the overwhelming agreement among Stalin's successors that it was absolutely necessary to substitute for "negative incentives" of terror a more positive pattern of rewards and incentives that might make life more pleasant, or at least more bearable. Stalin's system not only had made life nasty, brutish, and short but it had condemned the mass of the population to dire poverty and had made it impossible for even the privileged few of Soviet society to enjoy anything like a "European" way of life. Hence, a keenly felt need for improved industrial and agricultural efficiency and for a rise in the quantity and quality of goods ranked second only to a desire for personal security as a motive for reform. If successful, the reforms might invigorate Soviet society and bring about the replacement of apathetic conformity to the commands of authority by enthusiastic support and creative citizen participation in public life.

Such, at least, seems to have been the vision that inspired Khrushchev's drive for the "full-scale construction of communism" and his slogan of the "state of all the people." Today, some four years after the ouster of Khrushchev, it is clear that his successors are as committed to reform as he was. Indeed, the reform efforts of Brezhnev and Kosygin, of Podgorny, Polyansky, and Demichev, are, at least in principle, more fundamental and serious than those of Khrushchev, which focused mainly on administrative reorganizations and evangelistic sloganmongering. His successors have at last begun to undertake basic reforms of process and structure, especially in the ailing agricultural sector and also in the structure of wages, in prices, and in many other important fields.[27] The current introduction of a five-day week in industry is another important post-Khrushchevian reform. However, if one were to attempt to rate the respective contributions to reform made by Khrushchev and his successors, the palm for boldness would probably have to go to Khrushchev, who after all created the framework of receptivity to new departures, within which his successors operated, and also instituted many specific, important welfare measures such as the extension of social security coverage to the collective-farm peasantry.

Reform was necessary, but it created problems of incalculable and possibly illimitable dimensions. Perhaps only a tyrant can with impunity repudiate past policies. Khrushchev's reforms, like his not-so-secret "secret speech," challenged the useful myth of Stalin's infallibility and by extension the idea of the infallibility of the party. On a less lofty but not insignificant level, the breaking of precedents could be, and was, attacked by conservatives—such as Molotov, for example—as inexpedient and, indeed, dangerous. It is not surprising that, in order to justify himself and rally support for his innovations, Khrushchev felt compelled to smash the Stalinist idol and to substitute for the "cult" of Stalin a new Leninist cult, which was symbolized by Khrushchev's order abolishing the celebration of the anniversary of Lenin's death and introducing the celebration of the anniversary of his birthday.

Both Khrushchev and those who removed him from power were determined, however, not to permit reforms—whether in policy, organization, or doctrine—that might undermine the twin pillars of communist rule, namely, the unrestricted sovereignty of the party leadership and the unquestioned infallibility of Marxism-Leninism. Have they been trying to square the circle?

It is probably impossible to determine whether or not the dilemma of nonsubversive and nondestabilizing reform in the U.S.S.R. is insoluble. The difficulties are certainty formidable. For example—to point only to the sphere of economic policy— can the goals of the regime, in terms of welfare and even of efficiency, be achieved without granting a degree of autonomy to industrial enterprises and to labor, which would, to an intolerable degree, diminish the role of the party?[28] Can a party dedicated to "democratic centralism" permit the kind of freedom of discussion to which liberal professionals undoubtedly aspire? Can the regime allow citizens to enjoy genuinely the rights granted in the Soviet constitution, without allowing a degree of freedom that would destroy its power?

Despite the cautious control exercised by the party leadership over political outputs, input patterns, particularly in the sphere of interest articulation, have been altered significantly. A pattern, which might be described as one of contained diversity or limited pluralism, has begun to emerge. In connection with both the promotion and the implementation of many major reforms, brisk and business-like discussion of issues was aired in the press.[29] To be sure, even Stalin's political monolith was not without both symbolic and real dimensions of diversity. There was always the façade of a nominally democratic and federalist constitution. More important, of course, was the informal, largely illegitimate diversity of conspiratorial and subterranean factionalism. Something new, however, was added to the patterns of interest articulation and, to some extent, to those of aggregation in the post-Stalinist era. An astonishing range of opinions was aired in the mass media, and presumably an even greater variety and intensity of opinions was expressed in unpublished discussions, both official and unofficial. One interesting example of a bold but permissible public expression of opinion was the article by the factory economist O. Volkov in *Pravda* on August 23, 1964, which not only advocated that profit be used as the key economic index of performance for enterprises but also urged that manufacturing and trade organizations be "maximally independent" in bargaining for delivery and sale of their products and that they be to a certain extent independent in determining prices. That Volkov was really advocating bargaining—although he did not actually use this term—is indicated by the fact that he pointed out that in the socialist economy there existed a market—cleansed, to be sure, of the imperfections of the capitalist market—which could perform, much better than the capitalist market, the functions of controlling the quantity, quality, and variety of goods. Of course, the economic reform of September, 1965, reaffirmed at the Twenty-third Party Congress in 1966, did not go nearly so far in the direction of liberalism as Liberman, Volkov, Aganbegian, Birman, Kantorovich, and other advocates of the predominance of "economic" over "administrative" methods of economic leadership desired.[30] The reform, as adopted and as carried out thus far, has represented a compromise between the preferences of the "liberal economists," and their party-leader and economic-planner allies and supporters, and those more conservative administrators who desired to utilize improved cost-accounting and incentive methods and other economic indicators and controls, not to do away with "democratic centralism" and the principle of "the unified state apparatus of planning and administration of the national economy," but to render these principles, as a writer in *Kommunist* in the spring of 1967 put it, "more flexible."[31]

Unfortunately, despite the leadership's concessions to diversity in practice, it still clings, in the sphere of doctrine, to the myths of the possibility and desirability of complete agreement on social goals and the means of achieving them. Certainly the increasingly frequent but still not very numerous references in official Soviet sources to professional or other interest or opinion groups continue to be somewhat condemnatory. In a very important *Pravda* article published in 1965, the authoritative theoretician and central committee member A. N. Rumyantsev asserted that "groupism" (*gruppovshchina*) was incompatible with the proper behavior of Soviet intellectuals.[32] Since Rumyantsev, who has been characterized by the well-informed analyst Timothy McClure as a "moderate conservative," was actually advocating a substantial measure of increased autonomy for intellectuals, it would appear that his warning was directed not so much against vigorous freedom of expression as against actual or potential efforts of factions, especially in the field of literature, to do something that very few, if any, party executives, even the most open-minded and reformist, could be expected to favor, let alone to advocate, namely, to organize associational, even if only segmental, interest groups that might challenge the party's claim to be the final arbiter among all competing demands and aspirations in Soviet society. To put the matter somewhat differently, one might interpret the kind of sophisticated orthodoxy championed by Rumyantsev as a reminder to intellectuals that the political leadership not only was determined to carefully control, while broadening, the articulation of interests but was particularly concerned lest groups other than those designated by duly constituted authority make any move at all toward the drafting of programs or the creation of organizations for the aggregation of interests. The boundaries between permissible and impermissible individual or group discussion, lobbying, and other forms of interest articulation are fluid. In the field of literature and the arts, for example, the relative reasonableness of the Rumyantsev line was at least partially undermined by a "conservative resurgence" that began in the fall of 1965 and produced the notorious Sinyavsky-Daniel trial, the new statute of September, 1966, providing for fines or deprivation of freedom for "circulation of known falsehoods derogatory to the Soviet state and social system," even without proof of the malicious intent of their disseminators, and other unfortunate administrative, legal, and quasi-legal acts of repression.[33] However, this show of teeth has not proved to be a mortal threat to the creative autonomy of those writers, artists, social scientists, and natural scientists who were courageous enough to remain true to their convictions but shrewd and circumspect enough to conform at least to the letter of the law and to refrain from rashness in expressing moderate dissent.

Partly because the party thought that a measure of flexibility and tolerance paid dividends—in the form of performance by intellectuals and professionals which was useful to the regime— and partly because the intellectuals displayed considerable solidarity, courage, and resourcefulness in resisting official pressures, the post-Khrushchevian leadership, like Khrushchev, usually has employed persuasion and cajolery rather than repression to keep intellectuals more or less in line. Some sort of tacit bargaining process seems to have been involved in the situation of the last few years, in which loyal but relatively unorthodox poets, such as Andrei Voznesensky, were permitted to travel extensively in "bourgeois" countries and in which, to mention another characteristic episode, Ilya Ehrenburg chose to be absent from the country during the dreary May, 1967, Congress of the Union of Soviet Writers. Immediately after the Congress the world learned of Solzhenitsyn's courageous demand that censorship be abolished in the U.S.S.R., on both aesthetic and legal grounds. Among the many curious aspects of the contemporary politics of Soviet literature, of which no more than mere mention can be made, is the opportunity that the Sino-Soviet conflict has afforded for the safe voicing of unorthodox ideas disguised as criticism of Maoist extremists.

A considerable portion of our limited space has been devoted to the political aspects of Soviet literature because, as Victor Zorza pointed out in June, 1967, the Union of Soviet Writers, the official organization set up by the party in 1932 to control the writers, actually contains within its membership an "unofficial opposition."[34] Unlike incipient interest groups in other fields, the unorthodox writers—by no means fully homogeneous in outlook or cohesive in group structure, as has already been indicated—are in general, as Zorza notes, "divided into a Right and a Left wing, each with its own press organs, its own ideology, and its own supporters at the center of political power and throughout the country." Although Zorza's formula seems a bit oversimplified, it is, in this writer's opinion, generally correct and is particularly useful in raising the question of the links between segmental, or professional, groupings and the major factions at higher levels of the political system. Generally, signals from the top which reflect divided councils, the result, perhaps, of a leader's effort to gain support among the intelligentsia or even in mass opinion, have acted as "catalysts" for the formation and functioning of lower-level opinion and pressure groups.[35] Specific data on the communication links and patterns referred to above are very hard to come by, but scattered wisps of evidence gathered by alert foreigners, combined with inferences from the Soviet press, leave little doubt of their existence. Apart from such episodes as the denunciation of D. T. Shepilov in 1957, or the sudden dismissal of Rumyantsev as editor of *Pravda* shortly before the arrest of Sinyavsky and Daniel, one learns of assistance given by employees of party and government agencies in the smuggling of texts of confidential documents out of Russia. One hears from knowledgeable sources that members of various intellectual groups communicate openly at their favorite Moscow clubs and that the more unorthodox, "underground" intellectuals keep in touch (in semiclandestine fashion) through brief encounters—for example, in theater lobbies.

From time to time, *Pravda, Kommunist, Partiinaia zhizn',* and other important publications accuse "some comrades," or "some people," of such "petty bourgeois, anarchistic denial of the role of leaders" in Soviet life as would be involved in the setting up in the Soviet Union of noncommunist parties "financed by foreign capital and serving foreign interests." At times the party press has accused some people of seeking to serve the bourgeoisie by "hiding under the flag of nonpartisanship." Apparently the only high party leader in the post-Stalinist era who has been openly accused of offering a "platform" broader than that of the party, presumably in league with dissident intellectuals, was the forgotten and unfortunate Dmitri T. Shepilov, whose condemnation came in 1957.[36] On a much more subversive or "anomic" level, there were, of course—especially after the Hungarian uprising, and in connection with the Sinyavsky-Daniel affair—protest manifestations by students, including street demonstrations.

One can conclude only that, if neither Khrushchev nor his successors have been able to fashion sufficient uniformity of opinion in the top political command or to elicit voluntary harmony among Soviet writers, powerful and perhaps durable trends are at work.

Breaking the shackles of the "general line of the party" might or might not mean the abandonment of Marxism as the dominant philosophy of Russia. It would certainly mean a strengthening of the empirical and humanist links between Soviet thought and both Russian thought of the eighteenth and nineteenth centuries and the full heritage of Western culture. It would require the discarding of a mass of intellectual rubbish and stale formulas which choke and paralyze intellectual inquiry. It would permit and require clear thinking and honesty in history, the humanities, and the social sciences.

If writers and artists are, to some extent at least, protected against official repression for the reasons already adduced, and also because the U.S.S.R. is more sensitive to public opinon— especially that of communist intellectuals in Italy and France, in Eastern Europe, and generally wherever propaganda advantage can be gained by a semblance of liberality—than it was under Stalin, natural scientists must be treated with special respect, and even pampered, because national power depends so heavily upon the quality of their work, which in turn is influenced, directly or indirectly, not only by the facilities furnished to them but by their personal relations with the authorities and other nonmaterial factors. To a greater and greater extent Soviet natural scientists are wresting control of research institutes from party administrators and, as a recent study notes, have already "received authority to work as they wish."[37] There is a significant link between the struggle of Soviet writers and artists for freedom of expression and that of Soviet scientists for freedom of inquiry. Because of their great prestige and influence, and also because many of them are connoisseurs of arts and letters, Soviet scientists have, on a number of occasions, been willing and able to blunt the force of political pressures against unorthodox or experimental practitioners in these fields.[38]

Some features of the moving equilibrium in present-day Russia —an equilibrium between adaptive policy outputs and input demands which reflects a changing environment—have been identified. Among the many categories missing from our inventory on the input side is the broad range of anomic and, at least from the Kremlin's point of view, subversive activities by, or on behalf of, writers and artists which are known to have taken place in recent years, although information about them is tantalizingly incomplete. We do not know nearly as much as we would like to, for example, about the causes of the C.P.S.U.'s repressive actions in connection with such highly publicized affairs as those involving Boris Pasternak, Joseph Brodski, Andrei Sinyavsky, and Yuli Daniel, and we know less, little, or nothing about hundreds of lesser disturbers of official ideological tranquillity.

Almost entirely unrepresented in the foregoing discussion of trends in the developing Soviet pattern of interest articulation are reform proposals that, although legitimate, judging by their sponsorship and their coverage by the official media of communication, have no effect on public policy and, indeed, judging by what we can learn regarding their puzzlingly abortive history, may have had no impact at all. Proposals, perhaps launched as trial balloons but not implemented, may be indicators of predispositions that, although as yet not strong enough to elicit action, may someday become powerful forces. This surmise reflects some of the present writer's experiences in the Soviet Union and gleanings from others with experience in that country, which, taken together, indicate that there is not a complete lack of even rather fundamental alternative models for the present political system.

While it is probably true that political creativity and imagination are feebler in the Soviet Union than in any of the world's large nations, and far feebler also than in some small countries such as Yugoslavia, travelers' reports indicate that many Soviet intellectuals are favorably disposed to economic and social changes that might, if acted upon, have important political repercussions. These include the introduction of private enterprise into retail trade, some branches of light industry, and perhaps into agriculture.

This writer never encountered a Soviet citizen who advocated the replacement of the one-party political structure of the country by a multiparty system, or even a substantial institutional liberalization within the framework of the Communist party dictatorship. However, the fact that some Soviet citizens in relatively high positions think along such lines was indicated by the speech given by N. Arutyunyan, Chairman of the Presidium of the Supreme Soviet of the Armenian Soviet Socialist Republic, at the Fourteenth Congress of the Communist Party of Armenia, in 1966.[39] Arutyunyan is reported to have advocated the nomination of more than one candidate for a soviet—the context of his speech indicates that he was referring to local soviets—on the ground that electoral competition would increase the "political activity" of voters and the sense of responsibility of deputies to the electors. Although Arutyunyan wrapped himself in the mantle of Marxist-Leninist orthodoxy by including in his speech ritualistic statements about the superiority of "Soviet democracy" to its "bourgeois" counterpart, the liberal and indeed radical implications of his proposal were clear. Unfortunately, nothing was done to implement it, and it was not echoed at the Twenty-third C.P.S.U. Congress, which began a few weeks later. It also had no effect on the 1967 elections to the republic soviets. It is interesting to speculate about some of the possible reasons for a proposal that, in the Soviet setting, was a bold one. The Armenians, and also the Georgians, have a less despotic and a more cosmopolitan and individualist political culture than do the Great Russians, who dominate the Soviet Union. There is also in these countries—as in the Baltic region—resentment against Moscow's imperious interference in local affairs. Perhaps the Armenians, in particular, are more receptive than other peoples of the Soviet Union to the reformist and revisionist influences emanating from Yugoslavia and to a certain extent from Czechoslovakia, Hungary, and other East European countries where new ideas are either being tried out in practice or at least being talked about.[40]

Mention of Arutyunyan's proposal brings to mind the area of Soviet life in which, in proportion to the importance of the issues involved, adaptive evolution has probably proceeded most slowly, namely, that of political and legal institutions. The ticklishness of the problems involved in this sphere are indicated by the fact that some six years after Khrushchev's establishment in 1962 of a commission to propose reforms in the constitution of 1936—which, incidentally, until March 5, 1953, was often referred to in the press as the "Stalin constitution"— this commission, headed since December, 1964, by Leonid Brezhnev, had not reported. It would not be quite correct to say that complete stagnation has prevailed in recent years in the development of the formal structure of Soviet political institutions. Regularization and the modest revival of and increase in participation in political life effected at the upper and, to a certain extent, the intermediate and lower levels of party authority have radiated influences facilitating similar changes in the soviets, the ministries, the law enforcement agencies, and the other institutional structures of the system. The powers of the Supreme Soviet and of lower soviets, and in particular the functions of the standing committees of soviets at all levels, have become somewhat more significant. There has been an interesting revival of discussion of issues of constitutional law, for example, in connection with the powers of standing committees of the Supreme Soviet.[41] In law the reformist impulses of 1957– 58 have ebbed, but Khrushchev's successors did away with some of the worst features of "legal populism."[42] Although post-Khrushchevian progress toward legal liberalism has been marred by some retrogression (the aspects of which have been mentioned), an encouraging degree of freedom of public discussion among legal scholars and administrators has continued. However, as in the past, enthusiastic liberals in this field, as in others, are likely to be criticized for allegedly putting "group interests" above the "public interest."[43]

If progress toward the development of representative political institutions has been conspicuously absent, there has been some progress toward rendering the decision-making bodies of the party and the state somewhat more representative than they have been in the past. The significance of this pluralistic development is limited, however, by the control exercised over the state, cultural, and scientific agencies by the party, and by the particularly crucial functions of control over the party Central Committee exercised by its Secretariat, now headed by General Secretary Brezhnev. A recent analysis of the results of elections to the C.P.S.U. Central Committee and to the central committees of republic party organizations since 1954 reveals that there has been a reduction in the strength of the representation of professional party functionaries in these bodies, as well as a reduction in the representation of the police agencies. However, party officials still constitute the largest single group, and, as for the police, it would certainly be premature to remove them from the list of major factors in Soviet politics because of this decline in representation. In some ways, manifested for example in their glorification in the mass media, as in the cases of the exaltation of the exploits of Richard Sorge and Rudolf Abel, the police have scored a comeback since Khrushchev—even, in fact, since the last troubled years of Khrushchev's rule.

Surprisingly enough the 1966 party elections did not give representation in the Central Committee to any of the men directly associated with economic reforms, but "for the first time in the post-war period the ministers in charge of light, consumer-goods industries have been given a significant place among the party elite."[44] In terms of representation of the literary and scientific intelligentsia in the party Central Committee, recent developments have been mixed but perhaps, on the whole, encouraging. On the negative side of the equation, one must note the failure of the Twenty-third Party Congress to re-elect Tvardovsky as a candidate member of the Central Committee; this was balanced, however, by the failure to re-elect some conservative writers to their positions. A clearly positive trend is revealed in the increasing representation of distinguished Soviet scientists both in the party Central Committee and in the high councils of government. Thus, in 1961, the aerodynamicist Mstislav Keldysh became both president of the U.S.S.R. Academy of Sciences and a member of the C.P.S.U.

Central Committee. The October, 1965, session of the Supreme Soviet elevated to the post of Deputy Chairman of the U.S.S.R. Council of Ministers the outstanding physicist Vladimir Kirillin. In April, 1947, the atomic physicist Mikhail D. Millionshchikov was elected to the ceremonial post of Chairman of the R.S.F. S.R. Supreme Soviet. Another well-known and distinguished scientist-educator in the Central Committee is Minister of Higher Education Vyacheslav P. Elyutin.[45]

Even more important than the trends referred to above are the problems of the general political perspectives of the "World War II generation," to use Hough's expression, who are now increasingly well represented in the Central Committee and in leadership and administrative work at the *oblast* level, and the problem of turnover, which, for biological reasons, "must be faced in the next five years."[46] Hough is of the opinion that the emerging leadership probably does not have a "neo-Stalinist" orientation. This view, which seems to be well founded, tends to cast doubt on the possibility that a conservative coalition led by such men as Mikhail Suslov and Aleksandr Shelepin might overthrow the moderate Brezhnev-Kosygin-Podgorny leadership. Such a disaster probably will become less and less likely as the better educated, more open-minded men now in Soviet higher educational institutions or in junior executive positions come increasingly to dominate Soviet political life. As T. H. Rigby pointed out a few years ago, "About two-thirds of the middle jobs are now occupied by young men in their thirties and late twenties, and I suspect that many of these, particularly in the larger cities, feel they have more in common with the Evtushenkos and Voznesenskys than they have with their superiors in the apparatus."[47] Rigby had in mind general cultural trends, but one might also mention as a positive factor the effort—which, to be sure, will bear fruit slowly—to train Soviet officials in at least the rudiments of modern management methods and to reduce the ideological-hortatory element in the general political training of officials. A wide range of special courses and programs, to help both party and state executives, and, of course, production executives, engineers, planners, economists, and others adjust to the conditions created by economic reform, has been announced or reported in recent years.[48]   At least something of the spirit of American business administration and industrial engineering methods is beginning to permeate Soviet administrative life, and this can be very useful. Of course, neither inferences based on apparent developments in the recruitment and composition of the Soviet elite nor, for that matter, speculation based on other grounds can completely invalidate the hypothesis of a "conservative restoration" in the event, for example, that the economic reform failed disastrously or a serious deterioration occurred in the international situation.[49]

A full study of the relationship between elite recruitment and Soviet political development would, of course, require a degree of elaborateness and detail which is inappropriate here. The same can be said of emerging developments in the related process of political socialization and indoctrination.[50] On this vital subject, which unfortunately has been badly neglected, only a few impressionistic speculations will be offered. Socialization in the Soviet Union, as in all other political systems, is only partially successful. Although Stalin, and to a lesser degree Khrushchev, attempted to convert the school and even the family into pliable instruments of the party, it is obvious that neither achieved much success in creating the "new Soviet man." Growing specialization and stratification in the structure of society and increasing "feedback" from the international environment make it unlikely that this goal will be achieved in the future. Precisely among the most highly placed elements of the bureaucratic, artistic, and scientific elites it is possible, probably increasingly so, for parents to shield their children from the most numbing effects of the extremely conformist Soviet pattern of formal education.   Both reports brought back by Western social scientists in recent years and evidence contained in the Soviet educational and social science journals furnish grounds for thinking that the schools and other major instruments of socialization are likely, in the future, to put less emphasis upon rote learning and other features of the traditional Soviet pattern upbringing and to shift gradually to methods and patterns conducive to at least a measure of individuality, independence, and initiative.

CONCLUSIONS

In the political development of the Soviet Union since the death of Stalin, the proponents of adaptiveness and innovation have won some important victories over the defenders of traditionalist orthodoxy. There has been some movement away from the participating subject culture toward a pattern bearing some resemblance to the civic culture of the modern polities and mature industrial societies of the West. In this writer's opinion there probably will be further progress toward the "knowledgeable society" that Robert E. Lane sees developing in the United States. However, this progress may occur in fits and starts, and it may be subject to reverses from time to time.

The traditional political culture of Russia was centralist and authoritarian. Both "definitions of situations" and "standards of behavior," to use the language of Chalmers Johnson, were reshaped, though in some ways they were reinforced, by the triumph of the revolutionary "goal culture" of Leninism-Stalinism. Russianized Marxism took on the manipulative-coercive, mobilizational, plebiscitarian-elitist traits of the still dominant, if no longer completely unchallenged or unshaken, official doctrine of Soviet Marxism. The tenacious grip of the bolshevik syndrome on the Soviet mind, with its obligatory optimism, its intolerance, its moralistic self-righteousness, its contempt for "creeping empiricism," and its missionary zeal, is the product not only of deliberate policy decisions by the Kremlin but also of adverse circumstances and of massive, systematic indoctrination. Moreover, resistance to innovative and liberalizing reforms springs not only from emotional and intellectual commitment to established doctrines and rituals but also from the deeply rooted habits and vested interests of incumbents of elite status, who feel that their privileges and prerogatives are threatened. Deprivational changes, ranging from annoying losses of relative prestige to the humiliation of redundancy and re-training, or perhaps even worse, could befall various elite groups if rapid and fundamental reforms of the economic, political, and cultural life of the Soviet Union were instituted. The establishment of a "socialist market economy" would require a re-orientation of attitudes and a restructuring of the activities of the C.P.S.U. as a whole, and, in particular, it would affect the role of the party apparatus considerably. Fundamental economic reform also would impinge sharply upon the functions of state economic officials, plant managers, and other executive and professional personnel employed in the sphere of material production. Obviously, the replacement of the present regime of party dictatorship by a multiparty system, with provision for legitimate, open opposition, would deprive thousands of professional party functionaries not only of their job but even per-haps of much of the meaning and purpose of their lives. "De-ideologization"—an objective often attributed by Soviet propa-gandists to the policies of the "imperialist" governments of the "bourgeois" West—would affect not only editors, journalists, teachers in the "political enlightenment" institutions, and other professional communicators but also the political police, one of whose principal functions continues (as the Sinyavsky-Daniel affair demonstrated) to be the ferreting out and punishment of ideological heresy.

However, the balance of forces may be shifting gradually toward groups whose patterns of activity and professional con-cerns generate attitudes permeated by rationality and em-piricism. Institutional changes are usually preceded by intel-lectual changes. The re-examination of values by intellectuals is creating predispositions that may eventually undermine the traditional Soviet political system. Gradually, parochialism and fanaticism will wane. Neither ideology nor political structure, however, is likely to be swept aside by revolution, which is not likely to occur in a modern industrial society anywhere, given the resources of productivity and communication which modern technology places in the hands of political authorities and the resulting capabilities of governments for satisfying the material needs and the psychological aspirations of the majority of the citizens whom they govern. Of course, revolution, preceded by decay, is not impossible if Soviet leaders prove to be sufficiently unwise. In their partly open and partly behind-the-scenes bargaining with the Kremlin, Soviet innovative and creative intellectuals and professionals have already achieved considerable freedom to present their views and defend their interests. As a result, there has been some modest progress in Russia toward a wider shaping and sharing of values, to borrow a phrase from Harold D. Lasswell. This progress augurs well for the future. Of course, the position achieved to date by Soviet intellectuals, and by the citizenry in general, vis-à-vis their guardians and watchdogs, is a poor thing by Western standards, or by those of Yugoslavia. It is difficult to believe that the creative and productive elements of Soviet society will be content with the partial progress achieved to date. The impulse for further reform must be very powerful. National interest and national pride, as well as an awakened appetite for freedom of initiative and inquiry, impel both party and intelligentsia to heed the imperatives of economic and administrative rationality and of free and unfettered intellectual criticism. However, existing practices and structures, and the official ideology that legitimizes them, may increasingly serve as barriers to the completion of the modernization of Russia. Yet to modify, still more to discard, old practices is immensely difficult. The example of Yugoslavia, however, is encouraging to those who conceive of social change in piecemeal, or incremental, rather than in cataclysmic, "all or nothing" terms. Yugoslavia, a country ruled by Marxists, which has made considerable progress toward economic rationality, the rule of law, and ideological coexistence with the West, furnishes a model of ideologically legitimate social transformation. To be sure, it too has encountered problems in its reform efforts, and its relative powerlessness and lack of authority may limit its appeal to the proud and imperious Russians.

It should be clear that this writer does not expect to see in his lifetime a Russia blessed with the advantages—and the problems—of British- or American-style democracy. The

Western participant polity was the product of peculiarly felicitous circumstances. No lightning transformation, even granted the benefits of modern technology, can be expected in a society still largely preoccupied with pressing problems of economic development. However, the political maturation of the U.S.S.R. is slowly proceeding, and further progress, perhaps along the lines indicated in these pages, would appear to be in the interests of the world community. This essay will have served its purpose if it calls attention to some of the possibilities, problems, and modalities of a future that all nations must, whether they like it or not, share and jointly shape.

NOTES

1. A contingent approach was brilliantly applied by Zbigniew K. Brzezinski in his useful study "The Soviet Political System: Transformation or Degeneration," *Problems of Communism,* vol. 15 (January-February, 1966), pp. 1–15. In particular, Brzezinski ably argued the case of those who for various reasons seem to think that stagnation and disintegration are more likely than what is envisaged in the present study. One of the most plausible forecasts of relative stagnation is in John A. Armstrong's article "Party Bifurcation of Elite Interests," *Soviet Studies,* vol. 17, no. 4 (April, 1966). Carefully analyzing the age and background of the "territorial elite" in the R.S.F.S.R. and Ukraine, Armstrong foresaw a loss of economic efficiency for some years Thus far, the predictions of Armstrong, Brzezinski, Conquest, and others who stress the failure of the post-Stalinist, especially the post-Khrushchevian, leadership to dynamically improve elite recruitment practices or decision-making machinery have not, on the whole, been borne out by events, but, if sluggishness in these spheres persists very long or is aggravated, perhaps serious problems could develop. Also, it is not out of the question that men now in their middle and late forties and early fifties might not be content to "wait their turn" and, in challenging Brezhnev, Kosygin, and Podgorny, might precipitate new disruptions; however, in so doing they might also take measures to "rejuvenate" elite cadres. In general, the present writer feels that, even in the event of such disturbances, the present system is unlikely to be toppled or seriously weakened.

2. In general, the present author shares the perspectives regarding contemporary international developments, especially in the "third world," which are set forth in Marshall D. Shulman's study *Beyond the Cold War* (New Haven, 1966).

3. Lucian W. Pye, *Aspects of Political Development* (Boston, 1966), pp. 62–67.

4. Gabriel A. Almond and G. Bingham Powell, Jr., *Comparative Politics: A Developmental Approach* (Boston, 1966); see also David

Easton, *A Systems Analysis of Political Life* (New York, 1965), and Karl W. Deutsch, *The Nerves of Government* (New York, 1963).

5. A statistically ingenious but rather ethnocentric approach to political development is offered by Phillips Cutright in his article "Measurement and Analysis of National Political Systems," *American Sociological Review,* vol. 28, no. 2 (April, 1963), pp. 253–64.

6. Chalmers Johnson, *Revolutionary Change* (Boston, 1966).

7. *Ibid.,* chap. XIV. As Patricia Blake seems to suggest in her important article "This is the Winter of Moscow's Dissent" (*New York Times Magazine,* March 24, 1968), a dangerous desynchronization may already have developed in the U.S.S.R., between the values of the intelligentsia and the prerogatives of party and police.

8. Post-Khrushchevian conservatism was particularly apparent in the sphere of adult political socialization, where it involved, among other things, a reduction in the enrollment in the network of "Political enlightenment" courses and seminars from 36,000,000 in 1964 to 12,000,000 in 1966–67 and a corresponding elimination of non-party students from the program. See Ellen Propper Mickiewicz, *Soviet Political Schools* (New Haven, 1967), pp. 9–13. The persistence of conservatism in this sphere, very reflective of Kremlin moods and significant in shaping the future outlook of politically relevant strata, is indicated also by the reinforcement in adult political education of compulsion to study, as against Khrushchevian flirtation with voluntariness. See Christian Duevel's comments in *Radio Liberty Dispatch,* August 4, 1967, on the differences between the 1967 and 1965 editions of the *Handbook* for secretaries of primary party organizations, and also *Pravda's* September 4, 1967, article "Tirelessly Master Marxism-Leninism."

9. Theodore H. von Laue, *Why Lenin? Why Stalin?* (New York, 1964), offers the most stimulating presentation of the thesis that both the Bolshevik Revolution and the oppressive rule that resulted from it can be traced to interactions between the efforts of imperial Russian and Soviet leaders to achieve power and respect in the world and the "pressures of global politics."

10. On the wide range of ideas, attitudes, and outlooks among Soviet intellectuals, particularly in the field of literature, see Timothy McClure, "The Politics of Soviet Culture, 1964–1967," *Problems of Communism,* March-April, 1967.

11. See, for example, the speech of Y.C.L. leader Sergei Pavlov to the League's Fifteenth Congress, in *Komsomolskaia pravda,* May 18, 1966, or the article by Moscow Party First Secretary N. G. Egorychev, in *Kommunist,* no. 2 (March, 1965), expressing concern over the "disorienting" effect on the morale of Soviet youth allegedly caused by Alexandr Solzhenitsyn's depiction of the Stalinist era in his novel *One Day in the Life of Ivan Denisovich.*

12. Mickiewicz, *Soviet Political Schools,* pp. 14–15. See also in *Pravda's* previously cited September 4, 1967, article the demands for special attention to political indoctrination of young people and for militant struggle against "the ideological positions of imperialism."

13. *Twenty-third Congress of the C.P.S.U.* (Novosti Press Agency Publishing House, n.d.), p. 61.

14. See, for example, the "sociological" items in *Literaturnaia gazeta,* July 23 and July 26, 1966, and in *Politicheskoe samoobrazovanie,* no. 7 (July, 1966), pp. 122–26. The latter item notes that the vast majority of school graduates in a village where a study was made leave the village because of its "backwardness of culture and daily life."

15. N. Mironov, article in *Pravda,* May 17, 1967.

16. Article in *Pravda Ukrainy,* April 29, 1966, reporting that the Ukraine had forty dry cleaning and dyeing factories and that its public service enterprises offered three times as many services as they had three or four years previously. Also typical was *Izvestiia*'s editorial, September 17, 1965, "Service to Everyday Needs, in the Center of Attention."

17. Item in *Pravda,* June 30, 1965, from its Yerevan correspondent.

18. Report of speech by A. Shaginyan, in *Kommunist* (Yerevan), March 4, 1966.

19. See, for example, *Partiinaia zhizn',* no. 5 (March, 1967), editorial on "Speeches to the Toilers by Leading Officials," pp. 3–7.

20. P. Abroskin and S. Kamenitser, in an article on "Leninist Principles of Administration in Action," *Kommunist,* no. 6 (April, 1967), point out that Lenin was not ashamed to employ "bourgeois specialists" at high salaries, under the control, to be sure, of "the workers" (see p. 64).

21. This is indicated in such press items as F. Burlatskii, "Nauchnye osnovy politikii," *Sovetskaia Belorussiia,* September, 6, 1966, stressing the necessity of an empirical, pragmatic approach to public affairs, especially in economic policy, and sharply criticizing "skeptics" who cling to outmoded dogmas. I wish to express my appreciation to Professor Sidney I. Ploss for bringing Burlatski's article to my attention. The elimination, in the summer of 1967, of N. G. Egorychev as head of the Moscow city party organization and the apparent shackling of the energies of Aleksandr Shelepin, although difficult to definitively evaluate, probably should be regarded as victories of Soviet "middle-of-the-road" types over more militantly "anti-imperialist" forces.

22. Cutright, "National Political Systems," offers interesting evidence of connections between economic development—as well as noninvolvement in international conflict—and democratic political development.

23. Zbigniew K. Brzezinski, on the last page of *The Soviet Bloc* (Cambridge, Mass., 1960), identified the denial of victories and of enemies as the key to the erosion of ideology in the Soviet bloc.

24. See, for example, *Stroitelstvo kommunizma i mirovoi revoliutsionnyi protsess* (Moscow, 1966).

25. Almost everyone who has speculated about the nature and future of Soviet politics has something to say on the succession problem, but the basic study is Myron Rush's valuable book *Political Succession in the U.S.S.R.* (New York, 1965).

26. An eloquent and thoughtful but perhaps excessively pessimistic presentation of the outlook referred to above is Bertram D. Wolfe's article "Reflections on the Future of the Soviet System," *The Russian Review,*

vol. 26, no. 2 (April, 1967), pp. 107–28. In the present writer's opinion, Wolfe focuses his analysis too narrowly on the purely institutional aspects of political change in Russia and underestimates the significance of the changes that have occurred already in Soviet political life, despite the persistence of C.P.S.U. rule.

27. For a positive appraisal of Brezhnev's agricultural reforms, particularly guaranteed remuneration for collective farmers and increased democracy in collective-farm management, see Abudrakhman G. Avtorkhanov, "A New Deal for Collective Farmers?" Institute for the Study of the U.S.S.R., Analysis of Current Developments in the Soviet Union, no. 452 (April 25, 1967); for the Khrushchevian background to these developments, which helped to make them possible, see Sidney I. Ploss's important pioneer study, *Conflict and Decision-Making in Soviet Russia: A Case Study of Agricultural Policy, 1953–1963* (Princeton, 1965).

28. The voluminous Western literature on Soviet economic reform is replete with such questions. See, for example, U.S., Congress, Joint Economic Committee, *New Directions in the Soviet Economy,* 89th Cong., 2d sess., 1966, pt. 1, or such interesting recent studies as Gregory Grossman, "Economic Reforms: A Balance Sheet," *Problems of Communism,* vol. 15, no. 6 (November-December, 1966), pp. 43–55, and Alexander Erlich, "Economic Reforms in Communist Countries," *Dissent,* May-June, 1967, pp. 311–19.

29. For a fuller presentation of the general patterns of interest articulation, similar in approach to that sketched here, see chaps. II, V, and VII of Frederick C. Barghoorn, *Politics in the U.S.S.R.* (Boston and Toronto, 1966); see also the valuable works of Ploss, *Decision-Making in Soviet Russia;* Carl A. Linden, *Khrushchev and the Soviet Leadership, 1957–1964* (Baltimore, 1966); and Peter H. Juviler and Henry W. Morton, eds., *Soviet Policy Making* (New York, 1967).

30. An extraordinarily interesting analysis of the groups and issues involved in this dispute, which traces it to shortly after the death of Stalin and indicates that the partial victory achieved by the opponents of extremely centralized administrative controls can be credited to Kosygin, was the distinguished economist A. Birman's article in *Novy Mir,* no. 12 (December, 1965).

31. L. Abalkin, *Kommunist,* no. 6 (April, 1967), p. 78. Interestingly enough, the title of Abalkin's article is "Economic Laws, Interests and Methods."

32. *Pravda,* February 21, 1965.

33. The "conservative resurgence" is traced in considerable detail and with impressive documentation in McClure, "Soviet Culture," pp. 36–41.

34. Victor Zorza, "The Unofficial Opposition," *Manchester Guardian Weekly,* June 1, 1967.

35. The term "catalyst," as used in this context, was suggested to the author by Miss Anastasia Shkilnyk.

36. For some remarks on the role of Shepilov and related matters see Frederick C. Barghoorn, "Soviet Political Doctrine and the Problem of Opposition," *Bucknell Review,* vol. 12, no. 2 (May, 1964), pp. 1–29.

37. See p. 157 of Loren R. Graham, "Reorganization of the U.S.S.R. Academy of Sciences," in Juviler and Morton, *Soviet Policy Making*.

38. On the link between natural scientists and "abstract art" and modern Soviet writing see, for example, chap. XIX of Albert Parry, *The New Class Divided* (New York, 1966).

39. *Kommunist* (Yerevan), March 5, 1966, p. 4. The full text of Arutyunyan's speech was not published, and it is possible that it was even more innovative in spirit than the published report.

40. In connection with the above speculations the articles by Morton Schwartz, "Czechoslovakia: Toward One Party Pluralism?" *Problems of Communism*, vol. 16, no. 1 (January-February, 1967), and H. Gordon Skilling, "Interest Groups in Communist Politics," *World Politics*, vol. XVIII, no. 3 (April, 1966), are of interest.

41. See, for example, the review of the literature by L. Mandelshtam, in *Izvestiia*, July 30, 1966.

42. See, for example, Albert Boiter, "Comradely Justice: How Durable Is It?" *Problems of Communism*, vol. 14, no. 2 (March-April, 1965). The best general discussion of Soviet legal reforms is in Harold J. Berman, *Justice in the U.S.S.R.* (New York, 1963), esp. in chap. 2; see also Barghoorn, *Politics in the U.S.S.R.*, chap. IX. The contribution by Professor Leon S. Lipson to the symposium on Prospects for Soviet Society, to be published soon under the auspices of the Council on Foreign Relations, New York, will be very valuable.

43. "Some" legal scholars were accused of putting "group interests above the public interests," in *Kommunist*, no. 12 (August, 1964), p. 71.

44. Jerry Hough, "Groups and Individuals," *Problems of Communism*, vol. 16, no. 1 (January-February, 1967), pp. 28–35. This article, and Hough's study entitled "In Whose Hands the Future?" *ibid.*, no. 2 (March-April, 1967), as well as the article by Boris Lewytzkyj in *ibid.*, no. 1, provide valuable data on the composition and recruitment of the Soviet elite. For background see John A. Armstrong, *The Soviet Bureaucratic Elite* (New York, 1959), and Barghoorn, *Politics in the U.S.S.R.*, chap. VI. Useful elite studies have been prepared in recent years by, for example, Michael P. Gehlen and, in as yet unpublished form, by Jaroslav Bilinsky. The major elite study being readied for publication by Seweryn Bialer will add greatly to our knowledge of the dynamics of Soviet society.

45. *Izvestiia*, April 12, 1967. For a breakdown of the Supreme Soviet deputies by social status, occupation, and other characteristics see *Deputaty Verkhovnogo Soveta S.S.S.R.* (Moscow, n.d.), pp. 3–4.

46. Hough, "In Whose Hands the Future?" pp. 21, 24–25.

47. T. H. Rigby, "Western Experts and Soviet Reality," *Quadrant* (Melbourne, Australia), Winter, 1963, p. 13.

48. See, for a recent example, the C.P.S.U. Central Committee decree "Concerning Permanently Operating Courses for Re-training Leading Party and Soviet Cadres," *Partiinaia zhizn*, no. 2 (January, 1967).

49. That the problem of "representation" of various occupational and other groups in party decision-making bodies is a matter of perhaps increasing concern to the party leadership has been indicated in a number

of articles in major Soviet journals. See, for example, F. Petrenko, "Principles of Party Democracy," *Kommunist,* no. 18 (December, 1965), pp. 36–42.

50. Much valuable insight and information on some aspects of this subject are contained in Mickiewicz, *Soviet Political Schools, passim.* See also Barghoorn, *Politics in the U.S.S.R.,* chap. III, IV, and V and, in particular, the very valuable article by Jeremy Azrael, "Soviet Union," in *Education and Political Development,* James S. Coleman, ed. (Princeton, 1965), pp. 233–71.

The Party, Opposition, and Interest Groups in Communist Politics: Fifty Years of Continuity and Change

H. Gordon Skilling

A striking paradox of communist politics is the ceaseless flux of change beneath an appearance of changeless continuity in the forms and structures and in the communist theory of political power. Despite a succession of constitutions and even more frequent amendments of the party's own statute, the general structure of Soviet political institutions and of political processes as it exists in 1968 is not in its essential features unlike the order which emerged from the revolutionary events of 1917. There is now, as there was then, a single centralized and largely monolithic party, which enjoys a monopoly of political power and controls the representative institutions, the mass organizations, and the media of communication, and which seeks to direct and mold all aspects of society—the economic and spiritual as well as the social and political. Nonetheless, it is clear that beneath this surface uniformity there have been profound shifts in the way the system has actually operated at successive stages of Soviet history.

One could almost hazard a paraphrase of the old French saying *"plus c'est la même chose, plus ça change!"* Certainly it is appropriate to speak of a succession of Soviet political systems, from the Leninist through the early and the mature Stalinist to the Khrushchevian and post-Khrushchevian, each manifesting a distinctive style and substance of its own.[1] When one takes into account the other communist states of Eastern Europe, one encounters an even richer diversity, for these systems, once modeled on the Soviet prototype and still retaining the essentials of the old system, have in practice worked out many variations on the common theme.

Our awareness of the variety of communist politics has been dulled by the long existence of the mature Stalinist system in the Soviet Union and its full-blown imposition on Eastern Europe during the years 1944–48. Despite the Yugoslav exception after 1948, it was easy to equate communist politics with the forms and procedures characteristic of mature Stalinism and to ignore or minimize the possibility of alternatives. All communist systems, including even the Yugoslav, were classified as totalitarian dictatorships and, as such, were assumed to exclude group conflict and opposition, except at the very highest level among rivals for top leadership. Even after 1953 the totalitarian concept continued to blind Western observers to the possibilities of change and diversification in politics and in particular to hinder them in observing the emergence of new features. Only recently has it been widely recognized that policymaking in communist states, including the Soviet Union, takes place more and more within a context of sharp group conflict;[2] and still more recently it has been recognized that oppositional tendencies, never totally absent from communist policies, have assumed more vigorous and varied forms.[3]

Communist theory and practice have traditionally denied the legitimacy of any form of opposition or autonomous group activity. The doctrine of the proletarian dictatorship, as developed by Lenin and Stalin, conferred on the so-called party of the working class the exclusive authority to exercise political leadership and denied to other parties and groups the right to share this power or to counteract it. At the same time, the principle of democratic centralism assigned supreme authority to the top party leaders and required disciplined obedience of all lower officers and members.

As interpreted by Lenin, these theories led to the banning not only of "opposition," in the form of organized groups seeking to replace those in power, but also of "dissent," in the form of criticism of policies adopted or proposed by these leaders.[4] Carried to its extreme conclusion by Stalin, this strategy led eventually to the complete elimination of opposition in almost every form.[5] At the most, passive resistance or revolutionary conspiracy remained as the sole vestiges of opposition. In Eastern Europe this theory and its practice were introduced in full form after 1948, when complete communist power was everywhere established and the people's democracies were identified as forms of the proletarian dictatorship. Any opposition and any group activity, inside or outside the party, was thenceforth regarded as disloyal and impermissible.

In the years since Stalin's death there has been no basic change in the structure of the communist political systems, nor has the attitude of the leaders toward opposition in the abstract been essentially modified. Communist doctrine still rejects the rights of autonomous groups to articulate interests distinct from those of the party and still assigns to the party the exclusive right to aggregate, and even to articulate, the interests of all social groups.[6] Even in Yugoslavia, where the position and role of the party have been significantly modified, the idea of a multiparty system, or of an opposition party, has been explicitly rejected. Where other parties exist, as in Poland, Bulgaria, Czechoslovakia, and East Germany, they are loyal supporters of the ruling party and do not express basic opposition to it. Even in Poland, where other parties may in a limited degree express group interests and seek to influence public policy, they do not compete with the ruling party for power and do not form a political opposition.[7] In the U.S.S.R., needless to say, any such political competition is ruled out, and, indeed, any "narrowing of the role of the party, any restriction of its functions," is explicitly rejected.[8] In no communist country is genuine opposition inside the party permitted, and the existence of factions with "separate platforms" is forbidden.[9]

Nonetheless, in the U.S.S.R. and in all the communist countries of Eastern Europe, with the exception of Albania, there has been a noticeable rise in activity by interest groups and the emergence of political tendencies that can only be called "oppo-sitional." Leonard Schapiro, in his foreword as editor to the first issue of the journal *Government and Opposition,* referred to "the tentative process of loyal dissent" becoming apparent in one-party states.[10] Although the party retains its dominant position and the making of policy continues to be highly cen-tralized and authoritarian, with power resting in the hands of a few rule-makers at the top, political interest groups have been able to find means of articulating their own and others' interests and of expressing conflicting views on public policy. Especially in the phase of deliberation prior to the formal making of final decisions, and also in the later period of implementing them, such interest groups may interpose their own viewpoints, pre-senting alternative policies for consideration and endorsing or criticizing—sometimes opposing—the carrying out of policies already resolved upon. This development reflects a subtle but significant change in the party's attitude toward society and social groups and in its conception of the process of decision-making.

As we have noted, there has been no relaxation of the party's monopoly of political power and no admission of the desir-ability of political opposition as such. It is, however, no longer assumed that the party alone, and infallibly, knows the public interest and that all individual or group interests must be auto-matically and without question subordinated and sacrificed. There has been an increasing recognition that in a hetero-geneous society some conflicting interests will exist and that there will even be clashes between partial individual and group interests on the one hand and the broader national interest on the other. It is understood that public policy, if it is to be realistic and well based, should take these conflicting interests into account and should represent to some degree a reconcilia-tion or synthesis of them. The party increasingly performs the role of an aggregator of conflicting interests, rather than of the exclusive articulator of its own conception of the national in-terests.[11] This is not to say, of course, that the party passively accepts partial or conflicting interests; but in imposing its own decisive views it takes into account opposing concepts of the public interest as well as partial group interests.

Moreover, it is increasingly recognized that public policy must be "scientific," in the sense of being based not merely on Marxism-Leninism but also on the findings of scholarship and science on the matters under discussion. As a result the party has tolerated and, indeed, has deliberately encouraged wide-ranging debates among experts on certain policy issues such as economic reform or legal revisions.[12] This kind of discussion, permitting the expression of oppositional viewpoints on specific issues, is, needless to say, subject to strict limits, which will be discussed later. It has, however, created a new climate of policy-making and, without altering the essential forms of political action—in particular, the leading role of the party—has subtly and significantly modified the actual working of the political system.

It is necessary to define more precisely the exact meaning of "political opposition" within communist states. Some Western scholars have proposed a relatively simple dichotomy between "orthodox" and "unorthodox" dissent,[13] "dissent" and "opposition,"[14] or "control" and "contestation."[15] If such a classification is to be used, it must be understood not as a clear-cut demarcation of two sharply opposed forms but as a continuum stretching between two extremes, one seeking to change and improve the system, the other rejecting it absolutely. It may be more useful to employ a fourfold classification, defining several distinct types of oppositional tendency. The first, *"integral opposition,"* involves overt or covert disloyalty to the system; if expressed in action, it may take such forms as revolutionary conspiracies designed to overthrow it, or lesser forms of resistance such as sabotage or underground activity.[16] Carried on normally by anticommunist forces, it may also be manifested in the alienation of youth, the "inner migration" of intellectuals, or the rejection of communist doctrine by the religious. The second, *"fundamental opposition,"* involves opposition to, or severe criticism of, a whole series of the key policies of the regime, without, however, a rejection of the system itself.

Usually expressed by communists, it may take the form of resistance on the part of key interest groups, such as the party *apparatchiki* or the writers, who may divide (as we shall see later) into "hard" and "soft," "conservative" and "reformist," camps. The third, *"factional opposition,"* is conducted by individuals or groups within the highest organs of party and government, although support may be sought in broader social and political groupings. Although by definition identified with disloyalty to other leaders, and often embodying fundamental ideological rifts within the ruling elite, as between "nationalist" and "proletarian internationalist," or "leftist" and "rightist," this type of top-level opposition also does not represent opposition to the system as such. Finally, there may be opposition to specific policies of the regime, without a rejection of either the system or its incumbent leadership and their basic policies.[17] The chief exponents of *"specific opposition"* have been the professional groups, such as economists, lawyers, social scientists, educators, natural scientists, writers, and journalists. In the main this is a "loyal opposition," seeking to change or influence public policy by criticizing established policies or suggesting alternative measures or future courses of action. Although sometimes linked with, and even promoted by, top-level factional struggles, this form of dissent is normally designed not to secure power but rather to influence the actions of the existing powerholders.

It is not assumed that all of these oppositional tendencies will always be present in communist systems. Indeed, it can hardly be sufficiently emphasized that the individual communist systems will differ greatly from one another, and from one period to another, in the predominant types of opposition and in the intensity and forms of the various kinds of dissent. Moreover, the oppositional tendencies present at any time in a given country cannot be sharply marked off from one another and may to a considerable extent overlap or be combined. In particular, oppositional attitudes and behavior will vary with changing conditions. Specific dissent may develop into fundamental or even integral opposition and may merge with factional conflicts among leading groups. Integral opposition may recede with leadership changes and policy shifts and with increased opportunities for the expression of specific opposition. As will be discussed below, much will depend on the attitude of the ruling group toward opposition of varying forms, with intolerance of specific opposition generating fundamental or integral opposition.

Analysis is rendered difficult by the wide differentiation of the development in the communist countries, with the special circumstances and the peculiar traditions of each increasingly affecting the course of events. There is in fact a wide spectrum extending from Albania, where no basic change in the traditional Stalinist system has occurred and where coercion prevents all forms of opposition, to Yugoslavia, where the Stalinist system of the early postwar years has been modified since 1948 in fundamental ways and where opposition of certain kinds is permitted and encouraged. Between these extremes, each of the other countries has evolved a particular variation on the theme of de-Stalinization, least pronounced in the case of Rumania, East Germany, and Bulgaria, most marked in the case of Poland, Czechoslovakia, and Hungary.[18] The differences, however, are not clear-cut, nor are they fixed and changeless; on the contrary, they are smudgy and ever-shifting, so that the analysis of a single country—and even more so, generalization concerning them all—involves serious difficulties that are likely to be aggravated in the future as the individuality of each country becomes more pronounced.

Generalizing from differentiated and zigzag courses of development, one can say that integral opposition, after an initial outburst in Hungary, has everywhere declined, or at least does not usually express itself in overt actions of serious proportions. A significant exception is the case of the Polish Catholic church. Factional opposition, after intense activity in the early years of de-Stalinization, especially in Hungary, Poland, and Bulgaria, also has declined and has assumed more moderate forms. Fundamental opposition, again after an initial flourishing in the Polish and Hungarian crises, has subsided, but has recurred in Czechoslovakia and Poland in the sixties. On the other hand, specific opposition, extending over a whole range of issues, has greatly expanded in the more liberal states as the regimes have permitted and encouraged the expression of conflicting interests and opinions and as various occupational groups have taken the opportunity of expressing themselves vigorously on matters of public policy.

It should be clear that the forms of political opposition described differ profoundly from those characteristic of noncommunist states. In Western democracies, where opposition is an integral and legitimate part of the political system, opposition is normally institutionalized and based on constitutional foundations, and manifests itself primarily in competing political parties and in parliamentary or electoral procedures which guarantee the expression of dissent and opposition.[19] Political opposition of this orderly and peaceful kind is, however, a rare phenomenon in political experience, and governments have traditionally sought to suppress or contain it.[20] In other than democratic countries, opposition has normally been forced to assume a variety of nonlegal or illegal forms and to express itself in other than a formal and institutional manner. The crucial feature of opposition in communist systems is the absence of an institutionalized opposition expressed and guaranteed in constitutional principles or political custom.[21] In particular, this is manifested in the absence of two or more major and competing parties and in the limited degree of economic, social, cultural, and political pluralism. Although opposition in the sense common to Western democracies does not, therefore, really exist, oppositional tendencies have found other modes of expression, usually outside the normal channels of governmental action and deliberation.

Needless to say, revolutionary or conspiratorial forms of integral opposition are strictly curbed by law and by force. However, the advocacy of integral or even fundamental opposition by peaceful means also is not tolerated and can express itself only through subterranean channels. In varying degrees of vehemence, "hostile" ideas or domestic "enemies" within and outside the party are bitterly denounced and are often linked with outside "enemies," such as the Vatican, Radio Free Europe, or the imperialist bourgeoisie generally. Factional opposition also is taboo and must take place secretly at the top-most level of the party, among the high command of the Presidium and Secretariat. Although the Central Committee in some cases may have come to play a significant role in this respect, there is as yet no evidence (with the possible exception of Czechoslovakia) that this process of leadership conflict is likely to be institutionalized through a more genuine electoral or deliberative process within the party organs. Although purge of the old type is not as "permanent" a feature of communist rule as was once assumed, and usually is not accompanied by such draconic penalties for the defeated, factional struggle still remains a highly informal and illegitimate process of conflict, with the rival factions representing a weak surrogate for the political parties of a multiparty system. Such noninstitutionalized forms of conflict are likely to provide the framework within which other forms of group conflict will take place, with the leadership factions continuing to perform significant functions in articulating and amalgamating the interests of social groups whose support they seek in the interests of their own struggle for power.

Changes in the context of decision-making have been least pronounced in the functioning of the representative assemblies and of the mass or societal organizations. In the absence of genuine representative or legislative bodies, there is little opportunity for interest groups to function through the assemblies or for oppositional tendencies to be expressed in these bodies. The Supreme Soviet, for instance, or the party's Central Committee, is so constituted that certain social and occupational groups receive representation. In neither body, however, are the representatives selected by specific social groups or authorized by the latter to express a group position. Moreover, none of these organs, so far as can be seen, is influential in the determination of policy. Perhaps, in a modest way, certain group interests may be articulated in these representative organs, with members of the Central Committee voicing different opinions on the subjects under debate and deputies expressing regional and functional interests. The increasing role being given to committees of the Supreme Soviet and the practice of bringing in experts in various fields—sometimes formalized in advisory committees—for consultation with the committees and with the Soviet Presidium may bring professional groups closer to the locus of decision-making, although not as authorized spokesmen for the groups to which they belong.

In some countries of Eastern Europe there has been criticism of the inactivity of parliaments, and changes have been introduced to make the legislature and particularly its committees places of active and critical discussion. Plenary sessions have become longer and more business-like; committees are more active; time for questions has been introduced; the parliamentary responsibility of ministers has been proclaimed. The assemblies continue, however, to be the scene of unanimous approval of proposed legislation and do not offer a locus of serious opposition or a medium for articulating diverse interests and opinions. Only rarely, as in Czechoslovakia in June, 1965, is there a divided vote, and in the Czechoslovak case the legislation was passed, with the clause opposed by a majority unchanged. In the Polish Sejm, however, the legislative committees play an important role in the discussion of legislation.[22] Opposition is sometimes expressed in the plenary session, notably by the Catholic deputies, and negative votes are sometimes recorded. In Yugoslavia the assembly is an even more active arena of debate and of opposition, and the defeat of proposed legislation has occurred from time to time. In an event unique in the communist world, the government of the Slovene Republic was on one occasion compelled to resign as a result of an adverse vote, although it resumed office shortly thereafter.[23]

Efforts to invigorate the assemblies are likely to remain abortive as long as the elections themselves simply endorse the dominant position of the ruling party and exclude competition by opposition parties. In no country of the region have such parties been permitted to take part in electoral contests. A minor element of competitiveness has been introduced in Hungary and

Rumania, in the form of the legal possibility of multiple candidacies for office. Thus far this has not led to frequent electoral conflicts. Where other parties do exist, as in Czechoslovakia, Bulgaria, East Germany, and Poland, they are in all cases allies and partners of the ruling party and are not in any sense parties of opposition. At most they may give a modest expression of the interests of certain social or religious groups. Even in Poland, elections are not competitive but constitute what a communist theorist has called "semi-plebiscitary" or "consent" elections.[24]

Because there are more candidates than seats to be filled and because voters may express preferences in voting for certain candidates and certain parties, the elections provide "an opportunity to criticize the government policy by lowering the electoral acceptance of this policy."[25] In this way, Wiatr concludes, "the consent elections do not decide who will rule the country, but they influence the way in which the country will be ruled."[26] In Yugoslavia, where no other parties exist, but where a kind of national front in the form of the Socialist League plays a significant part, elections have assumed a somewhat different character in that recently the number of candidates has considerably exceeded the number of seats to be filled. As a result, at least a personal competition for office takes place, although this does not represent opposition in terms of policy.[27]

Traditionally lacking in communist systems has been an effective system of parliamentary control of the executive power. The danger of "uncontrolled power" has been recognized, and the need for a more powerful public opinion as a check on the abuse of power has been stressed.[28] Recent attempts to fulfill this function of parliamentary opposition in the form of a "question time" in the assembly or a more vigorous criticism of administration by deputies may have had some results, however minimal. Extraparliamentary "control" of official actions, through the press and special organs of popular control, have also been emphasized in recent years and may have accomplished something. Paradoxically, however, the chief source of criticism of executive arbitrariness or failures of administrative action has been the party itself, especially its top leaders and its organs, the Central Committee and the apparatus. This, of course, has been a traditional device characteristic of the times of Stalin as much as of the post-Stalinist period and represents a kind of "control from above" quite different from the control from below characteristic of more democratic societies. Even in Albania, for instance, in an open letter in March, 1966, the Central Committee censured the bureaucratic elite of party and state.[29] It is a curious paradox of communist systems that an important agency of "opposition" is the ruling party itself, which assumes the functions of supervising the actions of the executive or even of the leading figures of government or party and subjecting them to criticism.[30]

Similarly, the mass societal organizations and the broad social groups that they purportedly represent have not been able to find any effective means, except in a most informal manner, to express their interests through autonomous and overt political action. Broad social groups, such as the workers and peasants, the nationalities, or the religious denominations, are undoubtedly politically relevant in the sense that their needs and wants are in some degree or other taken into account by political leaders, increasingly so in the post-Stalinist period.

Certain important groups, such as the peasants, and even collective-farm chairmen or factory directors, find themselves in somewhat the same position as, say, the consumers in a Western democracy, possessing no formal institutionalized way of pressing their demands on the government. Even where mass societal organizations do exist, as in the case of the industrial workers or the youth and women, these associations are in the main unable to express or articulate autonomously the interests of the social categories concerned, but are designed rather to transmit the party's conception of the "real" group interest or more often the national or party interest to which the group interest is to be subordinated or sacrificed.[31] Even the intelligentsia has on the whole been unable to conduct political activity as a class or stratum, but can act only through groups representing the occupational interests or opinions of particular segments of the intelligentsia.

True, in the changed climate since Stalin's death there is some evidence that the mass organizations, especially the trade unions, sometimes provide a setting for the expression of a distinctive social-group interest.[32] Moreover, some of the political interest groups among the intelligentsia may articulate broader group interests—when, for instance, liberal writers express the interests of certain nationalities, or of the peasants, or of the intelligentsia as a whole.[33] As time goes on, the broad social groups may become better able to express their own group interests within existing organizations or even to form new associations for this purpose.

In most East European communist countries there has been outspoken criticism of the mass organizations for their lack of representative character and their lack of activity in the defense of group interests.[34] There have been frequent statements, official and unofficial, of the desirability of more vigorous expression of group interests by these organizations and of consideration of their special interests by the party in working out public policy in relevant spheres.

In most countries, special efforts have been taken to broaden the authority of the trade unions in particular and to encourage them to become more genuine representatives of the interests of the workers, especially at the local level, and to serve as consultants and advisers of the government and party at the national level. How far these principles will be applied is difficult to estimate, especially as the trade unions in all countries remain under the general direction of the party and are not regarded as independent pressure groups. In Yugoslavia, however, the trade unions have become much more independent and representative of the workers' interests and have on occasion exerted a considerable influence on the course of legislation. The national plan for 1965, for instance, was rejected by the trade unions and had to be revised extensively before parliamentary approval was gained. Moreover, strikes have occurred on more than one occasion and have been treated by the authorities as legitimate forms of oppositional action.

Apart from Yugoslavia the most notable action has been taken in Hungary, with the issuance in June, 1966, of a joint resolution of government and trade unions on the role of the latter. The trade unions are increasingly thought of, in Hungary at least, as having a dual function, taking account not only of the general interest as embodied in party and government decisions but also of the more partial and restricted interests of the workers. Conflicts of interest are therefore to be expected and supposedly are not to be automatically solved, as in the past, by the subordination of partial to general interests. Similarly, the trade unions are expected to serve as transmission belts operating in two directions, providing information needed by the rule-makers on the attitudes of the workers and funneling policy decisions and directives to the masses. This is not to say that the authorities will necessarily accept the workers' views of their own interests, or that the unions can be allowed to neglect the general interest. Indeed, as the first secretary of the Hungarian trade unions has explained it, the trade unions "represent and protect the individual interests of the workers on the basis of the interests of society as a whole."[35]

A more striking phenomenon has been the rise of activity by what may be called "political interest groups," acting sometimes outside, sometimes within, the formal structure of political power and normally seeking to influence and penetrate that structure in favor of their objectives.[36] Paraphrasing David Truman, we may define as such a group, persons who possess certain common characteristics and share certain attitudes on public issues and who adopt distinct positions on these issues and make definite claims on those in authority.[37] In the first place, *occupational interest groups* may be distinguished in that they are formed (a) by certain persons who occupy key positions in the power structure—what we may call *official* or *bureaucratic* groups, such as the party *apparatchiki,* state bureaucrats and managers, security police officers, and the military—and (b) by certain *professional* persons among the intelligentsia, such as the writers, economists, lawyers, educators, and natural scientists. It is assumed that each one of these broad occupational categories, bureaucratic or professional, may have certain common interests or attitudes and may press these upon the top rulers. At the same time, within each of these classifications *opinion groups* may be distinguished, having shared viewpoints on specific public issues that are more significant for their behavior and for communist politics than for the common interest of the whole occupational group.

Each of the two principal categories, the "occupational" and the "opinion," may be further broken down into a complex web of subgroups reflecting divergent aspects of occupational affiliation or outlook. Scientists, for instance, may be classified according to various criteria: institutional affiliation (Academy of Sciences, universities, other institutions); regional level of activity (all-Union, Union-Republic, provincial, or local); official or nonofficial employment (party apparatus, government department, or nonofficial institutions); geographical location of employment (Leningrad, Moscow, Novosibirsk); scientific field (biology, geography, etc.); function (pure scientists, technologists, governmental administrators); rank or position (full or corresponding member of the Academy, research employees), and so on. Each opinion group may also be analyzed as a complex network of subgroups exhibiting a wide variety of viewpoints. For instance, among the economists or writers it is possible not only to distinguish between "reformers," or "liberals," and "conservatives," but also to make narrower distinctions within these categories which will recognize differing degrees of liberalism or conservatism. Moreover, opinion groups, within the military for instance, may be based not on a liberal-conservative dichotomy but on other criteria, such as differing views of war strategy.

There is, then, a complicated patchwork of intersecting and overlapping groups; these in turn may form complex group alliances that give one another support in defense of common interests. There may be, for instance, alliances of differing professional or bureaucratic groups based on a common regional (e.g., Siberian) or ethnic (e.g., Ukrainian) interest or on a common functional interest (e.g., agricultural). A kind of military-industrial complex allying the military, heavy industry, and the party apparatus can perhaps be identified. Within several professional and bureaucratic groups there may be opinion groups that cut across occupational lines and link together, say, the liberal writers, artists, scientists, and lawyers in a common front on one or more issues.[38] Brzezinski has proposed a scheme for analyzing the spectrum of opinion in Soviet politics, ranging from the systematic left (radical reformists) to the systematic right (reactionaries) and including in the mainstream the left, center, and right.[39]

A striking feature of political interest groups in communist politics is that normally they are not formally organized, but are more often loose groupings of like-minded or like-interested persons. The paradox of the Soviet or communist context is that such informal groupings are more likely than organized groups to be active exponents of common attitudes and to assert demands for government or party action; in fact, such groups may come into existence because organized groups (e.g., the Union of Writers) do not perform these functions adequately. The more highly organized groups, such as trade unions or the youth league, express only in a limited degree distinctive interests of their own or of the social groups that they are supposed to represent. Although an interest group is not able to set up a formal organization of its own, it may work within a legitimate, officially established organization, if one exists, and may seek to use it to defend distinctive group interests. A whole occupational group, for instance, the writers, or a segment of it may express its views through the Union of Writers. In the same way, an interest group may express its views within official institutions—for example, the professional interests of all scientists through the Academy of Sciences, or the views of like-minded persons in the conservative military through the journals of the armed forces. In these circumstances the winning of key organizational positions, such as the editorship of a journal or an office in the leadership organs, takes on great importance, and the struggle may sometimes assume certain democratic aspects in the form of electoral rivalry.

Group theory in the West has tended to emphasize—or treat exclusively—private associations or so-called pressure groups, such as trade unions or farm organizations, and to exclude elements of the governmental structure. In the Soviet context, where the making of final decisions rests largely in the hands of a very small group of leaders at the apex of the system, there seems little reason to exclude group conflict at the next lower tier—that is, at the highest level of the party and state structures. Certain official or bureaucratic groups, such as party *apparatchiki,* state bureaucrats, managers, and the military, who possess official authority in varying degrees, are likely to have their own occupational-group interests and their own views of the general public interest, and may sometimes press these on the decision-makers. Within these power-holding occupational groups, as in the case of nonofficial groups, there are also likely to be rival and conflicting viewpoints on public policy, reflecting perhaps regional or functional considerations or ideological criteria. Moreover, the professional groups—for instance, writers or economists—often straddle the line between those who hold offices endowed with official powers and those who have influence without office. Some economists, for example, work for government departments or in party institutions; others are employed in the Academy of Sciences, the universities, or individual factories. In so-called private organizations, such as the Union of Writers or the Academy of Sciences, certain *apparatchiki* enjoy a good deal of semiofficial power, greater than that of the rank and file and perhaps sometimes equaling those with formal authority in government or party. Increasingly, both party and state have enlisted the services of professionals from the fields of scholarship in advisory capacities, thus bringing them closer to "officialdom" and smudging the boundary between official and nonofficial groups.

Although these groups are close to the strategic locus of decision-making and may therefore have a greater opportunity to press their views on the top leaders, the professional groups, because of their technical expertise, their indispensability to the ruling circles in framing policy, and their own access to influential media of communication, possess substantial influence. A most striking feature of the post-Stalinist scene in the U.S.S.R. and in all the European communist countries has been the rise of the intellectuals as a force capable of articulating not only their own professional interests but also the interests of broader social groups and of society as a whole. It would be a mistake to assume that the increased activity of the professional interest groups is simply a product of an official decision to widen the scope of consultation and the degree of freedom of discussion. Although official actions resulting from de-Stalinization have created an atmosphere more favorable to group activity and even to opposition, the professional groups themselves, taking advantage of this, have often expressed more radical oppositional views and as a result have been subjected to official criticism and restrictions.

For instance, during the critical early years of de-Stalinization in Hungary and Poland, the writers and journalists emerged as a powerful force seeking an acceleration of the process of liberalization and constituted a radical opposition to the existing regimes. In the case of Hungary, the literary community, together with other sectors of the intelligentsia, formed the spearhead of the subsequent revolution. Although the revolt was crushed, the liberal writers continued to act as an opposition, at first refusing to write for publication and later acting as spokesmen for greater freedom of expression. Similarly, the Polish writers, and intellectuals generally, without taking the road of violent revolt, were in large part responsible for the events of October, 1956, and thereafter continued to express their own views vigorously. Even with the reversion of the regime to stricter control of literature and the arts, the writers on more than one occasion defended their interests and protested against government actions.[40]

In Czechoslovakia, at a later stage, the writers and journalists became a significant political factor, pressing, in their associations and in their journals, for de-Stalinization and for greater freedom of expression and in some cases directly challenging the government and individual leaders.[41] The most celebrated case was the courageous attack by the Slovak journalist M. Hysko on Prime Minister Široký. Although Hysko was sharply censured by no less a person than the President and First Secretary Novotný, the removal of Široký testified to the effectiveness of his opposition. Most significantly, his article had been published in the organ of the Slovak Communist party, *Pravda,* which on that and other occasions served as the vehicle for oppositional attitudes. Other literary periodicals, in particular *Literární noviny* and *Kulturní život,* for years continued to be a thorn in the flesh of the regime, publishing critical articles dealing with all aspects of Czech and Slovak life and bringing down on their heads torrents of official censure.[42] A crucial aspect of this struggle was the membership of the editorial boards of these journals and the executive committees of the literary associations. Despite repeated condemnation and changes in leading personnel, the periodicals persisted in their oppositional attitudes.

Similarly, social scientists and other scholars have played an important role in the political life of certain countries. As in the case of the writers, the lawyers, economists, sociologists, and even historians and philosophers have constituted influential interest groups in their respective fields. "Opinion groups" within these occupational categories, conservative as well as liberal, have voiced conflicting opinions and thus have constituted important oppositions of varying kinds. In particular, the economists have played a significant role in criticizing the older planning system, in advocating economic reforms, and often in complaining about the slowness of the reforms officially adopted. Sharp cleavages have manifested themselves on the nature of the reforms among the economists and between economists and bureaucratic groups. Similar controversies among historians, in the course of a more objective re-evaluation of the past, often have had direct political relevance. Lawyers have been less influential but have actively contributed to the discussions of legal reform. The rise of the discipline of sociology has introduced a new and important element in scholarship which is capable of serving as an instrument in the formation of policy. A unique feature of certain countries, as distinct from the Soviet Union, has been the part played by philosophers in the expression of dissident views and in the advocacy of greater freedom of discussion. Indeed, a common point made by scholars in many fields has been the need for greater liberty of expression, in some cases going as far as a demand for absolute freedom.

Space prevents extensive analysis of the methods and channels employed by interest groups in articulating their interests and, where necessary, in expressing dissent. To a considerable extent, insofar as the discussions are conducted within the administrative institutions of party and state, the clash of opposing viewpoints takes place behind the scenes and is not subject to scholarly analysis. To some degree there may be efforts similar to what we know as "lobbying" in the West, when professional and even bureaucratic groups privately seek to exert influence on the appropriate bureaucratic office in the party or state. There is likely also to be a good deal of tension, and action and counteraction, between party and state offices, between individual departments of government, between central and regional agencies, and between central administration and local government agencies.

Most striking, however, has been the emergence, in a previously unknown degree, of public discussion, either in the main organs of communication, the newspapers, and to a lesser extent on radio and television, or, more surprisingly, in the scholarly and cultural media such as journals and conferences of scholarly associations, the literary journals and associations, or the books and plays of the writing community.

It should be clear that opposition of the kinds we have been discussing differs greatly from what would normally be regarded as legitimate opposition in a democratic political system. Such dissent has perforce to operate within strict limits, although they are not as strict as has customarily been assumed or as was once the case. The party's monopoly of the instruments of coercion prevents violent revolutionary opposition; and after the fiasco of Hungary a resort to force is not likely to occur, except in the eventuality of a serious future crisis. Moreover, although the coercive power of the regimes is exercised more lightly at present than in the past, and not in the form of outright terror, its presence still inhibits nonviolent opposition of a fundamental or integral kind. Similarly, the nature of the electoral system and single-party domination rule out effective parliamentary or electoral opposition.

The centralized and unified nature of the party sets strict limits on the functioning of factional opposition and usually blocks it in realizing its objectives. This does not exclude entirely the possibility of the replacement of leaders by oppositional groups through the secret processes of Politburo intrigue. The party's continuing claim to the exercise of total control over society, including the organized interest groups, circumscribes the overt autonomous action by such groups, although it does not entirely prevent it, as for instance in such cases as the Czechoslovak writers' association. The establishment of a single official theory, Marxism-Leninism, restricts the expression of oppositional views and requires a high degree of doctrinal conformity in voicing dissent. There is, however, wide latitude for various interpretations of the official doctrine, as in matters of economic reform, so that divergent viewpoints are not excluded.

The party's monopoly of the means of communication does not rule out the expression of diverse views on even sensitive issues such as literary or scholarly freedom, economic or legal reform. The party, while paying homage to the idea of freedom of discussion, never fails to stress that this freedom cannot be an absolute one and that criticism or dissent must be conducted within the framework of Marxism-Leninism and the general party line and cannot extend to include "bourgeois" or "anti-communist" views. If necessary, the party can resort to "administrative" measures, such as the closing down of a periodical, the removal of an editor, public censure of an offending critic, expulsion from the party, dismissal from posts held, or, in the most extreme cases, arrest and trial. This in turn may sometimes lead to continued resistance by the person in question and perhaps to protests by his colleagues. In some cases the expression of dissent may escape the control of the party and involve dissident views sharply opposed to the party's line. As in the case of the cultural periodicals in Czechoslovakia, a running battle may go on for some years, with the editors resisting heavy attack but not giving in to steady pressure.

How the process of opposition will develop in the U.S.S.R. and Eastern Europe in the future is difficult to predict. Owing to the difference of national backgrounds and the relative brevity of communist rule in the countries of Eastern Europe, the evolution of opposition is likely to exhibit features very different from those of the Soviet Union. Whatever occurs is likely to vary greatly as national traditions become increasingly influential factors in the political culture of each communist country. The tradition of the monolithic party and of the party's monopolistic position, however, is likely to die hard and to continue to set strict limits on the expression of opposition. But, if present trends continue, there are likely to be expanded opportunities for nongoverning interest groups to express dissent and to influence public policy through private pressure and public discussion. The party probably will remain the main mechanism of political control and rule-making, but its role will become increasingly that of an agency of conciliation and harmonization.[43]

There has been some speculation in the West on the possibility of the emergence of a kind of political pluralism and of an institutionalization of opposition in the Soviet Union and in East European communist countries.[44] The most optimistic forecast is that made by Ghita Ionescu, who, in his recent book, has analyzed the growth of "checks" and "dissent" in the European communist states and, citing Yugoslavia as a kind of model, has predicted their "institutionalization."[45]

Certainly there are possibilities of greater parliamentary participation in policy formation, as has occurred to some degree in Yugoslavia; of more effective parliamentary control of executive action; of electoral competition among persons sharing similar views; and of greater influence on decision-making by organizations such as the trade unions and other professional associations within their spheres of interest. Suggestions along these lines have been made with increasing frequency in the communist world, and the measures for moving in this direction have been introduced. But the likelihood that an advanced type of pluralism will emerge in the form of an effective multiparty system or even in a fully democratic exploration of policy alternatives, with wide opportunities for dissent, appears to be remote.

Nonetheless, the recent evolution of Czechoslovakia warns against dogmatic conclusions and suggests the possibility of unexpected alternatives in the future.[46] Until the end of 1967, Czechoslovakia had rightly been considered an extremely conservative bastion of Stalinist communism, where changes had been slow and halting and had not fundamentally changed the process of government. Nevertheless, dissent on specific aspects of life, such as economic policy, had been expressed openly and had led to the adoption of far-reaching economic reforms. Similarly, more fundamental opposition had been expressed by intellectuals, in particular by the writers, and had reached a culminating point at the Congress of the Writers' Union in the summer of 1967. Mass demonstrations by students in the fall, and the continued manifestation of discontent by the Slovaks, were further elements of fundamental opposition. Although in theory the party continued to reject the very idea of opposition and in practice sought to limit and suppress the expression of dissent, in fact, the Novotný regime was confronted over a period of years with a mounting tide of opposition sentiment articulated mainly by the intellectuals in their scholarly and literary publications. The crisis of late 1967, in which the many currents of dissent were channeled into bitter factional conflict at the top, led to the removal of Novotný from the first secretaryship and to the victory of the forces of opposition, as represented by a new leader, Alexander Dubček.

There followed a period of intense struggle during the early months of 1968, as the opposition sought to undermine the position of the remaining conservative forces in the top leadership, and in all organizations and institutions, and to assure the complete victory of reform. Almost full freedom of expression prevailed, and the press, especially the new organ of the Writers' Union, *Literární listy,* became the spearhead of dynamic change.

Radio, television, and public meetings also reflected the increasing radicalism of public opinion. Some of this dissent was very severe in its critique of many aspects of communism while favorable in its treatment of precommunist democratic and national traditions and verged, therefore, on integral opposition. In the main, however, this was criticism, by communists, of the evils and defects of communism as it had existed in the past, rather than a rejection of communism itself. The party, as was openly admitted, was divided between conservatives, "liberal" reformists, and centrists; conflicting views were expressed in party organs, such as *Rudé právo,* in local party organizations, and in the Central Committee. In an extraordinary process of public debate, sharp censure of the old order, and denunciation of certain key persons still in seats of power, were expressed, and demands for radical policy changes were raised. A climax came in the Central Committee at the end of March, 1968, when Novotný was displaced from the party's top organs and from the presidency, and when other discredited leaders were also removed, signaling a further triumph of the opposition.

The same session adopted an Action Program which proclaimed the target of a "socialist democracy" and set forth a sweeping agenda of political reforms, including a genuinely democratic electoral system; the revival of the National Front and the almost moribund noncommunist parties (Socialist and People's); a regeneration of mass organizations, such as the trade unions, as authentic pressure groups; legal guarantees of freedom of expression and association; and a restoration of the National Assembly as an organ of public debate and of control of the executive.[47] The "leading role" of the party was to be retained but was to be maintained by persuasion and justified through the winning of public support by the party's actions. This traditional doctrine was interpreted to exclude "a monopolistic concentration of power in the hands of party organs," and to include "a real discussion and exchange of opinions." The party itself was to be made democratic, with the free election of officers and free debate within its ranks, and with a reduction of the role of the apparatus. Above all, the power of the police was to be substantially reduced, and justice was to be assured through independent courts, thus excluding the possibility of a return to the terror of the fifties. Finally, a federal constitutional system was to be established, with far-reaching autonomy for the Slovaks. The implementation of this program would transform the political system in essential respects and would provide institutionalized guarantees of the expression of specific and even fundamental dissent in a manner never before attempted in a communist state.

Public discussion of the nature of "socialist democracy" was even more pregnant with revolutionary possibilities for the future. Several articles in the literary journals posed the central issue that a real democracy presumes the existence of two or more parties, including an opposition, and a genuine competition for power in elections, with the acceptance of the possibility of defeat by the ruling party. Without this, it was argued, other changes, such as the democratization of the Communist party, the revival of the other noncommunist parties within the alliance of the National Front, the restoration of interest associations, and even freedom of discussion, unlimited by censorship, would not guarantee a genuinely democratic socialism. "Indeed, it is possible to speak seriously of democracy," wrote one commentator, "only where the people have the possibility— from time to time—to choose freely who is to govern them. This presumes the existence of at least *two parallel alternatives,* i.e., of two autonomous, equal, and mutually independent political forces, both of which have the opportunity to become the leading force in the state, if the people so decide."[48]

The Action Program, however, excluded this radical possibility, arguing instead for a National Front as "a political platform which does not divide political parties into governing and oppositional in the sense that an opposition would be formed against the line of state policy, as the line of the whole National Front, and a political struggle for power would be conducted in the state." As one of the more liberal party leaders, Čestmír Čísar, put it:

Isolated opinions concerning the necessity of creating a new political party, with an opposition mission as a massive counterweight to our party, we do not regard as correct. A plurality of political parties competing for power so as to risk the very essence of socialism would contradict the need and interest of the people, would open the way to the possibility of a return to capitalism and create the danger of a violent struggle, and would call forth the need for a violent defense of socialism. The rise of an opposition party with an antisocialist program would mean the end of the Czechoslovak experiment of creating a model of democratic socialism.[49]

It hardly seems likely that the Dubček leadership, in spite of its dedication to basic political reform, would permit a free struggle of political forces leading to its eventual abdication from power. Yet the very raising of these issues, and the willingness of the regime to countenance and to sponsor somewhat less far-reaching, but in the communist context revolutionary, political reforms, had a potential for future development which could not be predicted, but which should not be underestimated. Old habits of thought and behavior, Dubček's natural reluctance to weaken or relinquish power, and pressures from the Soviet Union might slow down the course of change and in certain circumstances lead to the restoration of a system resembling the old one, as in the case of Poland since 1956. Soviet military intervention, as in Hungary, although unlikely, would turn the clock back decisively and would sow the seeds of an even more dangerous crisis in the future. On the other hand, the successful evolution of a unique, communist-ruled democracy in which freedom and dissent are institutionalized even more securely than they are in Yugoslavia, or even a peaceful transition toward full democracy under other than communist rule, should not be excluded from the range of possible alternatives.

NOTES

1. Robert Tucker's comment on Zbigniew K. Brzezinski, "The Nature of the Soviet System," *Slavic Review*, XX (October, 1961), 379–80.

2. See the present author's "Interest Groups and Communist Politics," *World Politics*, XVIII, no. 3 (April, 1966), 435–51. Cf. Carl Linden, *Khrushchev and the Soviet Leadership, 1957–1964* (Baltimore, 1966), Introduction, and Sidney Ploss, *Conflict and Decision-Making in Soviet*

Russia: A Case Study of Agricultural Policy, 1953–1963 (Princeton, 1965), Introduction and Conclusion.

3. See, in particular, the special issue of *Government and Opposition*, "The Dead End of the Monolithic Parties," vol. 2, no. 2 (January-April, 1967), pp. 168–80, and ensuing articles in the same issue. See also two earlier articles, one by Jerzy J. Wiatr and Adam Przeworski, "Control without Opposition," *ibid.*, vol. 1, no. 2 (January, 1966), pp. 227–39, the other by Ghita Ionescu, "Control and Contestation in Some One-Party States," *ibid.*, pp. 240–50. See Ghita Ionescu, "The Future of the Monolithic Party," International Conference of Futuribles, Paris (April, 1965), mimeographed. A fuller study by Ghita Ionescu, *Politics of the European Communist States,* has been published (New York, 1967). As this was not available at the time of writing, all references are to Ionescu's previously published works. In his new book, however, he has modified some of the concepts and definitions quoted here. See the present author's chapter on opposition in communist East Europe in the forthcoming volume by Robert Dahl, *Emerging Oppositions.*

4. See Leonard Schapiro, " 'Putting the lid on Leninism,' Opposition and Dissent in the Communist One-Party States," *Government and Opposition,* Vol. 2, no. 2 (January-April, 1967), pp. 181–203. See the fuller treatment in his book *The Origin of the Communist Autocracy: Political Opposition in the Soviet State. First Phase, 1917–1922* (London and Cambridge, Mass., 1955).

5. See Robert V. Daniels, *The Conscience of the Revolution: Communist Opposition in Soviet Russia* (Cambridge, 1960).

6. Frederick C. Barghoorn, *Politics in the U.S.S.R.* (Boston and Toronto, 1966), pp. 13, 20–21.

7. The Polish sociologist Jerzy J. Wiatr has called this a "hegemonical party system" rather than strictly a one-party system. See his "One-Party Systems—The Concept and Issue for Comparative Studies," in *Cleavages, Ideologies and Party Stytems: Contributions to Comparative Political Sociology,* ed. E. Allardt and Y. Littunen, Transactions of the Westermarck Society, vol. X (Helsinki, 1964), pp. 281–90.

8. *Pravda,* February 20, 1967.

9. In Hungary, for instance, the existence of "separate platforms" or "factions" within the party was explicitly rejected by the party daily newspaper, *Nepszabadsag,* May 16, 1963. Cf. the views of the Czech leader J. Hendrých (*Rudé právo,* February 10, 1967) that there can be "different opinions on different problems," but not "representatives of different ideologies." In Poland, in 1964–65, university students J. Kuron and K. Modzelevski were expelled from the party and later imprisoned for opposition activity, which had included an open letter condemning the entire Polish system.

In 1966 Professor L. Kolakowski was expelled from the party for a speech severely criticizing the regime's failures since 1956 (*New York Times,* November 1, 5, 1966).

10. Vol. 1, no. 1 (October, 1965), pp. 1, 3.

11. Cf. an elaboration of this theme by the Czech scholar Z. Mlynář, *Věda a Život,* no. 1 (1965). Mlynář has described the leading role of the

party as involving "the conscious embodiment of the interests of the whole society in its entirety, but also the deliberate harmonization of these interests." See his article "Problems of Political Leadership and the New Economic System," *Problemy mira i sotsializma,* no. 12 (December, 1965), p. 98. Hendrých, in his article cited earlier, referred to the party as "the bearer of the general social interests" (*Rudé právo,* February 10, 1967).

The Polish scholar Wiatr has referred to the party as "the forum of the expression of the non-antagonistic classes of interests of various socialist strata of the Polish society," and as "the platform where the divergent interests of the socialist society collide." Although the struggle of class interests takes place outside the party, the "resolution of conflicts which harmonize the interests of workers and their allies" takes place within the party and is guaranteed by intraparty democracy. See Jerzy J. Wiatr, "The Elements of the Pluralism in the Polish Political System," *The Polish Sociological Bulletin,* no. 1 (1966), pp. 22–23.

12. Z. Mlynář, in an important article already cited, rejected the "effort to solve these problems without discussions and controversies, without democratic deliberation of various possible alternatives, without serious scientific and theoretical elaboration of the perspectives of development" ("Problems of Political Leadership," p. 93).

13. Zbigniew K. Brzezinski and Samuel P. Huntington, *Political Power: USA/USSR* (New York, 1964), p. 105.

14. Schapiro defines *opposition* as "an organized political group, or groups, of which the aim is to oust the government in power and to replace it by one of its own choosing." Dissent, on the other hand, seeks "merely to criticize, to exhort, to persuade, and to be listened to" (" 'Putting the Lid on Leninism,' " pp. 182–83). Ionescu defines contestation as "the anti-system, basic and permanent postulates of any opposition on the grounds of fundamental dichotomic differences of opinion and ideologies" (*Government and Opposition,* vol. 1, no. 2, p. 241).

15. Ionescu and Wiatr use the concept "control" in this connection. Ionescu defines "political control" as *"non-constitutional* and *non-institutional* direct participation in, and influencing of, the decision-making processes in a non-parliamentary society by forces, groups and agencies indispensable to the running of that society" (*Government and Opposition,* vol. 1, no. 2, p. 240). Wiatr and Przeworski define control in the political sense as "the possibility of influencing those who hold power in such a way that they take into account the interests of groups exerting this control" ("Control without Opposition," p. 231).

16. This is close to what Robert Dahl refers to as revolutionary "structural opposition." See *Political Opposition in Western Democracies* (New Haven and London, 1966), p. 342. Cf. the somewhat awkward term "contestation" employed by Ionescu in "Control and Contestation in Some One-Party States, p. 241.

17. This is comparable to Alex Nove's "Dissent within Consensus," *Government and Opposition,* vol. 2, no. 2 (January-April, 1967), pp. 175–76. Cf. the term "orthodox dissent" in Brzezinski and Huntington, *Political Power,* p. 110.

18. See the present author's *Communism, National and International* (Toronto, 1964).

19. Dahl, ed., *Political Opposition in Western Democracies.*

20. *Ibid.,* pp. xi–xii, xiv.

21. See Wiatr and Przeworski, "Control without Opposition," and Ionescu, "Control and Contestation."

22. See V. C. Chrypinski, "Legislative Committees in Polish Lawmaking," *Slavic Review,* XXV, no. 2 (June, 1966), 247–58.

23. *East Europe,* vol. 16, nos. 1 and 2 (January and February, 1967), pp. 28 and 37, resp.

24. Wiatr and Przeworski, "Control without Opposition," pp. 238–39. A fuller analysis of Polish elections is given by Wiatr in his chapter, "Elections and Voting Behaviour in Poland," in *Essays on the Behavioural Study of Politics,* ed. A. Rannev (Urbana, Ill., 1962), pp. 237–51, esp. p. 239. For further discussion of the Polish system, see Wiatr, "One-Party Systems," pp. 287–89; Wiatr, "The Electoral System and Elements of Pluralism in a 'One-Party' System: Poland," *Transactions of the Fifth World Congress of Sociology,* International Sociological Association, 1962, IV, 381–86.

25. Wiatr, "Elections and Voting Behaviour in Poland," p. 251.

26. *Ibid.,* p. 239.

27. This has been called Yugoslavia's "1½ party system" (*New York Times,* May 29, 1966). See R. V. Burks and S. A Stankovic, "Jugoslawien auf dem Weg zu halbfreien Wahlen," *Osteuropa,* vol. 17, no. 2-3 (February/March, 1967) pp. 131–46. For further discussion of elections in communist countries of Eastern Europe, see the present author's book *The Governments of Communist East Europe* (New York, 1966), pp. 130–34.

28. For instance, see the articles by Miroslav Jodl, a Czech sociologist, in *Literární noviny,* November 13, 1965, and January 22, 1966. Cf. also the Polish discussion in 1965 of Adam Schaff's book *Marxism and the Individual* and of his concept of the power elite and alienation under communism. The Slovak M. Lakatos has written of the manipulation of the ruled by the rulers and has urged genuinely free elections as a means of preventing this (*Právny obzor,* no. 3, 1966, also translated in *East Europe,* vol. 15, no. 6 [June, 1966], pp. 22–23).

29. *Christian Science Monitor,* March 31, 1966.

30. The daily organ of the Hungarian People's Front, *Magyar Nemzet* (August 28, 1966), used this as an argument that an opposition party was not necessary. Criticism, it declared, is "the essence of opposition." In Hungary the party and the government criticize everything at all times, where things are not going as they should, and thus "supply the checking and criticizing functions of an opposition."

31. See Emily Clark Brown, *Soviet Trade Unions and Labor Relations* (Cambridge, 1966), especially chap. XI. Cf. her article, "Interests and Rights of Soviet Industrial Workers and the Resolution of Conflicts," *Industrial and Labor Relations Review,* vol. 16, no. 2 (January, 1963), pp. 254–78. Brown concluded that, although the unions are expected to protect the interests of the workers more than in the past, they still

function more as "arms of the government or party, carrying out policies established above, than as independent agencies representing the workers and their interests" (*Soviet Trade Unions,* p. 277; cf. pp. 80–85). They act "more like sections of a government department of labour than as independent trade union centres" ("Interests and Rights," p. 319).

32. This is particularly true at the factory and regional levels of the trade unions. At the national level the trade unions are consulted on labor legislation, and they issue, with government or party, joint decrees, but it is difficult to determine whether—and, if so, to what extent—they express a distinctive workers' interest in this activity. See Brown, "Interests and Rights," pp. 258–59, 261ff., 277, and *Soviet Trade Unions,* pp. 139ff. For a controversy over the role of Soviet unions, see the article by Paul Barton (*Problems of Communism,* vol. 9, no. 4 [July-August, 1960], pp. 18–27) and the ensuing discussion (*ibid.,* no. 6 [November-December, 1960], pp. 38–47).

33. Certain writers have directed attention to economic difficulties on the collective farms (Solzhenitsyn), or to the continued existence of anti-Semitism (Evtushenko).

34. Mlynář (*Rudé právo,* August 16, 1966). The same writer, in the international communist organ, argued that these organizations should not serve as mere transmission belts operating in one direction only (*Problemy mira i sotsialisma,* December, 1965, p. 97.) The Polish writer Wiatr has written of the dual function of various interest groups, serving not only as "pressure groups," which "represent the interests of their groups vis-à-vis the Party and the government," but also as "mobilizing groups," which mobilize their members to the tasks put forth by party and government ("Pluralism in the Polish Political System," p. 24).

35. S. Gaspar, *Nepszabadsag,* December 2, 1966.

36. For a fuller discussion see H. G. Skilling and Franklyn Griffiths' forthcoming book *Interest Groups in Soviet Politics.*

37. David B. Truman, *The Governmental Process: Political Interests and Public Opinion* (New York, 1951), pp. 33–37.

38. See, e.g., the letter of September, 1966, to the Central Committee, opposing the rehabilitation of Stalin, which was signed by leading writers, scientists, and artists.

39. Zbigniew K. Brzezinski, "The Soviet Political System: Transformation or Degeneration?" *Problems of Communism,* vol. 15, no. 1 (January-February, 1966), p. 10. Barghoorn also refers to a liberal-conservative continuum (*Politics in the U.S.S.R.,* pp. 180–81), with certain occupational groups tending to one or the other extreme.

40. For instance, the 1964 letter addressed to the government by 34 writers protesting censorship and paper restrictions.

41. See the present author's *Communism, National and International,* chap. 7, for a detailed discussion of these events.

42. See the Central Committee resolution on the cultural periodicals, *Rudé právo,* April 4, 1964, and subsequent official denunciations.

43. See the discussion on the future of monolithic parties on p. 1 of

the special issue of *Government and Opposition* cited in n. 3 above and the present author's *The Governments of Communist East Europe,* concluding chapter.

44. Brzezinski, "The Soviet Political System: Transformation or Degeneration?" pp. 1–15.

45. *Politics of the European Communist States,* pp. 80–85, 166–69, 190, 271–78.

46. For a fuller discussion see H. Gordon Skilling, "Crisis and Change in Czechoslovakia," *International Journal,* XXIII, no. 2 (Summer, 1968).

47. Text given in *Rudé právo,* April 10, 1968.

48. Václav Havel, "Na téma opozice" [On the Subject of Opposition], *Literární listý,* I, no. 6 (April 4, 1968), p. 4; cf. Alexander Kliment, "Aktivita nepojmenovaných" [Activity of the Unnamed], *Literární listý,* I, no. 3 (March 14, 1968), p. 4.

49. *Rudé právo,* April 29, 1968.

CHAPTER 2

Soviet Society

The Power Elite and Intelligentsia in Soviet Society

Boris Meissner

Function and Ideology in Soviet Social Stratification

Robert A. Feldmesser

The Power Elite and Intelligentsia in Soviet Society

Boris Meissner

FORMATION OF A NEW ELITE AND TRANSFORMATION OF THE SOCIAL STRUCTURE

The February revolution deprived of their social status and political power those members of the top-level bureaucracy and the officers' corps who, because they were mainly of aristocratic origin, were looked upon, like the nobility, as the chief supporters of the tsarist regime.[1] By far the majority of the state and *zemstvo* bureaucrats,[2] together with a large number of the newly developing soviet and trade-union organizations, ranged themselves on the side of the liberal democratic forces, the main supply base of which was the intelligentsia. The close links between bureaucracy and intelligentsia found expression in the formation of joint "Soviets of Deputies of the Working Intelligentsia."[3]

In the course of the violent transition from the bourgeois-democratic to the proletarian-socialist revolution, Lenin demanded the destruction of the existing machinery of government, including the abolition of the civil service and a standing army. He substantiated this point of view in greater detail in his well-known *The State and the Revolution,* written in the autumn of 1917. Yet he was realistic enough after the October Revolution to see that the Bolshevik party could not dispense with co-operation with the bureaucracy and the intelligentsia. He therefore decided to content himself during the transition period with "filling the most important key positions," which, in addition to the ministries, included the National Bank. The mass of the bureaucracy and intelligentsia, however, were not prepared to co-operate voluntarily in this.[4] Lenin first succeeded in crushing the opposition of the bureaucrats with the aid of the Cheka and then, in the course of the civil war, in bringing over to his side large numbers of the intelligentsia as well as the officers' corps.[5] While, owing to the difficulties in the food situation, the number of workers in industry dropped by half (1.5 million in 1920–21, compared with 3.0 million in 1917), the number of white-collar employees rose more than 60 per cent (2.4 million in 1920, as against 1.5 million in 1913).[6] The body of white-collar employees, which had absorbed the old bureaucracy, was composed, for the most part, of those members of the former upper social stratum (*lishentsy*) whose civil rights had been curtailed. Lenin was strongly in favor of employing those bourgeois specialists who had belonged to the old intelligentsia. In "Successes and Difficulties of the Soviet Power," which appeared in March-April, 1919, he wrote:

We must take possesion of the entire culture left behind by capitalism and build up socialism from it. We must take possession of the whole science and technology, of all knowledge and art. There is no other way of building up the life of communist society. This knowledge, technology and art, however, lies in the hands of the specialists and is lodged in their brains.

This is the assignment in all fields, therefore. It is contradictory, just as the whole of capitalism is contradictory, very difficult, but capable of being resolved. Not for the reason that in about twenty years' time we shall have educated newly minted communist specialists, the first generation of the communists without fault or blemish; no, allow me to say that we must organize all this here and now, not in twenty years but in two months, in order to contend with the bourgeoisie, with bourgeois science and technology all over the world. It is here that we must conquer. To force the bourgeois specialists into our service through the pressure of the masses is difficult, but possible; and if we do this we shall conquer.[7]

At the same time, Lenin strove to entrust political and economic leadership functions to workers, minor employees, and peasants, upon whom the Bolshevik party could better rely, thus enabling them to move up into the intelligentsia (*vydvizhenchestvo*). In January, 1921, the proportion of former workers among the top executives of the economy was 61.6 per cent, that of minor employees and other categories, 7.7 per cent. These included many metal workers. By the beginning of 1924, 51.1 per cent of the chairmen and 29.6 per cent of the administrative personnel of the industrial trusts were former workers.[8] The ratio of former workers among the chairmen of the metal and textile trusts was still higher (77 per cent and 62 per cent, respectively). Among the top-level political functionaries the ratio of former workers rose during the same period to 25 per cent, that of peasants to 3.7 per cent. Efforts to fill the "leadership cadres" with members of the Communist party, and to some extent with persons of proletarian origin who were not party members, were intensified still further after Lenin's death. They were to reach full development when Stalin's "revolution from above" started in 1928–29.

In view of this trend it is hardly correct to say that the existing government machinery was completely smashed after the October Revolution, although it was extensively reorganized with respect to its outer fabric and its internal structure. The development of a new "power elite" went hand in hand with the replacement of the former top-level bureaucracy by Bolshevik professional revolutionaries, who for the most part had belonged to the old intelligentsia. Among the top economic managers, however, former workers, the greater part of whom had joined the Bolshevik party only after the October Revolution,[9] outnumbered the "bourgeois specialists." Altogether, the latter were few in number and by no means all party members. The inferior educational background of the jumped-up proletarians made it imperative that large numbers of the petty bourgeoisie be entrusted with leadership functions in order that they build up the economy and, above all, rear a new intelligentsia at the universities and advanced technical schools.

Both processes were effected by the second Bolshevik revolution, triggered by Stalin in 1928–29, the goal of which was to speed up industrialization within the framework of an over-all planned economy. Through total socialization the petty bourgeoisie was thrust into the social group of the employees and workers. Since at that time it was customary to lump these two social categories under the general tag "proletariat," from the Soviet point of view the petty bourgeoisie had now become proletarianized. What the Bolshevik leadership overlooked was that artisans comprised only one part of the proletariat and that the state employees, insofar as they did not come from the former upper stratum, differed only slightly from the petty bourgeoisie in their social awareness and mode of living. Only when a former member of the petty bourgeoisie became an artisan did he become proletarianized; in his case the process generally took longer than it did with a peasant. He did not become proletarianized, however, if he was forced to give up his previous private employment in order to become a state employee. The assumption of new functions in the administrative field or in the organization of production meant just as great a rise in the social scale for some of the petty bourgeoisie as for workers who, as "practical intelligentsia," were entrusted with leadership functions. By the end of the first Five-Year Plan the number of these *vydvizhentsy* was to rise to almost one million.

In the course of the first two five-year plans the white-collar group, which in 1928 numbered 3.9 million people, rose to 9.6 million, fed by a growing stream of graduates from the universities and advanced technical schools—the majority of them from proletarian families—and by the process of incorporating large numbers of the petty bourgeoisie.[10] Between 1926 and 1937 this group increased considerably more rapidly than did that of the workers. After 1931 the white-collar employees, who had developed into a special social group distinct from that of the workers, came to be referred to as the "new intelligentsia," the "working intelligentsia," or the "socialist people's intelligentsia."[11] The crystallization of this trend—which was linked with the upgrading of the members of the "old intelligentsia," who were incorporated into the new group on the basis of equality—was marked by Stalin's programmatic speech before business functionaries on June 23, 1931.[12] Stalin said that no "ruling class" had ever been able to manage without its own intelligentsia. Accordingly, the workers must "create their own intelligentsia trained in production technique" while at the same time behaving with care toward the "old intelligentsia." In the same speech Stalin called for the abolition of marginal labor supply and of deviation from the party line. Work was to be paid for on the basis of results, and personal responsibility in the organization of production was to be increased. Under these auspices the introduction in 1929 of "uniform directory power" (*yedinonachaliye*)—that is, one-man management—in industry and other sectors of the economy acquired special significance.[13] It enabled a closely knit "leadership hierarchy" to form within the planned Soviet economy, and this became the starting point in a process of increasing differentiation within the "new intelligentsia."

The social upgrading of large numbers of white-collar employees, and therefore of the intelligentsia, resulted on the one hand from the natural cleavage between manual work and brainwork, and on the other hand from the effects of industrialization, especially in its planned form, upon the social strata. In 1935 the Bolshevik party leadership had encouraged this upgrading by doing away with the condition, imposed in 1928, that the body of students newly admitted to the universities and advanced technical schools should include a "core of workers" which was first fixed at 65 per cent and later raised to 70 per cent.

At the beginning of the upgrading process Bolshevik party leadership displayed a certain reserve toward the new intelligentsia. A change in this attitude came about only after the second generation began to infiltrate more heavily and after Stalin, in a speech to the graduates of the Army Staff College on June 4, 1935, coined the much-quoted phrase "The cadres are alone decisive." But for ideological reasons Stalin was not prepared to recognize the intelligentsia as a "class." In his report of November 25, 1936, on the draft of a new federal constitution for the U.S.S.R., Stalin defined the Soviet state as a socialist state of workers and peasants and described the "working intelligentsia" as a detached, intermediary social stratum. Although it possessed the same rights as the workers and kolkhoz peasants, its members did not constitute a class, even though they had very important functions to perform in the socialist society:

The intelligentsia has never been a class and cannot become one. It was and still is an intermediary stratum, recruited from all classes of society. In the old days the intelligentsia was recruited from the nobility, from the bourgeoisie, in part from the peasantry, and only to a very slight extent from the workers. In our times, in Soviet times, the intelligentsia is recruited mainly from the ranks of the workers and peasants. But, however it may be recruited and whatever character it may bear, the intelligentsia is still an intermediary stratum and not a class.[14]

Considering that by 1937 this group, together with its family members, already comprised 14 per cent of the total population, thus almost equaling the "liquidated" class of the "capitalists" in 1913, Stalin's line of argument was not at all convincing. The Bolshevik party leadership itself regarded the new intelligentsia as identical with the body of white-collar employees, the greater part of whom came from the petty bourgeoisie. In terms neither of their social function nor of their social awareness were they comparable to the old intelligentsia, which displayed predominately intellectual traits and looked upon itself as an order consecrated to the Revolution or to reform.[15] It may be that Stalin was conscious of these differences but considered that the time was not yet ripe for defining the intelligentsia in the constitution as an independent social group.

The Great Purge of 1936–38 brought about a complete change in the social makeup of the Bolshevik party, to the advantage of the intelligentsia. The liquidation of Lenin's fellow combatants, most of them intellectuals, was accompanied by widespread repression of the proletarian element in the party as a whole. In 1939, membership in the party totaled 2.3 million, of which the intelligentsia constituted 20 per cent. After the war this percentage rose to almost 50 per cent, while that of the workers, which in 1930 had amounted to 65.3 per cent, had dropped during the same period by more than half.

Categorized by their educational level, 54 per cent of the delegates to the Eighteenth Congress of the C.P.S.U.(B) in

March, 1939, belonged to the intelligentsia.[16] Stalin took this fact into account in granting the intelligentsia equal rights with the two "classes" and in abolishing all former restrictions on their admittance to the party—actions formalized in the party statute adopted by the Eighteenth Congress.[17] In practice this amounted to constitutional recognition of the leading social position of the intelligentsia vis-à-vis the workers and kolkhoz peasants. The term "proletariat" was dropped and the party was declared to be the leading force of "the entire Soviet people," not only of "the working masses."

THE TOP-LEVEL BUREAUCRACY AND INTELLIGENTSIA AS DISTINGUISHED FROM THE WHITE-COLLAR EMPLOYEES

Soviet society since 1939 has been characterized by a growing differentiation among the various major social groups, brought about chiefly by industrialization. In the late Stalinist period this process was for a time concealed by the trend toward a class state.[18] Part of the "de-Stalinization" was an effort to open up Soviet society from within by abandoning Stalin's policy of isolation, thus admitting a certain pluralism of the social forces. The appearance of a number of interest groups, combined with the rediscovery of sociology, revived discussion on the nature of the white-collar employees and intelligentsia as separate and distinct groups. The official class structure of Soviet society, which from the sociological point of view possesses only limited value as evidence, recognized as "classes" only the workers and the kolkhoz peasants. The third major social grouping, existing in fact but denied recognition as a "class" on ideological grounds, manifested itself in two forms— as white-collar employees and the "intelligentsia." What distinguishes these groups is not the function they perform but whether or not their labor is predominantly physical or intellectual. In the comments on the results of the Soviet population census of 1959, this criterion was explained as follows: "The employment of workers is understood as being employment which calls in the main for an expenditure of physical activity, and the employment of employees, that which demands in the main an expenditure of brainwork."[19]

From the vantage point of official Soviet statistics, the "employees form a separate social group which coincides with that of all "brainworkers" (20.5 million). The census of 1959 numbered the employees at 19.7 million. The remainder presumably belonged to the "worker" category. In recent Soviet writings the group of white-collar employees is designated as a stratum (sloi), where the application of social stratification to Soviet society was formerly rejected. The term "stratum" probably does not apply in blanket fashion to all the employees, who together with their families constitute one-fifth of the population. Soviet sociologists, however, do not yet dare to define multiple strata within the employee group.

The term "intermediate stratum" (prosloika), dating back to Stalin, is still used to some extent for the "intelligentsia." Before the war, as indicated by Molotov's remarks at the Eighteenth C.P.S.U. Congress in March, 1939, the intelligentsia was still bracketed with the white-collar employee group. This ceased to be the case in official statistics after Stalin's death.[20] In 1959, only 15.7 million (77 per cent) of the "brainworkers"—the white-collar employees in toto—were counted as belonging to the intelligentsia. The remaining 4.8 million (23 per cent) were distributed among professions that mainly had to do with the third-ranking category of public services. The Soviet sociologist Semyonov[21] is of the opinion that all those who pursue an occupation in "service work" (trud obsluzhivaniya) should be classed as employees not belonging to the intelligentsia. As distinct from the official breakdown, he also classes among them the 2.9 million office workers, thus including the lower bureaucracy.

Semyonov does not, however, go so far as to distinguish the intelligentsia from this special group of white-collar employees or to designate it as a separate stratum. Rather, he emphasizes the traits common to the two groups which unite them in one stratum and which are a function of the "nonphysical" work peculiar to both of them. As "nonphysical" workers (rabotniki *nefisicheskogo truda*) they are basically differentiated from the workers and kolkhoz peasants, who are the physical workers (*rabotniki fisicheskogo truda*). Rutkevich, on the other hand, singles out as intelligentsia only those specialists with university or advanced technical-school training, and not all gainfully employed persons who in the main perform brainwork.[22] Thus, in contemporary Soviet terminology the intelligentsia, as distinct from the employee group, may be subdivided in both a broad and a narrow sense.

On the basis of the 1959 population statistics, Semyonov subdivides the "intelligentsia" into the following groups:[23] (1) leading cadres of the government and economic administration, the party, and other social organizations, 2.4 million; (2) technical and economic intelligentsia, 5.0 million; (3) scientific and cultural intelligentsia, 5.3 million.

Thus, in 1959 the intelligentsia in the broad sense comprised 12.7 million, or 60 per cent of all the white-collar employees. At this time the total number of specialists was 8 million. Therefore, the following did not belong to the intelligentsia (in the narrow sense): (1) the leading cadres and subordinate bureaucracy without university or advanced technical-school education; (2) foremen and highly qualified skilled workmen, that is, the "workers' aristocracy," with employee status; (3) intellectuals without university or advanced technical-school education.

The total number of specialists, meanwhile, rose to 12 million (as of November 15, 1965), of which 4.9 million attended universities and 7.1 million the advanced technical schools.[24] A breakdown of gainfully employed specialists into professional categories and sectors of the economy or administration clearly demonstrates that the strength of the Soviet leadership cadres lies in the spheres of engineering and technology, medicine and education. The considerably lower number of economists, by comparison, and the far too few lawyers cannot fail to have a detrimental effect upon an industrial society that aims at a higher level of maturity.

Economists comprise only one-eighth of the specialists employed in the entire economic sphere, and lawyers only one-seventh of all specialists working in administration. Contemporary Soviet leaders appear, meanwhile, to have become conscious of the shortage of economists, but less so of the dearth of lawyers. Political economists and industrial managers cannot be produced as rapidly as is needed by a national economy that is undergoing a second industrial revolution and that shows a heavy pent-up demand in many sectors. The type entrusted with responsibility in politics, in public administration, and in the organization of production is still the graduate engineer, the total number of whom has risen to 1.6 million.

The "power elite," which includes both top-level bureaucrats and the corps of officers, coincides to a lesser degree with the intelligentsia (in the narrow sense) than is generally assumed to be the case. What is often overlooked is that the top-level bureaucracy is only a subgroup of the "leadership cadres," which in 1959 numbered 2.4 million. The number of top-level bureaucrats among these was 400,000, about half of whom belonged to the "party bureaucracy." Other holders of high-ranking government offices (lawyers, economists) numbered about 250,000.

The greater part of the "leadership cadres" consisted of the 1.7 million economic managers who may be regarded as the actual elite of the economic and technical intelligentsia. The prestige elite at the head of the scientific and cultural intelligentsia, consisting of writers, artists, and scientists, forms the other group of the intelligentsia (in the narrow sense). Because it comprises a higher ratio of university graduates, it carries more weight than is generally assumed. The top-ranking bureaucracy is recruited, for the most part, from the technical economic intelligentsia. This, however, does not help to remove the conflict of interests between the power elite and the economic managers. The top-level bureaucracy differs from the economic managers as regards both its composition and its functions. In the first place, it still consists, for the most part, of persons of proletarian or peasant origin with an educational background far inferior to that of the normal member of the intelligentsia. Secondly, it includes a number of "specialists" who joined the party before the war, most of whom have not enjoyed a thorough specialist's training.

THE NATURE AND CLASS CHARACTER OF THE TOP-LEVEL BUREAUCRACY AND INTELLIGENTSIA

The basic difference between the top-level bureaucrats and the intelligentsia lies primarily in the fact that the power of the former rests upon the ruling positions they hold, while that of the latter is rooted in the authority and prestige inherent in the social leadership functions they perform.[25] The basis of authority as well as of prestige in modern industrial society is specialized knowledge. This is as true in the Soviet Union as anywhere else in the world, although Soviet industrial society has not yet entirely shaken off the eggshell of its development. In the Soviet Union it is primarily the specialists with university or advanced technical-school training who possess that specialized knowledge which an industrial society needs in the nuclear age. Even if they do not occupy positions of power, their social functions are so crucial that they can influence, at the side of those exercising actual power, the determination of the social rules and sanctions of society. Ability based on specialized knowledge is not, however, the only avenue to the top positions in society. Another essential requisite is the ability to get ahead; here, personality, ability to adapt to the social rules prevailing in society, and personal connections are all important factors in the selection and promotion process, quite apart from the question of performance.[26] This way of getting ahead is practiced to a far greater degree in the hyper-bureaucratized Soviet society, with its totalitarian single-party system, than in democratic industrial societies. Contributing to the individual's success in this connection are a knowledge of ideological doctrines and power techniques and recognized service in the organization, on the one hand, and party patronage under the "nomenclature system" on the other.[27] The key position of the Soviet top-level bureaucracy rests primarily upon this type of ability to get ahead. The greater measure of power is not the only factor by which it differs from the Western power elites. It represents a foreign body in the fabric of the elite structure of an industrial society, since it does not submit, or submits only to a very limited degree, to the economic rationality that is characteristic of an industrial merit system. The goal of promoting the conditions for existence and growth in keeping with the community's requirements is only of secondary importance to it. Its primary objective is the consolidation and expansion of its power base.

Through its absolute monopoly of power and unrestricted control over all means of production, it is in a position to divert a disproportionately large share of the national product to this objective, and at the same time to secure a higher personal income for its members. Thus the ruling group derives considerable personal advantage from its power of disposition over state offices and therefore also over state property.

These advantages would be reduced if a larger proportion of the national product were to be diverted to economic investment and mass consumption. As a result there is a sharp conflict of interests within the "leading cadres," between the power elite and the economic managers, who aspire to a greater recognition of economic factors and to a consolidation and expansion of industrial autonomy as well as of "personal property." Even deeper is the conflict of interests between the ruling elite and the prestige elite, which seeks to enlarge the sphere of individual freedom through curtailment of the omnipotence of the state. The value concepts of Soviet society are in some instances shaped more strongly by the intellectual influences emanating from this prestige elite than by the accomplishments of the managers of the economy or the standards set by the ruling power elite and the bureaucracies dependent upon them. This fact is clearly borne out by a sociological study conducted by the Philosophical Institute of the U.S.S.R. Academy of Sciences in 1961–62, which deals with the value concepts and aspirations of an elite group of Soviet youth.[28] The economic managers and most members of the prestige elite hold state offices that place them in a ruling position. Nevertheless, they are much closer to the other strata of Soviet society than is the power elite, whose core is markedly parasitic in character. Thus we are justified in speaking of an antagonistic conflict of interests between the greater part of the power elite and the other strata of Soviet society. Because the technical intelligentsia forms the base group for the greater part of the top-level bureaucracy, so to speak, this conflict is far more pronounced in the case of the "creative intelligentsia."

From the sociological viewpoint can the ruling top-level bureaucracy be considered a "class"? Are we justified in speaking of Soviet society as a "class society"? These questions can be answered only on the basis of a class theory that takes into account the changed conditions of a developed industrial society, as well as the peculiarities of totalitarian rule. Neither of these considerations is to be found in the class theory of Karl Marx,[29] upon which Soviet sociologists constantly depend. This theory, moreover, is fragmentary in character, since the last chapter (52) of Volume II of Marx's *Kapital,* entitled "The Classes," was left unfinished because of Marx's death. Its significance lies above all in the fact that it draws attention to the reciprocal relations existing not only between the pattern of ownership and the social system but also between the power structure and the social structure. Marx defined classes as politically organized social groups determined by their awareness of a common class status and the common class interests resulting therefrom. The ultimate criterion in determining class differences was the extent to which they shared in, or were excluded from, private ownership of the means of production and the corresponding distribution of power which makes it possible to lay hands on the products of labor and thus to exploit the workers. According to Marx, the inevitable outcome of this unjust situation is class conflict, which takes the form of a deliberate showdown between two conflicting interest groups and triggers a revolutionary transformation of the existing social structure.

The weakness of Marx's class theory lies above all in the fact that power does not derive from private ownership alone, and that changes in the social structure cannot be attributed to class conflict alone. As Dahrendorf has put it aptly, to define power in terms of ownership is to define the general by the particular. Control over, and therefore power of disposal of, the means of production, which is not necessarily directly bound up with the title to ownership, is only one special case of power. Lenin's definition of classes in his essay "The Great Initiative," written in 1919, proved considerably more realistic:

Classes is the term for large groups of people differing from one another through their place in a historically determined system of social production, through their relationship to the means of production (to a large extent fixed and formulated by laws), through the role they play in the social organization of work, and consequently through their way of reaching social prosperity and the amount of this which falls to their share. Classes are groups of people, of which one, owing to the place it occupies in a given economic system, is able to misappropriate the work of the other for its own purposes.[30]

Lenin's definition of classes, to a far greater degree than that of Marx's, is keyed to the place, and therefore the rank, of the individual social groups within the framework of a given social system. This is clearly borne out by his thesis that, as long as conditions of power continue to exist in the Soviet Union, a similar system of placing and ranking of social groups will be found there too, which will manifest itself as class stratification. The only question is whether the class structure of the Soviet Union is dualistic or triplex. If Marx's conception of class is examined critically in the light of the insights it provides, it would seem obvious that power must be taken as the decisive criterion for establishing the actual class structure. This is the path followed by Dahrendorf in his theory of power and conflict.[31] Dahrendorf begins with the assumption that in an industrial society a number of power organizations exist which are more or less interlocked. Within each of these power organizations there will be two groups: (1) a group that holds power and is therefore interested in maintaining the existing power structure and consequently in preserving the social status quo; and (2) a group that is excluded from power and is therefore interested in transforming the existing power structure.

Dahrendorf, therefore, does not assume, as Marx did, that possession or nonpossession of the means of production is the decisive criterion of class, but holds rather that a share in, or exclusion from, positions of power is the real criterion. Because of the unequal allocation of institutionalized power, Dahrendorf assumes that a division into two groups exists in every society. As a result of the dichotomy of ruling positions and the concomitant social roles involved, two classes will always confront each other as the representatives of opposing interests—that is, of conscious policies.[32]

Applying this class theory to the Soviet Union, all those who hold official ruling positions—not only the power elite, but the whole of the intelligentsia—would form a closed "ruling class" confronted as opponents by their subjects, the popular masses. This conclusion certainly does not correspond to actual social conditions in Russia, which present a considerably more differentiated picture. The actual conditions can be understood only if a clear distinction is drawn between institutionalized power and social leadership. The question of the actual class structure of Soviet society may therefore be answered in the following way. If we take as the point of departure not only the distinction between positions of power and leadership but also the possibility of exclusion from both positions, we can arrive at a threefold division of society and thus at a triplex class structure. In this case the "ruling class" is composed of those who hold ruling positions that are not at the same time leadership positions within the meaning of the elite structure of modern industrial society. This means that only the core of the top-level bureaucracy is to be looked upon as the "ruling class." On the other hand, all those who hold purely leadership positions, regardless of whether or not they also hold ruling positions, form a second class, which occupies an intermediate position between the rulers and their subjects.[33] This second class, which is closer to the rest of the popular masses than to the actual power elite, includes by far the greater part of the intelligentsia and in particular the managers of the economy and the prestige elite. Whether in this case the remaining social strata may be considered to constitute a third class, or whether it is more correct to differentiate between an urban and a rural proletariat, are questions that may be left unanswered at this point. There is certainly no denying that social tensions exist between the intelligentsia and the popular masses as well as between the rulers and their subjects. The former, however, are mainly "nonantagonistic" in character.

In evaluating the possibilities of social change under the conditions of totalitarian rule, it is irrelevant, in the last analysis, whether the intelligentsia is viewed as a distinct class or whether its top group is looked upon as a counterelite. In either event the intelligentsia must be regarded as the force pushing the reform efforts associated with "de-Stalinization," which are in part openly directed against the party bureaucracy as the nucleus of the "ruling class." The conflict of roles which marks the existence of the intelligentsia has, to be sure, up to now prevented it from developing the dynamic force that would have enabled Soviet society to embark upon a post-totalitarian phase of evolution.

THE C.P.S.U. AS REPRESENTATIVE OF THE INTERESTS OF THE RULING POWER ELITE[34]

The social fabric of the C.P.S.U. reflects the changes in structure which have come about in the successive developmental phases of Soviet society. What was originally a dedicated and disciplined order, consisting mostly of intellectual professional revolutionaries with a strong proletarian element, has become a mass party headed by a cadre of bureaucratic professional politicians. In the party as a whole the body of white-collar employees and the intelligentsia predominate.

SOCIAL COMPOSITION OF THE C.P.S.U., 1917–67 (percentages)

Category	1917	1921	1924	1927	1930	1934	1956	1961	1964	1966	1967
Workers	60.2	41.0	46.0	56.0	65.3	?	32.0	34.5	37.3	37.8	38.1
Peasants	7.6	28.2	24.6	22.0	20.2	28.5	17.1	17.5	16.5	16.2	16.0
Intelligentsia and other employees	32.2	30.8	29.4	22.0	14.5	?	50.9	48.0	46.2	46.0	45.9
Total	100.0	100.0	100.0	100.0	100.0	100.0	100.0	100.0	100.0	100.0	100.0

If the educational level of the C.P.S.U. is taken as the base, the ratio of the employee group, and with it that of the intelligentsia, is considerably higher. The fully trained party members (at least high school graduates) who on January 1, 1967, composed 50.5 per cent, or half, of the party, are nearly equivalent to the intelligentsia (in the broad sense).[35] Those party members with incomplete secondary education (minimum of seven classes) are for the most part white-collar employees. It may safely be assumed that the percentage of communist white-collar employees today is about 60 per cent, not 45 per cent.

The proportion of specialists with university or advanced technical-school training increased between 1956 and 1965 from 26.0 per cent to 34.6 per cent. At the end of 1956 the communist specialists comprised 28.0 per cent of a total of 6.3 mil-

EDUCATIONAL LEVELS OF C.P.S.U. MEMBERS, 1956–66 (percentages)

Level	Jan. 1, 1956	Jan. 1, 1962	Jan. 1, 1965	March 1, 1966
University graduate training	11.1	13.7	15.0	
				18.2
Incomplete university training	3.6	2.9	2.6	
Advanced technical-school training	11.3		17.0	
		27.2		30.9
High-school education	10.8		13.1	
Total of advanced education	36.8	43.8	47.7	49.1
Unfinished high-school education	29.5	28.4	27.9	27.5
Total secondary-school education	66.3	72.2	75.6	76.6
Primary-school education	33.7	27.8	24.4	23.4
Total	100.0	100.0	100.0	100.0

lion specialists; by the end of 1964 the figure was 35.5 per cent of a total of 11.3 million. Thus one-third of the intelligentsia (in the narrow sense) are members of the party.

Of primary importance is the fact that the ratio of university graduates, who together with the top-level bureaucrats (mostly not university-trained) form the upper stratum of Soviet society, increased between 1956 and 1965 from 11.1 per cent to 15.0 per cent. It may be assumed that this percentage has risen still higher in the last three years. It is interesting that of the total number of university graduates the proportion of communist specialists is higher than that of communist specialists with advanced technical-school training. In 1956 it was 34.8 per cent of 2.3 million university graduates, and, in 1965, 39.1 per cent of 4.6 million. At least two-fifths of the university graduates, who form the actual nucleus of the Soviet intelligentsia, are members of the party. Among the rest of the party leadership the proportion of white-collar employees and intelligentsia is naturally higher than it is in the party as a whole. This is apparent from official statistics, which, since the late Stalinist period, have given no figures for production workers.

SOCIAL CATEGORIES OF DELEGATES TO PARTY CONGRESSES, 1924–66 (percentages)

Category	1924	1927	1930	1934	1952	1956	1959	1961	1966
Workers (Production workers)	63.2	71.0	71.2	60.0	7.6	18.5		22.3	
	(11.4	18.4	17.7	9.3)					
Peasants	5.4	5.7	6.7	8.0	7.8	13.8		10.6	
Total workers and peasants	68.6	76.7	77.9	68.0	15.4	32.3	31.4	32.9	34.3
Intelligentsia and other employees	31.4	23.3	22.1	32.0	84.6	67.7	68.6	67.1	65.7
Total	100.0	100.0	100.0	100.0	100.0	100.0	100.0	100.0	100.0

The statistics on educational levels bear out the fact that the percentage of intelligentsia and other employees among the party delegates was in actual fact considerably higher.

EDUCATIONAL LEVELS OF PARTY DELEGATES, 1924–66 (percentages)

Level	1924	1930	1934	1939	1952	1956	1959	1961	1966
University training or advanced technical-school education	6.5	7.2	10.0	31.5	66.5	64.5	61.1	72.8	79.5
High-school education	17.9	15.7	31.0	22.5	18.7	12.4	12.2	?	?
Total	24.4	22.9	41.0	54.0	85.2	76.9	73.3	?	?

The number of delegates at the last party congress who had completed a high-school education is not given, in order to conceal the fact that since 1961 practically all delegates to party congresses have come from the intelligentsia (in the broad sense) and thus belong to the employee group. Probably the percentage of 85.2 attained under late Stalinism in 1952 rose still higher in 1961 and 1966. Of the 3,248 (65.7 per cent) delegates to the Twenty-third Party Congress designated as intelligentsia, 2,315 (46.8 per cent) came from the power elite and the bureaucracies dependent upon it, 704 (14 per cent) from the economic managers, and 229 (4.6 per cent) from the prestige elite and other groups.

Under the heading of the ruling power elite, which this time provided almost half of the delegates to the Congress, the individual subgroups were represented in the following numbers:

COMPOSITION OF THE POWER ELITE AT THE TWENTY-THIRD C.P.S.U. CONGRESS

Subgroup	Absolute Figures	Percentages
Party functionaries	1,204	24.4
Government and economic functionaries	539	10.9
High-ranking military	352	7.1
Mass organizations	126	2.5
Cultural functionaries	94	1.9
Total	2,315	46.8

The party bureaucracy, which is to be regarded as the body actually responsible for totalitarian rule, predominated also at this party congress, comprising a fourth of all the delegates.

Whereas among the delegates to party congresses the power elite and the intelligentsia (in the narrow sense) are to a large extent identical, this appears to be the case hardly at all with members of the party committees, and still less so within the hierarchy of party secretaries and full-time party officials, concerning whose social background and education no official statistics exist.[36]

SOCIAL COMPOSITION OF DISTRICT AND TOWN COMMITTEES[37]
(percentages)

Category	1961	1965
Top-level bureaucracy	26.3	24.2
Intelligentsia	27.5	30.9
Other employees	8.3	8.5
Total of employees	62.1	63.6
Workers and peasants	37.9	36.4
Total	100.0	100.0

Of the 30 per cent of the intelligentsia on the district and town committees, including the revision commissions, 22.5 per cent belonged to the technical and economic intelligentsia and 8.4 per cent to the scientific and cultural intelligentsia. An analysis of the social composition of the Central Committee and the Central Revision Commission elected by the Twenty-third C.P.S.U. Congress shows clearly the preponderance of the top-level bureaucracy over the intelligentsia (in the narrow sense).[38] Among the full members of the Central Committee who belong to the ruling power elite, the number of state and economic functionaries, as well as of party ideologists and cultural functionaries, increased between 1961 and 1966. The proportion of foreign-service functionaries has also risen. The importance of party organizers and high-ranking military has, on the other hand, decreased proportionately. The number of Komsomol and trade-union functionaries has diminished.

From the ratio of top-level bureaucracy to intelligentsia (in the broad sense) among the rank and file of the party, among the delegates to party congresses, and among the 195 full members of the Central Committee, it can be seen clearly that the C.P.S.U. is primarily a body representing the interests of the actual power elite and that the technocrats, insofar as they do not belong to the top-level bureaucracy, show only a slender power base.

RATIO OF TOP-LEVEL BUREAUCRACY TO INTELLIGENTSIA IN THE C.P.S.U.

Intelligentsia in the Broad Sense (Exclusive of the Military)	Total in Millions 1959	Percentage of Party Rank and File 1961	Percentage of Congress Delegates 1966	Percentage of Members of the Central Committee 1966
Top-level bureaucracy	0.4	2.1	40.0	81.1
Technical and economic intelligentsia	7.0	24.7	14.2	2.1
Scientific and cultural intelligentsia	5.3	10.7	4.6	2.1
Total	12.7	37.5	58.8	85.3

The top-level bureaucracy (exclusive of the military) which, while constituting 2 per cent of the entire party, made up almost 40 per cent of the members of the party congress, is represented in the Central Committee with as much as 81.1 per cent of the full membership. The economic managers and the technical and economic intelligentsia—who, while constituting 25 per cent of the entire party, provided 14.2 per cent of the congress delegates—are represented in the new Central Committee with only 2.1 per cent of the membership. While it is true that the prestige elite and the scientific and cultural intelligentsia in general provide a higher proportion of members of the Central Committee than of delegates to the party congress, they carry less weight because they are almost exclusively writers, artists, and scientists, who act as auxiliaries to the official party cultural functionaries. It is remarkable that the "workers' class," which is alleged to lead the whole of Soviet society, provides a still lower percentage of Central Committee members than do the leadership groups of the intelligentsia; it represents only a little more than 1 per cent of the membership.

The sociological effect of the Kosygin economic reform was that the power position of the state and economic bureaucracy was greatly strengthened in relation to the party bureaucracy. This has restored the situation that existed prior to 1957. The industrial managers appear only as secondary beneficiaries of this development, which so far has not increased their influence on the policy-making process. The right of the prestige elite to greater social influence was indeed contested by the party. Several progressive Soviet writers, among them the liberal Tvardovsky and the conservative Surkov, were removed from the Central Committee. Thus nothing has been changed in the actual class structure of the party. The economic reform has resulted in a better balance within the top-level bureaucracy and has at the same time strengthened the position of the power elite as a whole. As the state and economic bureaucracy has gained influence, the "party organizers," who predominate in the party bureaucracy, have been reduced to their control function. The Twenty-third Party Congress revealed the effort of the "party ideologists," through stronger emphasis on ideological control, to preserve the primacy of the party bureaucracy and to give new confidence to the full-time party apparatus.

Whereas the supreme party leadership is recruited from the top-level bureaucracy, the intelligentsia is the key social group in the rank and file of the party. The conflict arising out of the party leadership's absolute monopoly of power is intensified by the conflict of generations resulting from the considerable age difference between the leadership and the rank and file. An age analysis shows that today 2.5 million (20 per cent) of the party members are under thirty years of age and 4.6 million (53 per cent) are less than forty years old. Most of the top functionaries, however, come from the older age groups of the middle generation (fifty-one to sixty years of age) and the older generation, which together make up only 22.1 per cent of the party. The younger generation, comprising over half of the party rank and file, has no representation in the top leadership at all. This group, in the main, consists of communists who joined the party in the "de-Stalinization" period—that is, after 1956—and who today comprise 47.1 per cent of the party membership.

In the intelligentsia (in the narrow sense) men and women are about equally represented. However, the influence of women in the leadership of the party is remarkably weak. Although women make up 20.2 per cent of the total party membership and constituted 23.3 per cent of the delegates to the Twenty-third Party Congress, only five (2.6 per cent) are full members of the Central Committee. No woman is now included in the party's supreme leadership.

All of these statistics demonstrate that the gap between the top-level bureaucracy and the intelligentsia, far from diminishing, has widened in recent years.

TRENDS IN SOVIET SOCIETY UNDER BREZHNEV AND KOSYGIN

Under Khrushchev's successors social conflicts have intensified to an even greater degree. This is borne out not only by the show trials of the Soviet writers Sinyavsky and Daniel and the criminal proceedings taken against other progressive writers but also by a study entitled "Russia's Path to Socialism," which appeared in the underground literary periodical *Phoenix 66,* issued under the editorship of the poet Galanskov, which is directed against the class dictatorship of the bureaucracy. The political significance of the antitotalitarian Soviet writers, who are also the *avant-garde* of the progressive intelligentsia, is, above all, that they give expression to the inarticulated opinion prevailing in the ranks of Soviet society and thus perform a quasi-parliamentary function, since there is no body which really represents the people in the Soviet Union. This idea has also been expressed in another way by Yevtushenko, who, in an interview which appeared in *Borba* on September 5, 1965, said: "In Russia the writers have always formed a government of the intellectuals. In contrast to an official government, whether here or elsewhere, this is always stable. It is not subject to dissolution, and it is exposed neither to attack nor to death. A head of state can be assassinated—but no one can ever kill this government!"

In view of the tense atmosphere, Brezhnev's and Kosygin's reluctance to accord more extensive rights to the factories and kolkhozy, and the fluctuations in their cultural policy, are understandable. The fact that the keynote of the Twenty-third Party Congress was one of strict orthodoxy was not, therefore, the result solely of the typically Russian bureaucratic apprehensiveness over the stirrings of independent intellects. This keynote found expression in a reversion not only to the traditional Marxist-Leninist dogmas but also to the emotional world of Soviet patriotism. The much-feared re-Stalinization, against which the party leadership was warned by twenty-seven outstanding representatives of Soviet literature, art, and science, did not come about. The offensive that had been launched at the end of 1965 by those who sought to restore Stalinism was soon brought to a halt by the opposition not only of the liberal forces but also of the moderate conservatives. "De-Stalinization" was not withdrawn at the Twenty-third Congress. The strength of the social groups interested in this movement made withdrawal impossible. It was, however, perceptibly checked. What mattered to Khrushchev's successors was the recovery of complete control over those intellectual forces which had been released by the two waves of de-Stalinization in 1956 and 1961. The halt called to de-Stalinization made itself felt most in the literary and artistic spheres. The anti-Stalinist "disclosure" literature threatened to undermine totalitarian one-party rule and to disturb the positions of those functionaries who had risen to power under Stalin, especially the party organizers who were preponderant in the existing party leadership. It further helped to disclose the close links between Soviet totalitarianism and militarism, which was frowned upon even by those high-ranking officers who had objected to Stalin.

After all, even those party ideologists who do not follow the ultraconservative line of a Suslov are still interested in a more intensive clamping down of the controls in the fields of social science and the arts, since, as the priesthood of the party, they need a mission that justifies not only their activities but also the right to the existence of the party itself. The retrogressive trend, therefore, was most pronounced in those parts of the Central Committee report which referred to cultural policy and the party. Since this "Party Congress of the *Apparatchiki*," the reins have been drawn in more tightly in the spheres of literature, art, and social science, and all thrusts against the intensification of censorship have been repelled. These efforts to tighten up the total controls "from above" are confronted by an increase in the centrifugal forces in Soviet society.

The power elite is no more a unified body than is the intelligentsia (in the narrow sense). Distinctions must be drawn, not only between the various subgroups of an institutional or occupational type and their placement at different administrative levels, but also between the special positions they occupy in the autocratic-totalitarian system of rule and the access they have to the actual holders of power. In the case of a multinational state, such as the Soviet Union, nationality also plays a special part. In addition to the general specialized elites, there are a number of interest groups that try to exert influence upon political and social developments.[39] The fundamental conflict in Soviet society, which lies between the ideological and organizational totalitarian claims of the party and the developmental requirements of a modern industrial society, finds expression in the struggle between the progressive and the reactionary elements. At the same time, minor social frictions come to the surface, in which the different strata and interest groups play a part. Finally, note should be taken of the constant conflict of roles existing between those sectors of the intelligentsia which hold state offices.

All of these conflicts contribute to a gradual social transformation. It would be a mistake, however, to assume that this development indicates that totalitarianism of the Soviet communist type is already coming to an end.[40] As long as the ruling bureaucratic class possesses the will and the power to exercise control over the autonomous social processes and forms of social spontaneity which it has encouraged in the interests of technical progress, Soviet society—despite a certain relaxation—will remain subject to totalitarian rule. There is still a possibility for the rulers in the Kremlin to build their domination increasingly upon the intelligentsia (in the narrow sense) and thus to check the fundamental social conflict. This would necessitate emancipation of appreciable sectors of social life from the control of the top-level bureaucracy.[41] If this were carried out at the right time, the decision, while not signifying the end of communist one-party rule, would finish off the totalitarian regime. This is a venture which alone can solve the growing conflict between the totalitarian state and a society that is on its way toward emancipation. It is, however, one that the present oligarchic leadership in the Kremlin, which, to a greater degree than Khrushchev did, looks upon itself as representing the ruling bureaucratic class, is neither willing nor able to embark upon.

NOTES

1. On the social structure of tsarist Russia see K. H. Ruffmann, "Der soziale Strukturwandel in Russland bis zur Oktoberrevolution" [The Transformation of the Social Structure in Russia up to the October Revolution], in *Sowjetgesellschaft im Wandel: Russlands Weg zur Industriegesellschaft* [The Transformation of Soviet Society: Russia's Way to an Industrial Society], ed. B. Meissner (Stuttgart, 1966), pp. 9 *et seqq.*

2. According to the population census of 1896 these numbered 151,345 (permanent civil servants 53,096; employees, 98,249). Officers and military officials numbered 52,471. In 1906, 25,429 persons earned over

2,000 rb. yearly as state employees (top-level bureaucrats), 65,775 between 1,000 and 2,000 rb., and about 100,000 under 1,000 rb. L. K. Erman, *Intelligentsia v pervoy russkoy revolyutsii* [The Intelligentsia in the First Russian Revolution] (Moscow, 1966), pp. 13–14 and 27.

3. See L. I. Smirnova, "O Sovetakh deputatov trudovoy intelligentsii" [On the Soviets of Deputies of the Working Intelligentsia], in *Iz Istorii Sovetskoy Intelligentsii* [From the History of the Soviet Intelligentsia], ed. M. P. Kim, P. A. Zhilin, and V. P. Naumov (Moscow, 1966), pp. 197 *et seqq.*

4. See M. P. Iroshnikov, *Sozdaniye sovetskogo tsentral'nogo gosudarstvennogo apparata* [The Formation of a Soviet Central State Organization] (Moscow-Leningrad, 1966), pp. 151 *et seqq.*

5. In 1921 one-third of the corps of commanding officers of the Red Army consisted of former tsarist officers and military officials. See N. I. Luchenko, *Sovetskaya intelligentsia* [The Soviet Intelligentsia] (Moscow, 1962), p. 6.

6. See P. Petrov and Y. Petrov, *Die wirtschaftliche Entwicklung der Sowjet-Union* [Economic Development of the Soviet Union] (Berlin, 1926), p. 69.

7. V. I. Lenin, *Werke* [Collected Works], vol. 29, p. 55; see also S. A. Fedyuikin, *Sovetskaya vlast' i burzhuaznye spetsialisty* [The Soviet Power and the Bourgeois Specialists] (Moscow, 1965).

8. Figures according to G. P. Andreiuk, "Vydvizhenchestvo i yevo rol' v formirovanii intelligentsii 1921–1932" [The Upgrading Trend and the Part It Plays in the Formation of the Intelligentsia, 1921–1932] in *Iz Istorii Sovetskoy Intelligentsii*, pp. 11, 17.

9. At the end of the NEP period the jumped-up proletarians included 80.4 per cent party members and 19.6 per cent nonparty members. In 1927 the 440,500 communist employees included 184,000 former workers and 56,000 former peasants. See *Iz Istorii Sovetskoy Intelligentsii*, p. 28.

10. See B. Meissner, "Der soziale Strukturwandel im bolschewistischen Russland" [Transformation of the Social Structure in Bolshevist Russia], in *Sowjetgesellschaft im Wandel*, p. 83.

11. See Molotov's report of January 28, 1935, in *Sowjetunion 1935* [The Soviet Union, 1935] (Moscow-Leningrad 1935), p. 82; J. Stalin, *Fragen des Leninismus* [Problems of Leninism], 11th ed. (Moscow, 1947), pp. 637 and 730.

12. "New Conditions—New Tasks in Economic Reconstruction," in Stalin, *Fragen des Leninismus*, pp. 402 *et seqq.*

13. See B. Meissner, "Die Entwicklung der Ministerien in Russland" [Development of the Ministries in Russia], *Europa Archiv*, 3rd year (1948), p. 1204.

14. Stalin, *Fragen des Leninismus*, p. 636.

15. Lenin put the intelligentsia on a par with the *literati;* see V. I. Lenin, *Polnoe sobranie sochinenii* [Complete Collected Works], vol. 8, p. 309.

16. Figures according to B. Meissner, *Russland im Umbruch: Der Wandel in der Herrschaftsordnung und sozialen Struktur der Sowjetunion* [Changing Russia: The Transformation of the System of Rule and

Social Structure of the Soviet Union] (Frankfurt on the Main, 1951), pp. 10 *et seqq.*

17. See G. Brunner, *Das Parteistatut der KPdSU 1903–1961* [Party Statutes of the C.P.S.U., 1903–1961] (Cologne, 1965), pp. 35–36.

18. See Meissner, *Sowjetgesellschaft im Wandel*, pp. 49 *et seqq.*

19. See *Itogi vsesoyuznoy perepisi naseleniya 1959 goda: SSSR* (Moscow, 1962), p. 10.

20. See the composition of the Soviet intelligentsia between 1926 and 1959 given by Meissner in *Sowjetgesellschaft im Wandel*, pp. 96–97.

21. See V. S. Semyonov, "Ob izmenenii intelligentsii i sluzhashchikh v protsesse razvernutogo stroitel'stva kommunizma" [Changes Taking Place in the Intelligentsia and the Employees in the Course of the Comprehensive Building Up of Communism], in *Sotsiologiia v SSSR* [Sociology in the U.S.S.R.] (Moscow, 1965), vol. 1, pp. 416 *et seqq.*

22. See M. I. Rutkevich, "Izmeneniye sotsial'noy struktury sovetskogo obshchestva i intelligentsia" [Changes in the Social Structure of Soviet Society and the Intelligentsia], in *Sotsiologiia v SSSR*, vol. 1, pp. 393 *et seqq.*

23. *Sotsiologiia v SSSR,* vol. 1, p. 418.

24. *Narodnoye khozyaystgo v 1965* [The National Economy of the U.S.S.R. in 1965] (Mosow, 1966), p. 573.

25. On the sociological importance of distinguishing between social leadership and institutionalized power see Meissner, *Sowjetgesellschaft im Wandel*, p. 107.

26. O. Dreitzel, *Elitebegriff und Sozialstruktur* [Elite Concept and Social Structure] (Stuttgart, 1962), pp. 75 *et seqq.*

27. See B. Lewytskj, "Die Nomenklatur: Ein wichtiges Instrument sowjetischer Kaderpolitik" [The Nomenclature System: An Important Instrument of Soviet Cadre Policy], *Osteuropa,* 11th year (1961), pp. 409 *et seqq.*

28. See G. Wagenlehner, "Die empirische Sozialforschung in der Sowjetunion" [Empirical Social Research in the Soviet Union], *Moderne Welt,* 6th year (1965), pp. 410 *et seqq.*

29. See R. Dahrendorf, *Soziale Klassen und Klassenkonflikt* [Social Classes and Class Conflict] (Stuttgart, 1957), pp. 5 *et seqq.*

30. V. I. Lenin, *Ausgewählte Werke* [Selected Works], vol. 2 (East Berlin, 1953), p. 570.

31. See Dahrendorf, *Soziale Klassen und Klassenkonflikt,* pp. 159 *et seqq.*

32. See R. Dahrendorf, "Zu einer Theorie des sozialen Konflikts" [Concerning a Theory of Social Conflict], *Hamburger Jahrbuch für Wirtschafts- und Gesellschaftspolitik* (Tübingen, 1958), pp. 84 *et seqq.*

33. The bureaucracy in the narrow sense can be regarded as belonging to the ruling class, but not, however, to each and every office-holder, as Dahrendorf ("Zu einer Theorie des sozialen Konflikts," pp. 84–85, no. 14) obviously assumes.

34. This chapter is based upon the following works of the present author: *Russland im Umbruch,* pp. 10 *et seqq.;* "Die soziale Struktur der KPdSU" [The Social Structure of the C.P.S.U.], *Osteuropa,* 16th

year (1966), pp. 599 *et seqq*. These also give the Soviet sources of the statistics.

35. See *Partiinaia zhizn'*, no. 7 (1967), p. 6.

36. Out of 200 members and candidates of the Political Office of the C.P.S.U. and the offices of the fourteen non-Russian central committees, allegedly 107 have enjoyed a university or advanced technical-school education; out of 139 first secretaries of the party committees at the republic, province, and district levels, 84 have attained this level. See B. Lewytskyj, "Generations in Conflict," *Problems of Communism,* January-February, 1967, p. 39, no. 6. Lewytskyj is right when he points to the inferior specialist training of the older top-level functionaries, a fact insufficiently taken into consideration by Z. K. Brzezinski and S. P. Huntington, *Politische Macht USA/UdSSR* [Political Power in the USA and the U.S.S.R.] (Cologne, 1966), pp. 181 *et seqq*.

37. Figures according to *Partiinaia zhizn'*, no. 1 (1962), p. 53, and no. 10 (1965), p. 17.

38. See B. Meissner, "Parteiführung und Parteiorganisation" [Party Leadership and Party Organization], *Osteuropa,* 16th year (1966), pp. 439 et seqq. (special issue: The Twenty-third Party Congress of the C.P.S.U.).

39. See H. Gordon Skilling, "Interest Groups and Communist Politics," *World Politics,* April, 1966, pp. 435 *et seqq*.

40. The despotic degeneration of totalitarianism into late Stalinism may no more be regarded a normal case of totalitarian one-party rule than the despotic form of absolutism may be viewed as that of an absolute monarchy. On the structural elements of post-despotic totalitarian one-party rule of the Soviet communist type see B. Meissner, "Wandlungen im Herrschaftssystem und Verfassungsrecht der Sowjetunion" [Changes in the Government and the Constitutional Law of the Soviet Union] in Boettcher-Lieber-Meissner, *Bilanz der Ära Chruschtschow* [A Balance Sheet of the Khrushchev Era] (Stuttgart, 1966), pp. 166 *et seqq.;* B. Meissner, "Totalitarian Rule and Social Change," *Problems of Communism,* November-December, 1966, pp. 56 *et seqq*.

41. If such a development were to be combined with increased liberalization, it would mean the transition from the totalitarian to an authoritarian system of rule.

Function and Ideology in Soviet Social Stratification

Robert A. Feldmesser

One of the most persistent and intriguing problems in the interpretation of the Soviet experience—and in the effort to anticipate its future course—is that of the significance to be attributed to ideology. The term "ideology" is used somewhat loosely here to mean the elements of more or less deliberate political choice based on ideas about "the way things ought to be" (or ought not to be), as distinct from the "functional" characteristics that we might reasonably consider requisite to any large-scale social system operating with a particular set of physiographic, demographic, historical, and cultural attributes. Of course, a tidy and conclusive separation of their respective effects is not to be expected. Aside from the difficulty common to all studies of Soviet society—the lack of crucial data—the concepts themselves are elusive.

In one sense all social action is "ideological," since it is always motivated by the desire to attain some preferred state of affairs. The goal being sought may not be verbalized, and it may not be achieved, but some goal is always present. Insofar as the action meets the needs of the institutional context within which it takes place, however, we are apt to call it functional; and, in turn, insofar as we can identify it as being functional, we are likely to suspect that it was undertaken precisely for its functional consequences and hence to call it "practical" or "pragmatic," implying some yielding of ideological principle. We should bear in mind, though, that the preservation of an institutional pattern may itself be the desired state of affairs.

Ideologically motivated action, in other words, can be quite functional; the strength of ideology is tested only when it entails functional costs. But test cases do not necessarily occur often enough to allow definitive conclusions to be drawn.[1]

How great must the functional costs be before we are entitled to say that an act or policy was inspired by ideology? The very existence of the system may be at stake, or the consequence may be only a lower degree of efficiency.[2] The former would be too severe a test; indeed, it would settle the problem by defining it away, since Soviet society has survived in recognizable continuity for fifty years. We shall use *functional* to mean "conducive to a high degree of efficiency," specifically in economic production.

Occupational stratification is an especially interesting context in which to examine the conflict, or potential conflict, between ideology and function in Soviet society, because of its central position in Marxist doctrine. An attempt will be made here, first, to analyze the present situation, with special reference to the composition of occupational groups, their distinctiveness from one another, and certain of the conditions of mobility among them. Later, an effort will be made to determine whether the future promises anything different. The most directly relevant ideological principles at issue are a belief in the superiority of industrial labor over other kinds of economic activity; egalitarianism, reconciled with the foregoing by the assumption that other kinds of work tend to become like industrial labor or to disappear entirely; and a preference for harmony ("collectivism") over conflict. As we might expect, though, the forced pace of industrial growth, and the authoritarian political system that made it possible, also bear upon the problem in important ways; the extent to which these, too, can be called "ideological" principles will be left to the reader.

I

In a common Soviet formulation, Soviet society is said to consist simply of two classes: the workers (*rabochie*), currently numbering about three-fourths of the population, and the collective farmers (*kolkhozniki*), or peasants, comprising about one-fourth.[3] They are differentiated, supposedly in accord with Marxist theory, by the form of property with which they produce—workers with property "socialized at the level" of the entire nation, peasants with property "socialized at the level" of producers' co-operatives as well as with "private" property in the form of individual plots.[4] This difference is held to be associated with certain others—the concept of workers as politically more advanced, for example, and the notion that they appear in the market only as buyers whereas peasants appear also as sellers and are therefore "interested to a certain degree in a high level of prices."[5]

Soviet usage also often distinguishes a subgroup among the workers whose generic characteristic is that their labor is non-manual. This subgroup is designated "employees" (*sluzhashchie*) and makes up a little more than 20 per cent of the population or roughly 30 per cent of the working class.[6] (Somewhat inconsistently, kolkhoz employees are generally included among them.) Sometimes a "stratum" (*sloi*) of "intelligentsia" (constituting about 60 per cent of the employees in 1959) is further separated out, which consists of those with professional or semi-professional training or those holding important technical or administrative positions, as well as people engaged in artistic activities.[7] Other occupational subgroups that occasionally have been utilized are "engineering and technical personnel" (ITR—*inzhenerno-tekhnicheskie rabotniki*), which evidently contains a mixture of workers and professionals in unknown proportions,[8] and "minor service personnel" (MOP—*mladshii obsluzhivaiushchii personal*), which embraces such people as sweepers, charwomen, guards, and watchmen.

More recently, with the thaw in the social sciences, the importance of still finer "intraclass" distinctions has been acknowledged. It has been said, for example, that "membership of members of the same class in groups of personnel of different skill, occupying different positions in the system of social production, now defines the social significance of the individual to a decisive extent."[9] In 1962 "approximately 30 to 40 per cent of [industrial] workers had low skill, 40 to 50 per cent middle, and 10 to 20 per cent high skill."[10] Each of these subgroups probably corresponds, but only roughly, to two of the six categories of the Soviet wage system. The overwhelming majority of kolkhoz peasants (at least three-fourths) are classified as having low skill or no special skill at all.[11]

This type of division of labor is broadly similar to that of all industrial societies. Nevertheless, Soviet analysts deny that it has similar consequences. Both class and intraclass differences are held to be, in the well-known phrase, "nonantagonistic contradictions." By this it is meant that the differences are outweighed by what all the groups have in common: freedom from exploitation, the obligation and right to work and to be paid commensurately with the value of their labor contribution, the same "conscientious attitude toward work," equal political rights, and a "community of fundamental social interests" in strengthening the Soviet state and in building communism.[12] Even the two major forms of property—industrial and kolkhoz —are essentially alike in that both are "socialized."

Whatever the validity of such an argument, the resemblances in form to industrial society should not blind us to the important differences. First, a relatively high proportion of the Soviet population works on the farm. This has not been primarily an ideological preference; on the contrary, Soviet values have harbored a deep suspicion of the peasantry as a "backward" and "obsolete" group. To the extent that the relatively large size of the peasantry can be attributed to unfavorable natural conditions for agriculture, it is functional. On the other hand, Western economists seem to agree that, even under these conditions, Soviet agriculture would be more efficient (and specifically, would use less labor) were it not collectively organized, and that the collectivist form of organization is an ideological preference as well as an indirect outgrowth of the forced rate of industrialization. (It is worth adding that the most efficient solution of the Soviet agricultural problem might well be the regular and large-scale importation of food products; the rejection of this solution also has important ideological components.)

There has been perhaps even greater ambivalence with respect to nonmanual employees. Increases in the number of people engaged in health, education, and science are often pointed to as signs of progress, and the numbers so engaged are relatively high on a per capita basis. At the same time, however, Soviet ideology has markedly favored activities directly linked to physical production, and *nonmanual* is sometimes taken as a virtual synonym for *nonproductive* or even for *decadent*.[13] This prejudice has had its most obvious effect in the periodic campaigns for staff reductions, but it is quite likely that it has also resulted in keeping the numbers employed in trade, services, and clerical and office work regularly below what they otherwise would be. Indeed, despite numerous criticisms (from both within and without) of the size of the Soviet bureaucracy, it is possible that it contains fewer people than would be optimally efficient in a state where decision-making processes are so highly centralized.[14]

Social and Economic Differentiations

Variations among the occupational strata in their circumstances of life are also of a familiar kind, but the magnitudes of variation are again not necessarily those we are accustomed to observing elsewhere. In educational attainments the differences appear to be rather great. According to the data of the 1959 census, and considering only those gainfully occupied, 63.5 per cent of the employees had completed some form of secondary education, compared with 7.9 per cent of the manual workers and only 3.2 per cent of the collective farmers; at the other extreme, the proportions with fewer than seven years of schooling were 10.7 per cent, 61.4 per cent, and 77.4 per cent, respectively.[15] The gap has been closed somewhat by now, but a number of sample studies show that it remains far from negligible. At the Nizhne-Tagil' Metallurgical Combine in mid-1962, 58 per cent of the employees had completed a secondary education or more (91.3 per cent of ITR), as against 20.9 per cent of the manual workers

(6 per cent of MOP).[16]   At the machine-building enterprises of Leningrad in 1965, administrative and professional personnel were found to have had an average of about fourteen years of education, while various groups of workers classified by skill averaged from six to nine years.[17] Meanwhile, at a state farm in the Kurgan *oblast* studied in 1963, almost two-thirds of *all* personnel had had four years of schooling or less. The same was true of the members of a collective farm in that *oblast* a year earlier; indeed, 8.2 per cent of the members were semi-literate or illiterate.[18]

The forces giving rise to these differences are complex, and of course precise weights cannot be assigned to them. The expense of providing education in sparsely settled rural areas—and perhaps the different attitude traditionally taken toward education by rural inhabitants—has in all nations led to a lower level of education in these areas, and the difficulty in the Soviet case is magnified by the sheer expanse of territory. On the other hand, the disproportionately old age-composition of the rural population may make the situation seem worse than it is. Still, it is hard to believe that peasants, and especially workers, could not have received more education than they did. The forced pace of industrialization is probably again partly responsible: an increase in education has held lower priority than an increase in industrial capacity, and resources have been invested accordingly. Indifference, if not contempt, toward the peasants has perhaps played a role in depressing their educational level even below that of the workers. In any event, the failure to raise the educational level of industrial and agricultural workers has exacted a functional cost, for often they are found to be unable to perform mechanized operations properly, let alone to learn new ones or make suggestions for improving old ones.[19]

About the same thing can be said of differences in *byt,* the conditions of everyday life: housing, food, recreational facilities, etc. The gap in these conditions between the peasant and even the unskilled worker has been notorious. As late as 1965, 12 per cent of the kolkhozy still lacked electric lighting.[20] Clubs,

libraries, theaters, shops, sometimes the most ordinary household needs—rural areas are less well supplied with all of these,
and neither the transportation system nor the road network is
such as to bring urban conveniences within easy reach. Work
is less mechanized, working hours are generally longer, and
much of the "free" time is taken up by the private plot. Young
people are eager to leave the kolkhoz, and the resistance to
being assigned there is a frequent topic of bitter commentary
in the press. For the urban worker, *byt* is also less ample than
it is for those higher in the occupational hierarchy, but this is
largely a matter of income.

With such a paucity of data, even those most skilled in the
complexities of economic analysis are hesitant to compare income distribution in the Soviet Union with that in other industrial nations. It is probably true that the gap between incomes on the collective farm and those in industry has been,
again, unusually wide,[21] though it is surely less now than it
once was. Within industry there are, of course, wage and
salary differentials of the conventional kind, but they ought not
to be overstated. An American economist found that the decile
ratio of earnings among workers—the ratio of income exceeded
by 10 per cent of the workers to the income exceeded by 90
per cent, and therefore a measure of the maximum spread—
was 328 in 1959, and wage reforms since then make it almost
certain that the figure is now lower. Average earnings of ITR
in 1960, according to his calculations, were only 50 per cent
higher than those of workers, and average earnings of employees
in 1955 were actually 12 per cent lower than those of workers.[22]
The study of Leningrad's machine-building enterprises showed
that the highest-paid group, "directors of shops, sections, and
enterprises," averaged 172.9 rubles a month—1.8 times the
average for unskilled workers in physical labor and 2.1 times
the average for the lowest-paid group, persons engaged in "nonphysical labor of middle skill (checkers, inspectors, office personnel, etc.)."[23] By contrast, the average yearly income of
managerial personnel in the United States in 1958 was 2.7 times
that of unskilled and service workers, who were the lowest-paid

nonfarm group.[24] And although Soviet authors may be inclined to exaggerate their significance, the so-called social funds—medical care, child care, education, pensions, low rents, etc., available to all without regard to income, or even scaled according to ability to pay—probably do moderate the monetary differentials more in the Soviet Union than do their equivalents in the United States. These funds were reported to constitute one-fourth of the "income" of all Soviet workers and employees in 1965.[25] Finally, whatever one thinks of the means used to bring it about, cyclical unemployment—still a hazard to workers in the Western world—has not been a serious problem in the Soviet Union. On the whole, the evidence appears to justify the conclusion that income differentials in urban areas, at least, have not been any wider in the Soviet Union than in the United States; if anything, they have probably been less.

In a cogent analysis of the question of stratified distribution, Gerhard Lenski points out that industrial societies generally have exhibited a lesser degree of inequality than have their agrarian predecessors, contrary to the previous historical trend and to his own prediction made on theoretical grounds. In searching for the explanation of this "reversal," he finds it attributable basically to the improved bargaining position of the working classes, which is a result of their increasing knowledge, skill, and productivity, their decreasing numbers (by virtue of birth control), and the institutionalization of democratic ideas.[26] None of these factors seems readily applicable to the Soviet case, where the workers are relatively unskilled and unproductive, where their numbers have (so far) been amply supplemented by transfers from agriculture, and where democratic institutions have had short shrift. Hence, it could well be expected that Soviet society would display *more* inequality than its industrial counterparts elsewhere.[27] What needs to be explained is not why it is so similar to them but why it is not more similar.

A glance at differentiation in political roles will help and will also amplify our picture of Soviet stratification. Workers and peasants in industrial societies are less active politically than other occupational groups, and the Soviet Union is no exception, though the differences in political organization should make us wary of direct comparisons. It can be estimated that in 1965 about 27 per cent of the employees, 8 per cent of the workers, and 5 per cent of the peasants were party members.[28] If these groups are subdivided, the variation is even wider, but the overlap among them also becomes evident. The study of the machine-building industry in Leningrad mentioned above found the following percentages of party members among (1) "directors of shops, sections, and enterprises," 54.4; (2) persons in "skilled mental labor (technologists, bookkeepers, etc.)," 19.6; (3) persons in "nonphysical labor of middle skill (checkers, inspectors, office personnel, etc.)," 7.8; (4) highly skilled workers "combining mental and physical functions," 23.4; (5) "workers of skilled manual labor operating machines and mechanisms," 12.2; (6) persons in "unskilled physical labor," 3.7. The range is narrowed when Komsomol membership is added—a justified procedure because of differences in age composition—but it remains substantial; the respective percentages for combined party and Komsomol membership are 60.8, 42.8, 27.1, 37.6, 34.5, and 13.8.[29]

Such variations are often regarded as a "defeat" for ideology, since the party was supposed to represent a dictatorship of the proletariat. There is undoubtedly much support for this interpretation, but some qualifications are also in order. That the ideology is not entirely dead is suggested by the party's successful efforts in the past decade to increase the proportion of worker-members. Furthermore, it was never unequivocally clear that Marx's concept of the proletariat was strictly limited to manual workers in industry, and it is even more doubtful that the dictatorship was meant to be exercised exclusively by the workers themselves. In any event, membership in a political party is not the only index of political activity, and probably it is not the best one in a society where such membership is deliberately restricted. Soviet doctrine has always laid great emphasis upon "public participation" for all citizens of whatever occupation, party and nonparty alike. In the Leningrad study, 35.1 per cent of even the "lowliest" group, the unskilled physical laborers, were reported to be participating in "civic work"; the highest frequency of participation was 84.2 per cent, among the directors.[30] A survey of Sverdlovsk *oblast* in 1965 was said to show that "from 50 to 73" per cent of the more than 46,000 members of various "public bureaus" were workers.[31]

But what is most important is the meaning of these data in the Soviet context. The civic activists are not making policy decisions, and it is doubtful that they are able to change substantially the allocation of the national product. Public participation is not the exercise of political power but the subjection to political obligations, to the demand that all citizens assist in the implementation of policies that others have set;[32] and, to the extent that participation is relatively equal, it is a sign that these obligations fall equally upon all. Something similar can be said about party membership: for the great majority, membership does not provide access to political power but is rather a more stringent form of obligation; and to the extent that membership is unevenly distributed, it signifies that the greatest obligations fall more heavily upon some than upon others.

An extension of this line of reasoning leads to the suggestion that, if Soviet income distribution is relatively egalitarian, it is because the higher occupational strata lack the power that has enabled their counterparts in other societies to obtain high returns. The party leadership could have paid them more, and without any reduction in efficiency—or possibly, to judge from the experience of other societies, with a functional gain. But it chose to use its power for egalitarian ends.[33] To put it differently, it is not the power of the working class which explains the relative equality of Soviet incomes, but the impotence of the higher occupational strata.

Since inequalities of power are essential to any definition of social classes, what this comes down to is the proposition that Soviet occupational strata are not social classes, and therein lies a major difference between the Soviet Union and Western industrial societies. It turns out that Soviet social scientists—and propagandists—really are not very far wrong in de-emphasizing the significance of class differences in the Soviet Union, though we may not agree with their explanation. From our point of view, the absence of class differences is the obverse of an authoritarian and totalitarian system, which keeps power in the hands of a small group of political leaders.[34]

Factors in Mobility

There is, however, one reason why Soviet society cannot be said to be completely classless. The family remains an important institution, carrying with it many of the differential advantages that are well known elsewhere and that have been acknowledged within the Soviet Union as well.[35] The ability of parents not only to win favored treatment for their children (e.g., in admission to educational institutions) but also to impart to them their own values, attitudes, and knowledge is of course a form of power, and the outcomes of its exercise are everywhere differentiated by occupational position.

Here again, we should be careful not to overstate the case. From the perspective of one familiar with the situation in the West, such data as are available on aspirations for, and entrance into, higher educational institutions and high-status occupations in the Soviet Union show a less-sharp differentiation by social origin, at least among urban residents.[36,37] Among the factors chiefly responsible are: the important influence exerted by extrafamilial agencies such as schools, youth groups, and the mass media of communication (the uniformity and ubiquity of these being another reflection of the political system); the extensive organization of in-service vocational training,[38] success in which may be more independent of family background; and the practice, apparently still relatively common in Soviet industry, of promoting bench-workers up through the ranks to even the highest positions (presumably because persons with the appropriate education are still scarce).[39] Nevertheless, the child's experience within the family continues to affect his later fortunes,[40] and, as long as the family has that kind of influence, Soviet society cannot be truly classless. The explanation for the persistence of the institution owes little, in this writer's view, to the regime's acceptance of the permanent indispensability of the family as such; Soviet values are hostile to the family as a child-rearing device on many counts. But there can be no doubt of the population's strong sentimental support for family living. The regime's yielding to this pressure can be considered functional, but, as Barrington Moore has pointed out,[41] it was also pushed in that direction by its reluctance to provide alternative child-rearing facilities at the expense of the industrial build-up.

II

For about a decade, active discussion has been going forward in the Soviet Union concerning the nature of communism, the form of society that, according to Marxist theory, is to succeed the present stage of socialism. It is true that Stalin spoke of the "transition to communism" as long ago as 1936; Geroid Robinson, in a regrettably neglected article,[42] pieced together a brilliant picture of what Stalin apparently imagined it would be like, and much of it can be found in recent discussions—without attribution, of course. But, with the adoption of the new party program in 1961 and the subsequent explorations of Soviet social scientists, a great deal less has been left to the imagination. Admittedly, Khrushchev's ebullience has now been replaced by the more staid pronouncements of Brezhnev and Kosygin, but this does not mean that the latter have abandoned the goal of building communism.[43] Even if it takes longer than expected and changes are made along the way, the statements about communism should give us some clues to the evolution we may look for in Soviet social structure; to ignore them altogether would place us, as Peter Wiles has put it, "in the position of a sociologist in a monastery who studies the kitchen but not the chapel."[44]

It will be pertinent, then, to see what, according to Soviet commentators, is supposed to happen to those characteristics of the stratification system which have been reviewed above. The particular objective shall again be an attempt to assess the ideological and the functional elements involved in the drive for the construction of communism. Since the functional interpretation here would be that "communism" is merely the Soviet name for "advanced industrialism," comparisons with the United States, an industrial society which is also moving into the "advanced" stage but which can hardly be said to be building communism in any deliberate way, will be introduced where they seem helpful.

The Division of Labor

By all odds the most widely discussed and agreed-upon feature of communism is a new kind of division of labor. This is expected to take a variety of interrelated forms.

1. As farming processes are increasingly mechanized and "chemicalized," as kolkhozes more frequently enter into combinations with one another and with local industries, and as agricultural property is converted into "property of all the people" (including the "withering away" of the private plot), the nature and status of agricultural work will be assimilated to those of industrial work.

2. Mechanization and automation of all production will lead to the elimination of unskilled jobs, especially those requiring heavy physical labor but also low-level nonmanual jobs—that is, clerical tasks will be performed by computers, and many waiters and salespeople will be replaced by vending machines or self-service restaurants and shops.

3. Each worker, instead of carrying out a single operation in the familiar system of the assembly line, will have a range of connected duties. He will have charge of a machine, a series of machines, or an automated line, he will set it up and test, adjust, repair, and maintain it as well as operate it, and he will clean his own workplace besides. Moreover, he will be capable of doing this not for one but for several related types of machinery; he will become, in a commonly used phrase, a "broad-profile" worker, approaching an engineer in his knowledge and skill. Production will be carried out by teams of such workers, who will rotate among jobs as required by absences,

product alterations, or simply the desire for variety. These teams will develop "collective" relations of mutual help and close friendship.

4. In addition, the worker will do a number of things that have hitherto been the province of "nonmanual" personnel: set his own norms and tabulate his own production; inspect his own work; suggest and initiate technological innovations; and pick up his pay without the need for a cashier.[45] In this and in the above is reflected the elimination of the distinction between manual and mental labor, one of the cardinal principles of communism. It implies that, eventually, workers will share in managerial responsibilities, extending "collective" relationships to the entire plant.

5. The foregoing might suggest the disappearance of "service" occupations, but on this point there seems to be disagreement. Relatively little hesitation is expressed about the continued growth of employment in science (though even this is not completely unambiguous, as we have seen); indeed, one academician "foresees a larger number of persons ultimately working in plant laboratories than in their production departments," and another has predicted that the "majority of the adult population in the future can . . . be engaged in the sphere of science."[46] Science is now often referred to as a "direct material force in production." But it is harder to make such an adjustment in the case of other services, so we continue to find statements like "the need for certain of the employees of trade and of public dining will decline with the degree of progress toward communism" and "the growth in the number of people engaged in commerce [which took place between 1939 and 1959] does not at all mean that our staffs in this field will have to swell to the colossal dimensions attained in capitalist countries."[47] On the other hand, this view is being increasingly challenged. "With the growth of labor productivity in material production, society receives the opportunity of increasing the number of personnel in the sphere of services, and consequently of improving services to the population."[48] Even more explicitly:

Each tailor shop in the U.S.S.R. has to service ten times as many people as in the U.S.A. At the present time, for every thousand people there are 16 persons employed in trade establishments in the U.S.S.R., and 76 in the U.S.A.; in laundries, 0.11 and 1.7, respectively. However, the increase in employment in material production and its reduction in the sphere of services is not infrequently pointed out as a special "advantage" of socialist economics in our economic literature. . . . We need now—and we will need still more in the future—tailors, shoemakers, hairdressers, personnel in public dining and trade, kindergarten teachers.[49]

One sociologist has gone even further in criticizing the old prejudice toward service personnel.

. . . an underestimation of the sphere of services, of workers in trade, of office clerks, of technical personnel is being expressed up to the present time. Through the efforts of certain people in the film, radio, and press we have created a humorous-neglectful attitude toward occupations in the sphere of services. *Systematically and seriously we now do not show their humanistic character, their growing role in communist construction,* and we are reaping bitter fruits.[50]

Kosygin himself told the Twenty-third C.P.S.U. Congress:

The rise in the living standards of the Soviet people largely depends on an improvement in the *service industries.* . . . the main thing is to enlist for the organization of these services enterprising and competent people who would know how to provide various amenities: renovate a flat swiftly and well; help move and settle in a new flat; deliver parcels home; repair footwear, clothing and household utensils quickly and at a low cost.[51]

And a resolution passed by the congress called for, of all things, more traveling salesmen (see *Twenty-third Congress,* p. 378). Perhaps, then, a re-evaluation is under way. For the time being, all that can be said is that such service occupations as do remain are expected to take on, like production occupations, a broader, more "scientific" character. The distinction between intelligentsia and employees would then disappear.

6. All of this would obviously require a rise in the educational level of the entire population. What is particularly emphasized is an increase in general education—"broad scientific knowledge"—rather than training for specific trades.

7. Finally, the "worker"[52] will also broaden the range of his nonwork activities: he will engage in the arts, write books, study and teach, and in general be a more "cultured" person. (Expectations are sometimes quite modest: the "new kind of worker" is occasionally spoken of as one whose "culture" consists of going to the movies or watching television, reading books or newspapers—or simply abstaining from "foul language.") He will also serve as a volunteer, helping civic organizations and public facilities do those jobs which require no special training. "Public participation" would become more widespread than ever; Khrushchev spoke of "drawing every citizen without exception into the management of public affairs."[53] There is no indication that this would mean more democracy than it has meant before.

It would be wrong to dismiss all of this as mere propaganda. We are entitled to be skeptical when we read about the coming of a "single homogeneous type of labor," but suggestions of that sort are the exception rather than the rule. More commonly, the discussions of labor under communism have a marked air of reality about them:

> The all-round development of the capabilities of man does not mean that he will have all-round capabilities for any kind of work. However broad the capabilities that a man acquires, he naturally limits his activity within the framework of his proclivities. . . . In any kind of socioeconomic conditions, all the types of concrete labor will never be reduced to a single one. Various types of concrete labor—and that means a division [of labor]—will always exist.[54]

In short, all that is envisioned, apparently, is that each member of the labor force will perform a set of operations sufficiently varied that it will no longer be possible to locate him definitely at any one skill level; and, as these "intraclass" variations proliferate and widen, the lines between classes or between "mental" and "manual" jobs become harder to draw and lose their social significance.

Some of these processes are already under way. In the enterprises of the former Central Ural economic region, the number of workers studying a second occupation ranged from 9,624 in 1957 to 39,103 in 1963; and in the Sverdlovsk medical preparations factory, three-fourths of the workers were said to have already mastered "related occupations." Among 692 workers of the Elektrosila factory in Leningrad questioned in 1961–62, nearly 35 per cent had two or more occupations (12.6 per cent had three or more). Half of the workers in the Novo-Gorky petroleum refinery (Gorky district) in 1963 possessed more than one skill.[55] A study of adults' time budgets in comparable cities in each of ten countries, carried out under the auspices of the International Social Science Council in 1965–66, showed that 44.8 per cent of the sample in Pskov were engaged in "continuing education and occupational training," spending an average of 4.9 hours a week at it; both figures were almost twice as high as the next highest figures.[56] (The corresponding figures for the American city in the study—Jackson, Michigan—were 8.1 per cent and 0.7 hours. These differences were maintained among virtually every category of respondent: single and married working men, single and married working women, and single and married nonworking women.)

It is striking to notice that what has been advocated as the division of labor proper to communism has been discovered to have functional advantages in American industry. The classic study of the automobile plant, *Man on the Assembly Line,* found that assembly-line workers, who were normally bored with their jobs and showed high rates of absenteeism and quitting, had devised, on their own initiative, methods for job rotation which made their work more enjoyable, with consequent benefits to productivity. Especially interesting was the case of the "utilityman," who was "a relief worker . . . competent to take over any job in his section for a longer or a shorter interval."

The job satisfaction of the utilitymen as a group was high. . . . According to their own testimony, their greater than average job satisfaction apeared to derive from their constant rotation among jobs. . . .

The utilityman is not, to be sure, a craftsman in the traditional sense. The work he performs . . . is strictly paced, repetitive, and routine. When he has mastered say twenty of these jobs, however, he *becomes* in a very real sense *a skilled workman.*[57]

Out of this study and out of experiments begun by "cost-conscious managements" who suspected that "a law of diminishing returns applies to the subdivision of operations, and to many other areas of extreme specializaton,"[58] emerged the concept of "job enlargement." In this form of the division of labor, each worker sets up his own machine from blueprints, operates the machine, sharpens his tools, and inspects his own work.[59] Or, as in a new power-generating plant, "the job of 'operator' [is] redefined and enlarged to include a knowledge of and responsibility for the three major parts of the production system rather than merely a specialized concern with boiler, or turbine, or electrical operations." Only three operating job classifications remained: A, B, and C power-plant operators, distinguished chiefly by their stage "in the process of acquiring proficiency on all the operations."[60] The results of such reorganizations have been not only greater job satisfaction but also reduced turnover and absenteeism, better quality of production and fewer rejects, greater flexibility of operations, less disruption due to absent workers—and, at the same time, higher wages for the individual workers, with no increase in unit costs. Moreover, the hierarchical organization of production becomes "simpler, more informal, better integrated," and voluntary collaboration among workers becomes more common. "In fact formal 'assignment' to tasks by the supervisor is not always necessary, as the employees know themselves where they are needed the most. Such free movement of employees promotes teamwork not formerly prevalent. When work is running smoothly, the operators rotate between machines according to their own collective choosing."[61]

Concern for long-run instead of short-run gains and the rising level of education of the workers thus apparently have reduced the suitability of the type of industrial labor of which the assembly line has been the epitome. The complex technology of the automated factory will probably make it positively dysfunctional. What now becomes efficient is a division of labor strongly resembling that of communism. It is easy to see how the "broad-profile" worker can be perceived as a reasonable approximation to "hunting in the morning, fishing in the afternoon, rearing cattle in the evening, and criticizing after dinner," though without the rustic and recreational overtones. It looks like a good instance of function reinforced by ideology—or maybe the other way round.

The more complex jobs now or soon to be done by the worker set the stage for another change in the division of labor. It becomes steadily less possible for those in charge of production to know and understand the work of their subordinates well enough to exercise unilateral authority over them. This trend already has led to the decline of the "entrepreneur," the person who asserts authority merely by virtue of ownership; the professional manager has taken his place. But now the latter's authority, too, has begun to run counter to the demands of efficiency: less and less often does he have the knowledge and information about those nominally under his control to be able to give them the "right" orders. Instead, he must seek their advice—in effect, make them part of the managerial decision-making process. The separation of ownership from control is succeeded by the merging of management and labor, with major consequences for the organization of industry. As John Kenneth Galbraith has written recently, decisions in the modern enterprise "cease to come from individuals."

They come necessarily, inescapably, from groups. The groups, as often informal as formal, and subject to constant change in composition, contain the men possessed of the information or with access to the information that bears on the particular decision. . . . Effective participation in such decision-making is not closely related to the individual's nominal rank in the formal hierarchy of the company or corporation. . . . Decisions require information, and some power will then pass to the person or persons who have this information. If this knowledge is highly particular to themselves, as in the case of sophisticated technology, their power becomes very great.[62]

Interestingly, "participative management" also has already been formally instituted in a number of American companies in the form of the so-called Scanlon plan. The results suggest that it leads to better morale, harder work, more co-operation among workers, higher output and efficiency—and, again, increased income for the workers in the form of production bonuses.[63] Equally interesting, the plan has not been adopted by a large number of American enterprises. Evidently both management and labor fear the loss of their prerogatives; that the two groups "ought" to have conflicts of interest is a firmly institutionalized ideological principle of the capitalist economy. Job enlargement has encountered similar resistance. Whether automation will force a change remains to be seen. Robert Blauner, upon concluding a study of an automated plant, has commented:

... with automation, the work of the blue-collar process operators becomes very similar to that of the white-collar staff—it is clean, includes record-keeping and other clerical tasks, and involves responsibility. Thus automation may eliminate the "innate" hostility of men who work with their hands toward "pencil-pushers" and administrators. And, conversely, white-collar employees will probably gain an enhanced understanding of, and respect for, the work of blue-collar men, since the office staff's contact with the plant and its production problems increases in automated firms, due to the greater need for checking and consultation.[64]

It is worth pointing out that the family farm, which enjoys considerable ideological support in the United States, nevertheless has almost disappeared. American farming *has* virtually been turned into a type of industry.[65]

It is not, then, difficult to believe that the division of labor in the Soviet Union will come to look the way it is supposed to look in communism. Ideology seems to point it precisely in the direction of advanced industrialism; and—partly because of that ideology, which stresses the harmony rather than the conflict of interests—there are no obstacles in the form of the institutionalized power of either trade unions or managers. The problem it does have is the habit of "command management" on the part of party functionaries; to the extent that the Liberman reforms break that habit, they may, surprisingly enough, be steps along the road to communism.

Distribution

Insofar as variations in pay are associated with the functional requirement of motivating people to take jobs with different

levels of knowledge and responsibility, the need for such variations becomes much less acute when the differences in level are
difficult to discern and carry little significance, all kinds of work
consisting of a broadly similar "mix" of duties. This is still
more the case if "unpleasant" jobs are rotated among members
of a work team or carried out by way of "public participation."
Moreover, under such conditions, the present principle of payment "according to work" would bring about a considerable
degree of equalization of incomes in and of itself. In these respects the Soviet Union has an especially long road to travel in
overcoming the gap between agricultural and industrial work.
However, the party now, at long last, seems quite serious about
attending to this. Guaranteed monthly wages are being introduced for collective farmers for the first time, and collective-
farm labor "is to be rated, organized and paid on lines running
ever closer to those of the state farms." Average earnings for
collective farmers (exclusive of income from the private plot)
are scheduled to rise about twice as fast as those of workers and
employees during the current five-year plan, and improvements
are promised in pensions, housing and the provision of household appliances, and "the building of schools, hospitals and
urban-type cinemas."[66]

But under communism, payment is to be made "according
to needs," not according to work, so that not even varying abilities to do the same sort of work will affect a person's income.[67]
This writer has speculated elsewhere on the form in which such
an idea might be effected.[68] A few directly pertinent remarks
are in order here. Distribution "according to needs" is definitely not used, in Soviet discussions of the subject, to mean
unlimited consumption or the indulgence of mere "whims."
Instead, one hears of "reasonable" needs and "scientifically
based rational norms" of consumption—or, in Khrushchev's
elegantly cryptic phrase, "the healthy needs of a culturally developed person."[69] One implication of this is that distribution
"according to needs" could be declared to have been attained
at a level of production that would be modest by Western
standards. This aspect of communism, therefore, may not be
so far out of reach after all.

The notion of "reasonable needs" is not foreign to other industrial societies, either. In his influential book *The Affluent Society,* Galbraith argued that production in the United States had gone beyond any real needs. "More die in the United States of too much food than of too little. . . . No one can seriously suggest that the steel which comprises the extra four or five feet of purely decorative distance on our automobiles is of prime urgency." In effect, "the marginal utility of present aggregate output . . . is zero"[70] and production is now valued more for the sake of employment than for the sake of consumption. Of course, the Soviet Union is far below such a level of production. But it is readily conceivable that, precisely for the reasons just presented, Soviet leaders would reject an American-style standard of living as a desirable goal: why should overeating and urban congestion be deliberately sought? Indeed, Khrushchev has said: "The concept of abundance as the limitless growth of personal property is not ours; it is a concept alien to communism."[71] William Turpin has given good reasons for thinking that the rise in the Soviet standard of living may instead take the form of increased leisure.[72] Some of this extra time might well be devoted to public participation.

A major instrument for achieving distribution "according to needs" under communism is to be the "social funds." In the Soviet Union and increasingly in the West, welfare services are recognized as a device for equalizing conditions of life among different occupational strata. The Soviet Union, however, with its admittedly and even proudly "collectivist" orientation, has much less ideological trouble with them than does the United States, with its traditions of individualism and self-reliance.

Welfare provisions commonly raise anxieties about motivations not simply for doing the "hard" jobs but for working at all, and this is apparently true in the Soviet Union also. If a person's needs are satisfied without regard to his work, what reason is there for him to do any work? The discussions of communism handle this in several ways. The maxim "He who does not work, neither shall he eat" is held to be applicable under communism and is constantly reiterated; presumably, the person who does not work "according to his abilities" not only will not receive "according to his needs"—he will not receive anything. Another reiterated theme is that communism will not be attained until work becomes a "vital inner need," "the prime necessity of life"—a matter of conscience and an absorbing interest rather than merely a way of earning a living. Research on attitudes toward work in the United States indicates that such a stage has already been reached there,[73] and further developments in the same direction are certainly possible.[74] Indeed, given the Marxist view that work should be a primary means of self-fulfillment instead of a dreary, externally imposed burden, one may wonder whether an ideological adjustment might not eventually have to be made when productivity reaches the point where labor time must be substantially reduced.[75]

But this point is not yet in sight; and meanwhile, warnings are frequently sounded against the "premature" introduction of income equalization either through money wages or through the social funds. The role of the latter, in particular, seems to have been deprecated of late. The 1961 party program anticipated that receipts from the social funds would rise steadily until they constituted half of the total income in 1980. Kosygin's report to the Twenty-third C.P.S.U. Congress, however, implied that the social funds would rise, during the current five-year plan, no faster than money wages, so that their share of the total income in 1970 would remain at the present 25 per cent; he also spoke of "the steady enhancement of the stimulating role of wages" as being the "principal feature of our wages policy," and he added: "It is essential to combine correctly systematic wage increases with the provision of priority incentives for those workers who make the biggest contribution to expanding and improving production."[76]

Nevertheless, it is no feat to imagine how incentives could be reconciled with distribution according to needs. If needs are to be "reasonable" rather than whimsical, "scientific" rather than subjective, Soviet history permits us to infer that they will be determined by the party. It would not be far-fetched for the party to "discover" that some people have greater needs than others. Nor would this contradict the principle of eliminating income differences among different kinds of labor, so long as the greater needs were attributed to those who worked best, whatever the content of their jobs.

If the party is to determine the nature of needs, and especially if these needs are to be satisfied out of the social funds, the freedom of the consumer is brought into question. The idea that communist distribution will take place through a kind of rationing is emphatically denied by Soviet writers on the topic, yet the inference is hard to avoid, and phrases like "tighter civic supervision over consumption" have in fact appeared.[77] No definite prediction is warranted, but it is relevant to point out that modern technology, requiring heavy commitments of resources long before a final product appears, turns consumer sovereignty into a potentially disruptive force. Consequently, there is a tendency to make consumers' wants depend upon producers' decisions, rather than the other way around. Galbraith has referred to this as the "dependence effect,"[78] and one cannot help but be struck by Kosygin's proposal to the Twenty-third Congress: "New types of goods must be introduced systematically and offered to the population, thereby creating a demand for them."[79] In the United States, consumer demand is managed by advertising, in which it enjoys an enormous head start over the Soviet Union—unless political propaganda can be modified to this end. If this is insufficient, and functional requirements lead to the need for more direct control over consumption, it is the Soviet Union which has the head start. From this point of view, those aspects of the Liberman reforms which are intended to heighten the consumer's influence over production may prove to be but a temporary retreat.

The Family

Ambiguity about the role of the consumer, however, is minor compared to that concerning the future of the family. By far the most commonly expressed opinion is that it will continue to exist under communism and will be even "stronger" then than it is now. The only major figure to take a contrary position is the venerable economist S. G. Strumilin, and he has been vigorously criticized for it. Yet concrete discussions of the institutions of communism invariably have more negative than positive things to say about the family, and there is ample ideological justification for that. The family is, in the Soviet conception, a "non-productive" unit, diverting time during the parents' "most mature period" away from more socially desirable activities.[80] Most of the services it does perform, it is held, could be carried out more efficiently by public enterprises, such as restaurants and laundries, thus freeing women for occupational work like that of men—and the elimination of this difference between the sexes is itself an often-stated goal of communism.

> The period of the construction of communism will see the transformation of household services into a branch of large-scale and highly mechanized social production. . . . Gradually, as the rapidly expanding network of household service enterprises is converted into one of the largest and most widely developed branches of public production, family housekeeping will be reduced to a minimum. No one will be compelled any longer to expend great labor upon the exhausting and unproductive work of the household. On the other hand, it is most unlikely that anyone will see her calling in keeping house, for the guiding life interests and strivings of the vast majority of Soviet people have long since emerged from the limits of the narrow scope of material welfare and homemaking.[81]

Juvenile delinquency and "such survivals of the past as religious prejudices, drunkenness, hooliganism, money-grubbing and incorrect attitudes to women and children"[82] are generally held to be the result of poor upbringing by parents and of their ability to resist interference by outsiders into the privacy of their homes. Finally, as was mentioned above, the family is seen as the source of unequal opportunities for children, and it is this which is particularly important for present purposes. Children reared in public institutions governed by uniform policies and run by uniformly trained personnel will be more likely to start out on an equal footing.

"The growing number of preschool institutions and boarding schools," declared the 1961 party program, ". . . will [by 1980] fully meet the requirements of all working people who wish to give their children of preschool and school age a public up-bringing."[83] Boarding schools for all children—the voluntary proviso notwithstanding, it was clear that they were intended ultimately to become universal—was one of Khrushchev's pet ideas, but it was subsequently dropped because it proved to be enormously expensive. A quite satisfactory compromise was evidently found, however, in the "prolonged-day schools" and "prolonged-day groups" at ordinary schools. Here the child attends for about 12 hours a day (including all three meal-times), leaving the parents to provide a place for him to sleep. Enrollment in such schools has risen rapidly, reaching 2.4 million in 1965–66. This is still only about 5 per cent of all school enrollments, but the new five-year plan calls for a doubling of this figure by 1970,[84] intimating that they have been accepted in principle. The concept of the preschool institution has not been challenged; about 7.5 million children are now enrolled in them, and the number is to increase to 12.2 million by 1970, which, according to Kosygin, "will, in the main, meet the urban population's need in these institutions and will considerably extend their services in rural areas."[85] Fees are charged for both types of institutions, but they are low and are scaled according to income, and, for those who need it, financial assistance is available through the trade union or other organizations.

That society is often ill-served by parental upbringing is no strange idea to the American of today.[86] The effects of the home environment on attitudes, aspirations, and measured intelligence, and thus on school performance and employment opportunities, are widely recognized, and so is the fact that it is usually the lower-class child who suffers. (Middle-class parents, incidentally, have long been served by nursery schools, kinder-gartens, and a great many after-school organizations.) Numerous programs, of which Head Start is perhaps the best known, have been instituted, with federal support, to reduce the amount of time that lower-class children of preschool and school age spend at home, and responsible proposals have been made for the extension and even for the universalization of such programs.[87] The ideological objective of equalization is part of the explanation of these trends in both countries, although there is probably also a functional concern for the utilization of otherwise unrevealed talents. But, once again, the United States has the handicap of a countervailing ideological principle: the privacy of the home and the restricted sphere of activity proper to the state. In Soviet ideology the family is essentially a stopgap. As Kassof has pointed out,[88] the authority of parents has always been held to be delegated, and it can therefore be withdrawn when something better becomes available.

There is, however, a further implication of public childrearing under communism. If all work is of equal interest and responsibility and if all needs are being satisfied, it is redundant to provide "equal opportunities" to all children, since all the statuses they might hold in later life would be equally desirable. Why, then, would it be necessary to abolish the family as a child-rearing institution? Even the desire to free women for work outside the home is not a sufficient explanation—first, because rising productivity will make them less needed outside the home; second, because the availability of domestic services and machines, combined with time spent in public participation, would make household work not very different from other work. Indeed, one might speculate that the sensible solution to childrearing might well be the conversion of motherhood into a paid occupation, with no other changes being necessary. But no such suggestion has been made in descriptions of the institutions of communism. One is bound to wonder whether control over the child-rearing process is not itself an important ideological desideratum.

CONCLUSIONS

We have seen that ideology played a continuous part in the shaping of the Soviet stratification structure, though with varying degrees of importance in its different parts. The Soviet regime has seemed willing to pay certain functional costs for the sake of implementing its ideology; this is even more true if one includes authoritarian control and the forced pace of industrialization as parts of "ideology." As we look toward the future, however, it appears that these costs will diminish: except for the attitude toward service occupations, and perhaps the stress upon work, the tenets of Soviet ideology may well be more compatible with the functional demands of the advanced industrialism that is emerging.

The truly advanced industrial society, the society of the future in both East and West, may be characterized as one in which the needs of "reasonable consumers"—as these are defined within the given culture—are fully satisfied. It is, then, a society in which the continued growth of production is no longer a primary concern. If all such societies do have any dominant economic concern in common, it is apt to lie in distribution rather than in production: the maintenance of a high and equal standard of living for all citizens—not an increase in the total volume of goods but the assurance that no individual will suffer a decrease in his share.

Convergence of systems is not an inevitable concomitant of advanced industrialism. On the contrary, precisely because it solves the basic economic problem, it allows greater choice than ever before.[89] But now it will be the Western democracies that will have to pay a price in efficiency if they insist upon their ideological principles. Advanced industrialism exacts a heavy premium for conflict, indecision, and spontaneity.

On the other hand, since advanced industrialism does offer a choice, convergence cannot be ruled out. It is possible, for example, that Soviet leaders might permit the dissipation of their power simply because they were loath to undertake the formidable task of centrally co-ordinating all the decision-making groups of so complex a society. Yet that does not seem like the most probable outcome: Soviet traditions, the unsettling effect of so great a change,[90] and the prospect of a fit between function and ideology which is better than ever before argue against it.

If there is to be convergence, it is more likely to take the form of movement toward the model of communism presented above. We need not assume that this would be entirely repugnant to Western values. For they, too, include a strain of egalitarianism, though its source is different. If, in the Soviet Union, the peasants and to some extent the workers have borne the costs of industrialization, the United States has its Negroes, its urban poor, and the hill-dwellers of the Appalachians. If advanced industrialism allows them to be given their due, it is hard to resist.

When one goes beyond such elementary demands of justice, however, dilemmas begin to appear. Where a Soviet ideologist might be expected to welcome advanced industrialism unflinchingly, one imbued with the Western democratic tradition would want to ask questions and explore the possibilities for alternative forms of advanced industrialism. What, for example, is to be done about the individual who *enjoys* routine labor[91] or who *wants* to specialize narrowly in one field of activity or to operate, even if briefly, his own small (and inefficient) business, or who quite possibly does not want to work at all? What about the person who finds public participation distasteful? How much control of consumption is really necessary or desirable? Ought parents perhaps be permitted to rear children in privacy, even if they do it badly? Is "collectivism" a cloak for authoritarianism? Are there not legitimate, even interesting, conflicts of interest? Under conditions of advanced industrialism, is co-operation morally preferable at all—"what superiority over individualism has the altruism of one millionaire working for another?"[92] Unfortunately, these questions, are not being raised in the Soviet Union, where advanced industrialism, rather than opening up new choices, promises to retain or intensify the old restrictions, now to be justified in the name of both efficiency and communism.

NOTES

1. Alec Nove, "Ideology and Agriculture," *Soviet Studies,* XVII (April, 1966), 397–407.

2. Jennifer A. Platt, " 'Social Stratification in Industrial Society': A Comment," in *The Development of Industrial Societies,* ed. Paul Halmos (Keele: University of Keele, 1964), pp. 137–38.

3. Tsentral'noe Statisticheskoe Upravlenie pri Sovete Ministrov SSSR, *SSSR v Tsifrakh v 1965 godu* (Moscow: Izdatel'stvo "Statistika," 1966), p. 12. Personnel of the state farms, as distinct from those of the collective farms, are included among the workers. There may also be a tiny class of individual peasants and artisans not in co-operatives—0.3 per cent in 1959, and given as 0.0 per cent for 1965—but there is virtually no information about them and they will not be discussed further.

4. Circumlocutions like "socialized at the level" are needed because, in strict legality, the land is nationalized along with all other means of production. Kolkhoz land, however, is deeded to the co-operative for its use "in perpetuity."

5. N. A. Aitov, "Izmeneniia sotsial'noi prirody i klassovykh osobennostei krest'ianstva," *Sotsiologiia v SSSR* (Moscow: Izdatel'stvo "Mysl'," 1966), I, 367.

6. According to one Soviet sociologist, about 10 per cent of the employees are actually "workers [*rabochie*] in whose work there is a relatively high proportion of mental work (a portion of the technicians and foremen, laboratory assistants, radiotelegraphers, telegraph and telephone workers, a portion of the personnel in trade and supply, a portion of the expediters, etc.)." (See M. N. Rutkevich, "Izmenenie sotsial'noi struktury sovetskogo obshchestva i intelligentsiia," *Sotsiologiia v SSSR,* I, 393).

7. V. S. Semenov, "Stiranie sotsial'no-klassovykh razlichii i perekhod k besklassovomu obshchestvu," *Voprosy filosofii,* no. 9 (1965), pp. 142–43.

8. N. G. Valentinova, "O psikhicheskikh osobennostiakh lichnosti rabochego, sviazannykh s soderzhaniem truda," *Sotsiologiia v SSSR,* II, 98–114.

9. O. I. Shkaratan, "Sotsial'naia struktura sovetskogo rabochego klassa," *Voprosy filosofii,* no. 1 (1967), p. 33.

10. V. S. Semenov, "Sotsial'naia struktura sovetskogo obshchestva," *Kommunist,* no. 11 (1965), p. 44.

11. N. A. Aitov, p. 386, and V. Semenov, *Voprosy filosofii,* p. 143.

12. M. T. Iovchuk *et al., Pod'em kul'turno-tekhnicheskogo urovnia sovetskogo rabochego klassa* (Moscow: Izdatel'stvo sotsial'no-ekonomicheskoi literatury, 1961), p. 17; A. K. Kurylev, *Preodolenie sushchestvennykh razlichii mezhdu umstvennym i fizicheskim trudom-problema stroitel'stva kommunizma* (Moscow: Izdatel'stvo Moskovskogo Universiteta, 1963), p. 73; M. N. Rutkevich, "Elimination of Class Differences and the Place of Non-manual Workers in the Social Structure of Soviet Society," *Soviet Sociology,* III (Fall, 1964), 5; V. Semenov, *Kommunist,* p. 41.

13. The ambivalence is nicely shown in the following: "From 1940 to 1962, the proportion of the working population engaged in the non-productive branches increased from 12.1 to 18.6 per cent. All of this growth came in education, health, and science. . . . A further increase

in the percentage of the working population engaged in the nonproductive sphere can evidently be expected in the future, although the relative share of doctors, teachers, instructors in higher education, etc., in the composition of the population has known limits. The hypertrophy of the nonproductive branches which is inherent in a decaying capitalism is not characteristic of socialism. . . . But technical progress in the conditions of socialism, too, demands of necessity both an absolute and a relative growth in the number of personnel in mental work in industry." (See Rutkevich, *Sotsiologiia v SSSR*, I, 395–96.)

14. Alec Nove, "Occupational Patterns in the U.S.S.R. and Great Britain: Some Comparisons and Contrasts," *Economic Rationality and Soviet Politics* (New York: Frederick A. Praeger, 1964), pp. 269–70, 274–76.

15. Tsentral'noe Statisticheskoe Upravlenie pri Sovete Ministrov SSSR, *Itogi vsesoiuznoi perepisi naseleniia 1959 goda SSSR (Svodnyi tom)* (Moscow: Gosstatizdat, 1962), p. 115.

16. Rutkevich, *Sotsiologiia v SSSR*, I, 403.

17. Shkaratan, p. 36.

18. F. I. Il'iashenko, "An Experimental Study of the Level of Culture and Technical Knowledge of Rural Working People," *Soviet Sociology*, III (Summer, 1964), 43–44.

19. *Ibid.*, p. 43; A. V. Vinokur and R. V. Ryvkina, "Socio-economic Problems of the Socialist Rationalization of Production," *Soviet Sociology*, III (Winter, 1964–65), 5–8.

20. V. Semenov, *Kommunist*, p. 41.

21. ". . . in 1958, only 40 per cent of the kolkhozy of the country had attained the level of pay of sovkhoz workers, and even at that, the level of earnings in the sovkhozy is lower than it is in industry. . . . even with [the addition of income from private plots], it appears that the national average of collective-farmers' income is lower than the income of workers. . . . Income received on the average by workers and employees in a form other than pay for work—expenditures of the state for pensions, health protection, education, culture, rest, everyday social services, etc.—is at present almost twice as great as for the peasants." (N. A. Aitov, pp. 379 and 384.)

22. Murray Yanowitch, "The Soviet Income Revolution," *Slavic Review*, XXII (December, 1963), 683–97; cf. Rutkevich, *Soviet Sociology*, p. 6.

23. Shkaratan, p. 36.

24. Gabriel Kolko, *Wealth and Power in America* (New York: Frederick A. Praeger, 1962), p. 83.

25. Tsentral'noe Statisticheskoe Upravlenie pri Sovete Ministrov SSSR, *SSSR v tsifrakh v 1965 godu*, p. 123.

26. Gerhard E. Lenski, *Power and Privilege* (New York: McGraw-Hill, 1966), pp. 308ff. A competing, if not more widely accepted, explanation has been that the absolute and relative rise in the material conditions of the working class has been due simply to the increasing volume of production (e.g., see John K. Galbraith, *The Affluent Society* [Boston: Houghton Mifflin, 1958], pp. 95–97). Yet, while this may have

made the change possible, it is hard to see how it alone could have been the cause. It is conceivable, after all, that, while output rose, the proportion of it received by workers could have declined, leaving them in the same absolute position as before and in a worse relative one. That, indeed, is along the lines of what Marx predicted would happen. The workers must somehow have been able to prevent it.

27. Lenski, incidentally, in *Power and Privilege,* pp. 311–13, also concludes that Soviet incomes are less differentiated than American, after a review of different kinds of evidence from that presented above.

28. Based on data cited in Tsentral'noe Statisticheskoe Upravlenie pri Sovete Ministrov SSSR, *SSSR v tsifrakh v 1965 godu,* pp. 117–18, 120, and *Twenty-third Congress of the C.P.S.U.* (Moscow: Novosti Press Agency Publishing House, n.d.), p. 121 (hereafter referred to as *Twenty-third Congess*); cf. Z. Brzezinski and S. Huntington, *Political Power: USA/ USSR* (New York: Viking Press, 1965), p. 100.

29. Shkaratan, p. 36.

30. *Ibid.*

31. L. N. Kogan, "Problema likvidatsii professional'noi ograni-chennosti rabochego," *Sotsiologiia v SSSR,* II, 71–72. A. K. Uledov, *Obshchestvennoe mnenie sovetskogo obshchestva* (Moscow: Izdatel'stvo sotsial'no-ekonomicheskoi literatury, 1963), pp. 176–84.

32. Howard R. Swearer, "Popular Participation: Myths and Realities," *Problems of Communism,* vol. 9 (September-October, 1960), pp. 42–51.

33. See Abram Bergson's *The Structure of Soviet Wages* (Cambridge, Mass.: Harvard University Press, 1946) for a demonstration that this also happened in the first decade of Soviet history.

34. Others have reached the same conclusion, though partly via different routes. (See Raymond Aron, *Le Développement de la société industrielle et la stratification sociale* [Paris: Centre de documentation universitaire, 1957], pp. 200–1, and "Social Class, Political Class, Ruling Class," in *Class, Status, and Power,* ed. Bendix and Lipset, 2d ed. [New York: The Free Press], pp. 207–8; and Isaac Deutscher, *The Unfinished Revolution* [New York: Oxford University Press, 1967], pp. 47–50 and 54–59.) Stanislaw Ossowski's comment in *Class Structure in the Social Consciousness* (New York: The Free Press of Glencoe, 1963, p. 117) is especially relevant; he writes that "the concept of the classless non-egalitarian society . . . within the frame of differing theories of social class is used for the characterization of one's own society in the leading countries of both the socialist and the capitalist world. . . . In both countries the view of their own society is based on the assumption that even widely ranging shares in the national income are not sufficient to establish social stratification, nor do they necessarily cause either class antagonisms or other symptoms characteristic of a class structure." The argument being made here is that the assumption is more warranted in the socialist world than in the capitalist. See also the interesting discussion by John Goldthorpe, "Social Stratification in Industrial Society," *The Development of Industrial Societies,* pp. 97–122.

35. See, for example, E. L. Manevich, "Abolition of the Differences betweeen Mental and Physical Labor in the Period of Full-scale Con-

struction of Communism," *Soviet Sociology,* I (Winter, 1962–63), 21; V. I. Selivanov, "Primary Rural Collectives and their Influence on the Formation of Personality," *Soviet Sociology,* V (Fall, 1966), 5; and V. N. Shubkin, "Molodezh' vstupaet v zhizn'," *Voprosy filosofii,* no. 5 (1965), p. 66.

36. Rutkevich, *Sotsiologiia v SSSR,* I, 410–13; M. N. Rutkevich and L. N. Kogan, "Methods of Sociological Study of Specific Phenomena," *Soviet Sociology,* I (Summer, 1962), 9–10; V. N. Shubkin, "Vybor professii v usloviiakh kommunisticheskogo stroitel'stva," *Voprosy filosofii,* no. 8 (1964), pp. 22–23.

37. In the study of the Leningrad machine-building industry, 54.2 per cent of the enterprise directors were found to have come "from families of workers of physical labor and of collective farmers; about half of them began their work careers as workers"; and in the entire sample the correlation between class origin and educational level was only .07 (see Shkaratan, pp. 37, 39). This does not negate the earlier point that those currently employed as workers have comparatively little education; the reference here is to the *children* of those in various occupations, and the low correlation simply means that the occupation and, by implication, the education of parents have little effect upon the educational level attained by their children. Unfortunately, serious technical defects in these studies prevent us from drawing precise conclusions from them. See also Robert A. Feldmesser, "Social Status and Access to Higher Education: A Comparison of the United States and the Soviet Union," *Harvard Educational Review,* XXVII [Spring, 1957], 92–106.

38. Manevich, *Soviet Sociology,* p. 24; S. B. Rozhdestvenskaia, "An Experiment in Computer Processing of Ethnographic Data," *Soviet Sociology,* III (Winter, 1964–65), 46; V. Semenov, *Voprosy filosofii,* p. 150; I. P. Trufanov, "O formirovanii i sovremennom sostave rabochikh kadrov leningradskogo zavoda 'Elektrosila' im. S. M. Kirova," *Sovetskaia Etnografiia,* no. 1 (1965), pp. 99–100.

39. At a major machine-building factory in Sverdlovsk, 22.4 per cent of the ITR in 1964 were *praktiki*—men who had no specialized education but who had learned their skill on the job (see Rutkevich, *Sotsiologiia v SSSR,* I, 405). According to Dewitt, 59 per cent of those classified as intelligentsia in 1956 had not had any specialized formal training: Nicholas DeWitt, *Education and Professional Employment in the U.S.S.R.* (Washington, D.C.: National Science Foundation, 1961), p. 482.

40. See especially the remarkable—and, so far as I know, unique—table in an article by I. M. Musatov, as reproduced in H. H.'s "Education and Social Mobility in the USSR," *Soviet Studies,* XVIII (July, 1966), 60. It shows, for example that, among secondary-school students in Novosibirsk in 1963–64, only 18.4 per cent of the children of unskilled workers had "excellent" or "good" academic records, compared to 54.4 per cent of the children of "highly qualified [nonmanual] personnel."

41. Barrington Moore, Jr., "Thoughts on the Future of the Family," *Political Power and Social Theory* (Cambridge, Mass.: Harvard University Press, 1958), pp. 160–78.

42. Geroid T. Robinson, "Stalin's Vision of Utopia: The Future Communist Society," *Proceedings of the American Philosophical Society,* 1955, pp. 11–21.

43. *Twenty-third Congress,* pp. 145, 147–48, 249, 253, 271–72, 279–80.

44. Peter Wiles, "The Pursuit of Affluence: The Economic Record," in *The USSR After 50 Years,* ed. Samuel Hendel and Randolph L. Braham (New York: Alfred A. Knopf, in press).

45. One aspect of this of particular interest to a sociologist is "mass participation" in social-science research: "Many hundreds and thousands of workers, peasants, office personnel, Soviet, party, trade union and Komsomol personnel circulate questionnaires, conduct interviews, serve as observers, etc. Thus, *the laboring population changes from a mere object of research into a researcher."* V. V. Mshvenieradze and G. V. Osipov, "The Principal Trends and Subject Matter of Concrete Sociological Research," *Soviet Sociology,* V (Summer, 1966), 21; italics in the original.

46. N. N. Semenov, as quoted in A. I. Aitov, "Some Peculiarities of the Changes in Class Structure in the U.S.S.R.," *Soviet Sociology,* IV (Fall, 1966), 4; and S. L. Sobolev, *Pravda,* September 1, 1966, p. 1.

47. V. S. Semenov, "Ob izmenii intelligentsii i sluzhashchikh v protsesse stroitel'stva kommunizma," *Sotsiologiia v SSSR,* I, 425; Rutkevich, *Soviet Sociology,* p. 10.

48. A. P. Osipov, "Teknicheskii progress i izmenenie professional'noi struktury rabochego klassa," *Sotsiologiia v SSSR,* II, 15.

49. E. Manevich, "Vseobshchnost' truda i problemy ratsional'nogo ispol'zovaniia rabochei sily v SSSR," *Voprosy ekonomiki,* no. 6 (1965), p. 30.

50. Shubkin, *Voprosy filosofii* (1965), p. 69; italics in the original.

51. *Twenty-third Congress,* pp. 244–45.

52. The Russian language has the advantage of a number of words for a "gainfully occupied person" that are not closely tied to the manual or nonmanual character of his work— e.g., *rabotnik, truzhenik.*

53. Charlotte Saikowski and Leo Gruliow, eds., *Current Soviet Policies IV* (New York: Columbia University Press, 1962), p. 103.

54. Osipov, p. 25; see also F. F. Korolev, "Rounded Development of the Human Personality—The Paramount Task of Communist Construction," *Soviet Education,* IV (January, 1962), 12, and Manevich, *Soviet Sociology,* pp. 18–19.

55. Kogan, *Sotsiologiia v SSSR,* II, 68–69; Trufanov, p. 99; Rozhdestvenskaia, pp. 46–47; see also M. T. Iovchuk, "Sotsial'noe znachenie pod"ema kul'turno-tekhnicheskogo urovnia rabochikh," *Sotsiologiia v SSSR,* II, 34; Rutkevich and Kogan, *Soviet Sociology,* p. 10.

56. Alexander Szalai, "The Multinational Comparative Time Budget Research Project: A Venture in International Research Cooperation," *American Behavioral Scientist,* X (December, 1966), 28.

57. Charles R. Walker and Robert H. Guest, *The Man on the Assembly Line* (Cambridge, Mass.: Harvard University Press, 1952), pp. 77–80, 110–11, 118–21, 148–50; italics in the original.

58. Charles R. Walker, *Modern Technology and Civilization* (New York: McGraw-Hill, 1962), pp. 77, 120.

59. *Ibid.,* p. 122.

60. F. C. Mann and R. L. Hoffman, "Case History in Two Power Plants," in *Modern Technology and Civilization,* ed. Charles R. Walker (New York: McGraw-Hill, 1962), pp. 169–70; also J. D. Elliott, "Increasing Office Productivity Through Job Enlargement," in *Modern Technology and Civilization,* pp. 129–34; R. H. Guest, "Job Enlargement: A Revolution in Job Design," in *Modern Technology and Civilization,* pp. 127–29, 134–35; Walker and Guest, p. 149.

61. Elliott, p. 130.

62. John K. Galbraith, "Planning and the Modern Corporation," *Atlantic Monthly,* vol. 219 (April, 1967), p. 56.

63. The Scanlon plan is essentially a scheme for sharing the benefits of reductions in labor costs among *all* the employees of an enterprise. Its main vehicles are a production committee in each shop and a screening committee for the whole enterprise, made up of representatives of both management and labor, at which suggestions for labor-cost reductions are considered. A few quotes will indicate how closely the behavior it fosters corresponds to the image of work under communism: "In the process of . . . debate [at the screening-committee meetings], almost every aspect of the business comes up for discussion. . . . The result is a dynamic, working unity. . . ." "Formerly, under the piecework incentive system, a highly skilled workman was reluctant to show a younger man the tricks of his trade. But today the older workers are eager to teach their skills, in order to raise shop productivity." (See Russell W. Davenport, "Enterprise for Everyman," in *Modern Technology and Civilization,* pp. 252–53.) "The janitor and the stenographer, as well as the engineer and the manager, can, and often do, exercise human ingenuity in developing improvements entirely outside the limits of their own job descriptions." ". . . the foreman ceases to occupy the impossible role that has been his . . . and becomes a manager in the real sense of the term. He is no longer caught in the problem of divided loyalties and conflicting pressures. . . . He ceases to be a paper shuffler, an ineffective disciplinarian, a 'master and victim of doubletalk,' and becomes a manager willy-nilly." "The pattern of managerial behavior which tends to emerge is remarkably close to that of the 'democratic' leader in the classic Lewin and Lippitt research. However, this term 'democratic' does not . . . imply that 'everyone decides everything.' Its essence is that it makes effective use of human resources through participation; it provides general rather than close supervision; it is 'employee-centered'; it encourages responsible behavior and tough-minded self-control rather than reliance on external authority." Two other remarks are especially provocative: "Competitive motivations . . . are not ignored. . . . However, instead of competing with fellow workers, or saying, 'To hell with the other department (or the other shift); I'm paid to do my job, not to worry about them,' the competition is with other companies in the industry. In a capitalist economy what could be more natural?" "[One benefit of the plan is] the education for all participants in the economics of enterprise. . . . through day-by-day

involvement in the problems of the enterprise. A casual conversation with Scanlon Plan company employees often reveals an understanding of our economic system which is uncommon even among college graduates. . . . Scanlon Plan company employees are believers in capitalism and they know *why* they are!" (See Douglas McGregor, "The Scanlon Plan Through a Psychologist's Eyes," in *Modern Technology and Civilization,* pp. 260–62, 263, 265.)

64. Robert Blauner, *Alienation and Freedom* (Chicago: University of Chicago Press, 1964), pp. 179–80.

65. ". . . In 1959 there were 408 farms in the United States each with sales of $1,000,000 or more, and another 800 with sales of $500,000 to $1,000,000. Many of these farms are operated like highly automated industries, with hired managers and full-time production workers increasing the resemblance. . . . *in the Soviet Union, as in other advanced industrial nations, the differences which historically separated farmers and peasants from urban workers seem to be disappearing . . . the farming or peasant class is in the process of being absorbed by other classes.*" Lenski, pp. 385–86; italics in the original.

66. *Twenty-third Congress,* pp. 216–17, 236.

67. L. M. Gatovskii, "Ob ekonomicheskikh osnovakh perekhoda k kommunizmu," in *Ot sotsializma k kommunizmu,* ed. P. N. Fedoseev *et al.* (Moscow: Izdatel'stvo Akademii Nauk SSSR, 1962), p. 58.

68. Robert A. Feldmesser, "Stratification and Communism," in *Prospects for Soviet Society,* ed. Allen Kassof (New York: Frederick A. Praeger, 1968).

69. Ts. A. Stepanian, "Osnovnye zakonomernosti i etapy formirovaniia kommunisticheskogo obshchestva," in *Ot sotsializma k kommunizmu,* p. 17; Gatovskii, p. 59; *Pravda,* March 19, 1966, p. 2; N. S. Khrushchev, "O kontrol'nykh tsifrakh razvitiia narodnogo khoziaistva SSSR na 1959–1965 gody," *Vneocherednoi XXI S"ezd Kommunisticheskoi Partii Sovetskogo Soiuza . . . Stenograficheskii otchet* (Moscow: Gosudarstvennoe Izdatel'stvo Politicheskoi Literatury, 1959), I, 95.

70. Galbraith, *The Affluent Society,* pp. 123, 160.

71. Saikowski and Gruliow, p. 66.

72. William N. Turpin, "The Outlook for the Soviet Consumer," *Problems of Communism,* vol. 9 (November-December, 1960), pp. 30–37.

73. Robert S. Weiss and David Reisman, "Work and Automation: Problems and Prospects," in *Contemporary Social Problems,* ed. Robert Merton and Robert Nisbet, 2d ed. (New York: Harcourt, Brace & World, 1966), pp. 555, 568–69.

74. To quote again from the reports on the Scanlon plan: ". . . the important points in the [screening-committee] debate are carried by the committeemen back into the shop, where they become the subject of further discussion—at the lunch hour, in the evening, or even at the union meeting. The result is that everyone . . . knows the business and takes pride in his particular contribution." "The plan . . . has completely solved the problem of 'controlled production'—that is, the policy, common to almost all labor, of holding back so that management will never know how fast a man really can work." (At one Scanlon-plan factory,

the engineers voluntarily gave up their vacations to work on a new machine design.) ". . . the workers . . . seem to enjoy working together and sharing the good and bad times. As one of them said, 'Formerly everyone was on his own. Now we all work for each other.' " ". . . a man who makes a good suggestion gets a profound satisfaction out of it; he carries the story home to his wife; he is admired and thanked by his associates," ". . . Union meetings . . . are heavily attended; and often enough most of the discussion is devoted to company affairs and how productivity can be increased." (See Davenport, pp. 252, 253, 254, 256.) "Examination of modern theories of motivation points up [that] Scanlon Plan production and screening committees, as well as the whole management-employee relationship which develops, provide ideal means for satisfying ego and self-actualization needs which are typically frustrated under the conditions of present-day industrial employment." (See McGregor, p. 264.)

75. In this connection, it is interesting to note that a proposal has recently been made for the resumption of unemployment compensation, which was abolished almost forty years ago (see Manevich, *Voprosy ekonomiki,* pp. 29–30).

76. *Twenty-third Congress,* pp. 236–37.

77. See Leon Lipson, "The Future Belongs to . . . Parasites? Commentary" (*Problems of Communism,* vol. 12 [May-June, 1963], p. 6n), quoting a speech by a borough party secretary; see also Feldmesser, in *Prospects for Soviet Society.*

78. Galbraith, *The Affluent Society,* pp. 152–60.

79. *Twenty-third Congress,* p. 206.

80. G. V. Osipov and S. F. Frolov, "Vnerabochee vremia i ego ispol'-zovanie," *Sotsiologiia v SSSR,* II, 238.

81. E. G. Balagushkin, "The Building of Communism and the Evolution of Family and Marital Relations," *Soviet Sociology,* I (Winter, 1962–63), 43; see also Gatovskii, pp. 63–64, and Manevich, *Soviet Sociology,* p. 16.

82. L. F. Ilyichev, "Current Tasks of the Party's Ideological Work," *Current Digest of the Soviet Press,* XV (July 10, 1963), 11.

83. Saikowski and Gruliow, p, 28.

84. Peter Juviler, "Soviet Families," *Survey,* no. 60 (July, 1966), pp. 53–56; Tsentral'noe statisticheskoe upravlenie pri sovete ministrov SSSR, *Narodnoe Khoziaistvo SSSR v 1965 G.* (Moscow: Izdatel'stvo "Statistika," 1966), p. 678.

85. *Twenty-third Congress,* p. 240.

86. See especially Moore, pp. 160–78, and Robert S. Morison, "Where Is Biology Taking Us?" *Science,* vol. 155 (January 27, 1967), pp. 429–33.

87. Henry Chauncey, "Report of the President 1965–1966," *Educational Testing Service Annual Report 1965–1966* (Princeton, N.J., 1967), pp. 26–27; *New York Times,* December 22, 1967, p. 20.

88. Allen Kassof, *The Soviet Youth Program* (Cambridge, Mass.: Harvard University Press, 1965), p. 33.

89. Peter Wiles, "Will Capitalism and Communism Spontaneously Converge?" *Encounter,* XX (June, 1963), 85–86.

90.   Peter Reddaway ("Aspects of Ideological Belief in the Soviet Union," *Soviet Studies,* XVII [April, 1966], 482) has suggested that a well-intentioned Soviet official might "feel that it was his duty to serve the party unquestioningly on the grounds that any political instability which might result from his challenging its methods could only involve increased suffering for the people."

91.   Valentinova, pp. 103–6, and Walker and Guest, pp. 52–55.

92.   Peter Wiles, *The Political Economy of Communism* (Cambridge, Mass.: Harvard University Press, 1962), p. 390; in this volume (see pp. 331–80), Wiles has offered a model of "full capitalism" or "affluent individualism," as opposed to that of "full communism." The labels might not be attractive, but the concepts merit attention, as does his analysis of the more strictly economic aspects of communism.

CHAPTER 3

The Military Establishment

Heresy Enshrined: Idea and Reality of the Red Army

Roman Kolkowicz

Soviet Military Policy at the Fifty-Year Mark

Thomas W. Wolfe

Heresy Enshrined: Idea and Reality of the Red Army

Roman Kolkowicz

INTRODUCTION

In charting the revolution of the proletariat, the Communist party's assumption of power, and the creation of a communist society, neither Marx, Engels, nor Lenin came to grips with the problem of the military and its role in such a post-revolutionary society. While they contemplated various "models" of such an armed force, both for revolutionary and post-revolutionary purposes, they were in agreement on one fundamental axiom: In a "communist society no one will even think about a *standing army*. Why would one need it?"[1] The existence of a standing professional army in a post-revolutionary society was viewed by them as an anathema, a heretical concept that contradicted and violated some fundamental tenets of the ideology.

Yet we have come to know that this heresy, the idea of a professional army in a "classless" communist society, has become a bald reality. Moreover, the Soviet military establishment has progressively assumed a larger role in the state and society, influencing and shaping important aspects of Soviet social, political, and economic life.

It is the purpose of this paper to trace briefly the genesis of the early nineteenth-century utopian ideas about the revolutionary armed forces, the transmutation of these ideas, and the emergence of a post-revolutionary armed force in the Soviet Union which has little in common with the original "models." It is not the intent of this paper (since it would be foolish to do so) to exhort the Soviet and other communists for having failed to live up to a remote and utopian idea born out of powerlessness, inexperience with political realities, ideas that were aimed at the destruction of established state orders rather than the maintenance of them. Rather, the intent is to indicate (1) that the initial distrust expressed by nineteenth-century socialists toward professional armies was borne out by events; (2) that Soviet Communist party leaders continue to be concerned with the role of the professional military in their state; and (3) that no satisfactory solutions have been advised for the thorough integration of the military professionals into the party-dominated political system.

The dilemma of the Soviet Communist party may be seen as a larger problem of the dictatorial and autocratic political systems of our time. The essential characteristics of such authoritarian systems are internal coercion and external militancy, and to achieve these postures the ruling elites had to maintain strong security organs and large military establishments. A vital difference, however, between the internal instruments of coercion and the military institutions in such states is that the former are usually organically a part of the ruling party's apparatus and intensely loyal to the dictator or faction, while the latter, though not necessarily disloyal, seek to disassociate themselves from the party apparatus and its controls, to cultivate their own professional and institutional values, and to remain aloof from politics and generally detached from society. Communist party leaders have found this propensity of the military a source of grave concern. Indeed, their inability to make the military a fully integrated part of the party-dominated system illustrates a vital defect in the structure of one-party autocratic systems.

UTOPIAN IDEAS: *VOLKSAUFSTAND* AND *BEWAFFNETES PROLETARIAT*

A basic axiom of early socialist views on the historical dialectic and class conflict was that the coming revolution of the oppressed lower classes would be achieved through a massive uprising of the people. In this they echoed the slogan of the French Revolution *"Levée en masse,"* expecting the armed people to sweep away the decadent and oppressive monarchic-bourgeois state and to usher in the millennium. In their utopian zeal the early socialists and social democrats saw little need for an organized professional army of the revolution, since a professional army was by definition an instrument of one class for the exploitation of another. Indeed, to Marx the monarchic-bourgeois state was synonymous with its army, which "is the organized power of one class for the exploitation of others,"[2] and that state was best exemplified by "the barracks and bivouac, saber and musket, mustache and uniform." To Marx, therefore, the *Volksaufstand* was going to be the vehicle for sweeping away the despised oppressive institutions of the state, including the army. Moreover, he maintained that in a future socialist society, which by definition would be classless, there would be no need for a professional army, since all means of production would be in the hands of the workers, thus negating any class differentials and, therefore, the need for any instrument of oppression by one class over another.

These utopian visions, however, were severely shaken in their first test with reality: the revolution of 1848. The defeat of the Paris uprising by the regular troops of General Cavaignac and the routing of the revolutionaries in the Baden uprising of 1849 forced Marx and Engels to draw some hard conclusions about the future of the revolution. They came to realize that "armed people are not yet soldiers . . . and most of all, [they] understood the great importance of proper military equipment."[3] Engels also observed that, although the Paris uprising failed, it held out much longer against a superior enemy, while the popular uprising in Baden failed miserably, where "everything was in disorder, every good opportunity missed."[4] He concluded that the proletarians of Paris had been better organized and were used to co-ordinated behavior because of their factory training and life, while the revolutionary liberals of Baden were marked by "brave stupidity," unco-ordinated action without any central leadership.

The events of 1848–49 led Engels, who had set out upon a program of self-education in matters of war and armies,[5] to reject the idea of a proletarian force that would come to power "through the use of modern means of war and modern military art."[6] However, once having realized the necessity for organized revolutionary action by a well-equipped proletarian vanguard, Engels and Marx continued to equivocate on issues involving the role of the armed force in a socialist society, the attitude of the revolution toward the "old army," and the strategy and tactics of a revolutionary force.

It was not until after the failure of the Paris Commune in 1871 that Engels and Marx finally and firmly rejected the "liberal" ideas of the social democrats and established several principles on the role of war, army, and the revolution—principles which were to guide Lenin almost a half a century later:

1. Rejecting the continued adherence of the social democrats to the idea of *Volksbewaffnung,* Engels and Marx strongly supported the idea of a class-based revolutionary force, the *Bewaffnetes Proletariat* (armed proletariat).

2. Engels and Marx disdained the social democrats' idea on the use of the existing armies of the state for the purpose of the revolution (after they have been indoctrinated and persuaded by revolutionary ideology) and instead urged the destruction of the existing "bureaucratic-military machinery" as a necessary first step in destroying the monarchic-bourgeois state.

The role of the armed forces in a post-revolutionary socialist society, however, was left undefined. Engels had rejected some of the ideas of the social democrats, such as the separation of state and army (along the lines of church-state separation) in a socialist society, and instead talked equivocally about closer integration of the armed forces and the party. This problem—the nature and role of the armed forces in the post-revolutionary socialist society—was one that was to plague Soviet leaders, one that has not yet been thoroughly solved.

THE REVOLUTIONARY CRUCIBLE

What Marx and Engels had bequeathed to the Russian revolutionaries, and what therefore links them rather intimately in this context, is (1) the idea of the deliberate use of power and organized violence for revolutionary purposes; (2) the idea that "war puts a nation to the test. . . . [it] imposes a death sentence on all social institutions which have lost their validity" or, in the Leninist rephrasing of the old Clausewitz maxim, that "war is simply a continuation of politics by other [i.e., violent] means"; (3) the idea that a revolutionary armed movement should be class-oriented, based on the proletariat rather than on the mass conscription of the people; and (4) the idea that the army of the *ancien régime* must be demoralized and destroyed as a functioning entity, to be replaced by a revolutionary, proletarian vanguard.

However, Lenin had to learn the bitter lesson on his own, as had Marx and Engels more than half a century earlier, about the uselessness of unorganized and unprofessional revolutionary forces when faced with professional soldiers of the oppressive regime. In 1903 Lenin was still adhering to the notion that "a standing army is an army that is divorced from the people and trained to shoot down the people." He reiterated that "a standing army is not in the least necessary to protect the country from an attack of the enemy; a people's militia is sufficient."[7] However, two years later he changed his mind as a result of the uprising of 1905: ". . . great historical questions can be solved only by violence, and the organization of violence in the modern struggle is a military organization."[8]

While the nineteenth- and early-twentieth-century socialists and communists were contemplating the role and nature of the armed forces in a future revolution, the events of October, 1917, suddenly brought the Bolsheviks face to face with the reality of a revolution's becoming victorious and with the near-intractable problems of running a state. Here ideas and reality clashed and in the process created the Red Army, an institution that is as remote from the utopian notions of the nineteenth-century thinkers as it is in some ways from the traditional military establishments of other large states. In 1917, as contemporary Soviet writers see it, "Lenin and the Communist party did not yet have a thoroughly formulated view of the methods and forms of the military organization of the proletarian state and of the principles of its military structure."[9]

Of one thing, however, the Bolsheviks were persuaded: the need to demoralize the old Russian army so that it would be useless to the provisional government in the fight against the revolutionaries. They therefore concentrated their major effort within the army on undermining the will to fight by promoting disobedience, spreading pacifist ideas, and otherwise stirring up the soldiers' imagination with simple, appealing slogans. Lenin's and Trotsky's political and psychological adroitness in so exploiting the mood and needs of the masses of the peasants in the army accelerated the corrosion of morale that was already underway. Mass desertions, fraternization with the enemy, and disobedience plagued the old Russian army, and the damage was only intensified by the futile disciplinary efforts of Kerensky and by Kornilov's brutal executions among disobedient units. In the fall of 1917 the Russian army ceased to exist as a viable military organization. To guard against the possibility of a revival, the Bolsheviks passed the decree on gradual demobilization in November, 1917, which was followed by decrees on the introduction of the elective-command principle and the equalization of ranks. The combined effects of these measures was to reduce the army in numbers and to remove the aristocratic and bourgeois officers from positions of authority.[10]

Having thus destroyed the old army, the Bolsheviks had to replace it with another military force if they were to be able to resist the onslaught of the counterrevolutionary forces. The existing Red Guards, although they had been adequate to deal with the garrisons of St. Petersburg and Moscow during the October Revolution, were "incapable of opposing enemy armies" because of "insufficient numbers . . . and the absence of proper centralization [of authority]."[11]

The new Red Army was at first far from the formidable military machine it was to become, for the Marxists' traditional distrust of standing professional armies as well as the near-anarchic condition of the country caused its founders to proceed cautiously. The plan was to decentralize the army, using the principles of voluntary recruitment and elected commanders. However, the divisive forces within the military—parochial interests, lack of centralized authority, multiple party committees and party cells, and friction between officers and enlisted men—nullified all efforts to turn the army into an effective fighting force. Consequently, in the "breathing pause" (*peredyshka*) afforded the party by the Brest-Litovsk peace treaty with Germany, Trotsky, with Lenin's approval, undertook to remove the internally corrosive and destructive elements from the Red Army and to transform it into an efficient professional force. Enjoying a broad mandate from Lenin, Trotsky sought to introduce some sweeping changes into the Red Army, thereby generating widespread debates on the proper role of the Red Army and incurring the wrath of many of his rivals in the party.

The many views and proposals advanced in the discussions over form and function fell into two main categories. The crucial question that divided them was whether the Red Army was to be a truly "revolutionary" army based on ideological tenets, or whether it should be a professional army unaffected by ideology. Advocates of the former favored (1) a minimum of centralized control and maximum reliance on local party control for military units (that is to say, a territorial militia as opposed to standing professional cadres); (2) the abolition of rigid discipline, ranks, and traditional military virtues and their replacement by a system in which commanders are elected and orders may be questioned; (3) voluntary recruitment as opposed to compulsory service; (4) local rather than central control of party organizations and political organs in the military units; and (5) revolutionary military doctrine in place of orthodox strategy.

By contrast, the proponents of a professional army of standing cadres advocated hierarchic organization, strict discipline, and centralized control in a military institution that would operate according to traditional strategic concepts.

The main protagonists in the debates were Trotsky and his followers, on the one hand, and the opponents of Trotsky's ideas, whose arguments centered on Stalin, on the other. Trotsky had proposed two stages of development for the military organism he was seeking to build. In the first, under pressure of counterrevolutionary threats within and without the Soviet Union, the party was to disregard ideological formulas and create a military force capable of fending off the enemy. In the second stage, after victory and internal stabilization, the party would be free to create, at a more leisurely pace, a truly revolutionary army guided by ideological imperatives.

For the first stage Trotsky urged rigid centralization of the military, the inclusion of officers from the old Russian army (*voenspetsy*), strict discipline in the units, the abandoning of the election of commanders, compulsory military service, and orthodox strategy. For the second stage he proposed transforming the Red Army into a territorial militia by decentralizing authority, minimizing the role of the political commissars, and doing away with the controlling power of the military over the secret police and political organs within the army.

Trotsky's recommendations for the first stage of the Red Army's development were based primarily on the urgency of the military situation and the acute need to preserve and expand the newly won Soviet power. His rationale for the second stage was similarly pragmatic: since the overriding problems (once the regime had consolidated its power and repulsed external and internal enemies) were economic, Trotsky argued the economic advantages of a part-time arrangement by which proletarians and "near-proletarians" could continue to work in factories and villages while spending part of their time in military training—an arrangement, he pointed out, that would be in closer accord with the model of the socialist system.

Though Trotsky's proposals had the support of Lenin, they generated widespread dissatisfaction and opposition in both the military and the party. This opposition consisted of divergent groups, the most prominent among them being the circle that gathered around Stalin. The latter, though a fervent advocate of a centralized standing army, saw his own position threatened by Trotsky's growing power and therefore found it expedient to attack him on the grounds that he would destroy the revolutionary army by including officers from the old army and adopting orthodox strategy. Other anti-Trotsky factions were those which interpreted the communist ideology very literally and opposed any measures tending toward militarization, the centralization of military authority, and orthodox strategy.

The widespread uncertainty and disagreement on the role of the Red Army was temporarily abated at the Eighth Party Congress, which met from March 18 to 23, 1919. The decisions of the Congress were (1) that the Red Army was to have a "definite class character"; (2) that it was to include military specialists; (3) that the principle of elected officers should be abolished; (4) that the army should be highly centralized; (5) that the army would be for the duration of the civil war a "standing and regular" one, after which it would take the form of a militia; and (6) that the role of the military commissars was to be enhanced.[12]

While the Eighth Congress thus strongly affirmed Trotsky's intention to create a professional military force and laid down some of its basic features, many members of the party continued to criticize and oppose its decisions. Until 1925, at the next five party congresses and on other major occasions, the party continued to suffer from the heated dispute over the definition of the Red Army. It was during this turbulent period that the eventual outline of the structure, internal organization, and political role of the military was developed. The utopian proposals of the left-wing communists, the Bukharinites, the "military opposition," and others fell by the wayside, and the Red Army came to reflect essentially a synthesis of the ideas of the two main protagonists in the conflict.

The basic agreement that made it possible for Trotsky and Stalin to arrive at a synthesis of their divergent viewpoints was on the immediate need for a disciplined and centralized professional army. But Trotsky envisaged a gradual changeover to an ultimately more "revolutionary," ideologically oriented army whereas Stalin and his supporters rejected that aim in favor of a permanent standing army. Trotsky, even though he introduced the political commissars into the Red Army, thought of them as playing only a limited role in the long run, while he favored increasingly wider functions for the intramilitary and local party organizations. Stalin, on the other hand, viewed the central political organs not only as playing a vital role during the formative period but as permanent instruments by which the party leader could keep the military under close control.

It might be said that the structure of the Red Army emerged from the crucible and turbulence of the Revolution owing mainly to three central factors: (1) Trotsky's capacity for pragmatic improvisation under stress; (2) Stalin's vast personal-power designs, combined with his practical understanding of statecraft; and (3) the conditions that prevailed at the army's birth—the political and military threats to the new Bolshevik government—which persuaded Trotsky and other party leaders to shelve the ideological preference for a people's army in favor of the more effective organism.

ABANDONMENT OF UTOPIA: IMPERATIVES OF POLITICAL REALITIES

If anything, Stalin was even more distrustful of professional military establishments than was Trotsky, and his advocacy of a standing, centralized army did not bespeak the militarist or martinet in him. Having created the Red Army, and having ousted or destroyed his rivals, Stalin was faced with the complicated task of retaining full political control over the military while extensively expanding its technical base and professional expertise. Stalin introduced strong political controls from the very beginning; he denied the commanders full authority (*edinonachale*), and he strengthened the security organs' authority in the military establishment. The military did win concessions from Stalin, but these were intended to keep the army loyal to his regime and to make it more proficient; they were far outweighed by measures and practices that resulted in severe curtailment of professional freedom, authority, and institutional self-esteem. Although the military emerged from the early postrevolutionary period with several gains, it found itself the captive of the party elite, living in an "atmosphere of an armed camp surrounded by enemies."[13] Its official role in the Soviet state, as it evolved in the early years, was to execute unquestioningly the policies and directives of the party; to protect the state and the regime and to put down challengers to the party's hegemony within and without; to accept and tolerate the presence of party functionaries in its midst, even at the expense of interference with military efficiency and authority; and to be a citizens' army, penetrated with egalitarian virtues while performing in a disciplined, effective manner.

It was becoming clear, however, that the Stalinist model of a submissive, malleable, and "faceless" army was in many ways, and different ways, as unworkable as some of the utopian schemes of the nineteenth century. What he failed to perceive was the fact that institutional and professional values were taking root in this essentially guildlike and closure-prone military society, and that certain values took hold among the emerging officer corps which transcended those of communist ideology. However, when these "alien" characteristics became noticeable in the late 1920's and in the 1930's, Stalin's distrust of the military intensified and his attempts to control it became marked by near paranoia.

Let us look briefly at the evolving Soviet communist model of a military institution and compare it with the "objective reality."

Although the party came to distrust most institutions and individuals, its apprehensions were unique in the case of the military because of the latter's structure, function, spiritual values, and, above all, certain inherent characteristics. The first of these is the vast physical power—the weapons, equipment, men, and logistic means—at the military's disposal. Second is the fact that the military mechanism, with its closely integrated organization, responds to commands and can therefore, in theory, be rapidly mobilized for action over large areas of the country. Third, the military tends to be a closed group and, as such, breeds elitist values; sharing the experiences, the schooling, and the jargon common to their career, its members are cliquish and have a strong sense of solidarity. Finally, its officers are trained to command, to demand obedience, and to respond to a chain of commands.

Indeed, as the party leaders realized, many of the Red Army's characteristics were those of all large professional military establishments, regardless of their politico-social environments: (1) high professionalization and demands for professional autonomy; (2) a professional ethos, including strict codes of honor and discipline; and (3) an organizational structure whose levels of authority are easily discernible and stable.

As these institutional characteristics and propensities of the military developed they clashed with the party's idea of the military as an open institution, one easy to penetrate and manipulate. While the party was attempting to alter these characteristics, it found its efforts less than successful, short of some radical measures; and it generally refrained from such radical measures lest these endanger the military's viability. Yet the party was also generally unwilling to accept their unchecked existence. This dilemma created difficult choices for the party, which accents this contradictory situation by denying the military an actual autonomy while firmly demanding from it the kind of results that could be achieved best if such professional autonomy were granted. It is almost as if the party leaders hoped to be able to create not only a "new man" but also a "new institution," which they expect to be *sui generis* in terms of organization, structure, and values, and yet to resemble other orthodox military establishments in performance.

The contradictoriness and incompatability of certain basic characteristics of the military and the features that the party would have it exhibit become readily apparent if one juxtaposes them as follows:

"Natural" Military Traits	*Traits Desired by the Party*
Elitism	Egalitarianism
Professional autonomy	Subordination to ideology
Nationalism	Proletarian internationalism
Detachment from society	Involvement with society
Heroic symbolism	Anonymity

That the military traits in the left column are indeed "natural" can be seen in the fact that they have tended to emerge whenever the military has been in a position which permitted it some freedom from the coercive controls of the party— in the early 1930's, during World War II, and in the brief period of Zhukov's tenure in the Ministry of Defense.

The incompatibility between the party's ideal model of a thoroughly politicized instrument of the socialist state (which must also be militarily effective and disciplined), on the one hand, and the military's "natural" tendencies toward orthodoxy, on the other, creates frictions and tensions between the two institutions which have continued to disturb party and governmental politics to the present.

Faced with this inherent incompatibility with the military professionals, an incompatibility which was viewed in exaggerated and paranoid ways by Stalin, leaders of the party in the past four decades have undertaken a variety of measures intended to keep the army "contained" without vitiating its capabilities or viability. The intensity of this policy of "containment" varied according to the internal strength of the party— the relative security of the Soviet Union, on the one hand, and the threat of war or internal party power struggles, on the other.

Faced with the specter of "capitalist encirclement," Stalin was forced to provide the Red Army with massive supplies of modern weapons and equipment, to give the military professionals a broad mandate to integrate the new weapons and equipment efficiently into the growing army, to train commanders and soldiers, and, generally, to provide a powerful shield against the gathering external threat to the state. However, he remained wary of the military's tendency toward elitism and exclusiveness, a propensity that grew with its professional renascence. So overwhelming did this distrust become that, at a time of acute danger of war in Europe, Stalin struck at the military in the massive purges of 1937.

Throughout his reign Stalin apparently looked upon the military as a giant on the party's leash. Hemmed in on all sides by secret police, political organs, and party and Komsomol organizations, the military's freedom of action was most of the time severely circumscribed. Whenever there was an external threat, or when it was internally divided, the party would slacken the leash and toss scraps to the military in the form of concessions and freedom to articulate their grievances. When the crisis had passed, the leash was tightened again, and many of the recently won privileges were rescinded.

However, the Red Army was progressively gaining a corporate image, a sense of apartness from the party-prescribed norms and processes for its existence. As long as Stalin's terror machine was in operation the military was not able to develop an active elite or spokesman for its interests, nor was it afforded an opportunity for articulating institutional views, objectives, and ideals. However, with Stalin's death and the division in party leadership that followed, the control mechanisms were weakened and the military's own interests and values emerged.

AFTER STALIN

The death of Stalin signaled the end of the military's very submissive role in the Soviet state. In the succession struggles of the middle 1950's the military assumed a major balancing role, directly or implicitly throwing its considerable support to certain personalities or factions within the party and assuming thereby an active role in Soviet politics. Moreover, in the person of Marshal Zhukov broad sectors of the military found their spokesman. Zhukov took advantage of the party's internal troubles to rid the military establishment of political organs' pervasive controls; he introduced strict discipline and the separation of ranks; he demanded the rehabilitation of purged military leaders and the punishment of their tormentors; he called for better pensions and higher living standards for the military; and he moved the military out of its social and political limbo and into the limelight. Above all, he dared to express, in public, opinions on major military issues which often deviated from the prevailing party line. The relationship between the party and the military changed from its previous benefactor-client form to one of a more equal distribution of roles. This relationship has become transformed into a dialogue of institutions, some of whose conflicting vital interests and values are in a constant process of adjustment.

The military's remarkable striving to free itself of ideologically and politically derived fetters generated deep concern in the party apparatus, whose members could only watch helplessly while Zhukov sought to destroy a control mechanism that had been carefully and meticulously built up during the preceding four decades. As long as the party leadership was locked in power struggles for the domination of the party and the state, the military enjoyed a relative freedom to set the historical record straight, to increase their authority, to reshape the internal structure of the armed forces, and generally to flex their muscles. However, after Khrushchev finally asserted his own dominating role in the party, by getting rid of the "antiparty group" in 1957 (with the help of the unwitting Zhukov), the *apparatchiki* were ready to deal with the specter of Bonapartism in the Soviet Union. The party's fears of the military's excesses are candidly reflected in the following remarks made at the Twelfth Party Congress:

A dangerous antiparty line and the Bonapartist policy pursued by ex-Minister of Defense Zhukov were nipped in the bud by the decisions of the [October, 1957, Central Committee] plenary session. How serious the situation was can be seen from the extent to which the role of the military councils, political agencies, and party organizations had been undermined and vitiated; absolutely all party criticism of shortcomings of behavior and performance of commanders of all grades was forbidden in the army; the party basis of one-man command was thrown overboard; arrogance, rudeness, arbitrariness, and intimidation were rife in the treatment of subordinates; dissension between commanding officers and political workers was cultivated. Party life and the work of political agencies were administered by fiat and were reduced to purely educational activity. The main political administration was slighted and downgraded. . . . There was a growing drift toward unlimited authority in the army and the country.[14]

While it is questionable that Zhukov and the military had Bonapartist designs on the state, there can be little doubt that

Zhukov used his authority as Minister of Defense to alter profoundly both the internal balance between military and political authority and the broader relationship between the party and the military. To the ultrasuspicious minds of the *apparatchiki* such a development harbored dangers to the party's hegemony in the state, and they therefore set upon some sweeping reforms to purge the military community of these dangerous ideas and practices.[15] In instituting these sociopolitical reforms the party sought (1) to minimize the conditions that breed elitism by forcing egalitarian collectivist procedures and values on the military community; (2) to "open up" the military community to the impartial and not necessarily sympathetic scrutiny of civilian party organs; (3) to deprive the officers of their automatic authority as commanders and force them in most instances to reclaim it from the collective authority of the party organizations in their units; and (4) to undermine the officers' security by exposing them in an intensified form to the ritual of *kritika/samo-kritika,* including the ignominy of criticism from the professionally and militarily lower-ranking Komsomols.

Both Zhukov's ouster and Khrushchev's ambitious plans to reform the officer corps were made possible because a large number of ranking military leaders who were Zhukov's personal enemies lent their support to Khrushchev and sought ultimately to replace Zhukov and his followers in the officer corps. These members of the so-called Stalingrad Group,[16] at the time a strongly pro-Khrushchev faction, did indeed achieve their objectives, but only at the price of renewed political controls and the sacrifice of some of the military's gains in professional autonomy and institutional independence.

In recent years, however, despite the setback suffered with the ouster of Zhukov and the military reform program of Khrushchev, the military has been advancing toward greater professional and institutional freedom. The reasons for this growing military strength lie less in deliberate attempts to oppose party controls, or in renewed Zhukovism, than in the profound changes in social and political conditions in the Soviet Union, in the changing international and strategic environment, and in the imperatives of modern military technology:

1. The officer corps is gradually being transformed from a body of interchangeable commanders with minimal skills into a group of more sophisticated, self-assured, younger specialists.

2. Individually and collectively, these technocrats are becoming indispensable to the effective maintenance of increasingly complex military weapons and equipment.

3. The Soviet Union's extensive politico-military commitments, both to the countries of the bloc and to the underdeveloped world and vis-à-vis the West, would be severely compromised by any serious crisis in the relations between the party and the military, thus making accommodation imperative.

4. A perceptible moderation in the party's methods of ruling and a general easing in the social life of the Soviet Union have permitted the ascent of professional managers, technocrats, and scientists, among others, as well as of the officer corps, which is becoming a professional group par excellence.

5. A growing antimilitarist, pacifist trend in Soviet society has prompted the party to try to enhance the military profession by paying greater tribute to officers and granting them concessions.

Moreover, the movement toward emancipation among former satellites and the split between the Soviet Union and Communist China contain a strongly nationalistic element. As Moscow's ideological and economic hold over these dissenters weakens, it may yet fall to the military to halt or even roll back the divisive trends in the communist camp. And finally, a corollary of the increasingly nationalistic orientation of the bloc countries is that the Soviet military is gaining stature as a major patriotic entity and symbol of the power of the C.P.S.U.

The cumulative effect of these and other developments has increased the military's internal role, one which they view as an active partner in policy-making in affairs which affect the security of the state. While it is unlikely that the marshals and generals seek Bonapartist objectives, but instead professional and corporate autonomy, they do not feel bound to refrain from criticizing party policies when such policies are seen to be destructive to the welfare and security of the nation. As an example of such public criticism of official policy by military people, one can cite recent demands by officers for a more adequate role in shaping strategic and economic policy as they affect the military establishments; demands for more authority to dispose of strategic forces and weapons, which the party jealously guards as its own prerogative; exhortations to revamp foreign policy along more militant lines, rather than continue those of blind adherence to *détente* with the West. These public criticisms by the military finally forced the party leaders to respond in public and to attempt to set the military straight by clearly asserting the party's legitimate rights and authority to manage and control the military establishment: [17]

Both World War I and World War II demonstrated that the leadership of an armed struggle could not be left in the hands of the military command alone.

Attempts to divorce politics from war and to prove that in a modern war the political leadership has possibly lost its role [have been decidedly refuted by logic]. . . . On the contrary: if the missile-nuclear war becomes a reality, the role of political leadership in it will grow substantially.

The military was lectured that "the time is long past when a general could direct his troops [while] standing on a hill" and that "Marxists-Leninists do not assign the roles of generals absolute importance." The party maintained that "the influence of brilliant generals was even at best limited to adapting the methods of warfare to new weapons and to new forms of combat." The military was also told that, "because of their destructive properties, modern weapons are such that the political leadership cannot let them escape its controls."

The military turns a deaf ear to these exhortations and admonishments by the party leaders, clearly rejecting such views as those exemplified in Khrushchev's statement that "I do not trust the appraisals of generals on questions of strategic importance" and arguing instead that "persons who dress up their superficial and primitive conclusions by referring to . . . 'strategic farsightedness' and who lack even a remote knowledge of military strategy must not be tolerated."[18]

PROSPECTS AND PERSPECTIVES

It is one of history's ironies that communist parties, which in principle condemn standing professional armies as an evil force of suppression, cannot do without such professional armies once they themselves have achieved political power, and, indeed, depend on the military to maintain them in power. Of course, there is nothing surprising about this turn of events, for political control of a state is impossible without some form of a military force. What is relevant, however, is the Communist party's difficulty in finding a stable form of "coexistence" with this necessary instrument of policy.

It is important to distinguish between two kinds of problems in the communists' attitudes toward their military professionals. One is *the need for ideological correctness in rationalizing the existence of a professional Army.* This is a relatively easy task, achieved by maintaining the doctrinal fiction of the eventual withering away of the state, of which the military is an important factor, and of the superfluity of a professional army in a classless society. Stalin devised the formula that the maintenance of a professional army was made necessary by the threat of "capitalist encirclement," and Khrushchev used the following rationale: "We are devoting great attention to our army only because we are forced to do so. Since the capitalist countries cannot think of existing without armies, we must also have an army."[19] Such avowed misgivings about the maintenance of professional armies, however, have been largely rhetorical statements for the sake of ideological continuity and legitimacy. A much more serious problem is *the party leaders' apprehension about the military's behavior and intentions within the present political structure of the state.* This concern is genuine and pressing and stems from the party's uncertainty about its ability to exercise constant and effective control over the "experts in violence," with their well integrated organization, whose institutional interests and values diverge in important ways from those of the party. The latter, to state the problem in its simplest terms, is a group of "experts in violence" of a much broader scope, who cannot tolerate any significant opposition to their hegemony within the state. Yet, while the party's fears of the men who carry guns, fly the planes, man the missiles, and command the obedience of millions of soldiers is real enough, they are finding themselves today more dependent on them than in the past.

The party's strategy toward the military has been one of containment, divisiveness, and integration: (1) *containment,* by imposing multiple shackles on the military community and by a ceaseless process of indoctrination; (2) *divisiveness,* by selective co-optation of certain trustworthy military leaders from the top hierarchy into positions of power and prestige, seeking thereby to prevent the military community from developing a focus, direction, and institutional identity of its own; and (3) *integration,* by denying the military a sense of apartness from society and by the establishment of multiple links between the military and society as a whole.

The objective of this strategy is simple and was best described in a terse statement by Mao: "Our principle is to have the party control the gun and never to allow the gun to control the party." The success of this strategy is considerable and has always enabled the Soviet party leaders to maintain their authority in the military and to reinstate it whenever such authority was temporarily weakened. However, the growing political and military commitments of the Soviet state, the lessening "charisma" of party leaders, the diminished role of the terror machine, and the imperatives of modern technology, among other factors, have favored the heightened professionalization and institutional loyalty of the officer corps. These developments present the party leaders with a dilemma that results from a delicate balance between two conflicting motivations: the desire for hegemony within the state and the need to maintain a strong military-political posture before the rest of the world. This balance is far from impossible, if the party leaders feel secure enough to trust the military to the extent of allowing them a modicum of corporate autonomy and a role in shaping defense policy. This the party fails to do because it assumes that generals cannot be trusted. In this mistrust the Soviet party leaders seem to reflect Engels' vitriolic comment on the earliest military professionals, who had joined the revolutionary movement of 1848: "This military pack . . . hate each other violently, are jealous like schoolboys of each other's smallest awards, but when it comes to people in mufti [*vom "Zivil"*] they are all united."[20]

One is tempted to employ the terminology and the deterministic formulas of the communist dialectic to describe the evolving role of the military in the communist state. One could say that the party has created the Red Army in order to use it for the furthering of its political and ideological interests. Having "given birth" to the Red Army, the party found itself progressively more dependent on it, for internal and external reasons. As the Soviet state assumed a larger and larger international political and strategic role, so did the party's dependence on the military grow, along with the latter's strength and influence. One may also speculate on the future "synthesis" of these "antithetical" forces, in which the two might merge, with the army "militarizing" the party and the military becoming even more "politicized." Such an eventuality would signal the ultimate death of the idea of the revolutionary vanguard of the proletariat (an idea that was moribund at its inception) without changing very much the political realities of the Soviet state.

The realities of current and future Soviet politics are strongly influenced—one is tempted to say "determined"—by certain developments that will force the party leadership to depend even more than in the past on the expertise, efficiency, and good will of the military professionals. These developments include the influx of modern military technology, which requires highly skilled military technocrats to maintain and operate the new sophisticated weapons; the breadth of Soviet political and military commitments to allies and proxies in various parts of the globe (such commitments are based on Soviet military counsel and support as well as on economic and political considerations); the "bloc-fatigue" problem, i.e., the erosion of alliance systems, coupled with a sharp renaissance of nationalism, both adding new significance and importance to an indigenous Soviet national armed force; and the problems of nuclear proliferation, which are viewed by the Soviets with grave concern and which will motivate them to seek preventive (as well as negotiatory) measures that will further enhance the military's role.

The problem of the professional army in a post-revolutionary communist state has come full circle from the utopian formulas of the early nineteenth century to the hard facts engendered in the responsibilities and problems of a modern superpower. The Soviet leaders, who frequently assert that historical determinisms are on their side, are facing new types of determinisms which cannot be wished away by a magic ideological wand. These determinisms derive from the fact that the Soviet Union and its leaders lay claim to being a global power and that, in seeking to maintain such a position, they must rely to an increasing degree on the main supporting instrument of that position—their professional armed forces.

NOTES

1. Cited in R. Kolkowicz, *The Soviet Military and Communist Party* (Princeton: Princeton University Press, 1967), p. xviii.

2. In Karl Marx and Friedrich Engels, *Selected Works* (Moscow: Marx-Engels-Lenin Institute, 1951), p. 43.

3. Reinhard Hoehn, *Sozialismus und Heer,* vol. 1 (Berlin: Gehlen Verlag, 1961), p. 43.

4. *Ibid.*

5. Marx, who had known even less about military matters than had Engels, urged Engels to keep him informed on his progress and to send him books and materials that might help him (Marx) in advancing his own knowledge. Among his reasons given to Engels, he mentioned the fact that he needed the occasional 10 pounds earned by writing articles on the subject. See *ibid.,* p. 61.

6. *Ibid.,* p. 52.

7. "To The Rural Poor," *Selected Works* (London: Lawrence and Wishart, Ltd., 1936), vol. 2, p. 281.

8. "Revolutionary Army and Revolutionary Government," *ibid.,* vol. 3, p. 313.

9. *KPSS i stroitel'stvo Vooruzhennykh Sil SSSR, 1918-iiun' 1941* (Moscow: Voenizdat, 1959), p. 11.

10. Kolkowicz, *The Soviet Military,* p. 37.

11. *KPSS i stroitel'stvo,* p. 11.

12. *KPSS o vooruzhennykh silakh sovetskogo soiuza: sbornik doku-mentov, 1917–1958* (Moscow: Gospolitizdat, 1958), pp. 49–63.

13. Carl J. Friedrich and Zbigniew K. Brzezinski, *Totalitarian Dictatorship and Autocracy* (New York: Frederick A. Praeger, 1956), p. 281.

14. *XXIIs'ezd: stenograficheckii otchet* (1962), vol. 3, p. 67.

15. Among the statutes and regulations of the reforms were: Statute on Military Councils (April, 1958); Statute on the MPA (April, 1958); Statute on the Political Organs (October, 1958); Changes in the Instructions to the Party Organizations in the Soviet Army and Navy (April, 1958). The last item refers to the change in Paragraph 2 of the original Instructions issued in April, 1957, during Zhukov's tenure as Minister; see Kolkowicz, *The Soviet Military*, pp. 139–42.

16. The Stalingrad Group consists of officers who allied themselves with Khrushchev during the battle of Stalingrad (where the latter served as political supervisor of that front) and who had risen with Khrushchev to top leadership in the Soviet military establishment. For details see "The Rise of the Stalingrad Group: A Study in Intramilitary Power Politics," *ibid.*

17. *Krasnaia zvezda,* January 5, 1967; see also *Krasnaia zvezda* of January 24 and April 6, 1967.

18. Marshal M. V. Zakharov, Chief of the General Staff, *Krasnaia zvezda,* February 4, 1965.

19. *Pravda,* February 16, 1958.

20. Engels, in a letter to Marx, cited in Hoehn, *Sozialismus und Heer,* p. 44.

Soviet Military Policy at the Fifty-Year Mark

Thomas W. Wolfe

The past half-century has seen the growth of the Soviet Union into one of the world's two strongest military powers, with an industrial-technical base commensurate to superpower status in the modern world. The Soviet armed forces themselves have not only met the supreme test of a great war but through fifty years of sometimes turbulent Soviet history they have remained the obedient instrument of the successive party leaderships that have controlled the destinies of the Soviet state. These are no mean accomplishments, and the present Soviet leaders may be pardoned if, as the Soviet Union celebrates its fiftieth anniversary, they tend to look back with pride and satisfaction at the military aspects of Soviet growth and development.

At the same time, however, the present collective leadership under Leonid Brezhnev and Alexei Kosygin can scarcely avoid giving sober thought to tasks and problems in the military field which bear upon the path the Soviet Union may follow in the years ahead. Indeed, as the Soviet Union has evolved into a more mature and complex society, placing subtle new demands upon those who direct its policies at home and abroad, so the problems of creating modern military power and of using it to political advantage have become more intricate and difficult.

In Stalin's day, following World War II, Soviet military policy had been oriented in a relatively straightforward way toward two primary tasks: the first and most urgent, to break the American nuclear monopoly; the second, to hold Europe hostage to preponderant Soviet conventional military power while the first was being accomplished. Comparatively little attention was given under Stalin to a number of more subtle problems, such as determining the political utility of military power in the nuclear age and developing a body of strategic thought responsive to the changing technological and political environments of the modern world. It was left largely to Khrushchev in the decade or so after Stalin's death to preside over the process of incorporating the new weapons of the nuclear-missile age into the armed forces, along with appropriate concepts for their use.

This proved, for various reasons, to be a somewhat painful process. For one thing, Khrushchev found himself wrestling with the paradox that, even as technology invested military power with an ever increasing destructiveness and coercive potential, constraints upon its use also grew apace, tending to multiply the risks and narrow the opportunities for turning military power to political advantage. Although this was a universal paradox confronting not the Soviet leadership alone, it had particularly damaging effects upon the doctrines of a Marxist-Leninist leadership elite schooled to take a tough-minded view of force and violence as agents of revolutionary sociopolitical change. It led to revision of such Leninist tenets as the inevitability of war between the rival systems, helping to persuade Khrushchev that a new world war was too dangerous to serve as the "midwife" for another round of communist advance, and that even lesser forms of revolutionary conflict might escalate into a large nuclear conflagration which could jeopardize the Soviet system itself.

In the immediate area of military policy, Khrushchev's role as revisionist and reformer likewise had a painful impact. The organizational and conceptual reforms that he imposed upon the Soviet military establishment were, at least in the eyes of conservative-minded elements among the marshals, too radical to be swallowed easily. Eventually, but not without generating a good deal of resistance, Khrushchev's military philosophy, based on the primacy of strategic deterrent power, won out. However, the military programs he sponsored had the side-effect of neglecting what many of his Soviet critics considered to be the need for "balanced, all-round strengthening" of the armed forces; moreover, even with respect to the strategic nuclear forces he favored, Khrushchev's programs tended to emphasize the *image* of strategic power at the expense of substance, and by the end of his rule the Soviet Union still found itself in a "second-best" strategic posture vis-à-vis the United States.

This then, in briefest outline, was the background against which Khrushchev's successors took over the responsibility for Soviet military policy. Since Khrushchev was removed from office in 1964, Soviet military policy under the Brezhnev-Kosygin regime has moved through an initial "standpat" period of reappraisal[1] into what may be described as the regime's own response to various major issues confronting it. Some of these are new problems growing out of developments like the war in Vietnam or the Middle East crisis; others, as we shall see, are mainly holdover issues from the Khrushchevian era, set perhaps in a new context.

Before taking stock of specific developments in the field of Soviet defense posture and policy under the Brezhnev-Kosygin regime, one should perhaps make the general observation that there has been no radical change of direction in Soviet defense preparations or in the strategic philosophy underlying them since Khrushchev left the scene. That is to say, the post-Khrushchevian period to date has been marked by no major organizational and theoretical reforms in the military domain comparable to what followed the death of Stalin. What has happened, rather, can be regarded as an effort to broaden Soviet military capacities in fields that suffered some neglect under Khrushchev's programs, while at the same time retaining the central feature of his military philosophy, the essence of which was to place primary emphasis on Soviet strategic nuclear-missile power. In this process, prompted perhaps by a belief of the present leadership that it must provide itself with a wider range of military options and divest itself of the political liability of having only a second-best strategic posture in future crisis situations, somewhat more attention has been given to strengthening the substance that stands behind the image, cultivated by Khrushchev, of imposing Soviet military power.

Although the Brezhnev-Kosygin regime may ultimately find that many of the military policy problems on its agenda will remain essentially intractable, nevertheless, the steps it has taken thus far are having significant effects on the Soviet defense posture and upon the military power relationship between the Soviet Union and the United States. Furthermore, changes in the Soviet Union's strategic position have been accompanied by the revival of internal discussion, and sometimes argument, over the doctrinal and policy implications of Soviet military development, as well as by the airing of questions pertaining to relations between civil and military authority. All of this not only testifies to the vitality of the issues involved but also suggests that a new chapter in the evolution of Soviet military policy has opened under Khrushchev's successors. Let us turn now to some of the pertinent developments of the past few years, beginning with a brief review of the question of defense claims upon Soviet resources—a perennial problem sharpened by the new regime's commitment to an ambitious program of domestic economic reform and improvement.

THE RESOURCE ALLOCATION ISSUE

Although the Brezhnev-Kosygin regime started out with the apparent intention of holding a ceiling on military expenditures (as indicated by its adoption of a 1965 military budget slightly smaller than Khrushchev's for the preceding year[2]), it rather soon became evident that the new leadership was to find no easy way out of the ever perplexing problems of economic-defense priorities. The details of early contention surrounding the issue of resource allocation may be found in a previous article by this writer;[3] here, suffice it to say that military spokesmen first surfaced the issue with a series of theoretical arguments in 1965 implying that one-sided emphasis on war deterrence, as practiced under Khrushchev, could lead to neglect of all-round strengthening of the armed forces and to questioning of "the need to spend large resources on them."[4]

At about the same time that military writers were suggesting that there are no ruble-saving short cuts to Soviet security, divergent views also showed up within the political leadership, with some leaders espousing resource priority for internal economic development while others stressed the need for further strengthening of Soviet defenses to meet the threat posed by a deteriorating international situation.[5] The extended crisis growing out of the war in Southeast Asia tended during 1965 and 1966 to buttress the position of the latter in the internal policy debate over economic-defense priorities. That they were gaining ground was indicated by a 5 per cent increase in the military budget for 1966 (to 13.4 billion rubles) and by Kosygin's observation at the Twenty-third Party Congress in April, 1966, that "aggravation of the world situation" had adversely affected Soviet plans for economic development, preventing the Soviet Union from making "a substantial reduction in military expenditures and correspondingly greater capital investment in peaceful sectors of the economy."[6]

By the beginning of 1967 it became still more clear that arguments for larger defense expenditures had prevailed, even at the cost of some setback of investment in other sectors of the economy. There was, for example, another increase in the published military budget for 1967—to 14.5 billion rubles, a boost of about eight per cent. These figures, it should be noted, are what the Soviet Union has chosen to announce publicly. Actual military expenditures, part of which are buried under other budgetary headings, are generally somewhat higher—at least one-third higher, according to competent Western estimates.[7]

As matters stand today, the supposition that military requirements are actually taking a bigger bite out of Soviet resources than the published figures indicate is strengthened by delay in ratifying the five-year plan for the 1966–70 period. The guidelines for this plan were issued in early 1966 and were discussed at the Twenty-third Party Congress in April, 1966, where

Kosygin said the plan should be ratified within four or five months by the Supreme Soviet. However, no new five-year plan was approved in its totality, suggesting that unresolved difficulties of resource allocation between military-space programs and civilian sectors of the economy stood in the way.[8] As we shall see later, one of the defense questions that have complicated Soviet planning appears to center on deployment of an ABM (missile defense) system, an undertaking that will involve substantial new expenditures at a time when other investment will also have to be stepped up to meet the economic goals of the five-year plan.

THE POSSIBILITY OF GENERAL WAR AND ITS POLITICAL UTILITY

It goes without saying that the urgency accorded Soviet military preparations depends in no small part upon what the Soviet leadership thinks about the likelihood of a major war in today's world, as well as upon its thinking on the question of whether war in the nuclear age has become obsolete as an instrument of policy. On the first issue, there has been a marked tendency in Soviet media since early 1965 to sound the theme that the "aggressive character of imperialism" is increasing, making it the "most important duty" of the Soviet party and other Marxist-Leninist parties "not to permit an underevaluation of the danger of war."[9] The new leaders themselves also have expressed concern that the danger of war has grown in light of U.S. "aggression" in Vietnam.[10] The critical point, however, is what distinction to make between Soviet declaratory utterances on the likelihood of war—which serve various purposes of internal argument and external propaganda—and the private convictions of the leadership.

Any opinion ventured on this subject is bound to be speculative. This writer would be inclined to believe that the incumbent Soviet leadership still considers a major war between the rival systems to be unlikely—if not thanks to benign U.S. intentions, then because of a combination of Soviet deterrent military power and the political forces generally described as the "world peace movement."[11] A qualification probably should be added, however, with regard to Soviet concern that a local war, such as the one in Vietnam, might get out of control, or that the policy of a resurgent Germany might one day draw the United States and the Soviet Union into war.

With regard to the second question posed above, it is a matter of some interest that doctrinal ferment has again arisen in the Soviet Union around the issue of war as a policy instrument. As one may recall, during Khrushchev's tenure there was a definite tendency to admit that nuclear war was likely to be militarily unmanageable and that Lenin's dictum on war as a continuation of politics was obsolete.[12] Since the fall of 1965, however, this view has been challenged frequently, beginning with an article by Lieutenant Colonel E. Rybkin in the semimonthly journal *Communist of the Armed Forces*.[13] The Rybkin article attacked by name such prominent Soviet writers as General Nicolai Talensky for having spread the "fatalistic" doctrine that it is no longer possible "to find acceptable forms of nuclear war." While agreeing that nuclear war would create great havoc and that one should do everything possible to prevent it, Rybkin asserted that one should not succumb to the doctrine that victory in nuclear war is impossible. To do so, he said, "would not only be false on theoretical grounds, but dangerous also from a political point of view."

He went on to argue that victory was feasible provided a country conducted a nuclear war so as to minimize damage to itself. According to Rybkin, there are two complementary ways to do this. One way lies in achieving "quick" defeat of the enemy, "which will prevent further destruction and disaster." The other lies in "the opportunity to develop and create new means for the conduct of war which can reliably counter the enemy's nuclear blows," an apparent reference to ABM defenses. At the same time, Rybkin warned that attainment of the requisite military posture would call for great effort, without which it would be a dangerous mistake "to assume that victory was reliably assured" simply because of the "innate superiority" of the communist system.

These views have been echoed in part by other military writers, but there has also been pointed criticism of certain aspects of Rybkin's argument. For example, in July, 1966, Colonel I. Grudinin joined the attack on the "no-victory" notion promulgated in the Khrushchevian era by people like Talensky but took Rybkin to task for adopting ideas that smacked too much of "bourgeois" theorizing about modern war.[14] In particular, he argued that Rybkin had strayed from Marxist-Leninist analysis by pragmatically stressing the material balance of forces, or what in the Western idiom might be called "hardware factors," while failing to give sufficient weight to the ideological advantages of the Soviet system.

Still another military theorist to be heard from on this subject was Lieutenant Colonel V. Bondarenko, who, writing in September, 1966, argued that the key to victory lies in a massive and imaginative research and development effort to assure military-technological superiority.[15] Asserting that a properly managed research program should avoid the dangerous mistake of concentrating merely on improvement of existing weapons, he advanced the thesis that new breakthroughs in weaponry "can abruptly change the relationship of forces in a short period of time." A further contribution to the discussion stimulated by these various military theorists appeared early in 1967 in an unsigned editorial in *Red Star*.[16] Noting that writers like Rybkin had taken a "creative, independent approach" to problems of modern war, the article stated at the same time that he and Grudinin unfortunately had skirted some of the changes to be taken into account under nuclear-age conditions. Although the article itself reiterated doctrinaire claims of communist victory if war should come, its main emphasis lay upon the need for "anti-imperialist forces" to oppose nuclear war "as a means for resolving international disputes," thus seeming to imply that theorizing on the prospects of victory should not be carried too far.

The revival in the Soviet Union of theoretical argument about modern war as a policy instrument does not necessarily mean that a hard-line element has begun to urge a current policy shift involving a much higher risk of war. The central point stressed by the various military theorists cited above does not seem to be that the present "correlation of forces" would offer a good prospect of Soviet victory if war should occur, but rather that future changes in the power relationship between the Soviet Union and its adversaries might do so. This suggests, in turn, that Soviet military theorists may believe that the programs being carried out by Khrushchev's successors have improved the propects of reversing the strategic power balance between the Soviet Union and the United States, making it worthwhile to reopen what had tended to become a closed chapter of discussion at the end of the Khrushchevian period. Let us look next, therefore, at some of the steps taken under the present regime to repair the Soviet Union's strategic position.

BUILD-UP OF STRATEGIC FORCES

Although Khrushchev's successors evidently came into office dissatisfied with the strategic balance as it stood under Khrushchev, it was by no means clear at the time what they proposed to do about it. Their initial approach did indicate, if nothing else, a determination to improve the technological base upon which any effort to alter the balance in Soviet favor would ultimately depend. Appropriations for scientific research were stepped up,[17] and, as made evident by the public display of new families of weapons,[18] among other things, the Soviet military research and development program was pushed even more vigorously than before. It was only after the new leaders had been in office for a year or two, however, that it gradually became apparent that they had committed themselves to a substantial build-up of Soviet strategic delivery forces.

As indicated by informed accounts that began to appear in the U.S. press in the summer and fall of 1966, an accelerated program of ICBM deployment was under way in the Soviet

Union.[19] By the beginning of 1967, according to some of these accounts, the number of operational ICBM's had reached around 400 or 450, and deployment was continuing at a rate of more than 100 a year.[20] These figures compared with a total deployment of less than 200 ICBM launchers during the entire Khrushchevian period. No less significant than the rapid growth of numbers was a shift to new types of missiles in dispersed and hardened sites, in contrast to the ICBM force of the Khrushchevian period, much of which consisted of early-generation missiles of "soft-site" configuration. In short, not only was the *rate* of operational deployment of ICBM's stepped up after Khrushchev's departure, but the *qualitative* character of the ICBM force had been improved as well.

Meanwhile, as emphasized in the late Marshal Malinovsky's report at the Twenty-third Party Congress in April, 1966, "special importance" has been attached to developing mobile land-based missiles for the strategic missile forces,[21] a step which would further diversify the Soviet Union's strategic delivery potential. The same report pointed out that the Soviet Union continues to count upon the additional contribution to its strategic delivery capabilities provided by long-range bombers equipped with air-to-surface missiles for "standoff" attacks against enemy targets and by missile-launching submarines.[22]

What the ultimate size and character of the Soviet strategic forces might be remains uncertain. It does seem clear, however, that the familiar situation of the past two decades, in which the United States enjoyed marked strategic superiority over the Soviet Union, is changing and that a new correlation of forces could emerge in the next few years. The precise nature of a new strategic balance is not predictable, but, if the programs undertaken by the present Soviet regime continue, a situation of "parity" or perhaps even some margin of "superiority" might be attained by the Soviet Union, depending in part upon what response the United States chooses to make.

A great deal of controversy, into which we shall not enter here, attends the questions of what constitutes "parity" or "superiority"; indeed, the point at which it becomes militarily meaningless to exceed a major nuclear adversary in numbers of weapons, megatonnage, or other attributes of strategic forces is something on which views differ widely, not only in the United States, but apparently in the Soviet Union as well.[23] Whatever the military merits of the argument may be, however, the political implications of the strategic-force equation are another matter. And it is in this regard that any substantial change in the previous strategic balance will be likely to pose far-reaching questions in the realm of Soviet policy. For example, in an environment of acknowledged strategic parity or superiority, will the Soviet leaders feel more secure and be inclined to play a more responsible and prudent status quo role in international politics? Or will they be prompted to seek fresh political gains from a more favorable correlation of forces, leading to pursuit of more aggressive policies, which could introduce new elements of turbulence into international relations? Only the future holds the answer to such questions.

THE ABM ISSUE

Another step taken by the new regime to bolster the Soviet strategic posture, and one which was held in abeyance under Khrushchev, relates to antiballistic missile defenses. As made known late in 1966 by the U.S. government,[24] after some months of speculation in the press that ABM defenses were being installed around such cities as Moscow and Leningrad, the Soviet Union has embarked upon deployment of an ABM system—the extent and effectiveness of which is still a matter of considerable debate in the West.[25] According to some accounts, it remains unclear at the moment whether the system is confined to Moscow alone, or whether another system covering a larger geographical area is also a part of the current ABM deployment.[26] Speculation about the effectiveness of ABM measures taken thus far by the Soviet Union has been further heightened by public expression of differing opinions on the subject among Soviet military officials.[27]

Why the present Soviet regime decided to deploy an ABM system and to claim a significant Soviet advantage in this field is not altogether clear. The Soviet leaders were undoubtedly aware that "first deployment" of ABM's has been widely regarded in the West as a step which could "destabilize" the strategic environment and set off a new round in the arms race. In light of the earlier example of the "missile gap" that in the late fifties and early sixties greatly stimulated U.S. missile programs and had the net result of placing the Soviet Union in a relatively unfavorable position with respect to strategic forces, one might have supposed that the Soviet leaders would think twice about stirring up an "ABM gap" psychology. However, Soviet predilection for building strategic defenses, combined with the possible overcoming of earlier technical obstacles in ABM development, seemingly prevailed over the economic costs and the risks of stimulating the strategic arms race, in the judgment of the present leadership.

Whether this decision will hold up in the face of American efforts to persuade the Soviet government to reconsider its ABM policy remains to be seen.[28] At this writing, nothing concrete has emerged from the exploratory U.S.-Soviet talks initiated in late February, 1967, apart from signs that the U.S. initiative may have aroused fresh internal policy debate within the Soviet government.[29] However, by agreeing to explore the matter, and by suggesting that any future negotiations should also take up the issue of strategic delivery forces, in which the United States still enjoys a putative numerical advantage,[30] the Soviet leaders at least seem to be giving second thought to the possibility of improving the Soviet Union's relative position via the arms-control route rather than banking solely on a further unilateral build-up of Soviet offensive and defensive strategic forces.

THE QUESTION OF PREPARATION FOR CONVENTIONAL AND LIMITED WAR

Under the Brezhnev-Kosygin regime, steps taken to bolster the Soviet strategic posture[31] have been accompanied by fresh attention to the possibility of nonnuclear warfare in various potential theaters of conflict, including Europe. Reflecting in part the pressure from some professional military leaders to achieve better-balanced forces than those inherited from the Khrushchevian period, and in part perhaps a reaction to such nonnuclear conflicts as those in Vietnam and the Middle East, there has been a tendency to recognize more explicitly than before that Soviet forces must be prepared for a wide range of situations involving either nuclear or conventional operations.[32]

With increasing frequency over the past year or two, Soviet military spokesmen have departed from the once standard litany of immediate strategic nuclear escalation, suggesting that hostilities involving possessors of strategic nuclear arsenals might not automatically call them into use. As some military men put it, Soviet military doctrine does not "exclude" the possibility of nonnuclear warfare or of warfare limited to tactical nuclear weapons "within the framework of so-called 'local' wars," which could "take place even in Europe."[33] Another writer— without, however, mentioning Europe—stated that Soviet military doctrine today calls for the armed forces to "be prepared to conduct world war as well as limited war, both with and without the use of nuclear weapons."[34] Among the more recent expressions of the view that nuclear weapons should not be treated as "absolutes," especially in theater-force operations, was that by Marshal I. I. Yakubovsky, newly appointed Commander of the Warsaw Pact forces, who asserted in July, 1967, that the efforts of the party and the government had improved "the capability of the ground forces to conduct military operations successfully with or without the use of nuclear weapons."[35]

Although there clearly has been recognition that the theater forces should be better prepared for situations in which it might not be expedient to bring Soviet strategic nuclear power to bear, this does not mean that reliance upon Soviet nuclear arms, in either a military or political sense, has been abandoned by the new regime, as some Western observers have tended to conclude from such articles as that by Yakubovsky.[36] Not only does the continuing large Soviet investment in a strategic-force build-up testify to the contrary, but even proponents of better-balanced forces still concede priority to capabilities for conducting general nuclear war.[37] Indeed, some Soviet professional opinion has insisted that any war in a place like Europe "would immediately assume the broadest dimensions,"[38] while such a well-known military authority as Marshal V. D. Sokolovsky has upheld the view that the responsibility of Soviet strategy is to properly plan for the use "above all of missile-nuclear weapons as the main means of warfare."[39] In an article in early 1967 not long before his death, Marshal Malinovsky, the Soviet Defense Minister, stated categorically that in Soviet defense planning "first priority is being given to the strategic missile forces and atomic missile-launching submarines—forces which are the principal means of deterring the aggressor and decisively defeating him in war."[40]

On the other hand, it should be kept in mind that the present Soviet regime, in surveying such policy commitments as those which it has taken on to back the Arab nations in the Middle East imbroglio or to support elsewhere what are known in the communist lexicon as "national liberation struggles," can scarcely afford to ignore the military implications of such commitments. One of these implications would seem to be that the Soviet Union must give further attention to the maritime-air logistic elements of power needed to project its military influence into local conflict situations without having to invoke the threat of immediate nuclear holocaust, a requirement congenial to the arguments of those who urge better-rounded forces. As a matter of fact, the present regime has moved in this direction, building on measures initiated in the Khrushchevian era to improve Soviet amphibious and airlift capabilities, to train the reactivated marine forces (naval infantry) in landing operations, and to secure base arrangements growing out of Soviet military aid programs abroad.[41] The dispatch of Soviet naval units, including special landing vessels, to the Mediterranean in connection with the Arab-Israeli crisis was a conspicuous example of this trend.[42] How far the Soviet leadership may be prepared to go, however, either in actually committing its own forces in local situations or in investment of the resources necessary to make such intervention effective, remains among the critical questions on its agenda.

THE VIETNAM CRISIS AND SOVIET MILITARY POLICY

The unresolved war in Vietnam has posed for the Soviet leadership a somewhat analogous policy problem, which is further complicated by the strained state of Sino-Soviet relations. although the Brezhnev-Kosygin regime has gradually increased its support of Hanoi's military effort during the past several years, especially by furnishing SA–2 missiles and other air defense matériel, it has not sanctioned the formal commitment of Soviet military forces to the war in Southeast Asia.[43] Presumably, in the interest of avoiding a direct confrontation with the United States, the Soviet leaders would prefer to keep their military involvement limited to furnishing equipment, technical advice, and training to Hanoi's soldiery, although they have occasionally spoken of permitting "volunteers" to participate, which would still be something less than formal intervention. Beyond experimenting with volunteers, however, the Soviet leadership's room for maneuver would seem to be constricted, not only by the risk of major escalation, but by the fact that geography makes direct Soviet intervention difficult. Charges of Chinese refusal to co-operate in the overland shipment of Soviet supplies to North Vietnam have pointed up this difficulty.[44]

With regard to China, the Soviet Union evidently has had to consider military problems potentially a good deal more serious than interference with shipments to Vietnam. In the spring of 1966, for example, the Soviet leadership reportedly felt obliged to castigate Peking for telling the Chinese people that "it is necessary to prepare themselves for a military struggle with the USSR."[45] Since that time, Sino-Soviet relations have grown still more inflamed in the climate of Mao's "cultural revolution" and amid rumors of frontier clashes and mutual military precautions in the border territories of the two countries.[46] Although an outright military collision between the two communist powers is still perhaps only a remote possibility, the new Soviet regime doubtless has been obliged to reassess its military preparations with such a contingency in mind. In this connection, according to Peking's allegations, there has evidently been some internal redeployment of Soviet forces in the Asian regions bordering China.[47]

Neither the Vietnam conflict nor friction with China, however, seems to have counseled any significant redisposition of Soviet military power deployed against NATO Europe. For the Soviet leaders to consider troop withdrawals in Europe while the war in Vietnam continues would, of course, leave them vulnerable to Chinese allegations of "collusion" with the United States to ease the European situation and permit the transfer of American troops to Vietnam.[48]

Sensitivity to Chinese criticism, however, probably has no more than an incidental bearing on Soviet military deployments in Europe. The main factor seems to be that, despite the war in Vietnam and the Soviet Union's increasing stake in Asian affairs generally, priority still applies to maintaining the Soviet Union's European power position and its ability to deal with the political and military problems of Europe, not the least of which, in Soviet eyes, is that of keeping a resurgent Germany in check. Indeed, Soviet spokesmen under the new regime have re-emphasized that the main focus of Soviet interest continues to lie in Europe, where, as the Kremlin sees it, the emergence of a closer U.S.-Bonn axis within NATO allegedly constitutes the greatest threat to Soviet security.[49]

SOVIET POLICY TOWARD THE WARSAW PACT

The military role of the Warsaw Pact in Soviet policy has changed considerably since the Pact was created in 1955, largely as a diplomatic counter to West Germany's entry into NATO. Originally the Pact played only a small role in Soviet military planning, which was predicated on the assumption that Soviet theater forces would bear the burden of any military undertakings in Europe in which the Soviet Union might become involved. Around 1960–61, however, Khrushchev instituted a new policy of closer military co-operation with the East European members of the Pact, aimed both at improving the collective military efficiency of the Warsaw alliance and at tightening its political cohesion in the face of "polycentric" tendencies in East Europe.[50]

This policy has been continued under the Brezhnev-Kosygin regime. In particular, the process of joint training and modernization of the East European forces, commensurate with their enlarged responsibilities, has gone forward. Today these forces total more than 900,000 men, organized in some sixty divisions, of which about half are at combat strength and readiness, according to Western estimates.[51] Taken together with the Soviet forces deployed in East Europe—which consist of twenty divisions in East Germany, four in Hungary, and two in Poland, plus sizable tactical air elements and tactical missile units—the aggregate Warsaw Pact forces in Europe today represent a rather impressive military potential.

From the Soviet viewpoint, however, the fruits of the new policy toward the Warsaw Pact have not been entirely sweet. While the military efficiency and capability for joint action of the East European components have been improved, the political aim of tightening bloc unity and cohesion through military integration seems to have gone somewhat awry. Instead of being bound closer to Soviet interests, the East European regimes have tended to press for a more influential voice in Pact matters affecting their own interests, such as the sharing of economic and military burdens, and for the formulation of alliance strategy. Rumania, first to jump the traces in the economic field, also has taken the lead in challenging Soviet control of military affairs.[52] Perhaps partly as a response to Rumanian recalcitrance, but probably more because the focus of Soviet political and strategic interest is directed toward Germany, a rather marked regional differentiation has emerged within the Warsaw alliance between countries of the "northern" and "southern" tiers.[53]

In sum, there is growing evidence that the Warsaw Pact is evolving into an alliance beset with the familiar interplay of coalition politics, rather than a fully compliant instrument of Soviet policy. It would probably be wrong, however, to jump from this to the conclusion that the Soviet Union has ceased to exercise a predominant role in the affairs of the Warsaw bloc. The residual animosities of the cold war, skillful Soviet play upon East European fears of a resurgent Germany, and, above all, the Soviet military presence in Eastern Europe, continue to place limits on the ability of the Warsaw Pact countries to shape their own policies independent of Soviet interests.

POLITICAL-MILITARY RELATIONS UNDER THE NEW REGIME

Finally, to complete this survey of Soviet military policy, a few words are in order on the state of politico-military relations, an area of recurrent tension in the fifty years of Soviet history[54] and one which has taken on new significance in light of special problems generated by the nuclear age. Broadly speaking, these problems fall into three categories: those of maintaining political control over the armed forces in time of crisis and amid the hazards which a nuclear-missile world may hold; those of meshing industrial-military planning to cope most effectively with the resource-consuming appetite of modern weapon systems; and those of balancing military influence on Soviet policy formulation against the need of political authorities to call increasingly upon the professional expertise of the military leadership.

Signs that all of these questions are alive in the Soviet Union have cropped up under the present regime. An unusual amount of attention, for example, has been given to the command and control problem under nuclear-age conditions, ranging from its technical aspects[55] to the need for creating the "necessary politico-military organs" to ensure co-ordinated leadership of the country in emergencies, taking cognizance of the fact that "modern weapons are such that the political leadership cannot let them escape its control."[56] Lessons drawn from mistakes committed by the Soviet leadership prior to and in the initial stages of the last war have been cited also to make the point that under modern conditions, especially in the event of a war's beginning with a surprise blow, the leadership's "correct and timely evaluation of the situation prior to a war and the reaching of initial decisions" have taken on greatly increased significance.[57]

The enhanced importance, under modern conditions, of tying together more effectively the economy and the planning and procurement of weapons for the armed forces has been a theme sounded frequently in Soviet writing, often with undertones of civilian-military competition for resources.[58] A suggestion that this issue might be creating pressure for the restructuring of traditional Defense Ministry arrangements along more civilian-oriented lines than has been the case in the past arose following the death of Marshal Malinovsky in March, 1967, when there was a spate of rumors in Moscow that his successor might be Dmitri Ustinov, a party civilian with a long career in the management of defense industry.[59] Had Ustinov taken over the post customarily occupied by a military professional with command prerogatives over the armed forces, it seems likely that rather sweeping organizational changes would have followed, perhaps with the effect of giving the professional military even less immediate influence on resource decisions than it now possesses. As it turned out, however, the regime shied away from such a radical step, if it had in fact seriously contemplated it, and after a delay of about two weeks Marshal A. A. Grechko was appointed in April, 1967.[60] Grechko's background as Warsaw Pact commander for seven years and his record as a middle-of-the-roader among the Soviet marshals made him an appropriate choice for the job, especially if the regime wished to avoid a controversy that might have exacerbated the issue of military influence upon Soviet policy.

That this issue, too, remains a live one under the present regime seems to be indicated by the reappearance in print of what was a familiar dialogue in Khrushchev's day between advocates of the case for a growing military share in the formulation of military doctrine and strategy and defenders of the principle of party dominance in all aspects of military affairs. Marshal Sokolovsky, an eminent spokesman for more professional military influence on the strategic planning process during the Khrushchevian era, was one of those who again pressed this viewpoint. By way of getting across the point that strategic planning in the nuclear age demands a high level of military expertise, Sokolovsky in April, 1966, cited the American case where, according to him, "direct leadership" of the top strategic planning body, the National Security Council, "is exercised by a committee of the Joint Chiefs of Staff," even though its nominal head is the President.[61]

The other side of the argument, to be sure, also was emphatically restated. Following a Central Committee plenum that met in closed session in December, 1966, a series of forceful reminders of the party's supremacy in military affairs appeared in the Soviet press. Among the most trenchant of these was an article in early January, 1967, by Major General Zemskov, who argued that the solution of the complex tasks of modern war involving great coalitions and the energies of whole societies "falls completely within the competence of the political leadership."[62] And, as if in direct rebuttal of Sokolovsky, the article pointed out that the need for a single "supreme military-political organ" through which the political leadership would exercise its role had been recognized not only in the Soviet Union but in other countries like the United States, where "the National Security Council, headed by the President, is such a supreme governmental military-political organ."

It would hardly be warranted, however, to suggest that sparring of this kind over the respective roles of the professional military and the party bespeaks a serious challenge to the policy prerogatives of the latter. The very fact that the party can summon advocates of its view at will from within the military establishment indicates as much. In short, insofar as the evidence of the post-Khrushchevian period permits one to judge, the Soviet political leadership still enjoys the last word, as was the case during the first half-century of Soviet history.

NOTES

1. For discussion of this initial period of policy reappraisal see the present author's "Military Policy: A Soviet Dilemma," *Current History,* October, 1965, esp. pp. 201–2.

2. The announced 1965 military budget was 12.8 billion rubles, about 500 million rubles less than Khrushchev's 1964 defense budget.

3. See *Current History,* October, 1965, pp. 202–5; see also the author's *The Soviet Military Scene: Institutional and Defense Policy Considerations,* The RAND Corporation, RM–4913–PR (June, 1966), pp. 62–72.

4. Colonel I. Sidel'nikov, "V. I. Lenin on the Class Approach to Defining the Character of War," *Krasnaia zvezda* [Red Star], September 22, 1965.

5. For details see *Current History,* October, 1965, pp. 204–5.

6. *Pravda,* April 6, 1966.

7. See, for example, J. G. Godaire, "The Claim of the Soviet Military Establishment," in *Dimensions of Soviet Economic Power* (U.S. Congress, Joint Economic Committee [Washington, D.C.: Government Printing Office, 1962]), pp. 35–46; see also article by Timothy Sosnovy, who argues that buried expenditures may again be as large as the published military budget, "The Soviet Military Budget," *Foreign Affairs,* April, 1964, pp. 487–94.

8. Among other problems holding up approval of the plan was apparently that of working out a pricing system for the economic reform program under which increasing numbers of Soviet enterprises are to be converted to a system using profitability as a criterion of economic performance.

9. For typical examples see General P. A. Kurochkin, "Strengthening of Aggressiveness—A Characteristic Trait of Contemporary Imperialism," *Krasnaia zvezda,* July 9, 1965; Fedor Burlatskii, "Lessons of the Struggle for Unity," *Pravda,* June 24, 1965; Marshal R. Malinovskii, "October and the Building of the Armed Forces," *Kommunist,* no. 1 (January, 1967), p. 32.

10. See speeches by Brezhnev, *Pravda,* September 11, 1965, and *Izvestiia,* October 24, 1965; by Kosygin, *Krasnaia zvezda,* July 1, 1965; by Suslov, *Pravda,* October 31, 1965; Kosygin interview with James Reston, *New York Times,* December 8, 1965; Garbuzov in *Pravda,* December 8, 1965; Brezhnev speech at the Twenty-third Party Congress, *Pravda,* March 30, 1966.

11. For an elaborate Soviet analysis of how the combination of Soviet military power and "peace forces" abroad act to prevent a world war see Major General N. Ia. Sushko and Colonel S. A. Tiushkevich, eds., *Marksizm-Leninizm o voine i armii* [Marxism-Leninism on War and the Army], 4th ed. (Moscow: Voenizdat, 1965), pp. 83–91.

12. For discussion of the debate on war as an instrument of policy during the Khrushchev period see the present author's *Soviet Strategy at the Crossroads* (Cambridge, Mass.: Harvard University Press, 1964), pp. 70–78.

13. "On the Essence of World Missile-Nuclear War," *Kommunist vooruzhennykh sil* [Communist of the Armed Forces], no. 17 (September, 1965), pp. 50–56. Rybkin, although not widely known outside the U.S.S.R., is author of an earlier book in which he also argued that modern war, no matter how destructive, is bound to have politically significant consequences; see *Voina i politika* [War and Politics] (Moscow; Voenizdat, 1959), pp. 25–26.

14. "The Question of the Essence of War," *Krasnaia zvezda,* July 21, 1966. Among other accounts critical of views expressed in the Khrushchevian period on the unsuitability of Lenin's dictum on war and politics by such people as Talenskii, V. Zorin, and N. Nikolskii see N. Ia. Sushko and T. R. Kondratkov, eds., *Metodologicheskie problemy voennoi teorii i praktiki* [Methodological Problems of Military Theory and Tactics] (Moscow: Voenizdat, 1966), pp. 33–34.

15. "Military-Technical Superiority—The Most Important Factor in Reliable Defense of the Country," *Kommunist vooruzhennykh sil,* no. 17 (September, 1966), pp. 7–14. For a detailed analysis of the Bondarenko article see Benjamin S. Lambeth, *The Argument for Superiority: A New Voice in the Soviet Strategic Debate,* Institute for Defense Analyses, N–419(R) (Washington, D.C., 1967).

16. "On the Essence of War," *Krasnaia zvezda,* January 24, 1967; see also Bernard Gwertzman, "Russians Debate Nuclear 'Victory,'" *Washington Star,* February 21, 1967. Since the present article was written, it has been made known that the Soviet ICBM force reached 720 launchers by November, 1967, and is expected to be about 1,000 by the end of 1968.

17. Published Soviet allocations for scientific research have risen as follows: 1963—4.7 billion rubles; 1964—5.2 billion; 1965—5.4; 1966—6.5; 1967—7.2. See *Pravda,* December 11, 1962, December 17, 1963, December 8, 1965, and *Izvestiia,* December 16, 1966. A substantial amount of spending for military research is evidently included in these figures. See discussion in Nancy Nimitz, *Soviet Expenditures on Scientific Research,* The RAND Corporation, RM-3384–PR (January, 1963), pp. 12–14.

18. For accounts of Red Square displays of new equipment see: *Pravda,* November 8, 1965; *Krasnaia zvezda,* November 10, 1965; *New York Times,* November 8, 1964, May 9, 1965, November 8, 1965.

19. Among such accounts see "Russian Missiles Estimated at 400," *New York Times,* June 9, 1966; Hanson W. Baldwin, "U.S. Lead in ICBM's Is Said To Be Reduced by Buildup in Soviet Union," *ibid.,* July 14, 1966; William Beecher, "Soviet Increases Buildup of Missiles and Deploys a Defensive System," *ibid.,* November 13, 1966; *idem,* "A New Round on Missiles," *ibid.,* December 18, 1966; see also *The Military Balance, 1966–1967* (London: Institute for Strategic Studies, 1966), p. 2.

20. Richard J. Whalen, "The Shifting Equation of Nuclear Defense," *Fortune,* June 1, 1967, p. 87; George C. Wilson, "New Arms Spiral Feared," *Washington Post,* April 9, 1967.

21. *Krasnaia zvezda,* April 2, 1966. For subsequent claims that Soviet development of a mobile, solid-fuel ICBM is among the factors

upon which alleged Soviet military-technical superiority rests see the previously cited article by Colonel V. Bondarenko in *Kommunist vooru-zhennykh sil*, no. 17 (September, 1966), p. 9, and Colonel S. Tiushkevich, "The Modern Revolution in Military Affairs: Its Sources and Character," *ibid.*, no. 20 (October, 1966), p. 23.

22. As is the Soviet custom, Malinovskii gave no figures for the size of the Soviet Union's long-range bomber and missile-launching submarine forces. According to recent Western estimates, the Soviet Union possesses about 200 heavy bombers (M-4 "Bisons" and TU-95 "Bears," some of which are used as tankers) and about 35 submarines capable of firing an average of three ballistic missiles each. In addition, about 40 submarines are equipped to fire cruise-type winged missiles, which could be used against land targets but which probably have a primary mission against the adversary's naval forces; see *The Military Balance,* pp 3, 5.

23. For a recent U.S. example of such controversy see the account in the *New York Times,* July 12, 1967, of a study by the American Security Council sponsored by the House Armed Services Committee, together with an answering statement by the Department of Defense. In the Soviet case, long-standing doctrinal commitment to the goal of both quantitative and qualitative superiority has sometimes been at odds with the view that among major nuclear powers "Superiority has become a concept which has no bearing on war" (see G. Gerasimov, "Pentagonia, 1966," *International Affairs*, no. 5 [May, 1966], p. 28).

24. The first official U.S. cognizance of "considerable evidence" that the Soviet Union was deploying an antiballistic missile defense system was given by Defense Secretary Robert S. McNamara in an interview on November 10, 1966; see the *New York Times,* November 11, 1966. Among earlier analyses of Soviet ABM activity see John R. Thomas, "The Role of Missile Defense in Soviet Strategy," *Military Review,* May, 1964. According to one estimate attributed to American officials in early 1967, the Soviet Union had spent up to that time from 4 to 5 billion dollars on development of its ABM system, compared with something over 2 billion dollars spent by the United States on development of the Nike-X missile defense system; see Hedrick Smith in the *New York Times,* January 29, 1967.

25. See, for example, Hanson W. Baldwin, "A New Round Begins in the Battle of Sword vs. Shield," *New York Times,* November 27, 1966; Henry Gemmill, "The Missile Race," *Wall Street Journal,* December 14, 1966.

26. For discussion of the question of whether the second system represents a defense against missiles or aircraft see Hanson W. Baldwin, "Soviet Anti-missile System Spurs New U.S. Weapons," *New York Times,* February 5, 1967; and articles in the *Washington Post,* February 22 and 23, 1967.

27. For several years Soviet military leaders have publicly advanced claims for Soviet ABM progress, varying from outright assertions that the Soviet Union had solved the ABM problem to more guarded statements like that of Marshal Malinovskii in April, 1966, that Soviet defenses could cope with some, but not all, enemy missiles. In February,

1967, the conflicting pronouncements of several Soviet military men on this subject assumed new interest in light of the opening U.S.-Soviet dialogue on halting a potential ABM race. Two Soviet officers, Generals P. F. Batiskii and P. A. Kurochkin, took the optimistic position that Soviet ABM defenses could reliably protect the country. Shortly thereafter, two other prominent and senior military men, Marshals A. A. Grechko and V. I. Chuikov, voiced the more sober view that the Soviet Union did not yet possess defenses capable "in practice" of intercepting all in-coming enemy planes and missiles. For press accounts of these statements see "Russians Say Anti-missile System Will Protect Them From Attack," *New York Times*, February 21, 1967; "Russians Concede Missile Net Flaw," *ibid.*, February 23, 1967; "Soviet Cities Vulnerable, Red Defense Chief Says, *Washington Post*, February 23, 1967.

28. U.S. hopes of persuading the Soviet Union to agree to a mutual "freeze" of some sort on ABM deployment were voiced by President Johnson in his State of the Union message on January 10, 1967. Since then, diplomatic soundings on the matter have proceeded in a climate of alternative doubt and cautious optimism about the prospects of reaching an understanding. The general Soviet tone, set by Kosygin in an interview in London on February 10 and again during his visit to the United States in June, 1967, has been on the cool side, although the Soviets have not closed the door to possible negotiations. See: "Kosygin Is Cool to Missile Curb," *New York Times,* February 10, 1967; "Soviet ABM Shift Denied," *Washington Post*, February 18, 1967; transcript of Kosygin's news conference at the U.N., *New York Times*, June 26, 1967.

29. Among such signs was publication of a *Pravda* article on February 15, 1967, in which Kosygin was made out to be more receptive to the idea of an ABM moratorium than his London remarks warranted. Two days later Western news agencies reported that the article written by Fedor Burlatskii had been repudiated by Soviet sources who claimed that the regime's position on ABM negotiations was negative, as would be made clear in a new article. The article did not appear, suggesting an internal policy hassle. In March a strong statement of the military case for going ahead with the ABM program appeared in a *Red Star* article stressing the importance of strategic defense measures. Both the article and its timing suggested an attempt to influence the policy debate over ABM; see Lieutenant General I. Zavyalow, "On Soviet Military Doctrine," *Krasnaia zvezda*, March 31, 1967.

30. See Hedrick Smith, "Soviet Would Widen Talks Asked by U.S. on Missiles," *New York Times*, February 22, 1967; Kosygin press conference, *ibid.*, June 26, 1967. The U.S. margin over the Soviet Union in intercontinental strategic missiles, according to published figures reflecting the situation as of October, 1966, was about 1,450 land- and sea-based missiles for the United States against about 470 for the Soviet Union, a ratio of about 3 to 1; see George C. Wilson's article in the *Washington Post,* April 9, 1967.

31. In addition to steps discussed in the text, two other matters with potential implications for Soviet strategic posture are worth mentioning. One is Soviet interest in the development of an orbital delivery system,

as evidenced both by statements of military officials and by the parade display of a large missile (SCRAG), claimed to have orbital capability. The other is renewed public emphasis on civil defense preparations, accompanied in January, 1967, by reorganization of the civil defense system. See the present author's *The Soviet Military Scene*, p. 101; Colonel General V. F. Tolubko's interview in *Trud* [Labor], November 17, 1965; Raymond H. Anderson, "Soviet Places a New Emphasis on Civil Defense," *New York Times*, November 23, 1966; Marshal V. Chuikov, "The Soviets and Civil Defense: The Business of All and of Each," *Izvestiia,* June 15, 1967.

32. It should be noted that arguments urging better preparation of the Soviet theater forces for conventional operations had begun to appear even before Khrushchev's political demise; see the present author's comments in *Current History*, October, 1965, p. 206.

33. See Colonel General S. Shtemenko, *Nedelia,* no. 6 (January 31–February 6, 1965), and Major General N. Lomov, "The Influence of Soviet Military Doctrine on the Development of the Military Art," *Kommunist vooruzhennykh sil,* no. 21 (November, 1965), pp. 16, 18. Other military writers, in discussing the possibility of postponing or limiting the use of nuclear weapons, made the familiar Marxist-Leninist point that this would depend on the class interests and political goals of those involved. See Colonel V. Morozov and Lieutenant Colonel E. Rybkin, "Problems of Methodology in Military Affairs," *ibid.,* no. 4 (February, 1967), p. 93; Sushko and Kondratkov, *Metodologicheskie problemy,* pp. 107–108.

34. Colonel N. Kozlov, "The U.S.S.R. Armed Forces in the Period of Building Communism," *Kommunist vooruzhennykh sil,* no. 4 (February, 1967), p. 80.

35. "Ground Forces," *Krasnaia zvezda,* July 21, 1967; see also Major General V. Reznichenko, "Trends in the Development of Modern Battle," *ibid.,* June 28, 1967.

36. See, for example, Victor Zorza's interpretation, "Soviet Defense Shift Seen," *Washington Post,* July 22, 1967.

37. See, for example, Sushko and Kondratkov, *Metodologicheskie problemy,* p. 299; Reznichenko, *Krasnaia zvezda,* June 28, 1967.

38. Major General V. Zemskov, "The Escalation of Madness," *Krasnaia zvezda,* August 3, 1965.

39. Marshal V. D. Sokolovskii and Major General M. Cherednichenko, "On Contemporary Military Strategy," *Kommunist vooruzhennykh sil,* no. 7 (April, 1966), pp. 59–66.

40. *Kommunist,* no. 1 (January, 1967), p. 34.

41. See the present author's *The Soviet Military Scene*, pp. 121–22.

42. See "Soviet Is Sending 10 More Warships to Middle East," *New York Times*, May 31, 1967; Hanson W. Baldwin, "Soviet Naval Power," *ibid.,* June 2, 1967; "Soviet Warships To Visit 2 Egyptian Ports Today," *ibid.,* July 10, 1967.

43. For a discussion of the Soviet Union's gradually increasing military aid to Hanoi see *The Soviet Military Scene*, pp. 109–24.

44. *Ibid.,* pp. 112, 173.

45. *Ibid.*, pp. 137, 174; see also *New York Times,* March 24, 1966.

46. See Victor Zorza, "Soviet Press Clamors Over Chinese Military Threat," *Washington Post,* November 10, 1966; "Chinese Report Soviet Border Clash," *ibid.,* February 14, 1967; Charles Mohr, "Observers Speculate That Tensions Along the Soviet-Chinese Border May Be Rising," *New York Times,* February 21, 1967.

47. See remarks on this question to a group of Scandinavian journalists by Chinese Deputy Premier Chen Yi, *New York Times,* July 21, 1966.

48. For a sample of such Chinese allegations see the *Peking Review,* no. 8 (February 18, 1966), p. 10.

49. See Gromyko's remarks before the United Nations General Assembly in New York on September 23, 1966, *New York Times,* September 24, 1966. Other Soviet commentary, such as a radio broadcast by Mikhail Stepanov in September, 1966, has cited the need to strengthen the Warsaw Pact forces in Europe as a "shield against U.S.-German aggression," on the grounds that despite the war in Vietnam the main focus of U.S. military strategy has not shifted from Europe to Asia, and therefore it would be an error to accept assertions in the Western press that the "situation in Europe has stabilized and there is no threat there to world peace" (Moscow radio broadcast, September 6, 1966). These assertions were part of a general Soviet propaganda broadside in the fall of 1966 and early 1967 against the alleged threat of a new Bonn-Washington axis; see, for example, M. Voslenskii, in *Krasnaia zvezda,* September 13, 1966; Anatoli Antonov's commentary, Moscow broadcast to North America, September 26, 1966; General M. Kazakov, "Fraternal Alliance," *Pravda,* May 14, 1967.

50. For a discussion of this policy shift see the present author's "The Warsaw Pact in Evolution," in Kurt L. London, ed., *Eastern Europe in Transition* (Baltimore: The Johns Hopkins Press, 1966), pp. 207–25.

51. *The Military Balance,* pp. 6–8; Raymond L. Garthoff, "The Military Establishment," *East Europe,* September, 1965, pp. 13–14. For a critical analysis of the much-publicized Warsaw Pact joint field exercises, which questions their military utility mainly on the grounds that they have been conducted by relatively small formations of Pact forces, in contrast with the NATO practice of wide-scale unit participation in annual exercises, see Stanley Dziuban, *The Warsaw Pact Maneuvers: Proof of Readiness or Psychological Warfare?* Institute for Defense Analyses, N–369(R) (August, 1966).

52. See the present author's *Soviet Military Power and European Security,* RAND Paper P-3429 (August, 1966), pp. 38–41. Among reported Rumanian demands was one that command of the Warsaw Pact forces be rotated to include non-Soviet officers. A delay of some three months in appointing Marshal Yakubovskii to succeed Marshal Grechko as Pact commander in July, 1967, tended to bear out speculation that the command issue had arisen within the Pact.

53. The "northern-tier" countries—East Germany, Poland, Czechoslovakia, and the Soviet Union—have frequently been alluded to by Communist sources as the "first strategic echelon" of the Warsaw Pact. These, of course, are the countries most immediately involved, politically and

militarily, with the question of West German aspirations in Central Europe. In the Vlatva joint exercise in Czechoslovakia in September, 1966, Hungary for the first time participated on a token basis with the other northern-tier countries, while Poland did not directly take part. Developments in Czechoslovakia in 1968 under the Dubček reform government, which occurred after preparation of this article, have raised a whole new set of problems for the Soviet Union, especially since the Czech crisis threatens the integrity of the northern-tier grouping.

54. For an exhaustive treatment of this question see Roman Kolkowicz, *The Soviet Military and the Communist Party* (Princeton: Princeton University Press, 1967).

55. See Tiushkevich, in *Kommunist vooruzhennykh sil*, no. 20 (October, 1966), pp. 22–23; Sushko and Kondratkov, *Metodologicheskie problemy*, pp. 69, 243–65, 279. In the latter volume it was stated that technical innovations in command and control constitute the third major stage in the military-technical revolution of modern times, the first two stages being the introduction of nuclear weapons and of missiles, respectively.

56. See Major General V. Zemskov, "For the Theoretical Seminar: An Important Factor for Victory in War," *Krasnaia zvezda*, January 5, 1967; see also Grudinin, *ibid.*, July 21, 1966; Lieutenant General Zavyalov, *ibid.*, March 31, 1967.

57. Marshal A. Grechko, "25 Years Ago," *Voenno-istoricheskii zhurnal* [Military-Historical Journal], no. 6 (June, 1966), pp. 10, 15.

58. An emphatic statement of the need to work out a co-ordinated "military-economic policy" to insure weapons production in "properly substantiated proportions" appeared in an April, 1967, article by Colonel A. Babin, who also stressed strict party control of such "complex tasks"; see "The Party—Leader of the U.S.S.R. Armed Forces," *Krasnaia zvezda*, April 6, 1967. A more recent treatment of the question, with emphasis upon "correct and effective use of resources" to "insure solution of all military-economic tasks," was offered by Colonel Ia. Vlasevich, "Modern War and the Economy," *Kommunist vooruzhennykh sil*, no. 12 (June, 1967), pp. 27–33; see also Malinovskii, *Kommunist*, no. 1 (January, 1967), p. 34; Sushko and Kondratkov, *Metodologicheskie problemy*, p. 79; Zavyalov, *Krasnaia zvezda*, March 30, 1967 (first of two articles).

59. See Stephen S. Rosenfeld, "Kremlin Looking for a McNamara To Rule Its Brass," *Washington Post*, April 23, 1967; Raymond H. Anderson, "Soviet Affirms Party Rule Over the Military Forces," *New York Times*, April 7, 1967.

60. At the same time that Grechko's appointment to succeed Malinovskii was announced on April 12, it was also made known that three other officers had been elevated in the Defense Ministry hierarchy. They were Marshal Yakubovskii and Generals S. L. Sokolov and I. G. Pavlovskii, men in their middle fifties. This move had the effect of introducing younger blood into the top military echelon, which has been dominated by an over-aged generation of World War II marshals.

61. Sokolovskii and Cherednichenko, *Kommunist vooruzhennykh sil,* no. 7 (April, 1966), pp. 62–63. Another example of the tendency to stress the importance of the military contribution to doctrine and strategy may be found in the book edited by Sushko and Kondratkov, *Metodologicheskie problemy,* pp. 93–95.

62. See the previously cited article by Zemskov, *Krasnaia zvezda,* January 5, 1967. Another emphatic restatement of the thesis of party supremacy appeared in Colonel Babin's article in *Krasnaia zvezda,* April 6, 1967. For a discussion of the similar dialogue in Khrushchev's day see the present author's *Soviet Strategy at the Crossroads,* pp. 100–9.

CHAPTER 4

The Soviet Economy

Structural Changes in Soviet Agriculture, 1917–67

Otto Schiller

Stalinist Industrial Development in Soviet Russia

John P. Hardt and Carl Modig

Structural Changes in Soviet Agriculture, 1917–67

Otto Schiller

Two distinct stages can be discerned in the agrarian policy of communist regimes: the initial stage immediately after the seizure of power, a stage which in given circumstances may last a number of years; and the second stage, in which the so-called socialist transformation of agriculture is effected. In the first stage the agrarian policy of communist regimes is determined by the revolutionary slogans used in propaganda or in underground activities prior to the seizure of power. It is inevitable, therefore, that structural changes which flow from such a policy do not accord with doctrinaire communist concepts of a socialist agrarian structural pattern. Communists can begin to implement these concepts only in the second stage, and even then they are obliged to make certain concessions—compromises with dogma in order to meet urgent, vital requirements of food supply for the population. The conflict between dogmatic goals and the need for pragmatic concessions to economic realities continues to characterize the agrarian policies of communist countries today.

THE POST-REVOLUTIONARY PERIOD

The agrarian structure in Russia at the time of the October Revolution was still largely feudalistic in character, although this traditional order had undergone some changes in connection with the gradual materialization of Stolypin's agrarian reforms announced in 1906. In the years before the Revolution in tsarist Russia there were 152 million hectares of land in the possession of landlords or nonpeasant landowners and 215 million in the hands of peasants, including 80 million hectares belonging to well-to-do peasants, or kulaks.[1] If agricultural land alone is considered, however, the percentage owned by the peasants was much higher, since a large proportion of the landlords' holdings consisted of forest land. The average size of a land-holding in 1905 was 534 hectares for aristocratic families, 655 for non-aristocratic landlords, and approximately 12 hectares for the peasants.[2]

Stolypin's agrarian reform did not result in major structural changes in terms of the size of operational holdings. These reform measures brought about a change first of all in the ownership structure, in that they aimed at a gradual abolition of the old Russian field community, the mir. Before the October Revolution more than 2 million peasants were freed from the ties of community ownership of land. Another 2.3 million peasants received their land as private property on the basis of the new legal provisions without specifically applying for it. Approximately 3 million peasant farmsteads did not belong to the field communities in the period prior to Stolypin's reform. Thus, at the end of the precommunist era less than half of about 13-14 million peasant farmsteads of European Russia were bound by the rules of the mir communities, which included periodic redistribution of land.[3] This fact is of some importance since it is fairly widely believed that because of the old tradition of community ownership of land the Russian peasants were mentally well prepared for the collective use of land subsequently introduced by the communist regime.

In the first days of the October Revolution the communist regime issued a decree abolishing landlord ownership immediately and without compensation.[4] The rights to land were basically regulated by the law of February 19, 1918.[5] Not all of the expropriated land was distributed among the peasants for individual use. Part of it remained under state administration.

Precise data are lacking in regard to the amount of land formerly owned by landlords which was distributed among the peasants for individual use at the time of the October Revolution. Moreover, the distribution of land was carried out not in a regulated fashion but chiefly through so-called black redistribution— another factor complicating any estimate of the amount of land involved. It has been estimated that approximately 50 million hectares in the European part of Russia were transferred to individual peasants. This means that for a significant part of the agricultural land a fundamental change in the size of operational holdings had taken place—that is, a transition from large-scale farming on big private farms to small-scale peasant farming. It must be borne in mind, however, that, even before the October Revolution, approximately half of the agricultural land held by landlords had been leased to peasants. For this part of the agricultural area, only a change of ownership rights took place, with little change in the actual size of the operational holdings.

THE WAR-COMMUNISM YEARS

After the October Revolution came the turbulent years of civil war and communist experiments with "war communism." At that time the boundaries of the territory under the communist regime were not definitely fixed, nor were conditions stabilized in the territory ruled by the communist regime. The changes which took place in the agrarian structure at that time can be described only in broad terms. It certainly was not possible to think of a total transformation of the agrarian structure in accordance with communist or socialist concepts—that is, to carry out a socialization of agriculture. Agricultural production was based almost exclusively on the small-scale peasant farms. Their productive potential was greatly reduced by rigorous measures for compulsory delivery enacted by the regime. Only a very small sector of agriculture was under state administration, namely, old state lands and some former private large-scale farms not redistributed among the peasants. State farms at that time cultivated less than 5 per cent of the total agricultural land.

Early experiments with the establishment of collective farms were carried out in this sector. A relatively small number of so-called agricultural communes were established on former private large-scale farms, using existing buildings. In accordance with the economic principles of war communism the methods adopted in these communes were genuinely communistic. The majority of the agricultural communes established by small groups of former participants in the war, or partisans, could be maintained only by permanent state subsidies. Their part in the total agricultural production was very small. But certain structural changes took place in the peasant sector of agriculture, too. Because of the disastrous economic conditions, a certain deurbanization had taken place—that is, a certain migration of the urban population to rural areas. The demands made on the land increased accordingly, and the number of small-scale farms increased while their average size gradually decreased.

Some other changes in agrarian structure evolved in the peasant sector, with partly unfavorable consequences. The population at the time was increasing by an average of 2.2 per cent annually,[6] and since there was almost no progress in industrialization, the additional population remained for the most part in the agricultural sector. The percentage of the total population that could be classed as agricultural was not any smaller at the end of this period (81.6 per cent in 1928) than it had been at the beginning[7] (approximately 80 per cent).[8] In absolute figures this meant an increase in agricultural population of about 7 million persons.[9] The number of peasant holdings increased from 21.0 million in 1918[10] to 25.6 million in 1928, and the average size of holdings went down from about 7 hectares to 4 hectares (4.3 in 1928).[11]

In the same period, in the peasant sector of agriculture a certain differentiation also had taken place, since it was possible for the active elements of the peasantry to increase the size of their holdings. Some scope for such increases was made possible by the fact that the peasants were permitted to lease un-used state land; and there were no restrictions on the increase of private animal husbandry, for which neighboring state lands could be used as pastures. In these circumstances a new upper stratum was re-established among the peasants—formed partly from the old peasant upper stratum—which resulted in a new group of relatively large peasant farms of some economic strength, the so-called kulak farms.

THE NEW COURSE IN AGRARIAN POLICY

Such a development unquestionably was not in accord with the conceptions of the ruling communist regime. When the New Economic Policy was abolished with the start of the five-year plans, an entirely new course of agrarian policy was also ini-tiated, characterized by compulsory collectivization. The pri-mary stated motivation for this policy change was the necessity to fight the kulak peasants. It was argued that these were counterrevolutionary elements representing a major threat to the Soviet regime. The present author, who at that time lived in a Soviet village, would like to say that one could not observe any conscious and active counterrevolutionary activity in the upper strata of the villages. The alleged sabotage of compulsory deliveries, especially grain deliveries, was probably not an or-ganized political action but mainly the result of the fact that economic and price conditions—especially the decrease in purchasing power of the chervonets existing at that time—were no stimulus for the peasant to produce more than he needed for his own and his immediate family's consumption.

The new course of agrarian policy started in 1929 brought a fundamental change in the agrarian structure. This was the most radical change in agrarian structure yet to have been effected anywhere in the world. Within less than five years the Soviet Union was transformed from a country primarily of small hold-ings into a country in which the agricultural area was almost exclusively operated by large-scale farms. In theory the process of collectivization of Soviet agriculture was concluded only at a later date. Soviet statistics have cited a residual group of individual peasant farms until quite recently. But from the statistical data given for these holdings it is evident that most of them existed only on paper. Since 87.4 per cent of the land in the peasant sector of Soviet agriculture was worked in collective farms in 1934,[12] it can be stated that the process of collectivization was for the most part concluded within the short period of five years.

Those five years were of decisive importance to the structure of Soviet agriculture. It was in those years that the institutional framework for collective agriculture was developed into what were for all practical purposes its final basic forms. In the initial stage of collectivization an intermediate form existed—a form in between individual and collective farming, the so-called co-operative for the joint use of land, or TOZ.[13] In this transitional form the peasant holdings, which up until that time were typical of Soviet villages, continued to exist; with the transition to the so-called artel these peasant holdings disappeared, except for a very small remnant of subsidiary private plots and private livestock. With the introduction of "Stalin's model bylaws of the agricultural artel" in 1935, the artel became the only valid institutional form for the collective farm, identical to what is usually called the kolkhoz.[14] The agricultural communes mentioned above were abolished at this time or were transformed into ordinary kolkhozy.

The result of this rigorous process of transformation of Soviet agriculture must be examined with reference to the changes in its size structure. It was a natural consequence that in the initial stage the operational units of collective agriculture were relatively small. The chairmen of the managing committees of the new kolkhoz units—the actual farm managers—at the beginning were for the most part ordinary peasants elected by the members. Certainly they had no experience in managing large-scale farms. The larger the size of the operational holding, the greater were the difficulties for these new kolkhoz managers, who were confronted with entirely new tasks.

In those parts of the country where relatively small villages existed, usually an entire village settlement was made into one collective farm. In the large villages of the steppe regions of the southern and southeast European parts of the country it was not unusual for more than one collective farm to be established in a village. After the completion of the phase of compulsory collectivization the Soviet agricultural sector in 1934 consisted of a total of 241,000 collective farms[15] created from 25.6 million previously existing peasant farms. This means that on an average approximately 100 individual peasant farms were amalgamated to form one new collective farm. At that time the sown area in a collective farm averaged approximately 400 hectares (421 hectares in 1934).

Changes also took place in the state sector of agriculture. In 1928 the sovkhoz share of the total sown area[16] was approximately 1.5 per cent, and the average size of these farms was about 1,200 hectares of sown area. By 1940 the share of the sovkhozy in the sown area had increased to 7.7 per cent and the average size of the sovkhozy to 2,800 hectares of sown area.[17]

As noted above, a small portion of the former individual farms remained untouched from the outset—the subsidiary private holdings of the kolkhoz peasants. The size of private plots—not privately owned, but privately used—was restricted to from 0.25 to 0.5 hectares, with up to one hectare allowed in exceptional cases, and private animal husbandry in these subsidiary plots was restricted by the provisions of model bylaws to, for example, one cow or two sows. It is often assumed that the subsidiary private holdings of kolkhoz peasants were introduced under the model bylaws of 1935;[18] in fact, they existed from the beginning of collectivization, as can be seen from the first model bylaws of 1930.[19] And a private sector still coexists with the state and collective sectors. Owing to its remarkable efficiency—much greater than in either of the other sectors—the private sector continues to play an important role in supplying the Soviet population with foodstuffs. It is significant that nearly all kolkhoz peasants make use of their rights to work a subsidiary private plot of land and to private animal husbandry. The number of subsidiary private holdings is nearly equal to the number of kolkhoz peasant households. In the last prewar years (1937–40) this number was approximately 18 million.[20]

Through the annexation of former Polish land and other territories of Eastern Europe where individual peasant farms prevailed, the number of peasant households in the postwar years increased considerably. From 1950 to 1956 this number remained more or less stable, at approximately 20 million households. Only in the last decade has it gradually decreased. In 1965 there were approximately 15.4 million peasant households with subsidiary private holdings.[21]

The size of the subsidiary private holdings of the kolkhoz peasants is restricted by the provisions of the bylaws within relatively narrow limits. Therefore, only minor changes developed in regard to average size. Exact data cannot be provided, because Soviet statistics do not include a separate figure for that part of the private sector which belongs to groups other than the kolkhoz peasants (to the sovkhoz workers and other rural or urban owners of private livestock). But it is remarkable that the average size of all subsidiary private plots was 0.49 hectares in the initial stage of collective agriculture (1938), 0.29 in 1955, and 0.26 in 1962.[22] Similarly, there are few changes to be noted in regard to private animal husbandry. In 1940 there were only 0.68 cows in one subsidiary holding; in 1953 there were 0.56 and in 1962, 0.59.[23] The figures indicate that the keeping of more than one cow, which under the model bylaws is allowed in certain regions specializing in animal husbandry, is restricted to a relatively small number of exceptional cases.

It is well known that in 1956, under a new legal provision, the kolkhoz farmers were given the right to effect limited modifications of their bylaws by decision of a general meeting.[24] Theoretically, therefore, it is possible to exceed the norms for the size of subsidiary plots and for the number of animals as defined in the model bylaws. That the kolkhoz peasants have made use of this right only to a very limited degree is clear from the statistical data on the average size of the subsidiary private plots and on private animal husbandry.

The new course of agrarian policy after 1929 resulted not only in compulsory collectivization of the peasant sector of agriculture but also in intensified activities in the state sector of agriculture. There was large-scale organization of new sovkhozy, which—unlike the old sovkhozy established in former private large-scale farms—specialized in certain branches of production, such as grain cultivation, dairying, the fattening of cattle and pigs, the production of poultry and eggs, and so on. Through such specialization, which is a typical feature of the new sovkhoz development, it was also possible to expand farms to a size beyond the previous norm. Confirmed communists are often inclined to believe that the bigger the farming units, the better able they are to apply modern techniques. But, undoubtedly, for the so-called economies of scale there is an upper limit. This is especially true of agricultural enterprises, where flexibility to adapt to such unpredictable natural factors as weather conditions is of greatest importance to the success of management. The idea of fixing an upper limit to the size of farming units at that time was not seriously considered by the Soviet leaders.

Special organizations, the so-called trusts, were charged with the establishment and guidance of new sovkhoz farms (as, for instance, the Sernotrust with the establishment of grain farms, the so-called grain factories). Some of these grain sovkhozy established by the Sernotrust in the steppe regions of southern and southeastern Russia were of very large dimensions. They typified the then prevalent trend toward making the farms as large as possible. The sovkhoz Gigant in the neighborhood of Salsk, in the Don region, became well known as an outstanding example of the grain factories. Through successive land allocations the size of this grain sovkhoz eventually reached more than 160,000 hectares.[25]

Only when, as a result of such exaggerations, the economic disadvantages and deficiencies of oversized farms became quite obvious were some countermeasures carried out. Stalin himself condemned the so-called gigantomania.[26] Oversized sovkhozy were subdivided into smaller units by developing their sectors or departments into independent sovkhozy. A similar situation developed in the sovkhozy that specialized in animal husbandry: the establishment of oversized farms created the managerial problem of nonsurveyable units, and the increased danger of disease had unfavorable consequences.[27] Certain norms were established for the size of sovkhozy, to be exceeded only in exceptional cases.

THE WAR YEARS AND THE EARLY POSTWAR PERIOD

During the war, basic changes in the size structure of Soviet agricultural enterprises obviously did not occur. For understandable reasons there are no statistical data available for these years. Only in the private sector of agriculture were there possibly some changes, since during wartime the Soviet authorities did not strictly oppose the tendencies of kolkhoz peasants to enlarge their private plots and private animal husbandry beyond the prescribed limits. In many places private plots were expanded through the individual initiative of kolkhoz peasants. After the war, special laws were enforced whereby all enlargements of private plots over the legal norm were nullified. The fact that such legislation became necessary shows how strong the tendencies of kolkhoz peasants to enlarge their private plots had been.

Through the incorporation in 1939 and 1940 of new peasant-farm territories in Eastern Europe, the peasant farmers' share of the total agricultural area increased to nearly 10 per cent. But this share was diminished again in the first years after the war, when agriculture in the new territories was collectivized in a relatively short period of time. As early as 1953 there were almost no peasant farms within the new boundaries of the Soviet Union.

Following the first years of the postwar period, the establishment of large-scale kolkhozy marked a new phase in the process of structural change. The result was a significant change in the size structure of Soviet agricultural enterprises. In the course of this process small kolkhozy were systematically amalgamated into larger operational units. This was the case especially in the regions of central and northern Russia, where up to that time relatively small kolkhozy had existed. Just as in these districts several village settlements belonged to one administrative village community, now some kolkhozy were merged to form one large-scale kolkhoz unit. This process was started in 1950, and in the course of a single year the number of kolkhoz units was reduced by nearly one-half—from approximately 250,000 to 123,000.[28] The amalgamation of the farms continued, with the number decreasing from year to year. Finally, in 1965 the astonishingly small number of only 36,000 kolkhozy existed.[29] Correspondingly, the average size of these farms increased steadily and reached approximately 2,800 hectares of sown area in 1965.[30] This average appears to indicate that in many cases the dimensions of a kolkhoz were much greater than is reasonable from the managerial point of view. The present author has mentioned this fact in earlier published articles and has expressed the view that a retrograde development may one day take place.[31]

It is astonishing that, despite the previously mentioned bad experience in the initial stage of establishing large-scale farms, similar tendencies toward gigantomania were fostered without hesitation after the war. The revival of gigantomania was especially evident in the state sector of agriculture. During the Khrushchev era two agrarian policy measures were working in this direction: first, the "new-lands campaign" in the steppe regions of northern Kazakhstan and southern Siberia, and, second, the systematic enlargement of the old sovkhozy through allocations to them of additional land out of the state fund or through new investments to increase their livestock. In the "new-lands campaign," preference from the beginning was given to the sovkhoz form of farm enterprise rather than to the kolkhoz form.

The regions where the new lands were reclaimed were sparsely settled areas where almost no permanent settlements had formerly existed, but where the land had been used for nomadic animal husbandry. There were, therefore, only limited possibilities for increasing the sown area by expanding the use of land in existing kolkhoz units. If for this purpose a new resettlement of people on the land was necessary, in most cases the sovkhoz pattern was more suitable because the new settlers belonged chiefly to the younger generation. Enlisted by the Komsomol, they came for the most part from urban environments and brought with them little of the old peasant tradition that in the long-settled areas still plays an important role among the kolkhoz population. Through these processes the number of sovkhozy has increased considerably since the beginning of the "new-lands campaign" in 1954.

The average size of the sovkhozy also has gone up. In 1955 there were some 5,100 sovkhozy in the Soviet Union, with an average sown area of 5,000 hectares; in 1965 the number of sovkhozy was around 11,700, with an average sown area of approximately 7,600 hectares.[32] As a result of this development the share of the sovkhoz sector in total agricultural production has increased considerably. In former years the share of the total sown area belonging to the sovkhoz sector remained fairly constant, at about 10 per cent, but after 1954 the percentage increased rapidly. This was attributed in part to the fact that for a certain period, from 1957 to 1962, an interesting process was going on which in Soviet literature has been mentioned only in passing—the so-called sovkhozization, or the transformation of kolkhoz into sovkhoz units. It is significant that 47 per cent of the sown area belonged to the sovkhoz sector in 1965, while in certain branches of production this percentage is still much lower—about 30 per cent in meat production, for example.[33]

The considerable expansion of the sovkhoz sector, which probably will continue in the years to come, is encouraged by the fact that the convergence of the two forms of farm enterprise has made appreciable progress. To date this has been reflected mainly in an evolution of the kolkhoz form towards the sovkhoz form, not the other way around. The wage system of the kolkhozy, for instance, has been changed by the payment of a guaranteed minimum as an advance for the final redistribution of profits. In practice this new system results, in many cases, in the kolkhoz peasants' being paid in a similar way and with rates similar to those of the sovkhoz workers.[34] The dissolution of machine-tractor stations, begun in 1958, and the purchase of machinery by the kolkhozy also resulted in a tendency of kolkhoz toward sovkhoz status.

The considerable growth of the sovkhoz sector should be taken into account in analyzing the unsatisfactory performance of the Soviet agrarian system. We are accustomed to using arguments that refer mainly to the peculiarities of collective, as compared with individual, farming. It must be recognized, however, that for the essential part of Soviet agriculture represented by the sovkhoz sector, another yardstick has to be used—namely, comparison with other state farms, of which a few examples exist throughout the noncommunist world. By this comparison it becomes evident that the unsatisfactory accomplishments of Soviet agriculture are attributable not only to the particular deficiencies of the kolkhoz system but also to general deficiencies of the Soviet system, deficiencies that have their counterparts in other branches of the Soviet economy.

ECONOMIC REFORM AND PRAGMATISM

The basic questions of economic reform which have been under discussion in the Soviet Union for the last few years, and which have already led to some practical measures, are of great importance for the further development of the size structure of the Soviet agricultural system. It seems to have been acknowledged that the concept of very large operational units of agricultural enterprises, under central planning and central administration, does not lead to satisfactory economic results. Steps toward decentralization were taken under the Khrushchev regime but were curbed again later.

New experiments are being carried out in the reorientation of enterprises away from the criteria of plan fulfillment and gross production, in the direction of marketed production and profit. Moreover, new emphasis is laid on the principle that, in the present phase of development, material incentives must be promoted by every possible means. In this connection the question has also been raised as to whether the size of agricultural enterprises accords with the requirements of the new orientation. For the first time the question of the optimal size of an agricultural enterprise has recently been discussed in a more or less undogmatic fashion in Soviet literature. Where in former years it was difficult to discuss this question with Soviet agricultural economists at international conferences,[35] such discussion now seems to be possible. There are some interesting recent Soviet publications in which it is frankly admitted that a number of sovkhoz and kolkhoz units are too large to operate profitably.[36] Thus, for instance, Rumyantseva states that the "great differentiation in the size of kolkhozy is not only based on objective reasons." It is, as well, the "consequence of the subjectivism with which the local authorities have decided the question of amalgamation of collective farms." As a result "there are at present many oversized kolkhozy which are difficult to manage." Rumyantseva says that in Kirov *oblast*, for instance, there are kolkhozy comprising more than 35 village settlements. Only 20 per cent of the kolkhoz units in that province are of the normal size. Half of the kolkhoz units in the Kirov *oblast* are said to be subsidized. The conclusion of the Soviet author is that "the superiority of the large-scale farms as compared with the farms of smaller size is obvious only up to a certain size limit." The author states that, therefore, "the very large farms often are less effective than farms of smaller size.[37]

These statements are quoted at length because it is significant for the present situation in the Soviet Union that even confirmed communists may arrive at such conclusions. The leading institute of agricultural economics, the "All-Union Scientific Research Institute of Agricultural Economics" (WNIIESCh), and the Institute of Economics of the Academy of Science of the Soviet Union have developed a joint study on the optimal size of agricultural holdings.[38] The concluding chapter of that book also takes up the question of how to effect the transition to agricultural enterprises of optimal size. The present author had the opportunity to discuss these questions with his colleagues in Moscow in 1966 and learned that here and there a reduction in the size of kolkhoz and sovkhoz units is already in progress. It is true that this interesting process apparently has yet to be described in Soviet writings. It is significant, however, that according to Soviet statistics in the last two years, the total number of agricultural enterprises has for the first time shown an increase. The following figures reflect this development:

	1962	1963	1964	1965	1966
Kolkhozy	39,700	38,800	37,600	36,300	36,500
Sovkhozy	8,570	9,176	10,078	11,681	12,196
Total	48,270	47,976	47,678	47,981	48,696

SOURCES: *Narodnoie khoziaistvo SSSR v 1962 godu*, p. 352; *Narodnoie khoziaistvo SSSR v 1963 godu*, p. 341; *Narodnoie khoziaistvo SSSR v 1965 godu*, pp. 405 and 422; and *SSSR v tsifrakh 1966 godu*, pp. 109 and 111.

An effort to deal pragmatically with the question of the optimal size of agricultural holdings is clearly a typical feature of the new course of Soviet agrarian policy. Symptomatic of the pragmatic approach are recent discussions of whether a subdivision of large-scale farms into relatively small work gangs or links may be advisable. The key question is how much independence such work gangs may be given without contradicting the still accepted principles of farming in large-scale units and of collective organization of agricultural work.

Experiments are being made with the organization of small work gangs or mechanized working links of not more than from four to six workers. The report of Saglada on such an experiment in a Ukrainian kolkhoz has been mentioned in the Soviet press,[39] and another experiment in a sovkhoz in northern Kazakhstan, carried out by chief agronomist Shulin, has also been recounted.[40] Both reports were given much attention in the Western press. A description of the discussion going on in the Soviet Union on the basic question of work gangs has been provided recently by R. Laird.[41]

Usually, however, the subsections—gangs or links—are still units of substantial size. It is reported, for instance, that in the sovkhozy of the new land region the gangs having from five to ten tractors are allocated an area of more than 1,000 hectares (in some cases more than 2,000) during the period of crop rotation.[42] Even the smaller units, the links (or *zveno*), usually work with from two to four tractors on a corresponding area of some 100 hectares.[43] It seems that some oversized farms are now reduced in size, and in some cases subsections may even become independent farming units.

The discussions in progress in the Soviet Union on the importance of the work links and the attempts to take advantage of land use in small groups by way of a subdivision of large-scale farms are instructive for an approach to the agrarian question in developing countries. Specialists in communist countries who are well trained in Marxist thinking are inclined to overestimate the advantages of economics of scale. It is significant, therefore, that the advantages of decentralization have recently come under discussion in these countries as well. It seems to have been realized that the smaller operational unit may sometimes be superior to the larger, oversized one and that use should be made of the incentive system to encourage personal interest if the work is done by small groups or by individuals in small units.

In connection with this new development in Soviet agrarian policy, there has been discussion in Western circles of whether a return to individual farming might be possible in the Soviet Union along the lines of developments in past years in two other communist countries, Yugoslavia and Poland. It has been asked whether this might not be considered a final remedy for the chronic shortcomings of Soviet agriculture. In previous writings the present author has expressed the view that such a development can hardly be expected, not only for political, but also for practical, reasons.[44]

It may also be stated that great changes in the size structure of the Soviet agricultural system are not to be expected in the foreseeable future. It can be assumed that in connection with the reduction of oversized sovkhoz units the number of large-scale farms may increase to a certain extent and their average size may go down. The tendency toward convergence of the two basic forms of farm enterprise may continue—with the state sector proportionately increasing—to a point at which there may be little difference between the state sector and the kolkhoz sector. Although at present the private sector is being promoted to some extent, it must be assumed that its share in the total production of agriculture will gradually decrease.

NOTES

1. "Tsentralnoe statisticheskoe upravlenie pri Sovete Ministrov SSSR," *Narodnoie khoziaistvo SSSR v 1958 godu* (Moscow, 1959), p. 345.
2. Geroid T. Robinson, *Rural Russia under the Old Regime,* 2d ed. (New York: Macmillan, 1949), pp. 134–35.
3. B. Brutzkus, "Agrarentwicklung und Agrarrevolution in Russland," *Osteuropa-Institut in Breslau* (Berlin), n.s., no. 2 (1925), pp. 94–96.
4. *Sbornik dokumentov po zemelnomu zakonodatelstvu SSSR i RSFSR 1917–1954* (Moscow, 1954), pp. 11–12.
5. *Ibid.,* pp. 23–32.
6. *Statisticheskii spravochnik SSSR za 1928 godu* (Moscow, 1929), p. 74.
7. At that time the rural population was almost identical with the agricultural population.
8. *Narodnoie khoziaistvo SSSR v 1963 godu* (Moscow, 1965), p. 7; Warren W. Eason, "Labor Force," in *Economic Trends in the Soviet Union,* ed. Abram Bergson and Simon Kusnets (Cambridge, Mass.: Harvard University Press, 1966), p. 72.
9. *Narodnoie khoziaistvo SSSR v 1963 godu,* p. 7.
10. V. P. Danilov, *Sozdanie material'no-teknicheskikh predposylok kollektivizatsii selskogo khoziaistva v SSSR,* Akademia Nauk SSSR, Institut Istorii (Moscow, 1957), p. 26.
11. *Statisticheskii spravochnik SSSR za 1928 godu* (Moscow, 1929), p. 82; *Narodnoie khoziaistvo SSSR v 1958 godu,* p. 345; "Narkomzem SSSR i Narkomsovkhozov," *Sel'skoe khoziaistvo SSSR, Ezhegodnik 1935* (Moscow, 1935), p. 12.
12. "Narkomzem SSSR i Narkomsovkhozov."
13. TOZ = *Tovarishchestvo po sovmestnoi obrabotke zemli.*
14. *Istoria kolkhoznogo prava,* vol. 1 (Moscow, 1959), pp. 427ff.
15. "Narkomzem SSSR i Narkomsovkhozov."
16. The present author is of the opinion that for the purposes of comparison the "sown area" (*posewnaja ploshchiad*) is the most appropriate criterion. Other criteria, such as "total area" or "cultivated" and "cultivable" area, may be neglected for our purposes.
17. "Tsentralnoe statisticheskoe upravlenie pri Sovete Ministrov SSSR," *Sel'skoe khoziaistvo SSSR* (Moscow, 1960), pp. 41, 128, 49, and 130, respectively.
18. *Istoria kolkhoznogo prava,* vol. 1.
19. Otto Schiller, *Die Kollektivierung in der Sowjetunion,* East European Studies, n.s., vol. 8 (Berlin: Ost-Europa-Verlag, 1931), pp. 117–23.
20. *Narodnoie khoziaistvo SSSR v 1958 godu,* p. 349.
21. *Narodnoie khoziaistvo SSSR v 1965 godu,* p. 257.
22. *Kolkhozy vo vtoroi staliniskoi piatiletke* (Moscow: Gosplan, 1939), pp. 9 and 11; see N. Jasny, *The Socialized Agriculture of the*

USSR (Stanford, Calif.: Stanford University Press, 1949), p. 341; *Narodnoie khoziaistvo SSSR v 1960 godu*, pp. 361 and 389; and *Narodnoie khoziaistvo SSSR v 1962 godu*, pp. 243 and 330.

23. *Sel'skoe khoziaistvo SSSR*, pp. 266–67; *Narodnoie khoziaistvo SSSR v 1962 godu*, pp. 225 and 303; and *Narodnoie khoziaistvo SSSR v 1958 godu*, p. 349.

24. Decree of the Central Committee of the Communist party and the Council of Ministers of the U.S.S.R. of March 6, 1956; *Izvestiia*, no. 60 (March 10, 1956).

25. Otto Schiller, *Das Agrarsystem der Sowjetunion* (Tübingen: Böhlau-Verlag, 1960), p. 31.

26. Decree of December 22, 1933; see Jasny, *Socialized Agriculture*, p. 255; *Sotsialisticheskoe zemledelie*, January 28, 1934.

27. Jasny, *Socialized Agriculture*, pp. 255–56.

28. *Sotsialisticheskoe zemledelie*, March 3, 1951; *Sel'skoe khoziaistvo SSSR*, p. 50.

29. *Narodnoie khoziaistvo SSSR v 1965 godu*, p. 405.

30. *Ibid.*, p. 413.

31. Otto Schiller, "Das Betriebsgrössenproblem in der sowjetischen Landwirtschaft," *Osteuropa-Wirtschaft*, no. 1 (1963), pp. 1–8.

32. *Narodnoie khoziaistvo SSSR v 1958 godu*, p. 521.

33. *SSSR v tsifrakh v 1966 godu*, p. 91.

34. Otto Schiller, "Auflösung der sowjetischen MTS," *Osteuropa*, no. 4 (1958), pp. 217–23, and "Grundsätzliche Fragen der MTS-Reform," *Osteuropa*, no. 7/8 (1958), pp. 489–92.

35. *Proceedings of the Twelfth International Conference of Agricultural Economists* (London: Oxford University Press, 1966), pp. 445–47.

36. G. Kotov, "Optimalnye razmery sovkhozov—vazhneishee uslovie ratsional'noi organizatsii proizvodstva," *Ekonomika sel'skogo khoziaistva*, no. 2 (February, 1964), pp. 54ff.; O. Simanovskii, "Spetsializatsia i razmery zemlepolzovania kolkhozov," *Ekonomika sel'skogo khoziaistva*, no. 5 (May, 1965), pp. 72ff.; see also nn. 37 and 38 below.

37. A. Rumyantseva, "Optimalnye razmery kolkhozov," *Ekonomika sel'skogo khoziaistva*, no. 5 (May, 1965).

38. K. P. Obolenskiy, G. Kotov, *et al.*, *Optimalnye azmery sel'sko-khoziaistvennogo predpriatiia* (Moscow: Izdatel'stvo' Kolos', 1965).

39. *Pravda Ukrainy*, July 28, 1962.

40. *Komsomolskaia pravda*, August 7, 1965.

41. R. D. Laird, "The New Zveno Controversy: Forerunner of Fundamental Change?" *Osteuropa-Wirtschaft*, no. 4 (December, 1966), pp. 254–61.

42. A. Cheskov, "Opyt raboty mekhanizirovanykh otriadov na tselinnykh zemliakh," *Ekonomika sel'skogo khoziaistva*, no. 8 (August, 1964).

43. M. Janushkin and M. Klinev, "Organizatsiia truda v kolkhozakh i sovkhozakh severnogo kavkaza," *Ekonomika sel'skogo khoziaistva*, no. 1 (January, 1965).

44. Otto Schiller, "Privates Grundeigentum und Private Landnutzung in den Reformplänen für die sowjetische Landwirtschaft," *Osteuropa-Wirtschaft*, no. 4 (1965), pp. 262–67.

Stalinist Industrial Development in Soviet Russia

John P. Hardt and Carl Modig

The purpose of this essay is to survey the industrial-development process in Russia for the first half-century of Soviet rule. Soviet industrialization was in part a continuation of trends and the fulfillment of aims predating the Revolution: the material preconditions for economic development and the necessary motivation were both present in 1913. This continuity explains the reference to Soviet Russia in the title. Our aim is to provide a brief survey of economic performance over the period and to give some understanding of the basic planning mechanism, rather than to analyze or indeed appraise the record against normative standards. In this, our focus is on those periods in which Joseph Stalin was the dominant figure and influence in the course of Soviet economic development. These were the periods in which a unique Soviet pattern was developed, distinctive from tsarist or Western counterparts.

THE LENINIST PATH FOR ECONOMIC DEVELOPMENT

The Leninist route to economic development has been the orthodox policy of the U.S.S.R. over the course of the first fifty years. In 1920 Lenin enunciated his formula "Communism is Soviet rule plus electrification of the entire country."[1] Electric power was broadly interpreted to refer to machine-building and, by official implication, to all energy and basic-metals output. Thus the economic conditions for attaining the ultimate historical stage of communism were economically dependent upon the expansion of heavy industry. From time to time these key sectors were given anatomical designations: machine-building was the heart, electric power the eyes, and steel the bread to feed the body economic. To be sure, the colorful references to the Leninist route for the attainment of communism invited incredulity, especially since they appeared to be stressed at times when attainment of the abundance of communism seemed least likely, e.g., in the early twenties, the first few years of the thirties, and immediately after World War II. Still, if there was a continuing thread throughout the fifty years, it was the devotion to the so-called Leninist path of heavy industrial emphasis in economic development.

The changes that took place during the fifty years could be divided into three periods or stages: 1917–28, 1928–55, and 1955–67. During the first period, a basically rural, agricultural Russian economy recovered from the devastation of war and revolution—the pre–World War I level of over-all economic performance of 1913 was reattained by 1928.[2] During the second period, dominated by Joseph Stalin, an urban industrial base was established in the Soviet Union. By 1955 the problems and opportunities had changed to those of superimposing an advanced industrial sector on the industrial base and of integrating the industrial base with neglected sectors such as agriculture and urban infrastructure. The fifty years are dominated by the middle Stalinist period: in the first period the base was refurbished for Stalinist development; in the third period new economic and political conditions led to modification of the Stalinist pattern.

The goal of the Stalinist period was the establishment of an industrial base in Soviet Russia. Many Russian leaders and economists considered this aim unattainable. Those politically divergent elements who felt that industrial development was necessary and attainable in Russia—Count Witte, M. Tugan-

Baranovsky, V. I. Lenin—did not represent a majority view.[3] The eventual Soviet establishment of an urban-industrial base fulfilled a Russian as well as a Soviet aspiration.

Industrial growth was narrowly defined in Soviet plans as the expansion of the production of basic metals, energy, and machines. This selective development laid the foundation for investing in additional productive capacity—capacity for meeting future requirements of either producers or consumers, as well as capacity for producing the sinews of war. Thus the high rate of increase in the output of steel, coal, electric power, and machine-building ensured in 1955 an absolute level of production well above that of 1928. Moreover, the urgency with which the selected sectors were developed was reflected in the geographical concentration of industrial capacity—the older, developed European regions continued to dominate the newer Siberian regions some distance away from the traditional centers.

To achieve the Stalinist goals of economic development, an urban industrial economy had to be established as a second, more advanced economy on the base of the rural-agricultural economy inherited from the tsars. The means for accomplishing this end may be summarized simply: the planners or economic sovereigns—in large part, Joseph Stalin, the autocrat— acted as if the maximum increase in the physical output in key industrial sectors in as short a time as possible were the *only* objective. All other economic choices were to be determined by their relationship to that central objective. To be sure, the needs of the military were set aside in this planning process at a given level, along with a minimum allowance for maintaining consumption levels and certain other communal activities. With this single-objective system, the value of all economic activity was imputed to, or derived from, its relationship to the aim of maximizing heavy industrial output. Indeed, the needs of *tempo*— rapidly expanding industrial output—tended to dominate all of Joseph Stalin's Russia.

Stalin may have outlived the political viability of his system. By 1955, the terminal year of the five-year-plan period in which he died, his central economic objective had been attained and the Soviet Union was ready for a new stage. The imperatives of the third stage were sharply competitive: (1) military-space needs called for a further advance on the narrow industrial base—the establishment of more sophisticated metals, energy, and machines beyond the traditional reliance on steel, coal, and general-purpose machines; (2) modernization of the established industrial base was required to improve the efficiency of labor, raw materials, and capital use; and (3) a widening of the economic-development process in the U.S.S.R. became necessary to broaden the industrial base and to integrate the rural-agricultural economy into the urban-industrial base created under Stalin.

The post-Stalinist period has been dominated by attempts to go beyond the industrial base established under Stalin, by simultaneously building on the base and widening its effective economic impact. The legacy of Stalin's model and the record of Soviet industrial accomplishment deserve a closer examination before appraising this current post-Stalinist dilemma in the options open to Soviet planners in economic development.

THE RECORD OF PERFORMANCE

The record of performance may answer four questions: How rapidly did the Soviet economy grow? What level did it attain? Where was the new productive capacity located? What was the type of economic activity which expanded? Thus the economic record examines the *rate, level, distribution,* and *composition* of development.

Rate

The accepted standard of national economic performance has come to be the Gross National Product average annual growth rate; for example, the U.S. rate during the last decade has been about 3.6 per cent, and from 1911 to 1966 about 3.1 per cent.[4] For the Soviet Union, however, there is no single agreed-upon GNP rate, but rather a range of estimates.[5] The Soviets say that from 1913[6] to 1963 their economy grew at an average annual rate of 6.85 per cent.[7] Some Western estimates are 2.1 per cent (Stanley Cohn),[8] 3.1 per cent (Warren Nutter),[9] and 4.8 per cent (calculated from data gathered by Peter Wiles).[10]

Such a fifty-year annual average includes periods of excessive economic dislocation—the First World War, the Revolution and Civil War, and the Second World War. Taking war and recovery periods out, the record improves to that shown in Table 1.

TABLE 1: AVERAGE ANNUAL GNP GROWTH RATES IN THE U.S.S.R., 1928–40 AND 1948–66 (percentages)

GNP Growth Rates		1928–40	1948–66	50-yr. av. 1913–63
Soviet data		13.3	9.2[a]	6.85
Western estimates	from	3.5	6.7[b]	2.1
	to	10.0		4.8

[a] 1945–66, 9.5 per cent; 1950–66, 8.9 per cent.
[b] 1948–64.

SOURCES
Soviet data. Calculated from national income data in *Narodnoie Khoziaistvo S.S.S.R.* [*The Economy of the U.S.S.R.*] (Moscow: Central Statistical Agency of the Council of Ministers, 1956), p. 36; *Strana Sovetov za 50 Let* [*The Country of the Soviets for 50 Years*] (Moscow: Central Statistical Agency of the Council of Ministers, 1967), p. 28.
Western estimates. 1928–40: Peter Wiles, "Statistics on the Soviet Economy," *The ASTE Bulletin* (The Association for the Study of Soviet-Type Economies, University of Pennsylvania), vol. IX, no. 2 (1967), pp. 10–11, which incorporates work by A. Bergson and S. Kuznets (1928–50, using both 1928 and 1937 weights) and Wiles 1926–29). 1948–1966: The datum "6.7 per cent" is a representative Western estimate for 1948–64. Most sources agree that the Soviet GNP growth rate after 1950 averaged about 7.1 per cent until the 1959–64 period, when it slowed to an average of 5.3 per cent (Stanley H. Cohn, "Soviet Growth Retardation: Trends in Resource Availability and Efficiency," in *New Directions in the Soviet Economy* [U.S., Congress, Joint Economic Committee (Washington, D.C.: Government Printing Office, 1966)], p. 107). For the postwar years before 1950, there are less data. Calculations from GNP indexes by Bergson indicate that the annual rate for 1948–50 was about 9.3 per cent. (A. Bergson, *The ASTE Bulletin*, vol. IX, no. 2 [1967], using 1937 ruble factor costs.)

More specifically than the GNP rate, the rate of growth of industrial production provides an important measure of performance. The avowed Soviet goal was not the general expansion of the GNP but the maximization of one narrow component of GNP: the heavy industrial sector. A Russian saying is *"ne vsyo merit' na svoy arshin"*—"don't measure everything by your own yardstick." Table 2 reflects the Soviet yardstick

TABLE 2: AVERAGE ANNUAL GROWTH RATES IN SELECTED SECTORS OF THE SOVIET ECONOMY (percentages)

Sector of Economy	1913–63	1928–40		1948–66
All industry				
Official data	8.2	16.8		13.2
Western estimates	4.7[a]	12.9[b]	(Hodgman)	9.6–9.9[c]
		10.5–11.0	(Jasny)	
		8.4	(Kaplan–Moorsteen)	
		6.3	(Nutter)	
All heavy industry (group "A" goods)	10.0	21.2		9.6
Machines and metalworking	12.7	26.3		13.0–15.0
Chemicals	11.2	22.3		14.6–17.4[d]
Electrical energy	11.2	20.7		12.4
Steel	6.0	12.8		9.9
Coal	6.0	13.7		5.9
Cement	7.3	10.1		15.0
Transport (volume)	6.0	—		—
Light industry (Group "B" goods)	6.0	—		—
Agriculture	1.6	—		—

[a] Warren Nutter, lecture at The Institute for Sino-Soviet Studies, The George Washington University, Washington, D.C., December 18, 1967.

by comparing growth in heavy industrial production with growth rates for various other sectors of the Soviet economy.

Although Western sources usually give lower estimates of these growth rates, Western and Soviet sources agree on one important point: heavy industrial production has steadily grown much faster than other sectors—almost one and a half times faster than the GNP and about six times faster than agriculture, according to Soviet data.

Moreover, an examination of certain representative five-year-plan periods, when growth was comparatively good, indicates even better absolute and relative industrial performance. Table 3 indicates growth rates during the second (1933–37) and fifth (1951–55) plan periods.

Level

The Russian economy inherited by the Soviets was overwhelmingly an agricultural one. In 1913 agriculture contributed over 56 per cent of the net national income, while industry's contribution was only 21 per cent.[11] About 75 per cent of the population was dependent on the agricultural economy. Moreover, in the first years, revolution and civil war slowed agriculture and paralyzed industry. As late as 1928 the share of industry in the Soviet economy was far less than that in other

---

[b] Calculated from compilation of indexes in Robert C. Campbell, *Soviet Economic Power* (Boston: Houghton Mifflin, 1966), p. 124.

[c] James H. Noren, "Soviet Industry Trends . . . ," in *New Directions in the Soviet Economy* (U.S., Congress, Joint Economic Committee, [Washington, D.C.: Government Printing Office, 1966]), p. 281, adjusted to 1948 with Warren Nutter, "The Structure and Growth of Soviet Industry," in *Comparisons of United States and Soviet Economies* (U.S., Congress, Joint Economic Committee, [Washington, D.C.: Government Printing Office, 1959]), p. 97.

[d] 14.6 per cent from 1950 to 1966; 17.4 per cent from 1946 to 1966.

SOURCES: All annual rates (except a–c above) calculated from Soviet data in: *Narodnoie Khoziaistvo SSSR* (Moscow: Central Statistical Agency of the Council of Ministers, 1956), pp. 63, 67, 71, 74, 79; *Narodnoie Khoziaistvo SSSR v 1964 godu* (Moscow: Central Statistical Agency of the Council of Ministers, 1965), pp. 59, 63, 157, 169, 174, 200; *Strana Sovetov za 50 Let* (Moscow: Central Statistical Agency of the Council of Ministers, 1967), pp. 29–30, 51–53.

TABLE 3: SOVIET AVERAGE ANNUAL SECTORAL GROWTH RATES,
1933–37 AND 1951–55

Sector	2d Plan 1933–37	Over-all Period 1928–40	5th Plan 1951–55	Over-all Period 1948–66
Steel	25.0	12.8	10.5	9.6
Electricity	22.0	20.7	13.4	12.4
Cement	9.5	10.1	17.2	15.0
Coal	14.8	13.7	8.5	4.9
Machines and metalworking	23.0	26.7	16.7	13.0–15.0

SOURCES: Calculated from Soviet data in *Narodnoie khoziaistvo SSSR* (Moscow: Central Statistical Agency of the Council of Ministers, 1956), pp. 63, 67, 71, 74, 79; *Narodnoie khoziaistvo SSSR v 1964 godu* (Moscow: Central Statistical Agency of the Council of Ministers, 1965), pp. 59, 63, 157, 169, 174, 200; *Strana Sovetov za 50 let* (Moscow: Central Statistical Agency of the Council of Ministers, 1967), pp. 29–30, 51–53.

economies at corresponding levels of development.[12] Thus the *level* of industrial output at the start of the Soviet period was extremely low. But, low as the industrial level was, most of the preconditions for building an urban industrial base on the predominantly rural agricultural underpinnings had been met by the time the Soviets took power. The tsarist legacy included a national railway network of 39,000 miles of track,[13] enabling the Soviets to keep construction of new mileage at the minimum necessary to support industrial expansion. There were also some established urban centers, a good communications system, a large government bureaucracy, and a sizable number of well-educated people.[14] Without the tsarist legacy of an industrial-urban infrastructure, the Soviets would have faced a double problem when they set out to build the industrial base: expanding fixed assets and building infrastructure. With sufficient infrastructure inherited, resources could be, and were, concentrated on direct industrial investment, as shown by the difference between rates of investment in industry and rates of investment in infrastructure from 1928 on (Table 4).

TABLE 4: GROWTH OF CAPITAL STOCK BY SECTOR

(1928 = 1)

Sector	1928	1940	1960
Industrial production			
Industry	1	6.4	28.0
Construction	1	25.3	188.0
Infrastructure			
Transport	1	2.9	9.0
Communications	1	10.0	19.0
Housing	1	1.8	4.0
Agricultural production			
Agriculture (excluding livestock)	1	1.8	5.0

SOURCE: Calculated from data in *Strana Sovetov za 50 let* [The Country of the Soviets for Fifty Years], Statistical Handbook, Central Statistical Agency of the Council of Ministers (Moscow: "Statistica," 1967), p. 34.

One measure of performance was the level of industrial output achieved by the middle 1950's, at the end of the Stalinist era, as indicated in Table 5. Such basic indicators measure industrial development—the "sinews of national power." By 1955, using these measures, we conclude that the basic industrialization stage of Soviet economic development was over. Figure 1 illustrates the resultant change in structure of the Soviet economy from 1913 to 1958.

Composition

The record of performance shows that the *composition* of industrial production remained relatively constant in at least two respects.

First, the structure of Soviet industry was resistant to rapid change. Production functions—the technology-governed formulas for producing various industrial goods—changed little throughout most of the Stalinist era. Since the "mix" of pro-

TABLE 5: U.S.S.R. LEVELS OF INDUSTRIAL OUTPUT, 1913 AND 1955; COMPARED TO U.S. INDUSTRIAL OUTPUT IN 1955

Industry	Unit of Measure	U.S.S.R.[1] 1913	U.S.S.R.[2] 1955	U.S.[3] 1955	U.S.S.R. World Rank 1955
Electric power	billion kwh.	2.0	170.0	629.0	2
Coal[a]	million short tons	32.1	304.0	493.0	2
Steel[b]	million short tons	4.7	50.0	117.0	2
Cement[c]	million short tons	2.0	24.8	55.0	2
Oil[d]	million barrels (1 barrel = 42 U.S. gal.)	74.0	508.0	2,484.0	3

[a] Excluding lignite and brown coal.

[b] Total crude-steel production (including ingots and steel for castings; excluding wrought iron).

[c] All hydraulic cement used for construction, including portland, aluminous, natural, etc.

[d] Including shale oil but excluding natural gasoline; U.S.S.R. data in metric tons converted to barrels using U.S. Department of Commerce conversion factor: 1 bbl. = 139.07 kg.

SOURCES

1. *Strana Sovetov za 50 let* (Moscow: Central Statistical Agency of the Council of Ministers, 1967), pp. 58–61.

2. *Narodnoie khoziaistvo SSSR* [The Economy of the U.S.S.R.], Statistical Handbook (Moscow: Central Statistical Agency of the Council of Ministers, 1956), pp. 63, 67, 69, 71, 79.

3. U.S., Bureau of the Census, *Statistical Abstract of the United States: 1957* (Washington, D.C.: Government Printing Office, 1957), pp. 947, 949–50.

ducers' inputs required to make a given industrial output changed slowly in response to technological innovations, proportions between various heavy industrial products tended to remain fixed. The Soviets preferred the large industrial output attainable by expanding an unsophisticated coal-iron-steel-cement economy. For example, the industrial base continued to be built on coal-derived energy sources long after a mixed coal-oil energy base became technically feasible. The quality of the mixed coal-oil base would have been higher in terms of efficient

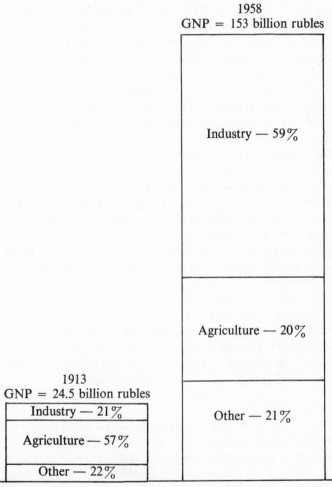

FIGURE 1
SIZE AND SOURCES OF SOVIET GNP
1913 AND 1958

1958
GNP = 153 billion rubles

Industry — 59%

Agriculture — 20%

1913
GNP = 24.5 billion rubles

Industry — 21%

Agriculture — 57%

Other — 22%

Other — 21%

SOURCES
1913 S. N. Prokopovitch, quoted in Peter Wiles, "Statistics on the Soviet Economy," *The ASTE Bulletin* (The Association for the Study of Soviet-Type Economies, University of Pennsylvania), vol. IX, no. 2 [1967], p. 25.
1958 Size: Nancy Nimitz, *Soviet National Income and Budget, 1956–58* (Santa Monica, Calif., 1962), in market rubles. Composition: *Narodnoie khoziaistvo SSSR v 1964 godu* (Moscow, 1965), p. 67.

use of resources, but the output—in terms of maximum possible immediate increase in BTU energy equivalents—would have been lower. Throughout industry, output of a relatively small number of products was maximized by using simpler production formulas, rather than accepting the loss of time inherent in the transition to new formulas that would be more efficient in the use of resources but initially less productive.[15]

Second, the blend of factors of production (materials, labor, capital) has also remained rather constant. Austerity was practiced in the use of scarce capital, but labor and raw materials were generally not economized. In capital terms this policy meant producing with older machinery for as long as possible. The emphasis was on repair, not replacement, of capital stock. Depreciation rates allowed on capital stock were low by Western standards, and obsolescence was a foreign concept.[16] In labor terms the policy meant increasing output by adding workers rather than by increasing the productivity of the individual worker, although industrial labor productivity also inevitably increased as the pool of skilled labor grew. Improved labor productivity was more the by-product of industrial expansion than the result of labor-saving investment.[17] Thus Soviet planners apparently preferred to sacrifice the variety of end products (on the industrial output side) and high-quality factors of production (on the industrial input side) in order to maximize output in a few heavy industrial sectors.

Distribution

In building their industrial base the Soviets could have altered the geographical pattern of the location of industry to insure a more even economic development of their country. Such a policy would have been in accord with Lenin's and Stalin's original declared policy on the nationalities, i.e., assuring the equal distribution of output through the development of the economies of all of the far-flung national areas of the new Soviet state.[18] But, in practice, such a policy would have sacrificed the advantage of inherited tsarist infrastructure, and the record of performance in this category shows that most of the industrial base was actually built where the skilled labor, cities, and transport already existed to some extent—in or adjacent to European Russia.[19]

The first Stalinist Five-Year Plan allotted more rubles for investment to the Leningrad area of European Russia alone than to all the regions of Siberia and the Soviet Far East combined. The following table provides details of the first Stalinist investment plan. In 1913, 95 per cent or more of industrial produc-

PLANNED CAPITAL INVESTMENT IN STATE INDUSTRY
1928/29–33[a]

R.S.F.S.R.	10,494
Central region	2,998
Leningrad region	1,055
Siberia region	662
Far East region	310
Ukraine	4,521
Total	16,548

[a] Millions of 1926/27 rubles.

SOURCE: *Pyatiletniy Plan* [Five-Year Plan], vol. 3 (Moscow: U.S.S.R. Gosplan, 1930), p. 568, cited in Violet Conolly, *Beyond the Urals* (Oxford: Oxford University Press, 1967), p. 68.

tion was in European Russia. As recently as 1960 the overwhelming bulk of such production was still in European Russia, counting the Urals (see Table 6). Even without production from the Urals, more than half of the production of most industrial sectors was in European Russia.[20]

As can be seen the geographical center of gravity of industry has moved somewhat eastward over the years. But this movement appeared to occur primarily in response to the strategic relocation of industry (e.g., during the German occupation of

TABLE 6: SHARE OF INDUSTRIAL OUTPUT PRODUCED IN EUROPEAN
RUSSIA, 1913–60 (percentages)

Industry	Production, Including the Urals			
	1913	1928	1940	1960
Steel	100.0	99.9	89.4	90.7
Iron	100.0	99.9	98.5	96.4
Rolled steel bars and shapes	100.0	99.8	88.7	88.6
Coal	92.3	86.0	71.3	64.1
Electric power	97.9	97.5	90.8	78.4
Chemicals				
Fertilizer	100.0	100.0	93.1	84.1
Sulphuric acid	100.0	100.0	95.8	81.3
Calcined soda	99.9	99.5	97.5	96.9
Caustic soda	100.0	100.0	100.0	90.9
Synthetic yarn	—[a]	100.0	100.0	81.5
Machine tools	100.0	100.0	98.4	92.9
Metallurgical equipment	n.d.[b]	n.d.	100.0	92.9
Tractors	—	100.0	100.0	87.3
Cement	95.2	96.5	86.5	78.6

[a] No production.
[b] Data not available.

SOURCE: *Strana Sovetov za 50 Let* [Country of the Soviets for Fifty Years]
(Moscow: Central Statistical Agency of the Council of Ministers, 1967), pp.
58–61.

World War II) and the comparative attraction of rich Siberian
resources, coupled with the gradual depletion of natural resources in European Russia. Such movement apparently did not
occur because of the Stalinist priorities but despite them.

THE STALINIST ECONOMIC MODEL

Representative Periods

What Soviet policies were responsible for the particular pattern of economic growth which has occurred? In our summary

of the record, we noted the significant industrial increments achieved during such periods as the second Five-Year Plan (1933–37) and the fifth Five-Year Plan (1951–55). Although these were not the only periods during which a normal[21] series of annual plans was carried through, they were, in our view, representative of the Stalinist system. In our attempt to describe characteristic economic processes, these two periods should be of particular interest, for Stalinist formulas were most operative in such periods.

Conceptual Model

All political leaders, in choosing among their economic policy alternatives, and economists, in solving their technical problems, are aided by economic models of varying sophistication. These models range from sophisticated mathematical models (such as those now employed in the United States and other industrialized nations for projecting national economic trends) to simple, conceptual models implicit in any decision-making process. Central to the conceptual model is the simplifying assumption, often postulated in economic theory in the "as if" form. For example, a basic premise in the study of Western market economics is that each entrepreneur acts "as if" the prime goal were the maximization of his enterprise's profits. And, although economists know that this picture of the firm does not fully correspond with reality, they often proceed "as if" it were so, for the sake of simplicity and because of the insights that the supposition allows.

Any model that the Soviets used under Stalin in guiding their economic policy must be described in this conceptual form. Under Stalin's planning, statistical discipline was too loose, conditions too chaotic, and revisions of plan targets too frequent to suggest seriously that an explicit, complex, and mathematically rigorous model was followed.[22] However, the general consistency of Soviet economic decisions suggests that it would be equally inaccurate to assume that there was no model at all. Rather, it seems to us that Soviet patterns of action very definitely conformed to a simple but inclusive conceptual economic model. It is in this sense that we refer to a "Stalinist" economic model and attempt to specify its central features.

Application of Tempo

Tempo, in Soviet usage, meant mobilization and concentration of resources to achieve one primary set of economic goals. In implementing the Stalinist economic model, Soviet planners have acted "as if" the maximization of output of only *one* sector of the economy—heavy industry—was important. They have acted "as if" the interest of the other sectors could be safely ignored or held constant (*ceteris paribus*) while heavy-industry output was expanded as rapidly as possible. And, finally, they have acted "as if" production of the other sectors was of value only insofar as it provided additional increments of materials, labor, and capital for the expansion of the heavy-industry sector. These "as if's" gave the Soviet planner a set of simple imperatives in planning resource allocation:

First, allocate to the military establishment the resources (labor, materials, capital) needed to fulfill strategic requirements.

Also, lay aside the minimum amounts of resources needed for consumption and for the preservation and necessary growth of the infrastructure.

Second, maximize the flow of resources into the heavy-industry sector.

Then, specify how resources are to be combined to maximize output. (The Soviet planner assumed that fixed, functional relationships held between units of steel, energy, and machine equivalents. A simple application of these production functions help him to determine the crude end-product mix as well as proportions among industrial inputs and proportions among factors of production. These production functions changed little over time.)

Third, distribute residuals of unrequired or unsuitable resources among other sectors such as agriculture and light industry.

Categorization by End Use

Viewed analytically, the aggregate of available factors of production was equal to the previous year's material product plus the total labor force and capital stock, and could be divided into three categories of use:

Available Resources = (1) Strategic Requirements +
(2) Consumption and Infrastructure +
(3) Heavy Industry.

Such a division corresponds to the Western practice of regarding the GNP as divisible into several categories by end use:

GNP = Consumption + Investment
         Public Private   Replacement Net Investment
         Defense
         Education
      Administration
         etc.

However, the Soviet planner in practice seemed to act as though his end-use categories were structured differently. The Western public consumption (defense) category was of such importance to the Soviets that it was brought out to stand alone as term (1). All other consumption, replacement investment, and net investment in nonpriority sectors became term (2). And net investment in heavy industry became term (3). The process to be performed on each of these terms differed in accordance with its priority. Resource allocation to (*1*) was stipulated to the planner "from above," (*2*) was to be held to the lowest level at which these sectors could still effectively support expansion of heavy industry, and (*3*) was to be maximized.

Application of the Plan

In the maximization process for heavy industry, limits were imposed by the maximum possible shift of new labor into the urban industrial work force from the countryside. A second limit was the availability of capital. Importation of foreign-capital goods was limited by the availability of Soviet agricultural and primary commodities for export,[23] and increments of domestically produced capital, by the rate of domestic saving which could be maintained. The third limit, of course, was the availability of materials, and the size of the supply plan was set largely by the previous year's production record.

In general, as discussed earlier, emphasis was on quantity of factors of production rather than on their quality. Hence production formulas that best utilized the available proportions of labor, capital, and materials were adapted, and these production functions then remained relatively fixed, tending to prefer the use of basic, undifferentiated materials and machinery to the proliferation of many highly differentiated ingredients in the production process. Since capital was the scarce factor while unskilled labor was plentiful, large-scale use of the latter was often made to conserve the former. Of course, with the passage of time the increased output of heavy industry itself increased the share of capital, and labor productivity inevitably went up. In general, however, the increase in productivity has been slow throughout the Stalinist era.[24]

Implementing the Plan: Control of the Industrial Sector

The basic simplicity of the procedure outlined above and the narrowness of scope of the sectors requiring detailed planning made centralization of planning both attractive and possible. A basic feature of the planning process was the optimal tautness of the production goals set. Soviet leaders were always optimistic to the maximum degree in setting targets; such planning "tautness" was then relayed down through the planning hierarchy.[25] The industrial sector was most heavily planned, with the most detailed control mechanisms governing its performance. However, control mechanisms were devised for nonpriority sectors as well; these mechanisms, although less numerous, were sufficient to insure that the other sectors made their necessary contributions to the main goal of building the industrial base.

In the industrial sector a set of annual plans for production, material, supply, labor, finance, and investment controlled in detail economic activity within the sector. The yearly elaboration and balancing of these plans was the responsibility of Gosplan, the State Planning Committee, which received each year a few dozen highly aggregated production[26] and investment targets from above and, in co-ordination with the branch ministries for each type of industry, distributed detailed individual plans to the basic industrial enterprises below. Gosplan did the planning largely by means of a crude but effective system of materials-balancing. At the Stalin-to-Gosplan level, tautness was embodied in the optimism of targets passed down and in the demand for very short construction times in building new plants. To the enterprise the plans appeared as a set of orders, hopefully co-ordinated, specifying what it was to produce, how much labor and materials it was entitled to acquire, from whom and at what prices, the buyer(s) of its production, how much they would pay, investment for expanding the enterprise, and so forth. At the planner-to-enterprise level, tautness was embodied in the high production quota assigned to the enterprise and the scanty allocations of materials, equipment, and labor with which the enterprise manager had to work.

Central planning in its strictest sense was limited to what were called *funded* items—producers' goods that could only be obtained by an enterprise or ministry if it had a *fund* or an allotment quota for the item in the form of an account of earmarked rubles in the state park.[27] Other items were centrally planned but were not strictly funded, and there were several thousand items in this second category. Between them, the two categories comprised the vast majority of all producers' goods.[28]

As can be seen, the Supply-Production Plan and the Finance Plan interlocked to control the individual enterprise's acquisition of the most important material inputs. Similarly, investment was controlled by the Investment Plan together with the Construction Bank. In order to sign a contract with a construction enterprise to begin an expansion in plant, a production enterprise had to have the project funded in the Construction Bank as well as approved in the Investment Plan.[29] The Investment Plan also covered much of nonindustrial investment; hence, its effect on the whole economy was to insure that heavy industry got all the increments of capital it could absorb, while within the industrial sector it distributed investment among alternative projects, thus substituting for the interest mechanism of Western market economies.

Implementing the Plan: Relaxation of Ceteris Paribus

Outside the industrial sectors the Stalinist economic model made less detailed but very definite demands on the other sectors in the name of heavy industry, and positive and negative mechanisms existed to make sure that these demands were met.

In agriculture the market mechanism was abolished in favor of negative controls that by direct procurement would better ensure adequate food supplies for urban workers, agricultural raw materials for industry, and grain for export—all at levels of compensation which did not increase the real income of the agricultural population, because procurement was not at market prices. The essential features of the agricultural mechanism were control of the agricultural plot through the collective-farm arrangements and fixed quotas of produce (chiefly grain) to be delivered to the state—at low, fixed prices set by the state. Applied rigorously, these instruments even decreased real per capita income of the rural population, thus serving as a positive incentive for the farmer to join the growing industrial labor force in the cities.[30]

In foreign trade the creation of a state monopoly over trade secured absolute control over imports and assured that capital goods imports were maximized and consumer goods imports were minimized.[31]

For labor the progressive, piece-rate system provided incentives without the necessity of increasing significantly the production of consumer goods. Low real wages[32] helped secure a high labor-participation ratio by making two- and three-worker households an economic necessity for most of the urban population. Labor unions, which had earlier secured wage increases in excess of productivity increases, were made an instrument of state policy.

Negative mechanisms included the worker's labor book, which tied him to his place of work, harsh legal punishments for absenteeism, and a labor draft that controlled an unprecedented shift of labor from agriculture to industry.[33]

Over the entire consumption sector of the economy the principal means of keeping consumption low and forced savings high were the low supply allocations, investment allocations, and targets for enterprises in the light-industry sector, on the one hand, and high retail prices to consumers on the other. While prices on producers' goods were kept low for the industrial buyer, the price of consumer goods was high because of an added "turnover" tax, which taxed away excess consumer purchasing power and at the same time was a principal source of revenue for the state budget, out of which most of the Investment Plan was financed. Throughout the Stalinist era, almost half of the money paid by the population for consumer goods was tax.[34] Moreover, differentiated retail prices increased consumers' preferences for such staple items as bread, which was relatively cheap and which, from the state's point of view, represented satisfaction of basic consumption needs at minimum cost to the state.

Negative mechanisms to enforce least-cost consumption included strict laws against black-market activities and, on occasion, revaluation of the ruble.[35]

The system followed the logic of building a narrowly defined industrial base on a rural-agricultural base in as short a time period as possible. The cost was high, but the objective was attained.

REVISIONS OF THE STALINIST MODEL

Post-Stalinist Environment[36]

The successful establishment of the industrial base by the early 1950's provided opportunities and necessities for further development. This development process required further expansion of the narrow industrial base and widening of the base to satisfy more completely the broad requirements of the economy as a whole. In effect the economic plan had to be simultaneously deepened and widened, and this new task made some modification of the Stalinist economic formulas necessary.

The military-space requirements demanded that new, unique, sophisticated industrial capabilities for modern weaponry be developed and added to the established base. Steel, coal, and simple machinery could not meet the needs of nuclear missilery as they had met the conventional requirements for rifles, tanks, and airplanes. Large-scale nonferrous metals, exotic fuels, and sophisticated machinery output had to be developed following the Soviet decision to exploit the strategic opportunities dramatized by their Sputnik success.

At the same time as an advanced tier of the Soviet industrial base was being established, the refurbishing and broadening of the existing base became imperative. It became increasingly costly simply to rely on increments of labor, raw materials, and capital from nonpriority sectors instead of shifting to more efficient factor combinations. Increases in industrial output had to come from an improvement in the efficiency of the use of labor and other factors rather than from the continued addition of the same resources. The delayed demographic impacts of the low World War II birth rate appeared in the 1950's as a trough in the annual number of males reaching eighteen years of age. Moreover, this effect coincided with the apparent exhaustion of the regime-defined surplus of peasants. The deceptively large rural labor force in agriculture included far too many grandmothers (*babushkas*), and even the available males were not easily trainable for required industrial tasks. Likewise, further deferment of investment in transportation, housing, and other nonpriority elements of the Soviet infrastructure could not be tolerated. Railroads bore the brunt of transport demands but continued to rely on coal-fired steam locomotion. As average hauls became longer—and even petroleum products were being hauled by rail (instead of by pipeline)—a point of negative economic returns may have been reached. Even the conventional industrial base still supporting military requirements was affected by labor-saving requirements: a series of reorganizations reduced drastically the number of men at arms. The army's conversion of rifle divisions into mechanized divisions was characterized by an exchange of added firepower and mobility for reduced manpower.

Beyond the deepening and widening of the industrial base there was a third, broader, more ambiguous requirement for meeting the demands of the economy as a whole. The integration of the broader needs of the economy challenged directly the central features of the Stalinist model.

First, military allocations levels can only provisionally set aside, both in the aggregate and in the trade-off between alternative military uses (e.g., missiles vs. conventional divisions). The fluctuating military budgets of Khrushchev and his successors bear witness to the fact that defense is now a variable rather than a preferred "given."

Likewise, consumption is no longer a nonpreferred "given." Production to provide for improved living conditions is a variable—if only as a stimulant to productivity.

Second, the simplifying assumptions of fixed product relationships are increasingly untenable as the structure of heavy industry becomes more complex, servicing technologically advanced space programs, traditional military and investment projects, and new requirements in the economic infrastructure.

Third, no longer can Soviet planners treat light industry, transportation, and agriculture as though they were primarily suppliers of "surplus" labor, raw materials, and capital for heavy industry—and consumers of whatever residuals are left after heavy-industry output is maximized.

Institutional Stagnation[37]

Likewise under challenge are the control mechanisms set up to meet the central objective of the Stalinist model: balanced estimates-planning, collectivized agriculture, foreign-trade monopoly, as well as the coercive institutions controlling urban labor and management. Institutions universally tend to outlive the original purpose for their creation, and the persistence of the administrative status quo in the Soviet Union is perhaps even stronger than it is in other societies.

The effectiveness of the Soviet institutions designed to implement the Stalinist model has turned on the participation of the Soviet Communist party. The role of the party under Stalin became closely interwoven with the institutions for economic control. Changes have been made—the labor camps have been closed and the application of terror to economic administrators has been reduced or virtually eliminated. Challenges have been permitted, even those directed toward the collective form of agriculture. But challenges are not changes: new central planning methods have yet to be adopted,[38] collectivization continues in agriculture, and foreign trade is still a monopoly. The institutional structure of Stalinism in economic development remains basically unchanged, if not unmodified.

The New Economic Stage

The Soviet Union may be characterized economically as three countries: an advanced urban industrial nation rivaling the United States and outstripping all other nations in strategic weapon and space technology; a developed industrial economy exceeding the industrial nations of Western Europe and Japan in output but lagging behind them in the broad range of industrial technology; a rural-agricultural economy with all the problems of the developing nations in the southern hemisphere of the world. The United States has largely integrated its variants of the three-tier Soviet economy. U.S. agriculture could be described, with some qualification for the subsistence-farming fringe, as a branch of industry. The advanced economy is less convertible than other sectors, but the technological gap between agriculture and other U.S. industry does not approach that existing in the U.S.S.R.

Perhaps the three Soviet economies can continue to coexist. The attendant problems of strategic considerations and regional differences may militate against compartmentalization. Even if the three-level economy continues, the choice among the sectors and within the sectors will be difficult. The Soviets cannot avoid the eventual substitution of a concept of optimizing—choosing among alternatives—to replace the concept of maximizing—placing primary emphasis on a single objective. Choices will be difficult. With a slowing growth rate all needs cannot be met. But how are the Soviets to allocate the shortfalls among defense, investment, and consumption? The best choices by any consistent application of criteria require better professional economic judgment than is possible while the institutional stagnation in economic administration continues. The pervasive role of the party in economic administration is at least partly responsible for the stagnation. But the party will hardly delegate away control that was carefully built up for it under Stalin, for the major economic decisions are too important. How the Soviets balance professionally derived efficiency and party control will determine the character of this latest stage in the development of the Soviet economy.

NOTES

1. V. I. Lenin, "Report to the Eighth All-Russian Congress of Soviets on the Work of the Council of Peoples Commissars," *Sochineniia* [Collected Works], 4th ed. (Moscow, 1950), vol. 31, p. 484; J. Stalin, *Economic Problems of Socialism in the U.S.S.R.* (New York: International Publishers, 1952), pp. 50f.

2. Abram Bergson, *The Real National Income of Soviet Russia since 1928* (Cambridge: Harvard University Press, 1961), p. 7.

3. Vladimir Il'ich Lenin, *The Development of Capitalism in Russia: The Process of the Formation of a Home Market for Large-Scale Industry* (Moscow, Foreign Languages Publishing House, 1956); M. I. Tugan-Baranovskii, *Modern Socialism in Its Historical Development* (London: S. Sonnenschein, 1910); Nicholas Spulber, *The Soviet Economy: Structure, Principles, Problems* (New York: W. W. Norton, 1962); M. I. Tugan-Baranovskii, *K luchshemu budushchemu* [Toward a Better Future] (St. Petersburg: Energia, 1912).

4. Average annual compounded rates of change in real gross national product expressed in 1958 dollars. U.S., Bureau of the Census, *Statistical Abstract of the United States: 1967* (Washington, D.C.: Government Printing Office, 1967), p. 322.

5. The results of various calculations for the Soviet GNP growth rate differ from one another because of differences in approach to such computational questions as: What year's set of prices should be used in calculating the total market basket of goods and services? What years are to be bases? How is double counting avoided? How should annexed territory be counted?

6. 1913 is chosen as an initial point rather than 1917 because of the better statistical data available for the prewar year.

7. As measured by Soviet data on national income (*proizvodstvo natsional' nogo dokhoda*). Since 1940 the GNP rate has varied from the national income rate by less than 0.2 per cent, according to Soviet data. *Strana Sovetov za 50 let* (Moscow: Central Statistical Agency of the Council of Ministers, 1967), p. 28; *Narodnoie khoziaistvo SSSR v 1964 godu* [The Economy of the U.S.S.R. in 1964], Statistical Yearbook (Moscow: Central Statistical Agency of the Council of Ministers), p. 59.

8. Stanley H. Cohn, "The Soviet Economy: Performance and Growth," in *Economics of the Soviet Union*, pt. II of *Promise and Realization: 1917–1967*, ed. Vladimir G. Treml, (New York: Praeger, 1968), p. 70.

9. Warren Nutter, lecture at The Institute for Sino-Soviet Studies, The George Washington University, Washington, D.C., December 18, 1967.

10. Peter Wiles, "Statistics on the Soviet Economy," *The ASTE Bulletin* (The Association for the Study of Soviet-Type Economics, University of Pennsylvania), vol. IX, no. 2 (1967), pp. 10–11, which incorporates work by: S. N. Prokopovitch (1913–28); Wiles (1926–29); A. Bergson and S. Kuznets (1928–38) with 1928 weights, 1937–50 with 1937 weights); and U.S., Congress, Joint Economic Committee, *Current Economic Indicators for the U.S.S.R.* (1950–1964) (Washington, D.C.: Government Printing Office, 1965).

11. Peter Wiles, "Statistics on the Soviet Economy," p. 25, quoting S. N. Prokopovitch, Birmingham Bureau of Research on Russian Economic Conditions, *Memorandum No. 3* (1931), p. 13.

12. Corresponding points in terms of per capita income. See Stanley H. Cohn, "The Soviet Economy: Performance and Growth," p. 83.

13. Holland Hunter, *Soviet Transportation Policy* (Cambridge, Mass.: Harvard University Press, 1957), p. 365.

14. Although only about one-quarter of the adult population was literate, the percentage of the population that had university training compared favorably with that of other European countries at the time. *Strana Sovetov za 50 let*, p. 271; Stanley H. Cohn, "The Soviet Economy: Performance and Growth," p. 65.

15. Michael Boretsky, "Comparative Progress in Technology, Productivity, and Economic Efficiency: U.S.S.R. versus U.S.A.," in *New Directions in the Soviet Economy* (U.S., Congress, Joint Economic Committee [Washington, D.C.: Government Printing Office, 1966]), pp. 150–53.

16. Richard Moorsteen and Raymond P. Powell, *The Soviet Capital Stock, 1928–1962* (Homewood, Ill.: Irwin, 1966), pp. 70, 81–84, 100.

17. Stanley H. Cohn, "The Soviet Economy: Growth and Performance," pp. 69–77.

18. A "Plan of Scientific-Technical Tasks," written by Lenin in 1918, outlines principles of national location of industry, i.e., the location of new industry closer to raw materials sources, reducing transport costs, and developing the "eastern regions" Lenin, *Sochinenia*, vol. 27, p. 288, April 6, 1918; see also *Pravda*, March 4, 1924). The party's declared policy conformed to Lenin's position in the early years: "It is the party's task to help the toiling masses in the non-Russian nations [within the U.S.S.R.] to overtake central Russia, which has forged ahead" (*Vse' soiuznaya KP v resoliutsiiakh i Resheniiakh s"ezdov, konferentsii, i plenumov Ts. Komitetov* [The All-Union Communist Party in Resolutions and Decisions of Congress, Conferences, and Central Committee Plenums], pt. I, 1898–1925 (Moscow: 1954), p. 559).

19. David J. M. Hooson, *A New Soviet Heartland?* (Princeton: Van Nostrand, 1964), p. 123.

20. *Strana Sovetov za 50 let* [Country of the Soviets for Fifty Years] (Moscow: Central Statistical Agency of the Council of Ministers, 1967), pp. 58–61.

21. *Normal* is used here in the conventional sense of nonwar, non-recovery, noncrisis, years.

22. For example, the second Five-Year Plan was begun in 1933 but was substantially revised after 1935. The fifth Five-Year Plan was to have started in 1951 but was not approved until 1952; then it was drastically altered in 1954, after Stalin's death. Edward Ames, *Soviet Economic Processes* (Homewood, Ill.: Irwin, 1965), pp. 24–30.

23. Another limit on imports was low agricultural prices in the world market, which was depressed at the start of Soviet industrialization. Soviet foreign trade was caught in a "scissors," as the prices obtained for their exports dropped and the prices of the capital goods they wished to import remained stable. Maurice Dobb, *Soviet Economic Development Since 1917*, 2d ed. (London: Routledge and Kegan Paul Ltd., 1951), p. 238.

24. The productivity of all factors of production combined actually took a downturn from 1937 to 1940; see Stanley H. Cohn, "The Soviet Economy: Performance and Growth," p. 77 (Table 10).

25. John P. Hardt, "Industrial Investment in the USSR," in *Comparisons of United States and Soviet Economies* (U. S., Congress, Joint Economic Committee [Washington, D.C.: Government Printing Office, 1959]), pp. 127–28.

26. In 1945 the basic list of production targets passed to Gosplan from above reportedly numbered twenty items. Ames *Soviet Economic Processes*, p. 28.

27. There were about 600 such funded categories of goods during the second Five-Year-Plan period in the 1920's, but by the fifth Five-Year Plan-period, in the early 1950's, the increased complexity of the economy had driven the number up to about 1200. Herbert S. Levine, "A Study in Economic Planning: The Soviet Industrial Supply System" (Ph.D. diss., Harvard University, 1961), pp. 43–44, 50–51, 53.

28. *Ibid.*

29. Ames, *Soviet Economic Processes*, pp. 145–146.

30. See Nancy Nimitz, "Soviet Agricultural Prices and Costs," pp. 239–76, and Lazar Volin, "Agricultural Policy of the Soviet Union," pp. 285–311, in *Comparisons of United States and Soviet Economies* (U.S., Congress, Joint Economic Committee [Washington, D.C.: Government Printing Office, 1959]). For a graphic personal account of collectivization and its effects on the average peasant, see Victor Kravchenko, *I Chose Freedom* (New York: Charles Scribner's Sons, 1946), chaps. 8 and 9.

31. See Frederick L. Pryor, *The Communist Foreign Trade System* (Cambridge, Mass.: M.I.T. Press, 1963), pp. 25ff.; see also Penelope H. Thunberg, "The Soviet Union in the World Economy," in *Dimensions of Soviet Economic Power* (U.S., Congress, Joint Economic Committee [Washington, D.C.: Government Printing Office, 1962]), pp. 413, 430–32; Alec Nove, *The Soviet Economy* (New York: Praeger, 1961), pp. 42–43, 193–94. David Granick, in his book on Soviet metallurgy, *Soviet Metal-Fabricating and Economic Development* (Madison: University of Wisconsin, 1967), suggests that the Soviets imported far more Western capital than they could use and more Western technology than they

could absorb (p. 262). But, of course, such an excess in implementation of the Stalinist model does not invalidate the utility or rationality—in terms of Soviet goals— of the model itself.

32. By 1937, real wages, including social benefits, were about 60-80 per cent lower than the 1928 level. They rose again from 1938 to 1939, but then declined again during the war, and in 1948 were considerably below the 1940 level. Steady improvement began only after 1948. Janet G. Chapman, *Real Wages in Soviet Russia Since 1928* (Cambridge: Harvard University Press, 1963), pp. 146–48.

33. Stanley H. Cohn, "The Soviet Economy: Performance and Growth," p. 83; see also S. Swianiewicz, *Forced Labour and Economic Development* (London: Oxford University Press, 1965), and, for a description of the impact of Stalinist labor policy at the worker's level, Kravchenko, *I Chose Freedom*, chap. 13.

34. Robert Campbell, *Soviet Economic Power—Its Organization, Growth, and Challenge,* 2d ed. (Houghton-Mifflin, 1966), p. 87.

35. Such a revaluation in 1947 deflated away considerable savings accumulated by the rural population during the last years of World War II. Ames, *Soviet Economic Processes,* p. 131.

36. See John P. Hardt, ed., *Toward a Soviet New Economics: Underlying Trends* (to be published in 1969).

37. Hardt, Treml, Gallik, "Institutional Stagnation and Changing Economic Strategy in the Soviet Union," in *New Directions in the Soviet Economy* (U.S., Congress, Joint Economic Committee [Washington, D.C.: Government Printing Office, 1966]), pp. 19–22.

38. For more detailed discussion of themes sketched herein, see Vladimir Treml in *Toward a Soviet New Economics: Underlying Trends.*

PART II

SOVIET FOREIGN RELATIONS

CHAPTER 5

The Rationale of Soviet Foreign Policy

Soviet Foreign Policy: Fifty Years of Dualism

Kurt London

Soviet Foreign Policy: Fifty Years of Dualism

Kurt London

The dualistic road of Soviet foreign policy began soon after the victory of the Bolshevik Revolution. It has remained, during its various periods and many oscillations, a remarkably continuous phenomenon throughout the half-century of Soviet rule. This is not surprising, for such political schizophrenia is the result of the inevitable contradictions between the roles of the Soviet Union as a nation-state and as a revolutionary power. It must remain a nation within the traditional framework of the meaning of this term until, as communist ideology proclaims, the "transition to communism" has been successfully achieved on an international scale; at the same time, its world revolutionary commitments must continue. It is led by a communist party that determines the course of Soviet internal and external policy and sees itself as the vanguard of an international movement against the same noncommunist states with which it maintains political and economic relations.

Inevitably, the principles of national foreign policy more often than not are incompatible with the goals of international communism. The attempts by Kremlin leaders to camouflage this dualism on the whole have been successful because of the failure of noncommunist governments to familiarize themselves with the body of doctrine which is inadequately called Marxism-Leninism.

This is not to say that all Soviet foreign-policy decisions are based solely on ideological precepts. Obviously, traditional goals are involved as well and must be weighed against revolutionary designs. It is to say, however, that Soviet policy should not be interpreted only as an extension of tsarist foreign policy. Rather, it is imperative to discern the extent to which inherited goals are made to serve ideological purposes. Even discriminating policy-makers familiar with the jungle of communist scholasticism often are hard put to separate revolutionary intent from old-fashioned power-balancing. It is like two sides of a coin—the face of revolutionary interests and that of state interests merge to make one unity, Soviet foreign policy. We cannot separate the sides, but from time to time we seem to see one more clearly or frequently than the other.

THE IDEOLOGICAL FRAMEWORK

For the Bolsheviks, the clash of tradition with revolution posed no problem. In their early history they were political iconoclasts who broke with the concepts of a tradition-minded law of nations as they adopted the thought of Marx and Engels and followed Lenin's practical interpretation of it. We have heard of these principles *ad nauseam,* but it is indispensable to recall them briefly if we wish to explore the whys and wherefores of the rationale of schizophrenic Soviet foreign policy.

The men who created the Soviet Union have claimed that the tools of dialectics enabled them to predict future developments in general terms. They analyzed situations, events, complications, and crises with what they believed to be "scientific" laws of the "objective" forces of history. This was made possible through the tool of dialectical materialism, revealing the drama of contradictory social systems as they have developed since mankind's beginnings. Within these systems, opposite elements struggle for predominance. In modern times these opposites have crystallized into socialist and capitalist antagonists whose beliefs and aims are irreconcilable. Armed with this weapon of Marxist dialectics, the leaders of the Revolution were convinced that they alone had the correct perception of the future that would inevitably be theirs. Lenin's work *Imperialism: The Highest Stage of Capitalism* extended the concept of the internal class struggle by applying it to the international arena and placing responsibility for war on the nature of capitalism. There can be no question that this Leninist thesis, first published in 1916, has directly or indirectly dominated or influenced the thinking of communist foreign-policy-makers ever since. It is obvious that the belief in these principles forecloses a pursuit of international relations in a fashion considered "normal" among Western states.

During the half-century of Soviet rule many changes have occurred, and the men in the Kremlin have acquired a more sophisticated approach toward the conduct of foreign affairs. But the modifications in Soviet government, economy, and society, introduced as necessary adjustments to new conditions, have not eroded the fundamental concepts of the Soviet leadership or modified their views of capitalism and imperialism.

The most important adaptation to new conditions resulting from nuclear technology is the rejection of Clausewitz' tenet that war is the continuation of policy by other means. The nuclear threat is understood in the Kremlin, and the only actions still permissible are self-defense against aggression and support of "wars of national liberation." But, in the latter event, risks that could lead to an escalation of local conflicts into larger— and possibly nuclear—hostilities must be avoided. World revolution as a concept has not been abandoned by the Soviet leaders but, since the twentieth C.P.S.U. Congress in 1956, it need not necessarily be achieved through a bloodbath. Instead, under the label of "peaceful coexistence," the struggle for a victory of "socialism" can be pursued, short of war, in the political, economic, social, and cultural areas.

Some scholars have stated recently that the Soviet Union has become a status quo nation. Were this true, the U.S.S.R. would be considered no longer a revolutionary power but rather a traditional nation-state. The present writer has seen no convincing evidence to that effect. On the contrary, dualism continues not only in policy-making but also in political substance. For example, the much advertised state interest for a relaxation of tensions goes hand in hand with the revolutionary interest, which, as Suslov has frequently stated, will continue, even though "peaceful coexistence" has become a major Soviet strategy.

As a result of this peculiarly communist logic the Soviet double standard, which started with Brest-Litovsk and has continued during the past fifty years, is now deeply ingrained not only in the older leaders but also in their successors, whose ability to understand the nonideological states remains very limited. The political and psychological climate of a closed society and the built-in antagonism toward Western political and societal concepts seem to have perpetuated themselves even among those leaders whose interpretation of the Marxist-Leninist gospel is less fundamentalist than that of the Bolsheviks.

It is essential to keep in mind these premises for the double standard of Soviet foreign policy when we consider some concepts and examples (of necessity, highly condensed) of dualism in foreign affairs during the most significant periods of Soviet history.

SOVIET CONCEPT OF INTERNATIONAL LAW

Law is the product of society. It grows out of the traditions and customs of the people who are subject to its rules, whether by free acceptance or by imposition. A nation's legal institutions reflect its political philosophy, economic organization, religion (if any), and moral concepts. Historical developments play a role in nonrevolutionary societies; genuine revolutions attempt to break with historical continuity.

The similarities among the laws of the nations of the Western world are greater than their differences: their cultural genealogy goes back to Greco-Roman and Judeo-Christian sources. Similarly, international law, first codified by the Dutchman Hugo Grotius in the seventeenth century, generally is based on these sources. So great has been the attraction of a universal law of nations that even non-Western countries have consented to Western concepts of international law, regardless of whether or not domestically they have adopted Western methods of political and social organization. Although international law for all practical purposes is not enforceable, and although its principles were frequently violated, on the whole the law of nations provided a universal platform on which to build relations among countries.

With the victory of the Bolshevik Revolution this legal one-world concept was ended. The leaders of the Revolution denigrated a law created by bourgeois-class states. But they were in no position to disregard this law and thereby isolate themselves from the rest of the civilized world. Their legal dilemma grew out of a political quandary: "If international law was socialist, it could not have antedated 1917 and could not bind capitalist states; if it was capitalist it could not bind the Soviet Union; if it was above class, it implied renunciation of a fundamental Marxist thesis."[1] The first Comintern Congress in 1919 had set the stage for this dilemma by proclaiming the fundamental antagonism of the proletarian dictatorship toward bourgeois democracy. This virtual declaration of war against noncommunist societies seemed to imply rejection of the body of private and public international law which, after two centuries of wrangling, was just being accepted as the nineteenth century yielded to the twentieth.[2]

However, it did not take the Bolsheviks long to realize that they lived in the world and not outside of it and that they must develop a Soviet legal concept which would relate to existing international law without compromising Soviet ideology. This was a difficult task, and the history of Soviet thought on international law is full of oscillations. Could a universal international law embrace both socialism and capitalism? Could devotees of the class struggle submit to laws written by class enemies, even if it served their interest to be protected from international lawlessness? Clearly, the existence of international law could not be denied, even though it was created by bourgeois states, albeit prior to the Bolshevik victory. The communists could not reject it altogether and thus become international outlaws.

The first communist textbook on international law, published in 1924, states that relations between Soviet Russia and the imperialistic states, large or small, depend on the view of the class structure of these states—this is part and parcel of the official Soviet doctrine, applied both to building up the structure of the Soviet republic and to its concept of international relations.[3] But, if international law is the product of class states, and if there exist such opposite economic and political systems as capitalism and socialism, the question remains whether the universality of the law can be admitted, even though there can be no international law without such recognition. In the beginning of Soviet history, this question was answered with a "temporary compromise between two antagonistic class systems."[4] World revolution then still seemed imminent, and the time span of the compromise was to be short. In fact, a few years later, even the concept of compromise was denied and replaced by the concept of struggle between the two systems of international law.

By the time Stalin had consolidated his position, repudiated Trotskyism, and proclaimed "socialism in one country," the need for a new formulation of the Soviet concept of international law arose again because the need for more-or-less normal trade relations had become vital to the survival of the Soviet state. It was based on the dualistic principle of co-operation and competition. This implied recognition of the universality of international law. Yet the need for a socialist international law has never ceased to occupy the minds of Soviet jurists, even when it was recognized that "contemporary international relations and the co-operation of states with different systems must be regulated by the same universally recognized norms of international law which are binding for all subjects of the law, no matter to which system they adhere."[5]

Written while Stalin was still alive, this statement sounds oddly reasonable. It must be analyzed in light of the fact that the class character of law was not to be forgotten. This dialectic situation could not help but develop the policy of dualism to a point of scholastic absurdity. On the one hand, the idea of co-operation—i.e., adherence to universality—was championed; on the other hand, the concept of competition between the old and new systems of international law was promoted. It is interesting and significant that the twofold Soviet concept of sovereignty relates to the dualism of international law. On the one hand, state sovereignty is regarded as a protective shield of the Soviet state and society; on the other hand, national sovereignty is held to be the legal basis for an aggressive self-determination that might be used to defend the doctrine of national liberation (and, in this connection, the national liberation wars).

This dualism of Soviet interpretation has the advantage of legally protecting the Soviet and other communist states from outside interference, while at the same time advancing a revolutionary interpretation of self-determination throughout the world. It is the key to understanding Soviet political strategy. A further consideration must be deduced from this position: the Soviet leaders have serious mental reservations toward any international organization whose members are divided by profound ideological differences, as their relations with the League of Nations and the United Nations demonstrate.

Khrushchev's elevation of the "peaceful coexistence" doctrine from a tactic to a strategy under which "international law must be interpreted and developed to service the interests of peace and socialism" has succeeded in consolidating many views and interpretations of international law. It combines co-operation with competition and propaganda.[6] Furthermore, peaceful coexistence "is the Soviet political and legal formula for international relations during the present epoch."[7] The dualism contained in the term was succinctly expressed by Khrushchev in his speech of January 6, 1961, when he claimed that "the policy of peaceful coexistence . . . is a form of intense economic, political, and ideological struggle of the proletariat against the aggressive forces of imperialism in the international arena."[8] Previously, the Statement of the 81 Communist and Workers Parties of December, 1960, had stipulated that ". . . the policy of peaceful coexistence is a policy of mobilizing the masses and launching vigorous action against the enemies of peace. . . . In conditions of peaceful coexistence favorable opportunities are provided for the development of the class struggle in the capitalist countries and the national liberation movement of the people of the colonial and dependent countries." Another indication of the dualistic Soviet interpretation of "peaceful coexistence" was contained in Leonid Brezhnev's Report of the Central Committee of the C.P.S.U. to the twenty-third Congress of the C.P.S.U., in which it was stated that the course of the party and of the state in foreign policy ". . . has been guided by the vital interests of the people of the Soviet Union and by a desire to ensure peaceful conditions for the building of communism and socialism in the countries of the world socialist community and to prevent the unleashing of a fresh world war."[9]

In terms of international law, "peaceful coexistence" is eminently suitable to serve the dual purposes of Soviet attempts to create a "socialist international law" and, at the same time, to convince noncommunist governments, with the help of traditional diplomacy and propaganda, that the Soviet concept is superior for the preservation of peace (though not for the prevention of cold war). Since the states of the Western alliance, including Japan, are politically far too sophisticated to accept this strategy, the main efforts of the Kremlin are directed toward the countries of Asia, Africa, and Latin America, in part through machinations in the United Nations. Thus the Soviet leaders have succeeded, with the help of their international jurists, in formulating a double-purpose doctrine of international law which serves them admirably in their formulation of foreign policy. In fact, this concept is far more sophisticated than that of the Lenin-Stalin era, during which the peaceful coexistence slogan was tactical in nature. At the Twentieth Congress of the C.P.S.U. in 1956, Khrushchev proposed a unity of opposites which would combine ideological with pragmatic elements of party and state policies. But his name was not mentioned in the Theses of the Central Committee of the C.P.S.U., "On the Fiftieth Anniversary of the Great Socialist October Revolution," published in *Pravda* on June 25, 1967, which made it clear that the foreign policy of the socialist countries

. . . is aimed at consolidating all anti-imperialist, peace-loving forces and at fighting the forces of reaction and war. An integral part of it is the course set toward peaceful coexistence of states with different social systems. This course is aimed against the unleashing of a new world war by the imperialists, against international provocations and the export of counterrevolution, at the creation of conditions favorable for the implementation by the peoples of their sacred rights of independently determining the road of development of their countries, at the development of mutually advantageous economic and scientific-technical co-operation, and at cultural exchanges between all countries.

And, in conjunction with this combination of contradictory goals, the dualistic concept of war is emphasized again: "While condemning predatory imperialist wars, Marxist-Leninists consider as just, and support, those wars which are waged in defense of the people's gains from imperialist aggression, wars for national liberation, and wars of the revolutionary classes repulsing attempts by reactionary forces to retain or restore their domination with the help of arms." This division between "just" and "unjust" wars has been part of Soviet foreign-policy doctrine throughout almost half a century and is a particularly apt demonstration of the Soviet concept of international relations.

EARLY BOLSHEVIK FOREIGN POLICY

The early Bolshevik leaders were strictly internationalist in outlook. Taking their cue from the decree of the French National Assembly of April 20, 1892, they looked upon themselves not as the citizens of Russia but as leaders of the world revolution. This attitude was reflected in the institution in charge of relations with foreign countries, the People's Commissariat for Foreign Affairs, of which Leon Trotsky was the first commissar. He summed up his view of the job by stating that he would "issue a few revolutionary proclamations to the peoples of the world and then shut up shop."[10] He dismissed Russian diplomats abroad, deputized a few unqualified individuals, and reportedly visited the office only once during his tenure.[11]

One could say that the only time Bolshevik policy pursued a single rather than a dual purpose was the strictly revolutionary policy of the period between the October Revolution and the second round of the Brest-Litovsk negotiations. The "Decree on Peace," issued by the All-Russian Congress of Soviets one day after the Bolshevik power seizure, appealing to the belligerents on both sides, fizzled. No revolutions occurred elsewhere. When armistice negotiations between the Germans and the revolutionaries led nowhere, the Germans began a new offensive, penetrating deep into Russian territory. In order to save the Revolution, the Bolsheviks, considering their state interest, signed an extremely unfavorable armistice in March, 1918. In this context it is revealing that Soviet dualism allows for flexibility and retreat. In commenting on the Brest-Litovsk peace, Lenin said to the Seventh Congress of the Russian Communist Party: "We must know how to retreat. . . . If you cannot adjust yourself, if you cannot bring yourself to crawl on your belly in the mud, you are no revolutionary, but a chatterbox. . . ."[12]

Since then, preoccupation with the success of world revolution and concern over national security have remained the essential ingredients of dualistic Soviet foreign policy. It had become clear that a weak state would be unable to protect itself against the hostile forces of "imperialism," that its security must be safeguarded by making it stronger politically, economically, and militarily. Trotsky became People's Commissar for War, and the sophisticated Gheorgy Chicherin replaced Trotsky as Commissar for Foreign Affairs. Chicherin, although a confirmed Marxist, began to shift slightly away from revolutionary aggressiveness toward diplomatic coexistence. But then, allied intervention, limited as it was, made such a position impossible.

Moreover, the success of the German revolution and the fall of the monarchy in November, 1918, was not tantamount to communist takeover in that country. In early 1919 two of the most prominent representatives of the *Spartakusbund,* which became the first Communist party of Germany, were assassinated—Karl Liebknecht and Rosa Luxemburg. The Social Democrats in power outlawed the party, which went underground. A revolution in Germany, which had been the great hope of Lenin, had become, in his words, a Kerensky type of revolution, totally unacceptable to him. Thus Soviet policy once again veered toward an unadulterated revolutionary stance.

Since Russia was completely isolated—shunned by the rest of the world—such a defensive reaction was to be expected. It is perhaps more than coincidental that the establishment of the Third Communist International (Comintern) took place at this time (March, 1919) and that it appealed to the proletariat of all countries to stand behind the Russian Soviets. These propaganda efforts were unsuccessful.

The Second Comintern Congress, of July/August, 1920, in an optimistic mood after the initial successes of the Red Army in the war with Poland, adopted the conditions of admission to the Comintern. Together, they were a blueprint for organization of international communism and also set forth the communist aspects of foreign policy. From then on, the Soviet concept of relations with bourgeois nations as devised by Moscow was imposed upon Comintern members, not all of whom accepted it with alacrity.[13] This revolutionary stance neither helped Soviet Russia to break out of its isolation nor invigorated the rather desperate economic situation. Abroad, a communist attempt to seize power in Germany ended in catastrophic defeat. Lenin, the revolutionary fanatic, could be pragmatic when necessary. To give the economy a breathing spell, he created the New Economic Policy, which the West wrongly interpreted as a "return to capitalism." With the help of a political adjustment to prevalent conditions, which did not diminish Comintern activities, Lenin sought to break out of isolation.

Britain

Although a trade treaty prohibiting political propaganda was signed with Britain in March, 1921, the Comintern blithely continued its subversive anti-British activities. In September, 1921, the British denounced the Soviets for having violated the provisions of the Trade Agreement. The Bolsheviks were accused of carrying on hostile propaganda against the British Empire in Afghanistan, aiding Indian revolutionaries against the British government, giving financial aid to a well-known Indian anarchist, pursuing a policy hostile to British interests in Persia, setting up schools in Tashkent for training Indian natives in anti-British propaganda, supporting Turkish nationalists (still then nominally at war with the Entente Powers) with money and munitions, etc. The Soviet reply denied the accuracy of these claims and admonished the British government not to identify the activities of the Communist International with the actions of the Soviet government. While it was true that some members of the Soviet government were also members of the Executive Committee of the Comintern, they were so only in their individual capacities.[14]

Germany

At the Genoa Conference of April, 1922, Russia and Germany, the one-time outlaws, were in effect reinstated as great powers (against France's vote), although the conference failed to achieve its predominantly economic purposes. During the conference, using an Easter recess, the German and Russian delegates met secretly in Rapallo and signed a treaty. The historic significance of this agreement lay not only in its provisions—it ended the isolation of the two ostracized powers.

Germany, in Bolshevik eyes, was considered then—and is considered now, despite its division—a country of prime importance. Lenin had always looked to Germany because of its advanced industrial capabilities and its revolutionary potential. This potential was overestimated then, as West German power is now. Rapallo may seem to have been a success of traditional diplomacy, but the Comintern Statement of May 19,

1922, referring to the Rapallo Treaty, made clear that it had no love for the German "bourgeois-Menshevik" government and regarded it as temporary: "The German working class will one day inevitably conquer power in their own country. Germany will become a Soviet republic. And then, when the German-Russian treaty brings together two great Soviet republics, it will provide such unshakable foundation for real communist construction that the old and outworn Europe will not be able to withstand it even for a few years."[15]

Chicherin and Joffe had done well by Soviet Russia the nation-state, but not too well for revolutionary Comintern purposes. Zinoviev, then still a very influential man in the Comintern, was more concerned with the consequences of Rapallo for international communism than with its world political implications. A schism was developing between Chicherin the diplomatist and Zinoviev the revolutionist and between their respective organizations, the Narkomindel and the Comintern. Radek, the representative of the Comintern in Germany, tried unsuccessfully to reconcile the two positions. By the end of 1922 Lenin had suffered his first stroke. Stalin at that time remained in the background. There were many crosscurrents in both the Soviet government and the Comintern.

Lacking Lenin's guidance, policy toward the German government and the German Communist party oscillated wildly. Trotsky and Zinoviev prevailed over Radek. As a result the German KPD leaders, after mapping their strategy under Soviet guidance, led an uprising in October, 1923, which collapsed. The KPD was outlawed once again but was permitted to resume operations about four months later. For the Russians a lesson was to be learned: "At long last the Bolshevik leaders abandoned the mirage of the German revolution. Never again were the expectations of an early revolution in Germany allowed to override the normal considerations of foreign policy. Never again would the Comintern pursue an independent policy of its own."[16] Rather, under Stalin's leadership, there would be an amalgamation of state and party considerations, forged in the Politburo. And, as the years passed, Stalin would strive to make the Soviet Union strong both as a nation, as the center of world communism, and, after the war, as the leading power of the "socialist camp." The foreign policy of the U.S.S.R. would remain two-pronged.[17]

After Rapallo, the failure of the German communist uprising, and the European proletariat's general lack of success in achieving a victorious revolution, the position and influence of the Comintern changed imperceptibly. At the Fourth Comintern Congress in November, 1922, it became clear that the Bolshevik Revolution's achievements in overcoming seemingly insurmountable difficulties at home and abroad had to be credited to Soviet state power rather than to international machinations of an organization set up to promote world revolution. Lenin, who previously had complained that the Comintern should be international rather than Russian, kept silent on this issue.

The fact was that the Comintern inevitably did become a Soviet-directed institution. After Lenin's death in 1924, and Stalin's takeover not long thereafter, it remained a suitable instrument of Soviet revolutionary and state foreign policy. Indeed, "henceforth the policy of Comintern would be fitted into the framework of Soviet foreign policy instead of Soviet foreign policy being fitted . . . into a framework of world revolution."[18]

To enhance international communist intrigue, new stratagems and organizational attempts were made, such as the establishment of the Profintern (Red International of Trade Unions) and the introduction of "united-front" tactics, presumably to supplement or implement Comintern directives. In any event, the years of European consolidation, including the *de jure* recognition of Soviet Russia by most industrial nations (except the United States), could not help but keep Comintern aspirations on a low level, the more so since the Bolsheviks, determining the country's foreign policy, were now in a sufficiently strong position to decide whether to use national or communist foreign policies or a combination of both.

Asia

What was true in Europe was no less true in Asia. Since Russia is both a European and an Asian power, the interests of the Bolsheviks in the Far East were secondary only to those in Europe. The dualistic course followed by Moscow, tempered by the influence of an active Comintern policy, created in China a situation that would have repercussions long after the events of the twenties and thirties. In 1919 the Kremlin officially had given up tsarist claims on China, but it soon retreated from its original concessions concerning the future of the Chinese Eastern Railway. Before long the Soviets successfully re-established themselves in the Far Eastern territories. More important, an autonomous Outer Mongolian republic had come into being in late 1921.

In China itself, the establishment in Canton of Sun Yat-sen's opposition regime, which was warring with the central government in Peking—then still universally recognized—did not prevent the Soviets from approaching Peking. The central government, however, did not succumb to Bolshevik blandishments, nor did it accept Moscow's proposals. While the Soviet missions to Peking failed, co-operation did begin between Moscow and Canton. The Soviet Russian representative, A. A. Joffe, reaffirmed to Sun on January 26, 1923, that the principles proclaimed by the Bolsheviks on September 27, 1920, concerning the abandoment of tsarist privileges in China were still in force, that the Soviet system was not applicable to Chinese conditions, that the Chinese Eastern Railway question could be solved by Sino-Russian negotiations, and that Russia had no imperialistic designs on Outer Mongolia.

In September of the same year, Moscow's Michael Borodin became Sun's political adviser. He organized the Kuomintang (KMT) along Communist party lines. But, although communists tried to infiltrate it, the KMT never became an arm of the Russian party. Although the Chinese Communist party had been established in 1921, Stalin considered it too weak to be useful and instead encouraged its members to seek individual membership in the KMT. When Sun died, Chiang Kai-shek took over. This radically altered Sino-Soviet relations. Chiang did not propose to tolerate communist subversion and gradually sought to wipe it out. After the 1927 massacres of communists,

Stalin was compelled to break relations with Chiang, only to restore them after Japanese forces invaded the Chinese mainland.

This greatly oversimplified picture of an extremely complex and often confused situation is projected for the purpose of demonstrating the Soviet technique of carrying out simultaneously both state and communist foreign policies on different levels and for different purposes. National security considerations vis-à-vis China had been important in traditional Russian policy considerations. After the Revolution they still loomed large, with the difference, however, that the Soviet leaders probably regarded communist sympathies as a safeguard against a clash between Russian and Chinese state interests. Thus they sought to spread the influence of communism throughout the Chinese political and social system. Sun Yat-sen was a politically naïve man and undoubtedly an idealist; Joffe and Borodin tried to take advantage of this state of mind. While Chiang, less the idealist, did manage to hold off communist influence for some years, he did not possess the wisdom and strength to cleanse his government and prevent it from eventual disintegration and defeat at the hand of Mao Tse-tung's forces.

NAZISM VERSUS BOLSHEVISM: NATIONAL SECURITY OR REVOLUTION?

In 1933, when Hitler came to power, Germany left the League of Nations. Japan had already left. The Soviet leaders correctly regarded this as a danger signal and earnestly considered a policy reversal toward the League. It may be useful to review briefly their position vis-à-vis that organization between 1919 and 1933.

In the early years of the Revolution, the League was called a "monstrous worldwide trust" which would exploit the world;[19] an imperialist instrument consisting of a temporary association of capitalist states for the double purpose of endangering the security of the Soviet state and stopping the advancement of the communist world revolution; an effort to crush the democratic forces of the proletariat. Lenin called it "an alliance of world bandits against the proletariat."[20] The orthodox Bolsheviks regarded the League as opposed not only to the proletariat in Russia but also to the working masses within the imperialist states. In their "Appeal for the Formation of the Communist International," Lenin and Trotsky opposed the "hypocrisy" of the League, which was organized to "strangle the revolution."[21] And Chicherin added that it was "a league of capitalists against the nations."[22] As late as 1927 Stalin remarked to a delegation of foreign workers that the Soviet Union could not take part in the League of Nations "because it [the Soviet Union] is against imperialism, against the oppression of the colonies and dependent peoples."[23]

The substantively most important objections were these: (1) Soviet Russia could not associate itself with a group of states of entirely different social structures; (2) sanctions could be undertaken against Russia with the goal of destroying communism; and (3) Soviet Russia regarded the mandate system as an exploitation of colonial peoples. However, these criticisms did not prevent Soviet representatives from participating in some international conferences organized for the League and dealing primarily with humanitarian, health, and communications problems. Yet, despite the fact that the failure of the Comintern to produce revolutions had led to a gradual lessening of its importance, and, further, that the Soviet economy needed a breathing spell very badly, no appreciable progress was made in the direction of a change in Soviet policy toward the League.

Only when Nazism became rampant did Stalin look to the League as an organization that might possibly "retard or prevent the outbreak of war." In December, 1933, he said, "It is not impossible that we shall support the League, notwithstanding its collossal defects."[24] Finally, on September 18, 1934, the U.S.S.R. requested membership and was admitted. It was on this occasion that Maxim Litvinov introduced the Soviet concept of international law as based on "peaceful coexistence of different sociopolitical systems at a given historical stage."

It appears that under internal and external pressures the Soviet leaders were willing to co-operate with the "imperialists" and accept the idea of collective security. They did this, no doubt, with many mental reservations. Without the Nazi, fascist, and Japanese threats, it is doubtful that they suddenly would have been so co-operative. But, owing to their strong feeling for formal legality, mingled with the tactical goals of their system, their attitude toward the League during the period of their membership was correct and their "record in the Council and the Assembly and conduct towards the aggressive powers were more consistent with the Covenant than those of any other great power."[25] Their objective was primarily the securing of a common front against Nazi-fascist aggression. When they felt they were making little progress toward this goal through collective security means, their disappointment, in conjunction with other factors, probably contributed to their decision to conclude a nonaggression pact with Nazi Germany in August, 1939. For the sake of national security, the Soviets had signed a pact with their mortal enemy. "In no sphere was the basic dualism between national and revolutionary policies revealed more clearly than in the contacts between Russia and Germany, and in none were its repercussions more lasting."[26]

Three months later, the Red Army invaded Finland. In December, 1939, the U.S.S.R. was expelled from the League for launching a war in disregard of the Covenant. Immediately, the previous Soviet hostility toward the League was restored.

The 1934 decision of the U.S.S.R. to join the League cannot be separated from the change of communist policy subsequently set forth by the Seventh Comintern Congress in 1935. Moscow's policy reversal of the previous year had to be explained and codified in international communist terms. In that meeting, the Bulgar Georgi Dimitrov, who was elected general secretary by the Congress, emphasized the need to use all means to vanquish capitalist imperialism. He called for subversion, citing as an example the technique used by the ancient Greeks to conquer Troy: the wooden horse. As the U.S.S.R. had joined a "front" of sorts in the League, so the communists should enter popular fronts, co-operating with all antifascist parties.

France serves as a good example of this policy in action, for it pioneered with a popular-front government. The communists not only tried to improve their relations with the Catholic church but also sought allies among the socialists and even beyond the moderate left. The Franco-Soviet Pact of May, 1935, helped this development, as did communist-socialist "co-operation" in the Spanish Civil War.[27]

Although chiding social-democratic leaders for their lack of revolutionary spirit, Wilhelm Pieck, a leading German communist, declared that "the idea that all bourgeois parties were Fascist [must be] denounced as a total misconception."[28] Rather, the working class was "exhorted to cherish every scrap of bourgeois democracy until it could be replaced by proletarian democracy."[29] Thus the establishment of "popular fronts" was approved so long as it was understood that ultimate communist leadership remained the goal. So understood, the technique was well used by the Soviets in World War II.

There also are good indications of the technique's particular usefulness in combining national feeling with the doctrine of class conflict. Thorez of France, Browder of the United States, and Dimitrov of Bulgaria introduced this aspect at the 1935 Comintern meeting. International interests, according to Dimitrov, could be defended by national forms of the class struggle, and "proletarian internationalism must, so to speak, 'acclimatize itself' in each country in order to sink deep roots in its native land."[30] This, in a sense, was a greater break in Leninist doctrine than the pragmatic change of policy vis-à-vis the League of Nations and the subsequent Molotov-Ribbentrop Pact. Lenin had called upon the vanguard to "lead," not to "acclimatize."

The use of nationalist tendencies by the Soviet leaders has been much misunderstood in noncommunist countries. The appeal to love of country has been subtly exploited by the Kremlin whenever necessary. Nationalism under a communist regime differs from that of other countries, for Soviet "patriotism" combines attachment to the motherland with dedication to the system under which it lives, and is equated with "proletarian internationalism." The amalgamation of communist doctrine with Soviet nationalism, or of internationalism with the Soviet commonwealth, is like the imprints on a coin: though different on either side, together they produce one coin. The Seventh Comintern Congress, perhaps more than any other communist congregation, contributed to this rather unique conceptual merger, which eventually became official Soviet policy at the Twentieth Congress of the C.P.S.U.

From the Comintern point of view, this was, of course, a tactic and nothing else. The newly advocated popular fronts were to help the united front of the proletariat in its antifascist endeavors. But the Kremlin's schizophrenic policies, veering between international communism and Soviet state interests, continued with emphasis on one or the other, as conditions warranted. Even while state or security interests may have had primacy during certain periods, they remained immersed in doctrinal party-oriented thinking, from which no Soviet leader, regardless of age, apparently can separate himself. Thus dualism has continued.

THE WAR: 1939–45

The German attack against Poland and the subsequent declaration of war on Nazi Germany by France and Britain were interpreted by the Kremlin—and by communists all over the world—as an "imperialist war." It was a conflict that might lead to exhaustion of the belligerents and cause revolutions similar to those in Russia of 1917. Hoping against hope that he might not be directly involved, Stalin embarked on a policy of territorial expansion in eastern Poland, the Baltic States, Finland, Bessarabia, and northern Bukovina. Further plans for an increase in Soviet spheres of interest, which eventually was to give the U.S.S.R. access to the Indian Ocean, were discussed in Berlin, Tokyo, and Moscow.

In June, 1941, when the Soviet Union was invaded by German armies, the war immediately became "just" and "patriotic."[31] Communist doctrine distinguishes between "imperialist aggressive, predatory wars . . . and defensive wars which the people are compelled to undertake in self-defense against aggression or intervention or counter-revolution. . . . Such wars, naturally, have the sympathy and support of communists, as of all honest and progressive people."[32] Lenin's theory of differentiating between imperialist wars—conflicts between capitalist states—and wars in defense of capitalist aggression against socialist countries dominated the thinking of the Stalinist era. Thus the outbreak of hostilities in 1939 between Germany and Poland, Britain, and France was regarded and labeled as an intercapitalist, imperialist war. Only after the Nazis had attacked the U.S.S.R. and the Western powers became allies of the Soviet Union did Moscow change the label of imperialist aggression to that of a defense against fascism. Later on, World War II became the "Great Patriotic War." In this switch from party to national label, Soviet dualism in the interpretation of war expresses itself with particular clarity.

While the war went badly, the East-West alliance prospered. But when it became clear after the British-American invasion of North Africa in November, 1942, and the Nazi surrender at Stalingrad in February, 1943, that the fortunes of war began to favor the Allies, political issues involving opposing views came to the fore again. Adherence to very general principles, such as the Atlantic Charter, was favored by Moscow as well as by Washington and London. But specific political issues could neither then nor later be resolved. They were bound to cause trouble after the end of the war.

It is significant that, while the Western leaders were primarily concerned with winning the war militarily, Stalin, even in the darkest days of the conflict, never forgot the political problems that would arise after a victorious end of the hostilities. These considerations became paramount when it was certain that the Allies were winning. The schism between the political concepts of the Western and Eastern allies was best illustrated in the debate about the future of Poland. Other controversial issues were the territorial and political aspirations of Stalin in Finland and Eastern Europe, postwar Germany, and the status of Japan and China.

The much-debated Yalta agreement, which granted concessions to the Soviet Union, the full meaning of which became evident only later, provided Stalin with an entree to Eastern Europe. "Not until later was it realized in the West that Hitler's tyranny had been replaced by another."[33] Soviet imperialism, guided by both *raison d'état* and ideology, attempted to advance the frontiers of "socialism" as far as possible.

Its territorial expansion after World War II provided the Soviet Union with more space in depth, either annexed or left under the rule of loyal communist vassals hewing to Moscow's party line. The development of Western nuclear arsenals stopped the further spread of Soviet territorial dominance, but not the attempts to subvert "noncommitted" areas or to infiltrate political life in other countries. Stalin was an ideological imperialist. He never lost sight of the need to strengthen his nation, but neither did he forget the fundamental principles on which it was built: to make the Soviet Union an unbeatable bastion of world communism. It is true that his successors did not approve of many of his policies and adjusted theirs to the nuclear age. But they stuck to the fundamentals. They continued the cold war that Stalin had initiated after 1945 and for which almost certainly he had prepared his plans even while his armies and those of his allies fought a common enemy.

STALIN'S COLD WAR: 1945–53

The war was won and the Soviet Union was on its way to becoming the second most powerful country in the world. More than that: with the acquisition of dominance over Eastern Europe and the subsequent victory of Mao Tse-tung's forces over Chiang Kai-shek, Moscow became the center of the "world socialist system." Flushed with their new status, convinced that Marxism-Leninism was the wave of the future, the communists resumed the struggle against "imperialism" full scale. The undeclared cold war broke out.

It was an East-West seesaw battle. There were failures on both sides, but perhaps the more serious ones were suffered by the Kremlin. The attempt to annex Azerbaidjan from Iran failed. So did the communists in the Greek civil war. American policy stiffened considerably with the adoption of the "containment" policy. Zhdanov countered by pronouncing that the world was now split into two hostile camps. The Cominform was established to conduct a well-co-ordinated campaign against the "capitalists." The Berlin blockade was set up but ended in failure. All these frantic efforts appear to have been heavily motivated by ideological considerations. The point could be made that *raison d'état* was subordinated to revolutionary activities, which, however, were largely unsuccessful in Western Europe, despite the growth of the communist parties in France and Italy.

At that time, the United States concentrated its efforts to rehabilitate Europe as well as Japan. Such extraordinary projects as the Marshall Plan did not help Moscow's designs to create unrest or, worse, revolutions. Like Lenin in the early twenties, Stalin probably expected a major conflict between the "imperialists." When it did not occur, and when the East-West stalemate in Europe hardened, he launched a "peace campaign."

The Soviets had not invented this stratagem. It had been started in Paris in March, 1948, by the "Combattants de la Liberté" led by Yves Farge, a communist opponent of De Gaulle. It was directed against "neofascists" and collaborationists. It did not begin as a "peace" organization, but it became such in August, 1948, when the Polish communists staged the "World Congress of Intellectuals for Peace." The Cominform took up the idea and helped spread it.

Peace meetings were held in both communist and noncommunist countries. Important peace congresses were arranged in New York and Paris. The establishment of NATO, feared and bitterly opposed by the Soviets, became one of the primary targets of these congresses. The main attack was directed against the Western governments, which allegedly prepared for a new war. Of all communist front organizations, the "World Peace Council" (W.P.C.) probably was the most successful in that it gained a great many noncommunist members. At least eighty countries opened branch offices; the entire organization was under Moscow-directed communist leadership and strictly followed Soviet policies.[34]

With Suslov in charge of the party, and Molotov of the state aspects of the campaign, the communist and workers' parties were ordered to give priority to the "struggle for peace." Next, the co-operation of all sympathizing elements of the populations was sought to fight anticommunist governments and to try to replace them, by constitutional procedures, with "peace-loving" governments. This campaign was marked by hostility toward America and Britain, who were "preparing for war against the Soviet Union, while the Soviet Union was pursuing a policy of peace."[35] Under organizational direction of the W.P.C. and with the political and financial support of the Kremlin, the campaign was steadily intensified and broadened to encompass anyone who was for "peace" and, therefore, by implication not anticommunist.

Particularly relevant is the comparison of Molotov's peace campaign policies with those of Suslov. Molotov, conjuring "peaceful coexistence" as the basic Soviet state policy, warned against imperialist war threats and demanded an ever more effective struggle for "peace," eschewing pacifism and suggesting the preparation for any military or political eventuality. His emphasis on military and ideological preparedness, on the one hand, and peace, on the other, is one more example of Soviet dialectics. The party spokesman Suslov, accusing the West of an unholy alliance of rightists and warmongers, mapped out a program of intensification of the peace campaign, supported by a combination of peace-supporting heterogeneous elements in a "united front from below" so as to tighten the unity of the workers. Moreover, he likened the peace movement to the "struggle for national independence," thereby creating a potent political weapon that was used against the bourgeois governments and became influential throughout the "third world."[36]

This state-party dualism on two fronts seemed formidable at the time, but repressive Soviet policies in Eastern Europe, stimulation of extreme violence in Greece, continued harassing tactics in Berlin, obvious Soviet support of the extremely hardlined French party (which attempted to sabotage the unloading of American weapons for France)—all these actions, combined with a steady stream of shrill and intimidating propaganda, did not have the effect Moscow had expected. The world remained largely unmoved by the Soviet effort. The signatures on the Stockholm Peace Appeal of 1950 were secured largely from behind the Iron Curtain. The campaign had been designed to counter Western military strength and, especially, the U.S. possession of the atomic bomb. The new weapon, although publicly denigrated by Stalin, presumably worried the Politburo and compelled it to assign priority to both the collection of information (including espionage) and the development of nuclear and space technology.

The World Peace Council, however, was only one of the mushrooming communist front organizations charged with providing a façade for spreading the Soviet-communist party line among the various professional and vocational organizations that have come under direct or indirect Soviet control or influence. These fronts were active both as national and as international bodies. Different from popular or united fronts, they were actually propaganda outfits that also undertook operational duties directly affecting the countries in which they were active. Apart from the World Peace Council, the World Federation of Trade Unions (W.F.T.U.) probably was the most important front because, through its members, it could interfere in the economy of noncommunist countries by means of strikes, civil unrest, and riots. It also served to reinforce leftist opposition parties and to stimulate infiltraton for purposes of subversion and espionage in noncommunist labor organizations.

A relative of the extinct Profintern, the W.F.T.U. was created in 1945. Russian, American, British, French, and Latin American labor unions joined. The first general secretary was Louis Saillant, a prominent French communist; thus, from the outset, communists led the organization. Only after several years did the noncommunist members recognize the character of leadership and purpose of the W.F.T.U. They quit in 1950. Since then, the W.F.T.U. has served as an uninhibited propaganda organ for Soviet foreign policy, thereby implementing dualistic policies rather than caring for the well-being of its affiliate branches. "The W.F.T.U.'s 'unity of action' campaign consists of appeals and invitations to its rival internationals for cooperation on such general problems as peaceful coexistence, opposition to the use of atomic and hydrogen weapons, and resistance to productivity drives in the West."[37] West Germany and colonialism also came under constant attack. As in the case of the World Peace Council, so the W.F.T.U. eventually became identified with communist aims that deprived both organizations of their original reputation of legitimacy.[38]

In addition to these two, there were other fronts, such as those for students, women, and the professions. In advanced countries, their influence has remained limited, even though some are still not generally recognized for what they are: instruments of Soviet propaganda among the intellectual circles. They have had somewhat better success in the developing countries of Africa, Asia, and Latin America, where they serve the purposes of the Soviet state and party. Since the early sixties, however, they have been hampered by the Sino-Soviet conflict and have been attacked by Peking, which is trying to set up rival organizations.[39]

During Stalin's cold war, "peaceful coexistence" was no more than a tactic to be used whenever opportunity arose. His peace campaign and the creation of other front organizations served as important implementers of a policy that attempted to prevent the cure of social and economic illnesses of the noncommunist world. Moreover, it was Stalin's belief that wars between the capitalist powers were inevitable; "peaceful coexistence" applied predominantly to relations between the U.S.S.R. and the imperialists—for the time being. He undoubtedly agreed with Lenin that an eventual clash between socialism and capitalism was unavoidable, but he was unwilling to accept such a clash in the atomic age. This is suggested by his policy in the Korean conflict, where he carried on the fight by proxy and subordinated revolution to national security.

Before he died, Stalin gained control of, or heavily influenced, the Eastern European states (except Yugoslavia), North Korea, and communist parties all over the globe. Almost all these states and parties did his bidding. Soviet foreign policy, as created by the Politburo, garnered much help and impetus from the parties that carried out Stalin's wishes, even if they were against the better interests of their own countries. It is doubtful that this tight political organization of the "monolith" has had a precedent in known history.

THE DUALISM OF KHRUSHCHEV'S PEACEFUL COEXISTENCE

Khrushchev immediately sought to modernize Stalin's sterile polices after coming to power in 1954. In 1955 he made a pilgrimage to Belgrade to patch up the quarrel with Tito; he signed the Austrian State Treaty, which had long been under consideration; he established diplomatic relations with West Germany, although the basic problems of Germany's diversion and the suspicions against that country remained strong; he engaged in summitry; and a few months later he restored Porkkala to Finland—all in the name of "peaceful coexistence."

The dualistic policies in these concessions were not at first apparent. But in 1956 the continuation of Soviet political dualism became quite clear when Khrushchev ushered in a new era of Soviet communism at the Twentieth C.P.S.U. Congress. It ended Stalinist communism and the cohesive force of the monolith, and it was to bring about important changes in the Kremlin's conduct of international relations. It successfully fused policies of national interest with those of communist internationalism adapted to the nuclear age.

One might say that the primary significance of the Twentieth Congress was its confirmation of "peaceful coexistence" as a basic political strategy. It is important to realize that the "peaceful coexistence" policy which dominated Soviet policies from then on—much to the discomfiture of the Chinese Communists—is one of the prime examples of a dual approach in the formulation of Moscow's national and revolutionary policies. "Peaceful coexistence between states with different social systems," in the Soviet interpretation, is an amalgam of traditional and revolutionary policies, Narkomindel plus Comintern, so to speak. Although the Soviets have said explicitly that competition and struggle are to continue, to the uninitiated, "coexistence" appears to signify peace and accommodation and so is deceptive.

The evolving nature of the international struggle, however, constituted a change brought about by the nuclear stalemate, for which no Marxist-Leninist doctrine existed. In addition to the denigration of Stalin, Lenin's expectancy of inevitable war was modified, as was the belief that revolution must necessarily be violent. This modification of an old ideological principle brought political benefits not only to the "socialist camp" (Red China excluded) and the communist parties all over the world. For, even though the Twentieth Congress's revelations ushered in the era of polycentric communism, they paid dividends in the improved attitudes of many noncommunist nations toward a presumably more moderate and realistic Soviet leadership.

Eastern Europe

The immediate aftermath of this apparent liberalization was the rebellion in Poland and the uprising in Hungary against their Stalinist leaders' reluctance to adapt their policies to Khrushchevian reformism. The events in Poland remained self-controlled; those in Hungary did not. The Kremlin did not hesitate to intervene when it appeared that Imre Nagy wanted more independence than the Soviets would allow. "Peaceful coexistence" did not seem to work within the socialist family, and the impact on the world of the Soviet slaughter in Budapest was deep. It would have been even deeper had not the Suez affair of 1956 diverted world opinion.

The Middle East

The subsequent alienation of the Arab world from the West made it possible for the Kremlin to pursue an old Russian dream with increasing vigor, namely, the penetration of the Middle East. To view such policy in the Soviet era as purely nationalistic or even imperialistic would not be accurate. If it were, it could not have succeeded in a world that had just emerged from an era of imperialism and still was very suspicious of it. Rather, Soviet national interests were matched with the message of socialism and national liberation. Thus "Arab socialism" was encouraged, and, regardless of the fact that Egyptian communists were incarcerated, the growing trend of the Middle East toward socialism greatly stimulated the readiness of Muslim nations to accept help and friendship from a Marxist-Leninist state.

The United States

Khrushchev's visit to the United States seemed to confirm his estimate that the terms "peaceful coexistence" and "relaxation of tensions" could be used to advantage by skillful diplomacy. The tendency of President Eisenhower to foster peace and to improve relations between the two great superpowers was cultivated by Khrushchev. In his statement on September 28, 1959, after his return from America, Khrushchev gave Eisenhower credit for his efforts in the pursuit of peace. But this propagandistic statement, which did not seem to be dualistic at all, was quickly discarded when at the Paris conference of May, 1960, perhaps because he realized that he could not expect Western concessions, Khrushchev seized upon the U–2 incident to torpedo the summit meeting. Subsequently, the rosy picture of the American president became tainted in Soviet propaganda, and a more belligerent language replaced the friendly references to the "spirit of Camp David," the existence of which, real or unreal, was the result of a deep longing for an end to East-West antagonism.

China

The Sino-Soviet rift, which contributed to Khrushchev's political downfall and greately affected Soviet relations with other parts of the world, especially the countries of the "socialist camp," is a telling example of intercommunist dualism. Its basic causes are both doctrinal interpretation and political-power disagreements.[40] Narrow dogmatic concepts and crude behavior in international affairs on the part of Red China stood against the far more sophisticated "peaceful coexistence" policy of Moscow. The theses of the Twentieth C.P.S.U. Congress were too advanced for the thinking of the Chinese Communist fanatics.

The quarrel, which became public record in 1960, forced the Soviet Union to be more permissive toward the East European countries and to increase political activities, economic assistance, and weapons deliveries in some countries of the third world. This policy was unsuccessful in Indonesia, suffered a setback in the Middle East, and did not get far either in Africa or in Latin America, with the sole exception of Cuba. While underplaying the revolutionary aspects of its efforts and trying to hide its political aspirations—which had become practically one and the same—Moscow emphasized its role as a humanitarian nation led by a humanitarian (communist) party and simultaneously launched a new propaganda campaign against the Western "imperialists" and "colonialists." It would be difficult indeed to analyze Moscow's state policies without assessing the impact of communist doctrine on these policies.

Cuba

Khrushchev's Cuban interests, which culminated in an adventure leading to the brink of nuclear war in 1962, are another example of a two-pronged strategy. The prospect of having a communist state ninety miles from the coast of the United States seemed an alluring opportunity. Equipped with medium-range missiles, it would create a serious threat to U.S. security and thus be useful as a *quid pro quo* in any major quarrel between Moscow and Washington. Moreover, as a communist-ruled state, Cuba would be an outpost of revolution in Latin America and would serve as a military and ideological base in the struggle against American "imperialism." But, when Khrushchev embarked on his dangerous scheme of exporting rockets, he went much further than he had gone in Berlin and elsewhere. It was not in the Soviet national interest to engage in a nuclear war with the United States at that time. The attempt, thanks to

President Kennedy's strong position, was abortive. It was a setback for both the Soviet state and party when the rockets had to be removed, but Castro remained in power. Indeed, Soviet influence waned in Latin America in favor of "Castroism." Perhaps Castro dreamed of assuming the leadership in Latin America as the leader of the Caribbean and Latin American communist movement. Since the Soviet party had become a socialist vanguard by reputation, but not in fact, Castro may have planned to establish his own vanguard in the Southern Hemisphere.

SOVIET POLICIES TOWARD THE THIRD WORLD

"National liberation" and self-determination in theory and practice have had a long and rich history, beginning, at least in Lenin's mind, even before the victory of the Revolution. The development and application of these theories by Lenin and Stalin to the "colonial and semicolonial areas" offer a classic example of dualism and show a double standard of implementation inside and outside the U.S.S.R. Stalin had once written about "Marxism and the National Question," proposing the right of national minorities to secede or, if they did not, to be granted recognition of their autonomy. But the promise was never kept. The resolution on the national question, as adopted by the pre-revolutionary All-Russian Conference of the Russian Social Democratic Labor Party of May 12, 1917—which was never abrogated—remained empty words.

However, Soviet propaganda in later years, presenting the U.S.S.R. as the supporter of "national liberation movements," has been generally successful. Its effectiveness has varied and has diminished somewhat as various developing nations acquired greater political sophistication. On the whole, however, it still appears attractive, particularly to those countries which once were part of European controlled empires and thus had had no right to determine their futures. It will take some time for those countries to realize that the chief effort of Soviet foreign policy is not focused on liberation for liberation's sake, but on the creation of a third—neutralist—camp that eventually may become a Soviet sphere of interest.

In May, 1925, Stalin outlined the revolutionary premises for national liberation in colonial countries. They consisted of political organizations for the purpose of winning over the working class "to the side of communism," against the bourgeoisie and imperialism, and "to ensure the hegemony of the proletariat." But the 1928 Comintern Congress established a new line: only communists could direct national liberation movements. Again, in 1935, the Congress reverted to a more opportunistic line by replacing the "united front from above" with the "united front from below." At that time the world political situation did not favor radical measures, nor were Soviet internal conditions very promising.

When Khrushchev took over he developed the three-camp theory, adding the third—that of the developing nations—to Stalin's and Zhdanov's two. In the aftermath of the war, more and more former colonial areas became independent nations, nations still resentful, however, of their former dependent status under colonial masters. Consequently, Soviet policies catered to their pride of newly acquired sovereignty, and to the appeal of revolutionary, anticolonial communism it added economic aid. This dual approach was at least partially successful—so long as Moscow's emissaries did not become too obvious in their efforts at infiltration, as was the case in Guinea or the Congo.

The United States, as the strongest of the Western powers, has acquired, among some quarters, the reputation of a "colonial" power mainly because of its alliance with the former colonial empires of Europe. All "colonialist" nations were considered to represent an exploitative capitalist system, which, to many third world leaders, is unsuitable for the economic development of a society without a middle class, without technological know-how, and without political education. On the other hand, the U.S.S.R. has no record as a colonialist power, even though there had existed since tsarist times an internal colonialism, which Stalin tried to deal with as the "national question." Moreover, communism, or "socialism," appeals to the poverty-ridden masses of Asia, Africa, and Latin America, who want to have a new lease on life and do not believe they can obtain it from Western forms of government and economics.

Khrushchev's political vision vis-à-vis the third world expressed itself in actions geared to offset the economic strength of the United States. The concept of "neocolonialism" was coined and was successfully incorporated in the dictionary of communist policies toward the underdeveloped countries. Khrushchev's successors, the new "collective leadership" under Brezhnev and Kosygin—a Khrushchev-Bulganin parallel—have continued his policies but have not been altogether successful. They have failed to achieve major influence in Africa and Asia; in Latin America they play second fiddle to Castro.

The Soviet policy-makers' goal in the third world is direct involvement in these areas in order not only to displace Western influence but also to set the third world against the West and so deny the rich resources of Asia and Africa to the West—a policy already suggested by Lenin at the Baku Conference of 1920. Of particular importance are Soviet attempts to penetrate the Middle Eastern region, the strategic link between Europe and Asia. Above all others, Egypt has remained the priority target. When the U.S.S.R. extended recognition to the new State of Israel in 1948, Soviet relations with the Arabs cooled. However, after the Bandung Conference of 1955 Moscow changed its policies and began to establish more persuasive political and economic bonds with Egypt, while the United States refused to help Egypt build the Aswân Dam.

When Nasser's closing of the Suez canal in 1956 resulted in the brief Anglo-French-Israeli war against Egypt, Moscow took advantage of the situation and has since maintained close relations with Nasser, regardless of the fact that he has jailed Egyptian communists. Nevertheless, Khrushchev, at the Twenty-first C.P.S.U. Congress in 1959, complained about the campaign of anticommunist elements against communists, "who are wrongly accused of contributing to the weakening or splitting of the national effort in the struggle against imperialism."[41] This position created some strain in Soviet-Egyptian relations.

It could be suggested that this was the result of revolutionary policies dominating national policies. Khrushchev had stated that "the Soviet Union has not interfered and does not intend to interfere in the domestic affairs of other countries," but he then added that "we cannot, however, fail to make clear our [view] that a campaign against progressive forces is being waged in some countries under the false slogan of anti-communism."[42] In this case, dualism, to say the least, was unco-ordinated and contradictory.

Soviet policies in the Middle East caused an even heavier involvement shortly before, during, and after the June, 1967, Arab-Israeli war. The Arab defeat, the loss of billions invested by the Soviets for armaments, primarily Egyptian, and the Soviet stand against Israel have forced the Arabs still closer to the Soviet camp. The Kremlin's dualistic policies in that area present a contrast between the "spirit of Glassboro" and the tough statements by Soviet Ambassador Fedorenko in the United Nations and by Premier Kosygin in his General Assembly speech and in his U.N. press conference. There is a revealing "unity of opposites" of Soviet strategic state interest in the Middle East and communist ideological interest in achieving an acceptance of "socialism" by osmosis, thereby overcoming local nationalism as well as Islam.

We have no clearer account of Soviet-communist policy toward the developing countries than that laid down in the C.P.S.U. program adopted at the Twenty-second Party Congress. It reveals better than most other statements the closely interwoven state and party policies, the dualistic approach of the U.S.S.R. toward the third world:

The C.P.S.U. considers fraternal alliance with the peoples who have thrown off colonial or semicolonial yokes to be a corner stone of its international policy. This alliance is based on the common vital interests of world socialism and the world national-liberation movement. The C.P.S.U. regards it as its internationalist duty to assist the peoples who have set out to win and strengthen their national independence, all peoples who are fighting for the complete abolition of the colonial system.[43]

CONCLUSION

The policy-makers of nations, capitalist or socialist, use (or abuse) many kinds of dualism. A misanthrope probably would say this was double-dealing, the stock in trade of the men in charge of foreign relations. But this essay does not deal with those duplicities of traditional foreign-policy-making which lie hidden under the cloak of diplomatic respectability. It does attempt to focus a spotlight on different levels of policy-making. In the case of communist-ruled states, policy-making is a matter of dualism—with the help of modern technology in weapons and communications—which seeks to combine traditional state-oriented foreign relations with the iconoclasm of the revolutionary communist gospel. "The duality of the Soviet Union as a state and as a party has long been recognized, and its behavior has always betrayed a certain amount of political schizophrenia,"[44] writes a sovietologist of repute.

But, while it is true that this recognition is of long standing, changes in both the U.S.S.R. and the international communist movement occurring since 1956 have tended to obscure the progressive merger of the two sides of Soviet foreign policy, chiefly because they are no longer organizationally distinct. As a result, some nations' appraisals of Soviet intentions have become somewhat euphoric. Moreover, since the rites of Moscow's secular religion are no longer as demonstrative as they once were, the prevalent view is that ideology is eroding and communism deteriorating. In the present writer's view, this interpretation is as faulty as is that which says that Soviet foreign policy expresses solely Russian national interests.

In a half-century in which events of great consequence occurred rapidly and frequently, conditions were bound to change. Had the Soviet Union not changed with them, it would have become sterile and brittle; that danger existed in the later years of Stalin's reign. But change it did. Khrushchev's reformism initiated a new era, discarding much that was useless and retaining what was considered essential. Many observers have been led to believe that these changes are fundamental, indicative of an evolution away from revolution. But when we look to the continuity of Soviet dualistic foreign policy, we realize that they are not. At best—not yet.

NOTES

1. Alexander Dallin, *The Soviet Union at the United Nations* (New York: F. A. Praeger, 1962), pp. 6–7.

2. Cf. Jane Degras, ed., *The Communist International, 1919–1943*, vol. I: *1919–22* (London and Toronto: Oxford University Press, 1956), pp. 7–24.

✓ 3. E. A. Korovin, *Mezhdunarodnoe pravo perekhodnogo vremini* (Moscow: State Publishing House, 1924), p. 32; see also M. Chakste, "Soviet Concepts of the State, International Law and Sovereignty," *American Journal of International Law*, 43 (1949): 24.

✓ 4. J. N. Hazard, "Cleansing Soviet International Law of Anti-Marxist Theories," *American Journal of International Law*, 32 (1938): 247.

✓ 5. Editorial, "Peaceful Coexistence of Two Systems—The Main Foundation of Contemporary International Law," *Sovetskoe gosudarstvo i pravo*, no. 4 (1952), p. 7.

✓ 6. See B. A. Ramundo's pioneering work *Peaceful Coexistence: International Law in the Building of Communism* (Baltimore: The Johns Hopkins Press, 1967), p. 8.

7. *Ibid.*, pp. 215ff.

′ 8. N. S. Khrushchev, "For New Victories of the World Communist Movement," *Kommunist*, no. 1 (January, 1961), as quoted by R. V. Allen, *Peaceful Coexistence* (Chicago: American Bar Association, 1966), p. 80.

9. Cf. *Moscow News*, supplement, April 2, 1966, p. 4; see also Allen, *Peaceful Coexistence*, p. 82.

10. E. H. Carr, *The Bolshevik Revolution* (Baltimore: Penguin Books, 1966), III, 28.

11. *Ibid.*

12. Jane Degras, ed., *Soviet Documents on Foreign Policy*, vol. I: *1917–1924* (London: Oxford University Press, 1951), pp. 57–58.

13. For example, the German communist Paul Levi, in a pamphlet entitled *Unser Weg* [Our Road], wrote that "the Executive Committee of the Comintern acts like the Cheka projected beyond the Russian frontiers" (Degras, *The Communist International*, p. 218).

14. Degras, *Soviet Documents on Foreign Policy*, p. 258.

15. Degras, *The Communist International*, p. 347.

16. E. H. Carr, *German-Soviet Relations Between Two World Wars, 1919–1939* (Baltimore: The Johns Hopkins Press, 1951), p. 76.

✓ 17. Cf. Elliot Goodman, *The Soviet Design for a World State* (New York: Columbia University Press, 1960), p. 169.

18. Carr, *German-Soviet Relations*, p. 446.

19. Bukharin and Prebrazhinsky, *Azubka* (Moscow, 1919), p. 92, as quoted by Goodman, *The Soviet Design for a World State*, p. 378.

20. K. W. Davis, *The Soviets at Geneva* (Geneva: Librairie Kundid, 1934), p. 4.

⎺𝑣 21. Degras, *Soviet Documents on Foreign Policy*, p. 136.

22. *Ibid.*, p. 117.

23. *Ibid.*, II, 274.

24. *Ibid.*, III, 45.

25. F. P. Walters, *A History of the League of Nations* (London: Oxford University Press, 1952), II, 585.

26. M. Beloff, *The Foreign Policy of Soviet Russia*, I (London: Oxford University Press, 1949), 56.

27. This episode offers a particularly good demonstration of the techniques of eventual takeover by communist cadres of all noncommunist elements.

⎺√28. Beloff, *Foreign Policy of Soviet Russia*, p. 190.

29. *Ibid.*

30. *Ibid.*, p. 192.

31. The present writer had some firsthand experience in communist "interpretation" of war when he taught at the College of the City of New York. Prior to the German invasion of the U.S.S.R., two of his students, obviously Marxist-Leninist in orientation, had condemned the war as "imperialist." After June 22, 1940, they kept quiet for a day and then, in a complete turnabout, supported the war as "just."

√32. O. V. Kuusinen *et al.*, eds., *Fundamentals of Marxism-Leninism* (Moscow: Foreign Languages Publishing House, 1963), p. 462.

33. G. von Rauch, *A History of Soviet Russia*, rev. ed. (New York: F. A. Praeger, 1960), p. 379.

34. See M. D. Shulman's excellent chapter "The Peace Movement as an Instrument of Diplomacy" in his *Stalin's Foreign Policy Reappraised* (New York: Atheneum, 1963), pp. 80ff.

√35. J. M. Mackintosh, *Strategy and Tactics of Soviet Foreign Policy* (New York: Oxford University Press, 1963), p. 64.

36. Cf. Shulman, *Stalin's Foreign Policy Reappraised*, pp. 118–120.

37. G. E. Lichtblau, "The World Federation of Trade Unions," *Social Research*, 25 (1958): 26.

38. Cf. Bernard S. Morris, "Communist International Front Organizations," *World Politics*, 9, no. 1 (October, 1956).

39. For a brief survey of front organizations see I. Phelps-Fetherston, *Soviet International Front Organizations: A Concise Handbook* (New York: F. A. Praeger, 1965).

40. Kurt London, "The Sino-Soviet Conflict," *Current History* (October, 1966), pp. 206ff.; see also the same author's "Vietnam: A Sino-Soviet Dilemma," *The Russian Review* 26, no. 1 (January, 1967).

41. Excerpted from Khrushchev's Report to the Twenty-first Congress of the C.P.S.U., in *Foreign Broadcast Information Service*, Washington, D.C., January 29, 1959.

42. *Ibid.*

43. As quoted by O. V. Kuusinen *et al.*, *Fundamentals of Marxism-Leninism*, p. 430.

44. V. V. Aspaturian, *The Soviet Union in the World Communist System* (Stanford, Calif.: Hoover Institution Studies, 1966).

CHAPTER 6

Soviet Relations with Eastern Europe

Soviet–East European Relations since World War II:
Theoretical Perceptions and Political Realities

Andrew Gyorgy

Soviet–East European Relations since World War II: Theoretical Perceptions and Political Realities

Andrew Gyorgy

THE PREWAR DECADES: DANUBIAN ALOOFNESS AND SOVIET REVOLUTIONARY INTENTIONS*

During the interwar years political contacts between the Soviet Union and the various East European states passed through several stages. The interrelationships between the Soviet Union and its European neighbors displayed, on the whole, a considerable amount of continuity because these connections were essentially of secondary importance to the parties involved.

Except for the first years of its existence, when it was preoccupied with frontier wars and boundary settlements, the Bolshevik regime focused its attention on relations with Western, and not Eastern, Europe. Soviet diplomatic activities in Eastern Europe were designed to neutralize the area through a variety of pacts and agreements so that it would constitute a barrier in preventing, or at least in delaying, "counterrevolutionary" aggression from Western Europe.

Bolshevik foreign policy, as we know, was conducted on more than one plane;[1] and while the Narkomindel pursued its essentially defensive relationships with legitimate governments, the

* This brief introductory section sets the stage for the more detailed treatment of the 1945–67 period in Soviet–East European relations which is the essence of this, paper. The author is indebted to the Lincoln-Filene Center of Tufts University, whose research grant made possible the completion of this paper, as well as its presentation at the Berlin Conference of September, 1967.

Comintern, at least in the early years, frequently worked at cross purposes, obstructing or undermining traditional foreign-policy processes. In terms of revolutionary as well as diplomatic aims, the East European countries were not considered nearly as important as Germany, France, Italy, or China. Only in Czechoslovakia was there a legal Communist party through which the U.S.S.R. could channel its operations. The Comintern actually ruined some promising situations in Danubia and the Balkans, largely through its failure to come to grips with that outstanding characteristic of interwar East European affairs: an exuberant and wholly undisciplined nationalism.

In addition to the relative aloofness that had pervaded Soviet–East European relations between the wars, nationalism provided the other major and recurring theme. On the Soviet side nationalism became an increasingly important policy guide and, indeed, it dictated most of the treaty relationships of the U.S.S.R. with its East European neighbors. Conversely, the rhetoric surrounding the peacemaking in Eastern Europe had left the new and dissected states all the more intoxicated with the politics and romanticism of national self-determination and ethnic vindication. Thus, in the decade after the war, each of the East European countries concentrated its foreign-policy energies on securing its position against real or imagined threats from hostile neighbors.

By 1928 the trends of the twenties reached their climax. Within the Soviet Union Stalin was firmly in control, and the drive toward building socialism in one country went into high gear with the introduction of the first Five-Year Plan. Thus the Soviet Union was even more interested in guaranteeing peace and in securing good commercial relations with the capitalist world. Since Germany was no longer isolated within Europe, the Narkomindel made more extensive efforts to develop collective security arrangements in Eastern Europe as a backstop for Soviet European policy. Yet, the closer the links between the exiled and illegal communist parties of Eastern Europe and the Soviet Union, the more unpalatable their activities became to the individual national regimes. Anticipating a new stage of crisis and war in the capitalist world, the Comintern program still prescribed a tactic of united front from below and no co-operation with bourgeois-democratic or socialist elements. Thus it perpetuated the isolation of communists from potential allies on the political left in Germany and Eastern Europe and opened the way during the depression years and afterward for intensified persecution of their representatives by the various right-radical regimes. At the same time, since it became more damaging and embarrassing for governments to maintain good relations with the Soviet Union, by the time the shift to pop-ular-front tactics was endorsed in 1935, too much damage had already been done for it to have much meaning in Eastern Europe.

The Comintern's popular-front policy did little to make the Soviet Union more acceptable to East European governments. It distinguished between friendly bourgeois-democratic and hostile fascist regimes, and, while East European governments did not fall neatly into the latter category, they were all, except for Czechoslovakia, intent on developing closer diplomatic rela-tions with Germany or Italy. Part of the new Comintern policy was to prepare the forces of revolution to take advantage of an inevitable war. Consequently, Comintern agents and emigré groups continued to be trained in the Soviet Union, and shuttled back and forth between Moscow and the East European coun-tries to agitate among the masses.

The *Anschluss* and Munich episodes are well known. They represented a serious blow to enduring Soviet efforts to secure peace, by preventing co-operation between Germany and the other capitalist states of Europe and by erecting a system of collective security. By joint agreement the capitalist states seemed to be directing aggression eastward, where Russia's fron-tiers were left exposed by her failure to secure an effective buffer. In the succeeding months the Soviets tried to salvage what they could by negotiating alternatively with the old but increasingly dangerous favorite, Germany, and the unreliable peace camp, France and Britain. The capitalist world would be divided, regardless of which negotiations succeeded, and in the end the choice hinged upon which side could offer to the Soviets their secondary, stopgap interest—a buffer zone along their vulnerable western frontiers. On the whole the bitter diplomatic frustrations that surfaced in 1938 during the *Anschluss* and at Munich, finally reaching a climax in the Nazi-Soviet pact of 1939, clearly proved that Soviet and East European political activities had been mutually self-defeating during the two decades of the interwar period.

1945–49: STALIN'S "REVOLUTION FROM ABOVE" AND THE TAKEOVER OF EASTERN EUROPE

"Soviet political ideology," Frederick C. Barghoorn observed recently, "is the product of the experience of an elite which was forced to perform many very difficult tasks under difficult conditions and in an excessively short span of time. Soviet ideology was the doctrine of an elite which made a revolution in the wrong country, under unfavorable conditions."[2] Indeed, Stalin's views on war and revolution, which in many ways set the stage for the turbulent world political scene of the 1940's and early 1950's, reflect the rigid and blind conservatism of a Soviet political elite accustomed to, and forged in the fire of, both ideological hardship and militant political realities. They have affected the tortuous political evolution of postwar Eastern Europe in an all-pervasive and frightening manner.

In Stalin's perspective, Danubia and the Balkans were an essential, even inevitable, sphere of influence, a *cordon sanitaire* developed to buttress the shaky and vulnerable western border zones of European Russia. In order to prevent future wars his brand of revolution would have to be exported to all of the East European countries. The suspicious dictator frequently pictured imminent military threats from the West, accompanied by the specters of "intervention" and "restoration," suggesting the return of an oppressive capitalist order in Russia. The Soviet leader turned to history and liked to dwell on past defeats suffered at the hands of invading Polish and Swedish armies, of Napoleon's invasion of 1812, and of Hitler's attack of 1941, which, after all, had almost succeeded.

In these Soviet nightmares Eastern Europe was portrayed as a strategic base exploited as an *ancillary* power-complex by the ultimate enemy, the Anglo-American world. Attacks would presumably be mounted and offensives launched from the Danube Valley or the Balkans by the Western "warmongers." The Soviet citizenry was therefore constantly reminded of the dangers of imminent war. As early as 1925, at the Fourteenth Congress of the Soviet Communist Party, Stalin had stated (and thereafter frequently repeated) that "two chief but opposed centers of attraction are being formed, and in conformity with this, two directions of gravity . . . throughout the world: Anglo-America and the Soviet Union." If, however, war originated from a westerly direction, Eastern Europe could be used by the Soviet strategic planners as a momentary shock absorber, a vulnerable "in-depth" buffer zone that would allow the U.S.S.R. some geopolitical elbowroom, a *Wehr-Raum* or military defense zone enabling it to delay as well as exploit an explosive Central European situation. Subsequently Soviet strength could be built up in such key areas as East Germany, Poland, Rumania, the Baltic States, and even Finland.

War Leads to Revolution

In the perspective of post–World War II Soviet–East European relations, Stalin and the Stalinoid types of the newly emerging satellite states viewed wars and revolutions as inextricably interrelated phenomena. Wars occurred in the external relations of nations, while revolutions appeared primarily as internal political events. In this context World War II was regarded by Stalin as the first step toward a successful revolution in Eastern Europe, with a concomitant strengthening of its proletariat and an inevitable destruction of its prewar capitalist systems. Eastern Europe's poor and downtrodden proletariat, he cynically pointed out, could only benefit from the ravages and destruction of such a war. It had little to lose and a great deal to gain, in stark contrast with the entrenched, prosperous, and successful prewar socioeconomic elites of the region which were now earmarked for careful and methodical destruction by the newly imported Muscovite communist leadership-groups.

War and revolution thus emerged hand-in-hand on the political landscape of Eastern Europe. Long before Khrushchev's highly publicized and globally applicable endorsement of "wars of national liberation," Stalin employed and exploited the concepts of "liberation campaigns," "anticolonial" conflicts, and "anti-imperialist" struggles waged or carried out in Central Europe and the Balkans. To the consternation of the far more sophisticated and considerably less cynical peoples of this region, his essentially contradictory views miraculously transformed the inevitable evil of war into a "purifier," a process that would accelerate the development of new "revolutionary and progressive" forces in the various East European states. Stalin's galloping schizophrenia pictured war as a repulsive imperialist evil clutching Eastern Europe, on the one hand, while portraying it as a glorious "revolutionary" struggle for all of its peoples, on the other. Such were the dialectics of Stalin's "inevitable war" theory as they affected the postwar course of Soviet–East European relations.

The Stalinist Revolution as a Theoretical Perception

Having rejected the Marxist thesis that proletarian revolutions could break out spontaneously, Stalin and his ideological coterie substituted for it the less revolutionary, but far more cold-blooded and militant, concept of staging an interrelated series of carefully *prefabricated* revolutions in Eastern Europe. In this "shatter-belt" of the old continent, the Muscovites believed, communist uprisings could succeed only if they were assisted by the power of Moscow, and if the Red Army were in a position to exercise direct control over the territory involved. Revolutions "from below,"[3] in the Stalinists' considered opinion, could never be carried out effectively by popular movements or genuine mass demonstrations. On the contrary, in order to succeed in the peculiar power constellation of the geopolitical zone immediately to the west of European Russia, they must be imposed by careful planning and brute force "from above."[4] Pre-revolutionary calculations for such Stalinist operators as Ulbricht, Gottwald, Rákosi, or Pauker generally speaking excluded the consideration of such factors as the spontaneous mood, instantaneous popular action, or expressions of mass opinion of the East Europeans themselves. The cautious planning of the chain reaction of revolutions must rest in the hands of a small and conspiratorial professional elite. Such revolutions may fail, however, Stalin warned, if "there is no revolutionary party of the proletariat sufficiently strong . . . to take power in its own hands."[5]

Thus, for Eastern Europe proper, the successful interplay of two major forces was deemed essential by the Soviet planners. One requirement was the existence of *at least* the nucleus of a fairly strong Communist party, operating either legally (as in Czechoslovakia) or, in countries where communism was outlawed (as everywhere else in Eastern Europe), through the instrument of small, fanatical, and highly trained underground groups. The second prerequisite was the massive presence of the Red Army, which had always played a central role in the Stalinist planning of such revolutionary "national uprisings," amounting actually to carefully premeditated military seizures of power. With the exception of Czechoslovakia, such military support then produced the political takeover of individual East European countries which occurred step-by-step and country-by-country during the 1944–48 period of Soviet expansion.

Political Reality: The Takeover of Eastern Europe

On the whole, Stalin's views on revolution were reflected more in their practical execution than in fanciful theory. To discuss the "takeover process" is merely to state in other terms that, from Communist China to the Elbe River in Central Europe, Stalin was instrumental in successfully exporting his own brand of revolution. Thus, despite intriguing local variations on the theme, the end product was everywhere Soviet rather than communist. Consequently, Stalin's postwar empire was ruled by the same techniques that on the home front had already become painfully familiar—throughout at least two decades of steady experimentation—to all Soviet citizens. Rather than describing at length the individual techniques of this total dictatorship—

ranging from police terror through purges and economic exploitation to rigid political indoctrination—this essay will attempt to systematize the unsystematic and to examine three key "takeover" theories that scrutinize the same problem from different perspectives. Essentially, to paraphrase Professor Hugh Seton-Watson's felicitous statement and to expand on it somewhat, post–World War II Soviet intervention in East European affairs has been of four major types: the application of military force; direct political action, or at least the threat of it; various forms of indirect political action; and economic action.[6]

THE "CHRONOLOGICAL SEQUENCE" THEORY

One approach to the Soviet takeover process stresses chronological interrelationships and tries to find a common denominator among the East European victims of Stalinization on that basis. The 1944–48 period is consequently divided into four subphases during which approximately the same events took place concurrently in the various countries.

Phase One: Liberation (1944–45). Using the Soviets' extravagant and misleading phrase, the first period is politically the simplest to describe: the Red Army swept through Eastern Europe in lightning fashion and exploited its crude military influence to put "friendly" regimes in power and to integrate at least the foreign policies of the Danubian and Balkan countries with those of Moscow.

Phase Two: Retribution and Reparations (1945–46). Although this brief "interlude" witnessed primarily the punishment of foreign and domestic war criminals, it foreshadowed a suppression of the anticommunist opposition, a liquidation of its leaders, and the assessment and collection of enormous reparations, including the wholesale confiscation of the so-called Nazi assets. Last, but not least, the characteristically concomitant features of this process were also immediate drastic limitations on the freedom of the press and on the key political rights of free speech and assembly. Under the guise of warcrimes trials many innocent anticommunist political figures were carefully liquidated by the various Ministries of the Interior, which were, by and large, already Moscow-dominated communist organizations.[7]

Phase Three: Engineered Disruption (1946–47). This period can be aptly summed up as one of endlessly recurring domestic crises (invariably fomented from the outside) that set the stage for the inevitable communist party coup and the ultimate violent seizure of power. The principal item in this third phase—indeed, a prerequisite for the operation of a long-range communist formula—was the pressure to gain control of key posts in the coalition- and national-front governments temporarily prevailing throughout the area. This process involved, beyond the highest priority—the Ministry of the Interior's control of the entire police system—such other sought-after political prizes as the Ministries of Information, Education, National Defense, and Foreign Affairs. But we must emphasize that throughout this short-lived phase, despite the clearly "engineered disruption," the coalition governments were carefully maintained and their principal functions scrupulously observed until the moment arrived when a former *minority* dramatically transformed itself into a full, ruling *majority*.

Phase Four: Monolithic Communist Party Control (1947–49). The logical last step in this chain of events was the removal and liquidation of all actual or potential opposition. The emergence of the truly monolithic phase implied the establishment of total control by local Communist party leaders, primarily of the nonnative or Muscovite variety. The "takeover" process was now completed, the "people's democracies"—better known to posterity as a series of abject Stalin-created satellites—were born, or rather launched by the tremendous power and overwhelming central authority of the U.S.S.R.[8]

THE "DECISIVE ELECTION" THEORY

Professor C. E. Black's useful account of the role of key elections in Eastern Europe carries the "chronological sequence" approach a considerable step further.[9] As a final confirmation of their seizure of power, suggests Black, communist leaders everywhere insisted on holding general elections. These also heralded the introduction of new constitutions that had been hastily drafted to legitimize the new regimes. By that time the temporary "people's fronts" had served their purpose and were tolerated only as "part of the trappings of the transition period to full socialization."[10]

In the over-all context of the takeover process, these general elections were decisive in two different directions. First of all, the voters were subjected to direct compulsion to join in a mass vote of confidence expressed vis-à-vis the newly emerging and already predominantly communist regime. Secondarily, the over-whelmingly favorable percentage of the vote was then used to accelerate the destruction of the very "coalition" government (or popular front) for which the vote itself was originally planned and which was supposed to be buttressed by the mass expression of a "free" public opinion.

The specific results of these crucial plebiscites were the following:

PLEBISCITE ELECTIONS: EASTERN EUROPE

	Decisive Communist-Controlled Elections	People's Front Majority (percentage)
Yugoslavia	November 11, 1945	89
Albania	December 2, 1945	93
Bulgaria	October 27, 1946	78
Rumania	November 19, 1946	80
Poland	January 19, 1947	90
Hungary	August 31, 1947	60
Czechoslovakia	May 30, 1948	89

Three countries formed an exception to this general pattern, as Professor Black observes. These were Czechoslovakia, Finland, and East Germany. In the first case the communists of that country had to resort to an open threat of force, while in the second the successful resistance of the Finns to communist pressure frustrated and postponed indefinitely the holding of "decisive" elections. East Germany, in turn, had to be treated differently from the beginning and, as occupied territory—in West German parlance, SBZ or *Sowietische Besatzungs Zone*— and only the fragment of a once-larger state, it did not qualify even for such mock-plebiscites as characterized most of the neighboring satellites.[11]

THE "FOUR AREA" OR FUNCTIONAL TAKEOVER THEORY

This interpretation of the takeover process emphasizes a substantive and functional breakdown of this complex phenomenon rather than chronological or electoral details. It suggests that, played against the ominous and permanent background music of a strictly secret-police-patterned occupation (in the best Stalinist sense of this term), four parallel subprocesses were put into operation along simultaneous lines. These were the following, placed in a tentative order of importance:

Politically speaking, several of the more prominent opposition forces, particularly the groups of urban middle-class liberals, peasant parties, and the socialist parties, had to be destroyed or at least silenced and gradually forced into a minimal degree of passive co-operation. While this goal was accomplished only with the greatest difficulty in such countries as Poland, Hungary, and Czechoslovakia (in which traditionally powerful anticommunist elements held out in firm opposition for brief periods of varying duration), the destruction of the political opposition was easier to carry out in Bulgaria, Rumania, and Yugoslavia. There, either the anticommunist forces had been disastrously weakened by World War II, or procommunist and pro-Russian forces proved to be more numerous. The habitual techniques accompanying the politics of this takeover ranged from fraudulent elections through political assassinations and mass kidnapings to a ubiquitous police terror. The entire procedure was subjected to the careful threefold scrutiny and supervision of a Red Army marshal or general, a well-trained "Muscovite"-type leader, and a legion of Soviet civilian "occupation experts."

In the realm of *economics* the Soviet Union exacted particularly harsh tributes from its would-be satellites. Stalin demanded heavy war reparation payments for their participation in the war against Russia. There was a wholesale dismantling of industry and the physical removal of entire factories, including their labor and management personnel, to Russia. In the 1945–49 period, this ruthless dismantling process removed about ten billion dollars' worth of goods and products from East Germany alone. "Joint companies" were established between the Soviet Union and the satellite, by which the Russians gained control of all resources and industries that could contribute to Soviet military and economic strength. High on the list of these resources were the uranium deposits of Czechoslovakia and East Germany, the bauxite of Hungary, the oil and petroleum products of Rumania, and control of the Danube River. Stalin's revolutionary blueprint required the weakening of a country's economic base to the point where the politics of communism could be forced upon a defenseless and demoralized population, despite its anticommunist feelings.

Culturally the "takeover" process involved equally drastic measures. A direct challenge to organized religion, particularly of the Roman Catholic church, was one of the first steps taken by Stalin's local communist forces. The fight against religion was most bitter and protracted in Hungary, Poland, and Czechoslovakia, where a large majority of the population was Catholic. Despite the confiscation of her large land estates, parochial schools, seminaries, and even her churches, the Church was not silenced. Following a series of viciously false trials of leading cardinals and archbishops throughout Eastern Europe, there was a temporary lull in the bitter church-state relations, a moment of truce, but there was never a permanent accommodation between the two antagonists. Other religious groups fought equally spirited battles against the frightening impact of atheistic Stalinism. The small Jewish colonies of Eastern Europe acted as temporary barriers to the "takeover"; and the Protestant church of East Germany was particularly noteworthy in its unyielding resistance against the encroachments of the puppet regime of Walter Ulbricht in the Soviet-occupied zone of Germany.

Another aspect of Stalin's postwar "revolution" was the intensive drive toward at least a cultural and ideological Russification of the entire East European area. For the youngster in grade school and for undergraduate and graduate students through the Ph.D. level in the universities, Russian language and literature became compulsory subjects. Thousands of Soviet "specialists" swarmed over the occupied countries and sought to transform their educational, technical, administrative, and governmental patterns to conform to the Soviet model. A Russian form of communism was imposed upon the satellites and, despite tremendous national variations (particularly in non-Slavic and anticommunist Hungary, Rumania, and Finland), all of them were gradually forced into the Stalinist mold. The mold was a comprehensive one; the same elements were soon apparent in each satellite. Rule over each country was exercised by a small clique of "Muscovite" communists; and Stalin's own favorite and inimitable style of architecture was a common sight. Larger-than-life reminders of the leader—Stalin in picture, bas-relief, and statue—appeared everywhere.

Last, but certainly not least, a *militarily* imposed "takeover" process frequently formed part of the establishment of Soviet control. Local armies were demobilized and carefully purged of all noncommunist elements. New and politically pliable officers were given the more responsible command positions, while top-level assignments were held by officers from the Soviet army. A network of Soviet "Chiefs of Armies" developed throughout Eastern Europe: Stalin's trusted emissaries, who were strategically located to enforce the dictator's military demands.

One of the notorious military occupation "specialists" was Marshal Konstantin Rokossovsky, a World War II hero of the Red Army. In November, 1949, Stalin dispatched Rokossovsky to Warsaw to be Poland's Minister of Defense and the Chief-of-Staff of the Polish Army. Rokossovsky, in the uniform of a Soviet marshal, was declared by governmental edict to be a Polish citizen. The Poles regarded Rokossovsky as an "outsider"—he was born in Poland but had been taken to Russia when he was less than a year old—and resented his holding the powerful political-military posts of their country. Similar Rokossovsky types were active during this era of all-out Stalinism (approximately 1949–53) in the neighboring Central–East European countries. In East Germany, Marshal Grechko was responsible for the bloody suppression of the June 17, 1953, rebellion. Equally sinister was Marshal Konev, the troubleshooter of the Soviet military, who presided over periodic army purges in Czechoslovakia and Bulgaria. Such favorite Stalinist techniques were relentlessly employed and forced upon half of the European continent; and through the victory of Chinese communism similar patterns were subsequently extended over at least one-third of the Asian continent.

1950–67: DEEPENING CONFLICT BETWEEN IDEOLOGICAL PERCEPTION AND POLITICAL REALITY

In the past two decades one of the most salient features of the East European landscape has been the immensely close interaction pattern between domestic and foreign issues. Primarily in order to divert attention from their rapidly multiplying domestic problems, both economic and political, the various communist regimes of the area have frantically focused on foreign developments. In turn, these external factors, particularly in the form of crisis developments, have exerted a significant impact at home, on the domestic life and internal ideological evolution of the once-satellite nations of Danubia and the Balkans. These focusing and refocusing processes have been particularly obvious during the last few years of the Stalinist period, when the satellites of Eastern Europe were in a truly dependent state, and, in turn, have asserted themselves dramatically in the "New Course" era of Khrushchev's initial rule and the post-1956 years, which have gradually witnessed the evolution of these countries into more or less vigorous ex-satellites.

This intricate interaction of domestic and foreign considerations affects equally the perception level of regime-developed and promulgated party lines as well as the firmer foundations of popularly accepted political realities. Take the American involvement in Vietnam as an example. The artificially construed official perception publicized by the various communist regimes peremptorily rejects all American policy advances toward Eastern Europe, stating: "You cannot build bridges here and destroy them in North Vietnam at the same time!" Angry anti-American campaigns thus tend to organize diversion from the vicissitudes of the home front to the foreign shadow of the "imperialist aggressor." The actual popular view of Vietnam is entirely different. It can be briefly summarized as follows: "We like the West and admire America. Furthermore, we are Europeans, and who cares what happens in an obscure part of Asia?" Thus the popular reaction tends to be totally different from the regime's view: wherever possible a basic friendliness and spirit of hospitality shines through the opaque communications curtains.

Domestic Issues

We shall turn now to an examination of three major and persistent domestic issues, keeping in mind both the "interaction" or "organized diversion" concept and the sharp dichotomy between perception and reality.

GENERATIONAL CHANGE

The theoretical postulate in this context is deceptively simple: there is no conflict and there can be no disharmony between the succeeding generations in a Marxist-Leninist society. The image of a successful relay race is conjured up, one in which the batons of communist ideology and Marxist practice are smoothly passed on from fathers to sons. The time factor is often stressed as a supporting argument in defense of this inter-generational harmony viewpoint—namely, that after more than two decades of communist rule a large sector of the population has acquired a vested interest in the continuation of the system, with ever fewer opposing forces and operational problems to upset members of an increasingly indoctrinated society. To some extent this point is well taken. The longer communism survives in Eastern Europe, the more sporadic and atomized will be popular and social resistance to it.

The level of reality is far different from the harmonious structure of theoretical perceptions. Throughout the entire region there is a convulsively obvious generational change consisting of an ever-widening communication gap between the "old stalwarts" and members of a new *avant-garde*. There is indeed a mute confrontation between components of the original "revolutionary" generation[12] and the current "post-revolutionary" age group, the children of the "New Class," so to speak. The sociological symptoms of this clash are manifold; juvenile delinquency, drunkenness, looting, the stealing of state property, and immoral behavior are the characteristics of a process of social erosion. They denote a growing sense of frustration on the part of this "posterity" with lagging political and economic progress. In a recent radio broadcast a Hungarian author bitterly blamed the "post-revolutionary generation" for having given up their ideals and for turning bourgeois:

The young man . . . who watched the world and humanity, and who wanted to become an intellectual . . . has turned into a narrow-minded, uninteresting adult who does not care about anything that happens in either East or West, not farther than, perhaps, 500 kilometers from him. . . . His seemingly broad outlook is, in reality, narrow-mindedness and provincialism.[13]

The author then goes on to analyze some of the preconditions for shaking the new generation out of its "withdrawn" state into a more conscious, creative, and united posture. Is there a solution for this particular ill of a communist society? A partial possibility exists, indeed; since active loyalty (defined by one writer as an "active stand for the cause and concrete deeds") is too much to ask for, the concept of passive loyalty is being debated in countries such as Hungary or the U.S.S.R. Even this becomes an optimum goal, since reality usually will stress more the passivity than the loyalty of this generation. "Agree and ignore" would be a motto for this pattern of behavior.[14]

VARYING PATTERNS OF NATIONALISM

The past decade and a half of Soviet–East European relationships has been increasingly affected by two major patterns of nationalism. Indeed, the communist societies of Europe today present a fascinating mixture of *traditional* and *novel* types of nationalism. Of the former, three dominant varieties seem to be in existence, namely, political, religious, and romantic, while among the latter we shall review briefly the economic and utopian subpatterns. Since the present author has examined political and religious forms of nationalism elsewhere in some detail,[15] we must turn here first of all to a sketching of the romantic, nineteenth-century, or antediluvian[16] category.

"Romantic" nationalism directly affects the ideological and strategic position of the U.S.S.R. in both the northern and southern tiers of Eastern Europe. It asserts itself on the political landscape simultaneously in at least three different directions.

Firts of all, by clinging to the grandeur of a more majestic "glorious past," it tends to revive old and sensitive nationality issues. Recent references to "Macedonian chauvinism" again project, for example, the age-old specter of this irredentist and truly revolutionary problem area.

As a second possibility, touchy linguistic cleavages again begin to raise the question of certain particularistic trends in *regional* nationalism, divided within itself, and thus add fuel to the fire of smoldering Balkan and Danubian conflicts. The reemergence of an old Serb-Croat linguistic feud was succinctly covered by the *New York Times* recently: "The call for discipline has grown out of a campaign against communists suspected of promoting *regional nationalism*. In Zagreb it was announced today that 15 party members had been expelled and 24 disciplined for having signed a manifesto calling for more emphasis on the Croatian language."[17]

Finally, nineteenth-century nationalism is quite capable of arousing, and then of accelerating, certain geopolitical issues that lay dormant for the first two decades of post–World War II communism but that have suddenly displayed a potentially explosive territorial menace. Transylvania, Bessarabia, and

Bukovina immediately come to mind here, but other conflict zones could easily enter into the limelight in the foreseeable future.

These expressions of "romantic" nationalism were truly unheard-of and unimaginable as long as Stalin lived and Stalinism held sway. Today they are potentially "all there" and threaten to become inconveniently postdiluvial in terms of Soviet plans, intentions, and expectations in Eastern Europe. The events of 1968 in Czechoslovakia would truly fit several competing patterns of nationalism. The sudden political rehabilitation of President Thomas G. Masaryk, the reopening of the "murder" case of his son, Foreign Minister Jan Masaryk, as well as freer references in the press to the late Edouard Benes, are important individual case studies of *romantic* nationalism, although in a more limited and compressed framework of time. On the other hand, the sudden dismissal of Antonin Novotny from both the presidency and the office of Secretary General, and particularly his dramatic replacement by Alexander Dubček, a much younger and far more liberal Slovak party official, might well have practically *utopian* connotations for the Czech public at large. Utopia, in this case, implies significant liberalization within the system rather than the liquidation of a Marxist-Leninist ideology or of a communist governmental organization on Czechoslovak soil.

This brief summary cannot encompass all the variations on the theme of East European nationalism. What is important to observe, however, is that these multiple patterns have only recently come into their own again—with the relative but relentless weakening of the fabric of an alien-imposed ideological system. In effect, to the delight of the Western social scientist, there seems to be a *direct* correlation between the deterioration of a central, controlling authority and the slow re-emergence of native political forces and endemic socioeconomic drives.

Economic nationalism, currently paralleling political nationalism as an equally significant motivating phenomenon in Eastern Europe,[18] is itself the result of two factors working in close combination: (1) certain specifically local circumstances (dissatisfaction with their own and Soviet leaders, etc.) triggering fundamental and long-term popular complaints; and (2) a set of globally existing conditions, namely, the sweep of a world-wide "revolution of rising expectations" which has emerged in Eastern Europe in recent years in a vigorous fashion similar to that of Africa, the Middle East, or Latin America. While the East European variant is generically similar to such economic waves of revolutions elsewhere, it has certain special and distinctive features of its own because it is, after all, an economic revolt under the umbrella of communist ideology. By definition communism and genuine popular mass aspirations conflict rather than coincide in purpose or ultimate fulfillment.

Within this frame of reference the economic nationalist—be he of Rumanian, Hungarian, or Yugoslav national background —is apt to define the current stage of his country's socialist development as based on a national "community of economic interests," on a large degree of "economic autonomy," on a hopefully high degree of industrialization, and—wherever possible— on a more or less subtle resistance to Soviet plans for dictated economic integration (viewed here as semicolonial subservience).[19] The ultimate goal is obvious to all: it is the projection of the image of an economically unified and relatively independent state.

The phenomenon of economic nationalism is also confronted by the perception-versus-reality dichotomy. The theoretical (party line) dictate suggests the need for, and the communist acceptance of, the primacy of the supranational interests of a socialist world system, a modified and up-to-date version of an East European "socialist commonwealth." Simultaneously, practical political realities increasingly demand the placement of the ex-satellite's activities and operations within the framework of an independent *national* economy. These two extremes are almost impossible to reconcile; it is clear, however, that throughout the past few years economic nationalism has already erupted in at least subtly anti-CEMA—if not in directly and openly anti-Soviet—trends, moves, and aspirations.

Utopian nationalism, the other nontraditional pattern, is anxious to reconcile loftily defined national interests with the long-range goals and glowing promises of Marxism-Leninism. In this context a nationally oriented utopia is carefully meshed with an apocalyptic vision of a future communist world in which the contradictions of the "world and society" will be absorbed and all forms of class struggle peacefully resolved, even while the country's "national history will be newly born . . . and the history of humanity aims at new things."[20]

While the type of nationalism we are discussing here is extremely ambitious in scope and ubiquitous in its existence, it is utterly impossible to visualize such a two-dimensional reconciliation of what the communists call "socialist patriotism" with the mandatory spirit of "socialist internationalism." This self-contradictory double goal indeed confirms Anatole France's well-known aphorism that "history is not a science, but an art."[21] Applying it more closely to the Soviet position in Eastern Europe, here is the crux of the "built-in" problem from the perspective of the colonial power, the U.S.S.R. Essentially supranational in orientation, the current Soviet overlordship, or "stewardship," must incorporate a sufficient scope and variety of concrete national interests into its institutional bases to satisfy even the most deviation-prone member of the alliance system. Whenever such satisfaction is not forthcoming, as is obvious in the cases of Rumania and Czechoslovakia, such diverse Soviet endeavors as the Warsaw Treaty Organization and CEMA have come close to failure.

It is not easy to categorize the current Czechoslovakian position in Eastern Europe. Formed in January, 1968, the new leadership of Dubček and General Svoboda has been clearly intent on rectifying at least the most obvious domestic iniquities of the worst period of Stalinist and post-Stalinist oppression. Czech and Slovak nationalism denote, in this case, primarily a *domestic* explosion against the Soviet overlord, although, despite careful and judicious moves by the Czechs in foreign political, military, and economic matters affecting the communist bloc of Eastern Europe, they could not avoid the ruthless, direct military intervention of the U.S.S.R. The ugliness of the five-nation Warsaw Pact invasion of late August, 1968, raised the specter of another Hungary or Poland *à la* 1956. Despite these dramatic events, it is still probable that Czechoslovakia will eventually approximate Rumania's place on this spectrum or, what is more likely, will move slowly along the Yugoslavian "road to socialism." Conversely, Bulgaria and East Germany have obediently followed the dictates of this internal antagonism, and thus stand at the other end of the spectrum from the Rumanians and Czechs. Steadily rationalizing their own problems and increasingly concerned with their *over-all* relationships to the U.S.S.R., Hungary and Poland would probably stand at the midway point on this dubious spectrum of Soviet-directed loyalties, from the perspective of national aspirations vis-à-vis communist international organization.

Summing it up briefly, this pattern of utopian nationalism is both highly optimistic in nature as well as flexible in its ultimate expectations. It is firmly based on the popular assumption that the status quo is unsatisfactory,[22] and proceeds from there to hope for a return to *both* a precommunistic national spirit and a post-communistic (post-diluvian) ideological renaissance. Communist operators, of course, aspire to a Marxist version of utopia. A Hungarian ideologist recently suggested that the ultimate ideal image of the Danube basin will be a "changed world," where people will have "attained their rights, their common ideals in the socialist revolution," have set their aims clearly, and have "created the preconditions for a brotherly coexistence."[23]

IDEOLOGICAL FATIGUE

Last but certainly not least among major domestic issues, we must stress the myriad psychological implications of a widespread popular feeling of ideological "fatigue" or "erosion" which has strikingly emerged throughout this region in recent years. People are desperately tired of Marxism-Leninism and genuinely sick of the incessant din of daily propaganda surrounding communist doctrinal pontifications. The rejection of ideology cannot be frank and open; rather, its results resemble that sentiment of "internal emigration" which had characterized certain anti-Nazi German intellectuals in the early Hitler period. The feeling is well articulated in an article in *Neues Deutschland* by a leading East German poet, Paul Wiens, who is also chairman of the Berlin chapter of the GDR's "Writers' Union": ". . . This does not mean, however, that I would like to end every poem with the formulation: 'Besides, I approve of our society!' *Tenaciously repeated declarations of creed and love, even if expressed in imaginative variations, soon get on everyone's nerves.*"[24]

Placed in the context of the "perception-versus-reality" conflict area, there is the excitingly communicated official party line concerning a second—possibly even opposition—party and, ultimately, free elections. These perceptions are articulated for the "foreseeable future" especially in such countries as Czechoslovakia, Yugoslavia, and Hungary. Writing recently in *Pravny obzor,* a Slovak scholar has publicly argued that some representative government based on free elections is a *sine qua non* for a just socialist society. "Public participation in government," he stated specifically, "must reflect the popular will, and the popular will can best be expressed by free elections."[25]

In Yugoslavia numerous voices have been raised in favor of massive internal ideological liberalization in the form of a second party and free elections. *Praxis,* the revisionist Zagreb philosophical bimonthly, has repeatedly urged that an "organized political grouping" be created as a "second party," even if it were not much more than a small group gathered around the editorial board of a periodical (i.e., *Praxis* itself). The crux of the notorious Mihajlov case, and the true reason for the protracted persecution of the young author (sentenced in April, 1967, to a further four and a half years in jail), was not so much his attempt to launch a new periodical as his thesis that "there would be no real liberalization in Yugoslavia as long as the party held a monopoly of power. *The solution . . . was to have an opposition party and an opposition press.*"[26]

Existing communist realities obviously and sadly contradict these loudly claimed perceptions. Not only does Mihajlov's Djilas-style "publish and perish" treatment underscore practical reality, but, in addition, the March 19, 1967, Hungarian elections may also serve as a useful case study. In these elections 340 single-ticket candidates were elected to the Parliament, and in the nine elections where there were "unofficial" second candidates the official candidates won in every case. Not one of the nine "special" contestants made it. In the final analysis Communist party electoral lists won in 349 out of 349 cases, and, while the mere fact that nine unofficial candidates were in the running might be interesting to note, one qualified observer rightly suggested that "the election, played up with a great deal of excitement, was in fact a repetition of ancient comedies."[27]

Such reactions are not confined to the urban white-collar intelligentsia but are symptomatic also of the more youthful generation and of such other significant categories as the skilled industrial workers and the rising group of noncommunist technocrats who have come to occupy important positions in economic life. Silence, boredom, apathy, indifference, and attitudes of remoteness from the tortuous daily battles of ideological—or partisan—politics are some of the emotional variations on this popular theme.

Changing Problems in Foreign Policy

POLYCENTRISM AND THE IMPACT OF THE
SINO-SOVIET DISPUTE

Before turning to specific factors of disunity, one important generalization must be kept in mind. While the latitude in action or mobility of the individual East European states has increased since the death of Stalin, and was certainly further affected by the revolutionary events of 1956, this mobility is still forcefully restricted and circumscribed in the three key fields of military, economic, and foreign policies. On the whole, there is much more elbowroom for the satellites in domestic relations than in foreign affairs. *Domesticism,* the ability to navigate on one's own initiative and momentum in domestic matters, is an increasingly meaningful term in Soviet–East European relations. Thus *polycentrism*, impling one's own brand of noninternationally-minded communism, has in recent years evolved primarily into a domestically oriented term. Polycentrism cannot, at least not at this writing, be defined as a concept affirming national independence, since the "independent" actions and policies of the East European countries are severely curtailed and restricted by Soviet-controlled foreign, military, and economic policies. There is indeed a temptation to set up slogans applicable to the current situation on two parallel levels: (1) in the foreign field, unity over diversity, bloc relations over polycentric communism, while (2) in domestic affairs, diversity over unity, polycentrism over bloc loyalty. Since we are compelled to draw tight lines around the recent phenomenon of East European diversity, it must also be admitted that many of the regional changes we witness there are little more than cleverly contrived optical illusions.

Proceeding now from this narrowed-down definition of polycentrism, we must stress a few of the major factors militating against bloc unity in its operational context. At the present time, essentially three major forces seem to be working toward an acceleration of latent polycentrism, both of the institutional and of the ideological variety.

The first of these is the organizational weakness of the Soviet leadership in its external relationships as the guiding center of world communism. The inability to direct, to impose its will regardless of consequences, is particularly evident in the C.P.S.U.'s relationships with the French and Italian Communist parties, but it also surfaces in the faltering and ambiguous connections with Cuba, Yugoslavia, and Albania. The independent and often even truculent postures of these leaderships clearly reflect the prestige- if not the power-decline of the C.P.S.U. hierarchy. In turn, the internationally weakened position of Brezhnev and Kosygin not only affects their westward dialogues with such fellow communist leaders as Luigi Longo or Waldeck Rochet, but also tends to weaken their eastward rapport with Gomulka or Ulbricht.

A second, closely related power factor is the tremendous pull of the European Common Market, which, as a case study of runaway capitalist prosperity and organizational accomplishment, has exerted a pervasive impact on all East European countries as well as on the uneasy neutrals poised on the ECM periphery, namely, Austria and Finland. Despite Kosygin's rudely applied pressure on the Austrian government and the Soviets' vetoing of Austrian membership in the EEC, and notwithstanding Great Britain's continued exclusion as well as General de Gaulle's increasingly peculiar tactics on an all-European stage, for such geopolitically suitable countries as Yugoslavia or Hungary, EEC membership at some future date would loom as a profitable and desirable prospect. In the meantime the C.P.S.U.'s negative attitude toward the Common Market continues; it will probably keep Finland out of the Western organization as well. Nevertheless, the magic attraction of the Inner Six (soon to be substantially enlarged anyway) is bound to generate further and considerable divisive forces within both the northern and southern tiers of Eastern Europe—forces that for primarily economic reasons (capitalist wealth vis-à-vis Marxist-Leninist shabbiness) are inescapably headed in the direction of weakening the military infrastructure of the region.

Third and last, but not necessarily least, the fear of a resurgent West Germany—especially of the precedent-breaking Kiesinger-Brandt coalition government—can assume unexpected expressions as far as the national interests of Soviet foreign policy are concerned. This anxiety and deep-seated concern with the "colossus again" complex may well lead the Greeks, Dutch, Danes, Norwegians, Belgians, and even the French to "link up" in some shape or form with the Czechs and Poles, in particular, to prevent by joint and collective efforts the future realization of any pattern of West and East German reunification. The polycentric impact of such an all-European movement could only weaken the communist organization in general, and the East European power position of the U.S.S.R. in specific terms. Thus the fear of Germans, and more directly the latent European suspicions of Kiesinger's *Ostpolitik,* may in the long run tend to weaken rather than strengthen the Warsaw Pact system. In the short run, however, the specific fear of the Federal Republic is clearly bound to cement and weld together the strategic northern-tier nucleus of the Warsaw Treaty Organization: the Poles and Czechs in close alliance with the U.S.S.R., including also (more for tactical reasons) the East Germans. These are the nations, after all, which have suffered most directly and considerably from the wartime record and behavior of Nazi Germany.

Our discussion of polycentrism would not be complete if we did not briefly consider certain background forces working subtly and indirectly against the phenomenon of communist polycentrism. There are two principal factors asserting themselves against any major institutional and/or ideological linkage between East and West. The first of these, in order of current importance, is the war in Vietnam. The war in Vietnam, as Marshall D. Shulman observed: ". . . *introduced a qualitative leap forward for the Soviet Union in Western Europe,* partly because of the unpopularity of the American position in Viet Nam, but even more because the war occupied so much of our attention and energy. . . . The Soviets have intensified their efforts to weave a network of technological, trade, cultural, and political relationships with the major countries of Western Europe, as well as with Canada and Japan."[28]

The seriousness of an all-communist bloc reaction to the entire Vietnam issue cannot be minimized. In addition, it must be stated that the Soviet backing of Arab countries in the Middle Eastern war of June, 1967, has greatly complicated the original "Vietnam complex." The joint and continuing impact of the escalating American war effort, on the one hand, and the indirectly and informally pro-Israel stance of the United States, on the other, have in effect succeeded in transforming two originally "red herring"-type problems into major, and truly divisive, issues. Not only have the reactions to Vietnam and to the Middle Eastern war solidified the variegated membership of the East European bloc, but even after a settlement of this Southeast Asian conflict, East-West—and, more specifically, U.S.–East European—relations are not likely to return to the friendlier 1963 or 1964 status quo. The Soviet leadership, making the most of this antipolycentric and communist-unity-building argument, has angrily equated the Johnson Administration with war and conquest in Asia while wistfully identifying the late President Kennedy with policies of peaceful accommodation.

Beyond the Vietnam and Middle Eastern issues, there looms an almost equally important politico-governmental link between the U.S.S.R. and Eastern Europe. This consists of the proliferation of major Soviet governmental and political institutions throughout the entire area. It implies an intricate network of interconnecting "national" Communist parties, which are more or less slavish imitations of the structure of the C.P.S.U., with parallel administrative procedures and personnel policies. On the whole, during the past twenty-three years the U.S.S.R. has "succeeded first in transplanting and then in proliferating Soviet Russian governmental, bureaucratic, police repression, and economic patterns of operation in a wholesale manner."[29] Clearly, the antipolycentric and pro-U.S.S.R. forces of communist cohesion have derived considerable benefit from the basic fact that Eastern Europe's local replicas, as variations on a general theme, reflect many similarities and instinctive duplications of the Soviet original.

Turning now specifically to the impact of the Sino-Soviet dispute, during the first few years of its emergence into the open, the disruptive conflict between these two communist giants has had a fourfold influence on Eastern Europe. It has presented these countries with the following alternatives:

1. to support Communist China unequivocally to the point of precipitating an open break with the U.S.S.R. (a dubious choice made only by Albania, which severed relations with the Soviet Union in the 1960–61 period);

2. to gain an area of political maneuvers and material advantages by playing off one of the major ideological antagonists against the other (an alternative attempted in a modest way by several of the East European countries but exploited only by

Rumania, which has played the bribery-bargaining-exploitative game with acrobatic skill and great national satisfaction);

3. to pledge complete loyalty to the U.S.S.R. in the hope of gaining sizable political rewards and economic concessions thereby; (Although Bulgaria has been the most loyal to the Soviet Union, Hungary, East Germany, Poland, and Czechoslovakia have certainly echoed this policy in its military, economic, and diplomatic aspects, insisting in turn on a "most favored satellite" treatment from the Muscovite leadership. By now all of these countries, except Albania, have profited either directly or indirectly from the communist camp's internecine power struggle.) and, finally,

4. to establish the lone outpost of a truly Balkan independence, as has emerged in Tito's Yugoslavia. (This country's foreign policy posture can only be described as a "plague-on-both-your-houses" approach to the problem, punctuated with occasional pro-Soviet noises,[30] but with an essentially aloof attitude toward the day-by-day vicissitudes of the dispute itself. Although Yugoslavia nominally favors the Soviet side, its diplomats are primarily intent on going through the "correct" motions of support rather than taking a substantive side in the conflict. Indeed, a cleverly contrived isolationist aloofness would be the most appropriate descriptive term categorizing the Titoist posture. It is *de facto* nonaligned in the context of Tito's frequently enunciated foreign-policy dictum of the 1950's and early 1960's.)

U.S.–EAST EUROPEAN RELATIONS: THE IMPACT OF AMERICAN FOREIGN POLICY

In conclusion, certain new East-West stirrings must be recorded in the expectation that a minimal rapprochement between the two sides may alter somewhat the future course of East European politics. Theoretically the lines of approach were drawn in President Johnson's New York speech of October 7, 1966, which stressed a theme of Western flexibility toward the communist East and talked in terms of "bridge-building" and "peaceful engagement." In actual practice, however, both the German Federal Republic and De Gaulle's France have taken much fuller advantage of the more liberal political atmosphere of Eastern Europe. Chancellor Kiesinger's coalition government, in its trade policies, its cultural exchange, and its tentative diplomatic relations, and General de Gaulle's Fifth Republic, in commercial and political matters, have successfully undertaken the widening of existing bridges as well as the vigorous construction of new ones. These bold and important Western initiatives not only have helped to erode somewhat Moscow's control over the once homogeneous communist nations of Eastern Europe but also have tended to accelerate the latent polycentric trends typical of the *new* European communisms.

A student of East European affairs has recently outlined three alternative courses for American policy in Eastern Europe.[31] The first of these harks back to the 1940–50 period and seems to be dictated by the realities of the cold war of the immediate post–World War II era. Its actual policy lines involve a stepped-up pattern of economic and political warfare against the "satellites" (the assumption being made here is: once a satellite, always a satellite!), a ringing declaration that captive peoples must be freed and that such an aggressive policy on the part of the West would require the maintenance of large military establishments in Europe on a continuing basis. Conversely, this policy dictates the reduction of trade and cultural relations with the Eastern bloc practically to a minimum and even foresees their eventual discontinuation.

The second policy line attempts to draw a distinction between Eastern Europe proper and the U.S.S.R., intending to weaken their connection and ultimately to lure the individual countries of Danubia and the Balkans away from their Soviet "colonial protector." Emphasizing the budding national independence of the "ex-satellites," the hopeful expectation is to create a series of Finlands, Yugoslavias, or even neutral Austrias, and to involve them in both European Common Market and U.N. activities. The goal clearly is to expand the scope of Western influence in Eastern Europe without necessarily antagonizing the Soviet Union.[32]

The third approach would treat the Soviet Union and the countries of Eastern Europe alike, assuming a *general* "easing of tensions," an infectious and over-all spirit of "peaceful co-existence," without drawing sharp distinctions between the Soviet and East European patterns of Marxism-Leninism. This view insists on a contrast between the U.S.S.R. and Eastern Europe, on the one hand, and a truculent Communist China (unalterably opposed to the very spirit of "peaceful coexistence"), on the other. As a governmental policy this line would take temporary advantage of the growing ideological hostilities created by the Sino-Soviet dispute.

Obviously, there are no quick and easy solutions for such a complex problem area. The U.S. government seems to follow a policy that combines the second and third courses. Despite the unpleasant realities of our Vietnam venture and continuing Soviet-American policy divergencies in the Middle East, we have not given up the pursuit of "building bridges" in Eastern Europe or of peacefully engaging in the cultural and commercial affairs of the region. We do this, not as a result of softness toward communism, but as a matter of practical, national foreign-policy considerations.

NOTES

1. For an excellent analysis of the continuing "political schizophrenia" characteristic of Soviet foreign policy see Kurt London's "Soviet Foreign Policy: Fifty Years of Dualism" on pp. 327–63 of the present volume.

√ 2. See F. C. Barghoorn, "Observations on Contemporary Soviet Political Attitudes," *Soviet Studies,* vol. XVIII, no. 1 (July, 1966), p. 68.

3. For further discussion of the revolutions "from below" see the present author's article "Die Rolle des Nationalismus in Osteuropa," *Osteuropa,* February-March, 1966, pp. 113–27.

4. The Stalinist revolutions "from above" are analyzed in some detail in several of the contributions to *Eastern Europe in Transition,* ed. Kurt London (Baltimore: The Johns Hopkins Press, 1966); see esp. the present author's article on nationalism, pp. 3–18.

5. Cited with editorial comments by George A. Morgan, "Stalin on Revolution," in *The Soviet Union, 1922–1962: A Foreign Affairs Reader.* ed. Philip E. Mosely (New York: F. A. Praeger, 1963), pp. 237 *et seqq*

6. See Hugh Seton-Watson, *From Lenin to Malenkov: The History of World Communism* (New York: F. A. Praeger, 1953), esp. pp. 253–66.

7. For further discussion of the chronological theory in general, and of this point in particular, see Andrew Gyorgy, *Governments of Danubian Europe* (New York: Rinehart, 1949), esp. chap. II, pp. 37–68.

8. A perceptive analysis of these stages is to be found in Franz Borkenau's monumental *European Communism* (New York: Harper and Brothers, 1953), esp. chap. XIX, "Popular Democracies," pp. 484–516.

9. See C. E. Black's excellent discussion entitled "Confirmation of Communist Control in People's Democracies—Eastern Europe," in *European Political Systems,* ed. Taylor Cole, 2d ed. (New York: A. A. Knopf, 1959), esp. pp. 775–79.

10. *Ibid.,* p. 776.

11. Chronologically, the plebiscite elections were not, on the whole, the first elections after World War II. As second or "follow-up" spectacles they were used as acts of confirmation of communist control in the newly promoted "people's democracies." For an excellent commentary see Black, "Confirmation of Communist Control," pp. 776–77.

12. The term "revolution" is used here in a narrow Stalinist sense. These revolutions were far from being massive popular explosions; rather, they were artificially planted communist movements forced upon captive peoples by the occupational might of the Red Army. Thus they were truly revolutions *from above.*

13. Gyula Fábián, "Meditations," Radio Kossuth, Budapest, February 13, 1967, analyzed in *Hungarian Press Survey*, Radio Free Europe (Munich and New York), February 28, 1967, pp. 2–5.

14. This discrepancy further enhances the dichotomy between Communist party and nonparty masses. The communist ideal is a far cry from sordid reality. "A communist," states a recent Hungarian article, "has to agree actively, meaning that at his own post he contributes with active deeds and work to the implementation of party resolutions" (Jenö Faragó, "Upholding the Banner for Communism," *Népszabadság* [Budapest], February 21, 1967).

✓15. See especially "The Role of Nationalism in Eastern Europe: From Monolith to Polycentrism," in *Eastern Europe in Transition*, pp. 3–18, and the present author's introductory chapter, "Eastern Europe in Historic Perspective," in *Eastern European Government and Politics,* by V. Benes, A. Gyorgy and G. Stambuk (New York: Harper and Row, 1966), pp. 1–22.

16. *Diluvian* in this case denotes the onrush of the communist flood tide after 1944. The post-diluvian (or utopian) form of nationalism is at present only a hypothetical mirage for the average East European.

17. *New York Times,* April 20, 1967.

18. This pattern of nationalism inevitably produced economic reforms in Eastern Europe. "The Year of Economic Reform" throughout communist Europe was 1965; it is ably analyzed by Gregory Grossman in his "Economic Reforms: A Balance Sheet," *Problems of Communism,* November-December, 1966, pp. 43–55.

19. These phrases are taken primarily from Rumanian sources, such as Constantin Vlad, "The Evolution and Role of the Nation in Socialism,"

Contemporanul (Bucharest), no. 31 (1966), with detailed comment in *Rumanian Press Survey*, Radio Free Europe (Munich and New York), no. 650 (August 22, 1966).

20. See *Hungarian Press Survey*, Radio Free Europe (Munich and New York), January 25, 1967.

21. We are confronted here with modern communism's ceaseless "Operation Rewrite." As one Hungarian historian recently phrased it, evaluation of the "historical past must change in accordance with the interests of the momentary power" (see *Hungarian Press Survey*, Radio Free Europe (Munich and New York), December 15, 1966, esp. p. 3).

22. Complaints abound specifically about the Soviets' cultural backwardness. "Are these the people who want to be leaders of the world?" the Poles or Hungarians ask incredulously. The answers to this question are uniformly depressing throughout Eastern Europe.

23. See István Szirmai, "Our Party Policy Liberated the Forces of the Intellect," *Népszabadság*, February 12, 1966, pp. 1 *et seqq.*

24. See *Neues Deutschland*, September 18, 1966, as analyzed by Dorothy Miller, in "The First Annual Conference of the East German Writers' League," *RFE Research Bulletin*, November 9, 1966, esp. pp. 2–3; italics added.

25. See M. Lakatos, "Some Problems of Socialist Democracy from the Viewpoint of the Citizen's Position in Our Society," *Pravny Obzor*, no. 3 (1966). For detailed comment see "Czechoslovak Writer Calls for Free Election," *Czechoslovak Press Survey*, April 20, 1966, pp. 1–2.

26. See Richard Eder, "Mihajlov Is Given New 4½ Year Term By Belgrade Court," *New York Times*, April 20, 1967, pp. 1 and 14; italics added.

27. See *News From Hungary*, Free Europe, Inc. (New York), March 31, 1967, p. 1, under the title "Not a Single Opposition Candidate Is Elected Deputy."

28. See his article " 'Europe' Versus 'Détente'?" in *Foreign Affairs*, April, 1967, pp. 389–402, esp. p. 395.

29. For further discussion of this point see particularly chap. I, "Eastern Europe in Historic Perspective," in Benes, Gyorgy, and Stambuk, *Eastern European Government and Politics*, esp. pp. 10–12.

30. It must be stressed, however, that in the course of 1967 Tito's approach to the U.S.S.R. became more than casual or perfunctory. The apparent establishment of a joint Soviet-Yugoslav military mission would indicate a major rapprochement between the two nations and a significant ideological twist of the previously meticulous neutrality of Yugoslav foreign policy.

31. See John C. Campbell, *American Policy Toward Communist Eastern Europe: The Choices Ahead* (Minneapolis: University of Minnesota Press, 1965), esp. chap. VI, pp. 83–107.

32. For a discussion of these policy alternatives see Michael B. Petrovich's "United States Policy in East Europe," *Current History*, April, 1967, pp. 193–99 and 243–44.

CHAPTER 7

Soviet Relations with Germany

The Soviet Union and the Germans

Klaus Mehnert

The Soviet Union and the Germans

Klaus Mehnert

The definitive work on Soviet-German relations since the victory of the Bolshevik Revolution has yet to be written, although this problem has remained a major concern for the past half-century. The existing monographs and memoirs, some of which will be mentioned below, are valuable contributions, but they do not offer a comprehensive in-depth analysis. The present author will resist the temptation to add yet another personal account to the literature on the subject. Rather, he will deal briefly with ten main factors that in our time have affected the attitudes of the U.S.S.R. and Germany toward each other, in an attempt to throw some light on the dimensions of this many-faceted problem.

GERMANY AND LENIN

There might still have been a revolution in Russia if there had been no Germany (even this, one may doubt, looking at the close intellectual and political relationship between the two countries), but without Germany there surely would have been no Lenin. Lenin's entire intellectual and revolutionary history is closely linked with the intellectual and revolutionary development of Germany. That was true before he went to Germany and especially so after his first visit there, in 1895. During his Siberian exile (1897–1900) his friends arranged subscriptions for him to *Die Frankfurter Zeitung* and *Archiv für Soziale Gesetzgebung und Statistik.* Apart from some Russians, notably G. W. Plechanov and L. Martow, Lenin's most important teachers, friends, and foes were Germans. In checking the two volumes of indexes to Lenin's *Works*[1] one can see at a glance that the most frequently mentioned political and social thinkers or doers—in addition, of course, to Marx and Engels—include, in this order, Karl Kautsky, Rosa Luxemburg, Eduard Bernstein, Karl Liebknecht, August Bebel, Philip Scheidemann, and many others, as well as Feuerbach, Hegel, and Kant. It was in Germany and in the two neighboring German-speaking countries, Austria and Switzerland, that Lenin spent most of his time during his years abroad.

True, we know that Lenin's political Weltanschauung was not exclusively of German-Marxist origin, that a number of Russian traditions and schools of thought contributed to his mental outlook. But among the Russians most often named in Lenin's writings, those influenced by Marxism and German thought are by far in the majority, and there is little doubt that German thinking with its various ramifications occupied a dominant place in Lenin's thinking. Khrushchev was quite correct when in 1955 he reminded Chancellor Adenauer in Moscow that, after all, the man who was so greatly responsible for the shaping of the U.S.S.R., Karl Marx, had been a German.[2]

The government of the kaiser took upon itself the responsibility of transporting Lenin and other Bolsheviks, including Grigory Zinoviev and Karl Radek, through Germany to Sweden (and Russia) in the spring of 1917, enabling Lenin to overthrow the Russian government in order to knock Russia out of the war and thus to free German troops for the Western front. To what extent the German government had supported Lenin's movement financially before and after the journey of the "sealed car" is still not completely clarified, and may never be, but there is no doubt that German money was involved, and it is equally clear that Lenin did not feel in the least obliged to the imperial German government for its aid.[3] The label of German agent, however, has long clouded Lenin's reputation.

Of the ensuing events, we can omit, from the vantage point of today, the last phases of the Russo-German war as well as the Brest-Litovsk treaty; these were episodes that left no lasting traces. To be sure, in Brest the Soviet government ceded the western and southwestern territories of the tsar's empire—Finland, Estonia, Latvia, Lithuania, Poland, the Ukraine, Transcaucasia—but the first five might have obtained their statehood and independence without Brest (though probably not without the war with Germany), and the latter two were to lose it again.

THE SPLIT BETWEEN RUSSIAN AND GERMAN MARXISTS

Lenin's intellectual and political development occurred in a constant dispute (*Auseinandersetzung*) with the German Social Democrats, which gradually grew into conflict and finally into open hostility. This process, so decisive for the future of Russia and for her relations with Germany and with the world socialist movement in general, has been much discussed and described.[4]

Today we possess new insight into this rift, in light of the split between the Russian and the Chinese communists. In reading Peking's attacks against Moscow, particularly since 1962,[5] one is struck by the extraordinary similarity of Mao's anti-Soviet vocabulary with the language used by Lenin in his polemic against the SPD (Social Democratic Party of Germany) forty-five years earlier. Indeed, the Chinese Communists have accused the Soviet leaders of being "disciples of Bernstein and Kautsky,"[6] because they are following today the road of the SPD, which Lenin abhorred.

The very term "revisionism," which the Chinese constantly hurl against Moscow, is but an echo of Lenin's accusations against the German comrades,[7] who in the process lost the prerogative of being called comrades, just as the Russians have lost it in the eyes of the Chinese today. In Lenin's view, the German SPD had abandoned its revolutionary fervor to become an organization of reformers, even traitors; as far as the Maoists are concerned, exactly the same is true of the Soviet leaders today.

Lenin spoke about an eastward movement of the revolutionary center, and the Maoists have made this thesis a part of their ideology. Lenin was right then, as Mao is now. The reason, of course, is not that "the east wind prevails over the west wind"—as Mao claimed in November, 1957, in a speech to the students of Moscow University—but that the radicals of underdeveloped Russia then were more radical than those of highly developed Germany, just as the radicals of underdeveloped China now are more radical than those of the highly developed, largely saturated Soviet Union.

Friedrich Ebert, the sober leader of the SPD, with his strong sense of responsibility for his country and for peace in general, the man who said—before taking office as the first Chancellor of the German Republic in November, 1918—that he did not want a social revolution, because he "hated it like sin," was just as different from Lenin as the technobureaucrat Kosygin is from Mao.

The split of 1919 (when Lenin founded the Communist International in opposition to the SPD-led Socialist International) engendered a deep hostility. We feel it still today, after almost half a century, personified especially by the two men who for a long time were in charge of the two halves of this much tormented city of Berlin—Willy Brandt and Walter Ulbricht. All through the years of the Weimar, and again of the Bonn, Republic, the German socialists have been the most bitter enemies of the German communists, whom they considered—with much justification—the Russian communists' fifth column in Germany.

THE GERMAN RIGHT AND MOSCOW

During the Weimar period of Germany it was not the socialist left but the German right, especially the German *Reichswehr,* which was seeking contacts and even allies in Bolshevik Russia. The German right was traditionally anti-West and became even more so after the Treaty of Versailles of 1919; it was also—as a result of the territorial losses in the East—anti-Polish. For these reasons it was inclined to look toward Russia, even Bolshevik Russia. Between 1906 and 1914 one of the German right's major prophets, Arthur Moeller van den Bruck, published twenty-three volumes of Dostoyevsky in German, explaining specifically that the Germans needed this anti-Western Russian as a counterweight against Western influences.[8] To give an ideological foundation to this strange bedfellowship, the West was painted as decadent while the Russians were counted among the young nations.[9]

The German National Bolsheviks, as some of them called themselves, did not leave much of a mark on German-Russian history, because Lenin was not interested. He did not follow the lead of Karl Radek who—in Berlin and in Moscow—was pleading for co-operation with the German nationalists of the right, just because they were anti-Western and thus essentially anti-capitalist.

What Radek advocated with regard to Germany, Stalin and his successors later carried out by creating alliances with anti-Western bourgeois nationalists—starting with Chiang Kai-shek (1923–27), and more recently with Nasser. Lenin understood, of course, the political implications for Russia of the German nationalists' opposition to Versailles and the Western powers, but he did not think much of the political influence of the anti-Western German rightists.

Yet the infatuation of German rightists with anti-Western Moscow has left some traces to this day: the present-day German nationalists, the NPD (National Democratic Party of Germany), have been demanding close political co-operation with anti-Western China. The U.S.S.R. itself, as a status quo power in control or in possession of large German territories, does not exercise much influence on German nationalism today.

A much more effective and lasting form of understanding between German nationalism and the Soviet Union was the long though secret co-operation between the *Reichswehr* and the Red Army. Today we know the forms and the extent of this co-operation.[10] Fear makes things loom larger than they really are, as one might translate the Russian proverb *U strakha glaza veliki*. The fear of German rearmament made German-Soviet military collaboration appear larger than it was. But it was big enough. For the young and threatened Soviet state it was important that Germans build armaments plants in the U.S.S.R., and for the *Reichswehr* it was most valuable that its officers could be trained in Russia with weapons forbidden to Germany —planes and tanks. Many years later Göring and Guderian were to say that the arming of Hitler's *Wehrmacht* after 1935 could not have proceeded so quickly without the long years of preparation on Soviet territory.[11] If this statement is correct, the *Reichswehr*–Red Army deal has had very significant consequences indeed.

Another effect of this deal has by now practically disappeared: the close personal links of German and Russian officers. Yet, the present writer knows a high officer in the *Bundeswehr* who still remembers with a good deal of warmth the year of training which he spent in Russia in the early thirties, before Hitler ended the military co-operation with the U.S.S.R. But not many are left—on either side—and too much has happened since.

RAPALLO

While German-Russian military co-operation was a fact of considerable consequence, the Treaty of Rapallo was more a myth than a political force. The main significance of this treaty, concluded on Easter Sunday, 1922, has been symbolic. The two countries—the pariahs of Europe, as Lloyd George called them—had found the way to each other. The contents of the treaty itself were harmless enough, and it contained no secret clauses. Still, the name of the small Italian resort where the treaty was hurriedly signed stands to this day for German-Russian anti-Western collusion, if not conspiracy.

It was largely because of the attitude of the Western powers —Great Britain and France in particular—that the treaty assumed a significance quite out of proportion with its wording. Rapallo is still a political term, like Munich; the big difference, of course, is that Munich did have profound consequences, while Rapallo did not.

The mere fact of mutual diplomatic recognition, brought about at Rapallo, would not have meant very much; it did not mean much twenty-three years later, in 1955. The fact that it did have some consequences—surely more, at least, than in the period after 1955—was largely attributable to a German diplomat who by his remarkable personality and will power was able to create the image of something close to a German-Soviet alliance (which did not, in fact, exist) and to set a style of political relationship which was to last until 1941. Count Ulrich von Brockdorff-Rantzau, an eccentric and most complex man, succeeded during his six years in Moscow in establishing excellent contacts with the leaders of Soviet foreign policy, with Foreign Commissar Gheorgy Chicherin in particular, both of aristocratic mind and background and both being fond of work at night.

Brockdorff-Rantzau established the tradition of a close, frank, and, if need be, tough relationship between the German Embassy in Moscow and the Soviet government, a tradition which was continued by his successors, Herbert von Dirksen and Count Werner von der Schulenburg. (Rudolf Nadolny, the man in between, left following a quarrel with Hitler and Foreign Minister von Neurath after a very brief stay, but he, too, adhered to this line.)

Needless to say, none of these noblemen had the slightest sympathy for Bolshevism or for Stalin, but all of them were fascinated by the phenomena of the Russian Revolution and the Soviet state and were dedicated to their assignment, which was the establishment of close relations between their fatherland and the growing giant in the East. This also became the attitude of their staff members, some of whom have achieved considerable prominence: General Köstring, long-time military attaché and symbol of excellent relations between the military; Gustav Hilger (Moscow-born, like Köstring), the soul of the German Embassy and close personal friend of many prominent Soviet leaders (including Mikoyan), author of a book on German-Soviet political relations, as Köstring was of one on German-Soviet military relations;[12] J. Herwarth von Bittenfeldt, now

German Ambassador in Rome; Fritz von Tvardovsky, later Ambassador to Mexico, still active in Bonn; Otto Bräutigam, after World War II the Consul General in Hong Kong, now retired but participating in the German discussion on *Ostpolitik*, with emphasis on improving relations with the U.S.S.R.; Peter Pfeiffer, now head of the world-wide cultural activities of the Goethe Institute in Munich; and, of course, Otto Schiller, after 1931 (and again after 1956) German agricultural attaché, now professor at Heidelberg.

On the whole, the German Embassy during the almost two decades prior to the invasion by the *Wehrmacht* into Russia, was the most competent and devoted of all foreign missions in the Soviet capital, and only during the brilliant Bullitt-Kennan-Bohlen-Durbrow period of the U.S. Embassy (after 1934) did it have a serious rival. Even under Hitler, Schulenburg managed to keep this spirit alive; and after 1955, when diplomatic relations were resumed during Adenauer's visit to Moscow, the tradition was quickly revived—under Ambassadors Wilhelm Haas, Hans Kroll (a particularly articulate advocate of German-Soviet rapprochement, whose book on the subject appeared in 1967), Horst Gröpper (now Ambassador to Turkey, who had the bad luck of serving in Moscow during a phase of sub-zero relations between Bonn and Moscow), and Gebhardt von Walther. The last two, incidentally, had served in Moscow under Schulenburg.

CRITICAL UNDERSTANDING

The Brockdorff-Rantzau spirit also affected the German correspondents in Moscow, of whom Paul Scheffer and Arthur W. Just were the best known, while Wilhelm Baum, the long-time representative of the German News Agency, was less known to the general public; Baum committed suicide in 1942, out of despair over Hitler's Eastern policy. The spirit of friendly though critical understanding came to life again after the Second World War, in the person of Hermann Pörzgen, who had worked in Moscow in the Schulenburg days and who, despite hard years in Soviet prisons from 1944 to 1955, returned to Moscow (for the *Frankfurter Allgemeine Zeitung*) in 1956, now the dean of German correspondents in the U.S.S.R.

Even the Russian and East European studies at the German universities fitted into this picture of critical understanding. The men who set the pace in this respect were Otto Hoetzsch, professor of East European history, and his Russian history colleague, Karl Staehlin, both at the University of Berlin. Berlin was, during the twenties and early thirties, a center, perhaps *the* center, of what now is known as sovietology. It had many students, now scattered all over the world (George F. Kennan among them), several journals, such as *Osteuropa* and *Ostwirschaft,* and a good deal of cultural exchange. A bibliography of books and articles on the Soviet Union printed in German outside the U.S.S.R., published in Berlin just before Hitler's ascent to power, included 1,900 titles.[13]

In 1925 numerous German scholars, including noted scientists such as Max Planck and six university presidents, participated in the 200 years' celebration of the Academy of Sciences, then still in Leningrad. In the following years two Soviet weeks were held in Berlin, one on natural sciences (1927) and one on Russian history (1928), both attended by famous Soviet scholars—the latter, for example, by M. N. Pokrovsky and S. F. Platonov; in 1929 a German Technical Week was organized in Moscow.[14] Activities on this scale came to a stop after Hitler took power and were resumed in West Germany after 1945. But the tradition of the Otto Hoetzsch school of critical understanding is very much alive in the German *Ostforschung* (Eastern research) of today.

The Germans who were active in these contacts during the twenties and thirties were not "pinks"; in fact, Otto Hoetzsch was a respected member of first the *Deutschnationale,* then the *Jungkonservative* party, both quite far to the right. But they considered the Soviet Union a fact of life, of great interest in general and to the Germans in particular.

THE GERMAN COMMUNISTS

From the outset the relationship between the Germans and the Soviet government has been adversely affected by the presence of a Communist party in Germany. This, of course, can be said of almost any other country's relationship with Moscow. But the Germany of Weimar was particularly unstable, and hence her Communist party was of special importance. Lenin's hope to win "the German proletariat" away from the SPD and into the KPD (Communist party of Germany) did not materialize. The SPD remained—from Bismarck's time until the present—the party of the German workingman. The KPD's emphasis on violence and revolution did not endear it to a nation that was not very revolutionary-minded. Its ill-fated uprisings, particularly in 1923, as well as the revolutionary activities of its predecessor, Spartacus, made it unpopular and suspected. Yet the KPD was at times one of the biggest vote-getters among the vote-conscious Germans, and during the depression years the party obtained up to six million votes (1932) in a Germany which at that time had close to six million unemployed and several million more underemployed.

This is not the place to discuss the general attitude of the Germans toward democracy; but there is no question that the German laborer has a long democratic tradition. It was he who fought—successfully—for an enlargement of his democratic rights against Bismarck and against Wilhelm II, thereby identifying his cause with that of democracy. Lenin's antidemocratic attitude, his emphasis on a conspiratorial elite with which to lead "the masses," the unpleasant sight of a dictatorship which was precisely not *of* the proletariat but *over* the proletariat, the many accounts of violence, terror, and destruction during the Revolution, the civil war, the collectivization, the purge—all this repelled the great majority of the German workers. They also resented the KPD's obvious servility to Moscow. Sooner than the proletariat in other countries, the German working class understood that, especially under Stalin, the KPD was simply an auxiliary of the Kremlin, that Stalin, not Ernst

Thälman, was its boss, and that it acted not in the interest of the German workers, nor even of the party itself, but of Moscow's foreign policy—official and otherwise. At a time when nationalism was in the air, the very "masses" whom the KPD wooed began to turn away from it to vote, and march, for the man who aroused their nationalistic passions and who in addition promised "socialism," bread, and security. While the SPD on the whole succeeded in holding its members and voters, many desperate KPD voters, though not many KPD cadres, turned to Hitler and Goebbels.

A major blunder committed by Stalin added to the estrangement between the KPD and the SPD. In 1924 he declared: "Social democracy and fascism are twins,"[15] and he reiterated this misanalysis until the bitter end. As a result, there could be no question of antifascist co-operation between the two Marxist parties of Germany. Disunited they stood, and separately they were destroyed by Hitler's liquidators. In April, 1933, weeks after Hitler had come to power (with the Reichstag burned, the KPD leaders in prison or dead, the SPD just about eliminated), the Central Committee of the KPD branded the SPD "the main support of the capitalist dictatorship," and the Executive Committee of the Communist International proclaimed that the time had finally come to drive the last nail into the SPD's coffin. It was George F. Kennan who proclaimed Stalin's responsibility for the failure of the Weimar Republic.[16]

In the concentration camps and in exile there occurred some co-operation between German communists and socialists, but hardly was Hitler defeated and dead when the old struggle was resumed. Wolfgang Leonhard and some others who were in Berlin during the first phase after the end of the Second World War have interpreted the new split[17] as a result of Walter Ulbricht's efforts to monopolize control over the left wing in Germany and over state power in the Soviet-occupied zone. Had it not been for Ulbricht and his like, there might have emerged in all Germany a united leftist party, as there did emerge a united Christian party encompassing Protestants and Catholics. These, after all, had fought each other for over 400 years, while the division between communists and socialists had lasted only a quarter of a century. As a result, the SPD, under the tough leadership of Kurt Schumacher, turned out to be the communists' most dangerous foe in West Germany. And in the Soviet-occupied zone many of the staunchest and most determined opponents of Ulbricht's rule were men from the SPD.

One is tempted to ask what would have happened if Lenin in 1919 and Ulbricht in 1945 had not split the German left, just as one might speculate, by the same token, on what might have happened if Mao in the 1960's had not split world communism.

GERMAN BUSINESS AND THE BUILDING OF SOVIET INDUSTRY

The economic co-operation of the two "pariahs," established by a number of agreements, the first of which was concluded on May 6, 1921, was slow in starting. Various attempts were made which came to naught. At first the Russians were willing to make economic concessions to German (and other) firms; but, being extremely suspicious of "foreign capitalists," they held them in a very tight grip, which obstructed effective operation. One example was the huge forest and lumber concession *Mologales*. It ended in failure—like all the others—because of basic disagreements between the Soviets and the German concessionaires. The greatest relative success was achieved by the mixed German-Soviet air-transport company *Deruluft*.

The chief obstacle to trade was the Soviet trade monopoly, which functions to this day, although with some modifications. It gave the Soviet government an advantage over its foreign partners—a state monopoly versus innumerable foreign firms. The German side later countered the Soviet move by forming, in Berlin, the *Russlandausschuss der Deutschen Wirtschaft* (Russian Committee of German Industry), which tried to co-ordinate some of the German firms' activities; it also provided them with relevant information to help them avoid unexpected traps. From 1926 on, the German government gave guarantees to German firms that sold goods to the Soviet Union on credit. This operation worked well; the Soviet government could not fail on a single payment without at the same time losing all creditability.

It was only during the early thirties that German-Soviet economic co-operation reached sizable proportions. At that time two factors coincided: the enormous pace of Stalin's industrialization and the depression in the West, which forced German firms to look for orders in countries not affected by it. In February, 1931, one of the most illustrious industrial delegations ever to travel abroad from Germany went to Moscow; it included, among others, the representatives (often the heads) of Krupp, Klöckner, Vereinigte Stahlwerke, Demag, Borsig, AEG, MAN, and Otto Wolff. During that year Soviet orders in Germany totaled almost one billion German marks, while goods worth about 750 million marks were delivered to the Soviet Union. German specialists by the hundreds went to the U.S.S.R. to work on Soviet projects, enough to force the German Embassy in Moscow to open a school for its children. Gustav Hilger recalls that, during his vacation in Germany, representatives from 200 firms visited him in Berlin in the course of ten days, to inquire about exports to the U.S.S.R.[18] In the midthirties the present writer, visiting the huge Soviet factories of the first Five-Year Plan, walked—so it seems in retrospect—miles and miles among machines with German labels.

Curiously, this economic co-operation continued after Hitler came to power in 1933. Hitler's government granted the Soviets large credits, which were scrupulously repaid. It is well known that huge Soviet shipments were on their way to Germany when the *Wehrmacht* started its invasion of the Soviet Union on that early June morning in 1941.

FROM EISENSTEIN TO YEVTUSHENKO

Outside of the U.S.S.R. there was no country where Russian *and* Soviet cultures were more highly esteemed than they were in the Germany of the nineteen twenties—at that time the intellectual clearinghouse of the world, a position she lost in the thirties and forties and still has not regained. At that time there was no UNESCO to record annual statistics of cultural exchange among nations; but it is the impression of those who lived in the Berlin of the Weimar period that the city was then a show window of Russian art and literature. German intellectual life was sufficiently vigorous not to be afraid of foreign influences—from Russia or anywhere else.

The Soviet theater—including that of Stanislavsky and Meyerhold—was frequently on tour in German cities; Soviet films, at that time worth applauding, were shown to large audiences with great success, Eisenstein being the favorite. Soviet literature was much translated and read: Sholokhov's *And Quiet Flows the Don*; Gladkov's novels of "socialist construction"; Ilya Ehrenburg's innumerable works; Aleksey Tolstoy's *Peter the First*; much of Gorky, although his main works were written before the First World War. Zostchenko's satirical short stories—especially the collection under the title *Sleep Faster, Comrade!*—were favorites of the German public, as were the caustic novels of Ilf and Petrov. Many of these authors later on found their way into other parts of the West. A number of noncommunist German and Austrian publishers specialized in the works of Soviet authors.

At the same time, the Russian classics—in music and literature—had their renaissance, partly owing to the many refugees from the Russian bourgeoisie and aristocracy who had made their homes in Germany and who had brought a good deal of Old Russia with them. The Don Cossacks were among the many artists who enjoyed some of their earliest triumphs in German concert halls.

Some people may have found the way to communism through Soviet art. But with the great majority this was not true; most saw in it the spiritual emanation of a strange but great revolution, and while few approved the revolution, least of all its brutality, they were fascinated by its artistic expression. Post-Wilhelmian Germany was hungry for experimentation; while it took a leading place with its powerful school of expressionism, it was willing to learn from everybody, including the Bolsheviks.

The decline of Soviet culture under the frost of Stalinism began at a time when the Germans started the banning and burning of books; hence it remained more or less unnoticed, except by specialists. The beginning was marked, however, by the resolution of the Central Committee of April 23, 1932, and the founding of the Soviet Writers Union shortly thereafter. The Second World War was not conducive to cultural interchange. Many treasures of art and history were destroyed, some on purpose, others not: Lev Tolstoy's estate, Yasnaya Polyana, was respected, not desecrated, by its German occupants; the burial of some German soldiers near Tolstoy's grave seemed a desecration to the Soviets, but surely was not so intended by the Germans who buried their comrades.

After the war was over the Russians were in possession of a large part of Germany, including intellectual and historical centers such as Weimar and Potsdam, Wittenberg and the Wartburg, Leipzig and Dresden. They then had an extraordinary chance to exert their cultural influence on the Germans; they used it to a large extent, but with rather modest success. At first the Germans showed a remarkable willingness to devour—after years of cultural seclusion and barrenness—anything that was offered to them from abroad. There existed a genuine desire to know many and, if possible, favorable facts about the new masters. But the old saying held true: "It was too much of a good thing."

One might compare the ill effects of overexposure to Russian propaganda in the Soviet-occupied areas of Germany after 1945 with those in China after 1949. At first there was much eagerness to absorb and learn—language, literature, music, history, even ideology—but then followed all the signs of overeating: satiety, lack of appetite, and finally revulsion. Something of this nature also happened in the Western-occupied zones with regard to American, French, and British culture, but less drastically because the overfeeding was not so forced and the fare was more varied. For the Germans of the Soviet zone it did not take long to realize that what they were being fed was plentiful but very monotonous—except, of course, for the classics, which remain popular to this day, although even they have suffered somewhat from the too-much-of-a-good-thing syndrome. Apart from Gorky and Mayakovsky, socialist realism predominated, at any rate until the mid-fifties. By the time post-Stalinist literature and art began to trickle in, the novelty had worn off.

Interest in Soviet literature was low in West Germany after 1945, and with reason; however, the classics were much read, with Nikolai Leskov experiencing a vogue not known before. Things changed in the post-Stalinist era; recent Soviet novels and poetry are appearing in increasing numbers and editions. In 1965 West Germany alone published fifty-nine titles of *belles lettres* translated from the Russian.[19]

It is noteworthy that today there seems to be more genuine interest in Soviet culture in West Germany than in the Soviet-occupied zone; precisely because no one tried to push it down the West Germans' throat they are more relaxed about it. But in both parts of Germany, interest is far below that of the twenties. Yevgeny Yevtushenko is without doubt the best-known and most popular Soviet author in the Federal Republic, especially among the younger generation. His popularity may be ascribed partly to his personal appearance in German lecture halls, which were always filled to overflowing.

THE BLACK YEARS

Hitler, his attack against the U.S.S.R. in 1941, the dreadful occurrences of the following years—in short the black years of 1941–45 and their aftermath—are by far the most important items on the list of events since 1917 to affect present-day German-Soviet relations. Centuries of good relations, of "traditional friendship" even, the alliance in the War of Liberation against Napoleon, Bismarck's emphasis on co-operation with Russia, dozens of German-Russian royal and princely marriages, more than a century of mutual cultural stimulation (from Schiller to Rilke), of scientific collaboration (since Lomonosov) —all this was completely overshadowed if not altogether canceled by the horror of those years. But one remarkable fact is to be stressed: out of all this hardship and pain there emerged on the whole a surprisingly friendly feeling between the Russians and the Germans. Tens of thousands of Germans have traveled as tourists in the U.S.S.R. without experiencing unfriendliness on the part of the population.

THE TWO GERMANIES

The single most lasting effect of Hitler's *Ostpolitik* was the truncation of the German Reich prior to and in Potsdam, with the U.S.S.R. taking over part of East Prussia, including Königsberg, and giving vast areas of Germany to Poland—up to the Oder-Neisse line, with rump Germany subdivided once more along the Elbe and Werra Rivers and with West Berlin cut off from West Germany.

It is the truncation of Germany which has had by far the most important and most burdensome impact on the relations between the U.S.S.R. and the Germans, though not all aspects of the division have been of equal weight. Least onerous has been northern East Prussia. It is hard for the Germans to acquiesce in the loss of the "city of the kings," where the Prussian kingdom started and Kant taught, but it is equally hard for them to imagine that this part of the Reich, formally handed to the Russians in Potsdam by their fellow victors, will return to the German colors. It is not mainly of Königsberg that the Germans think when they speak of their nation's future.

The areas which at Postdam were given to Poland are quite a different matter. Millions of Germans from Silesia, Danzig, Pomerania, Brandenburg, East and West Prussia, have not abandoned hope that somehow they will return to their homes. Yet, while they realize that it is Russia rather than Poland which is responsible for their flight and expulsion, they are inclined to think more of the Poles than of the Russians when they deliberate the difficulty of ever seeing Breslau or Posen. They consider the Polish state as an entity in its own right, not simply as a satellite of Moscow.

What makes German-Russian relations almost hopeless for the time being is neither Königsberg nor the Oder-Neisse line, but Ulbricht's regime and its pressure—increased again at present—on West Berlin. True, voices in Germany may speak up for "two German states"; such calls may come from individuals, from groups, perhaps eventually even from a political party. But the Germans as a nation will never accept their division as a lasting fact; and as long as Walter Ulbricht—unpopular in both parts of Germany—is in power they will consider the Kremlin to be the obstacle to reunification or at least liberalization in "the other Germany."

To Moscow, on the other hand, the German desire for reunification appears as revanchism and revisionism (revision of the frontiers, that is) and therefore aggressivism. To the men in the Kremlin the part of Germany temporarily ruled by Ulbricht is a state by itself, like Switzerland or Austria, therefore any open desire for German unification represents a "threat of aggression." It is impossible at this time to say how the gap can be bridged. Moscow is so fearful of German reunification that it does its utmost to bedevil the Federal Republic. No Soviet leader speaks on any subject without attacking the West German government bitterly and profusely.

For the moment there is not much that West Germany can do to change matters. One might even doubt whether Bonn-Moscow relations would improve if Bonn were to recognize East Berlin as another German capital of another German state. Quite likely the Kremlin would sense in such an action nothing but an ominous sign of West German intent to bring about German reunification by other means than those hitherto employed without success. After all, when Bonn did what the Soviets had urged it to do for many years, when it tried to improve its relations with Eastern Europe, when it succeeded in exchanging ambassadors with Rumania, the Kremlin did everything in its power to prevent other East European capitals from following Bucharest's lead.

It is the basic disagreement over the future of the German nation that separates Germans and Russians today. As long as this fundamental discord continues, it is hard to imagine a spectacular improvement in the relations between the Soviet Union and the Germans. The soundest solution of the "German question" in this writer's view—a solution acceptable to the

Germans as well as to their neighbors and, if they are wise, also to the Russians—would be the integration of Germany (or of two Germanies, for that matter) in a United States of Europe.

NOTES

1. V. I. Lenin, *Werke,* translated into German from the fourth Russian edition, 2 vols. (Berlin: Register, 1964).

2. Konrad Adenauer, *Erinnerungen 1953–1955* (Stuttgart, 1966), p. 519.

3. Z. A. B. Zeman, ed., *Germany and the Revolution in Russia* (London, New York, and Toronto, 1958); and W. Hahlweg, *Lenins Rückkehr nach Russland 1917* (Leiden, 1957).

4. For a good summary see Dietrich Geyer, "Lenin und der deutsche Sozialismus," *Deutsch-russische Beziehungen von Bismarck bis zur Gegenwart,* ed. Werner Markert (Stuttgart, 1964), pp. 80–96.

5. For the most important anti-Soviet statements from Peking in 1963 and 1964 see *Zentralkomitee der Kommunistischen Partei Chinas: Die Polemik über die Generallinie der internationalen kommunistischen Bewegung* (Peking, 1965).

6. *Ibid.,* pp. 404–9.

7. For a useful collection of Lenin's writings between 1899 and 1923 against revisionism see V. I. Lenin, *Gegen den Revisionismus: Eine Sammlung ausgewählter Aufsätze und Reden* (Berlin, 1959). The contents of this book now form the anti-Soviet bible of Peking.

8. Introduction to vol. I, Dostoyevskii, *Sämtliche Werke* (Munich, 1906), p. 1.

9. Moeller van den Bruck, *Das Recht der jungen Völker* (Munich, 1919).

10. For a good summary see F. L. Carsten, "The Reichswehr and the Red Army," *Survey,* nos. 44–45, October, 1962, pp. 114–32.

11. Ernst Köstring, *Profile bedeutender Soldaten* (Frankfurt am Main n.d.), p. 47.

12. Gustav Hilger, *Wir und der Kreml* [The Incompatible Allies], (Frankfurt am Main–Berlin, 1955); Köstring, *Profile bedeutender Soldaten.*

13. Klaus Mehnert, ed., *Die Sovet-Union, 1917–1932* (Berlin-Königsberg, 1933).

14. *50 Jahre Osteuropa-Studien: Zur Geschichte der Deutschen Gesellschaft zum Studium Osteuropas und der Deutschen Gesellschaft für Osteuropakunde* (Stuttgart, 1964), pp. 8–15.

15. J. W. Stalin, *Werke* (Berlin, 1952), VI, 253.

16. George F. Kennan, *Russia and the West under Lenin and Stalin* (London, 1961), p. 291.

17. Wolfgang Leonhard, *Die Revolution entlässt ihre Kinder* (Cologne-Berlin, 1955).

18. Hilger, *Wir und der Kreml,* p. 231.

19. *Buch und Buchhandel in Zahlen 1966* (Frankfurt am Main, n.d.), p. 95.

CHAPTER 8

Soviet Relations with the Middle East

Soviet Policy in the Middle East

John A. Armstrong

Soviet Policy in the Middle East

John A. Armstrong

I

Although perennial Middle Eastern crises arouse passing interest in Soviet relations with that area, in-depth studies of the U.S.S.R.'s foreign policy have tended to neglect the Middle East.[1] Indeed, Soviet surveys of international relations themselves assign a relatively small place to the Middle East.[2] For example, the recent three-volume treatment *International Relations after the Second World War* devotes fewer than 90 of its 2,100 pages to the Middle East.[3] In the first years of Soviet foreign relations, however, the Middle East absorbed a much higher proportion of Soviet attention, and very recently the U.S.S.R. has once again been ascribing more importance to its Middle Eastern contacts.

Analytically, one may distinguish two sets of factors influencing any regional aspect of Soviet foreign policy. One set of factors may be termed "strategic." It comprises relatively permanent elements of the situation: geography, including especially crucial communications routes and natural barriers; natural resources; traditional cultural influences; and developed economic, military, and political power. Soviet perception of the importance of these factors is, of course, influenced by the regime's over-all international objectives, such as expansion of Soviet-controlled territory and opposition to powers (mainly the principal Western states) regarded as "imperialist," since these objectives must be pursued within a framework of strategic resources. Generally speaking, however, non-Leninist analysts would evaluate these strategic factors in much the same way that Soviet analysts perceive them. The set of factors related to social, economic, and political change in the Middle East is perceived in a more distinctive manner by Soviet analysts because of their adherence to Leninist theory. Although this theory is itself subject to some change, conceivably it does continue to affect Soviet perceptions of internal developments in the Middle Eastern state system.

While the interplay of these two sets of factors affects Soviet policy-making for all parts of the world, it is especially significant in the Middle East. Strategic factors there exert a direct impact on Soviet interests because (in contrast to Latin America, Africa, and Southeast Asia) the Middle East lies on the Soviet frontier, and because (in contrast to Europe and the Far East) the Middle Eastern countries adjoining the area of Soviet domination are neither powerful nor, for the most part, internally stable. One should not fall into the widespread error of believing that, until recently, the U.S.S.R. confined extension of its power, even in military form, to adjoining countries; Spain in 1936–38 and Israel in 1948 are examples to the contrary. For a land-based power like the Soviet Union, however, such extensions are risky and difficult. The advantages of operating in a contiguous area were evidently greatest when Soviet Russia was a weak state struggling to establish itself in the international arena. It is hardly surprising that the first sizable dispatch of Soviet arms abroad, in 1921, was to the Turkish Nationalist forces.[4] Similar assistance was extended during the early 1920's to Afghanistan, another Middle Eastern neighbor of the Soviet state; the third neighbor, Iran, was extended minor assistance. Then, and for many years thereafter, the non-contiguous Arab countries received very little attention from the U.S.S.R.[5] In Leninist theory the Arab countries were also involved in the "national liberation" struggle against "imperialism," but the limited resources and relatively weak international position of the U.S.S.R. demanded that it concentrate on the safer and more promising adjacent states. In the early 1920's Turkey and

Afghanistan, and to a lesser extent Iran, were in fact opposed to Great Britain, which the Soviet leaders regarded as the main power of the "imperialist camp." Consequently, assistance to these countries would contribute in some degree (doubtless Lenin and most of his associates exaggerated the effect) to weakening imperialism and would serve as symbols of Soviet sympathy for other "colonial and semicolonial" nations. Equally important, friendly (and, if possible, dependent) regimes on its Middle Eastern border would directly enhance Soviet internal security. From its inception Soviet Russia has been a Middle Eastern power, not only geographically, but ethnically and culturally as well. Most of its Caucasian territories and all of Soviet Central Asia are Muslim in religious background, and the peoples of these areas are often indistinguishable historically and linguistically from those of Iran, Turkey, and Afghanistan. This cultural overlap facilitated Soviet penetration of the neighboring states, but it could just as easily make them dangerous bases for disrupting Moscow's tenuous control of its borderlands.

From the purely strategic standpoint, Soviet interests in the adjoining Middle Eastern countries could be secured either by collaborating with friendly regimes or by forcefully dominating them. The alternatives are clearly illustrated by Soviet-Turkish relations, as indeed they were during the preceding century in Tsarist-Ottoman relations. By 1936 Turkey was definitely aligned with Great Britain, though not necessarily hostile to the U.S.S.R. In the Soviet perception, however, Turkey had shifted from anti-imperialism to support of the imperialist camp, especially through her key role in the 1937 Saadabad Pact. Though this nonaggression treaty linking Turkey, Iran, Iraq, and Afghanistan was designed to protect the northern part of the middle East against fascist and Nazi threats, it was also a barrier to Soviet penetration. Although Turkey was officially neutral during World War II, Soviet statements have consistently charged that she favored the Axis powers and even contemplated invading Soviet Caucasia. Stalin's response to this alleged threat was moderate while the war with Germany continued; but immediately afterward he sought to gain his strategic objectives—military bases on the Straits and in the Kars and Ardahan border districts—by threat of force. If he had not been thwarted by Turkish determination (backed by Britain and the United States), he would have attained the purely strategic objectives that the U.S.S.R. had earlier sought through collaboration with anti-Western Turkish nationalists. From the defensive standpoint, control of the Straits would have protected the Black Sea coast of the U.S.S.R. and its new Balkan satellites, and Kars and Ardahan would have served as a glacis for Caucasia. Since these acquisitions would have made Turkey an impotent satellite, the U.S.S.R. could also have utilized her as an access route to the Arab Middle East.

During the 1940's, reliance on military force was a general characteristic of Soviet policy in Europe and the Far East as well as in Turkey. The Red Army was also the key to extension of Soviet influence in Iran during the war period, as a leading Iranian communist bluntly admitted:

Each victory of the Red Army meant at the same time a weakening of the imperialists. Moreover, the contradictions between the imperialists themselves and the crisis of the colonial system favored the struggle of the oppressed peoples. All these developments, and the presence of Soviet armed forces in Iran, gave a new impulse to the striving of the masses for a fundamental change in relationships in Iran. . . . In the north, where the forces of the Red Army were stationed, they [the "imperialists"] sought to incite unrest; and in the south, where the imperialists had a free hand, they unleashed brutal terror against all progressive forces.[6]

While the strategic implications of Soviet moves were less sweeping in Iran than in Turkey, if successful they would have gained a broad glacis for much of the Central Asian as well as the Caucasian frontier. Moreover, Soviet control of Iran would have given the U.S.S.R. direct access to the Arab countries, would have given it control over major oil fields, and would have brought Soviet forces very close to the remaining Persian Gulf oil resources. Soviet indignation (in 1946, and in retrospective treatments) over British threats to reoccupy southwestern Iran if the Red Army did not withdraw from the north suggests that the Soviet regime has been well aware of the real value of Iran as a boulevard to the Persian Gulf—a suggestion which is much strengthened by the fact that after this threat the Red Army did withdraw from Iran. It is important to note, however, that, in contrast to its 1945 position toward Turkey, the U.S.S.R. did not rely entirely on military power to subject Iran, but had potent internal Iranian forces working in its favor.

Apart from their position on the Soviet frontier, the northern-tier countries of the Middle East differ from the Arab countries to the south in three major characteristics: (1) in contrast to the ideal tank-maneuvering grounds of the Fertile Crescent and Egypt, their mountainous terrain poses a serious obstacle to modern military forces; (2) their populations are greater than those of most Arab countries and, at least as far as the Turks and Afghans are concerned, traditionally are more warlike; (3) except for the Iranian oil fields (which, as a matter of fact, are in an area that resembles the Arab world both in terrain and in ethnic composition), the northern tier contains few natural resources important to the "imperialist camp." When the Soviet regime was formed, Middle East petroleum was relatively unimportant except for British naval requirements derived from the Iranian fields; but during the next forty years Western Europe became increasingly dependent on Persian Gulf oil and on the pipelines conveying it to the Mediterranean. Simultaneously, the Red Sea–Suez sea route through Arab territories became even more important than it had been in earlier decades. It is hardly surprising that, by the 1940's, Soviet strategy, while continuing to concentrate on the northern countries, was coming to regard these countries as stepping stones to a more seriously disruptive offensive against the Western powers. In Palestine in 1947–48 the U.S.S.R. made its first serious attempt to bypass the northern barrier and establish influence athwart the major communication lines of the lower Middle East. Clandestine aid to the Palestine Zionists represented a "target of opportunity," and a transient one at that. Military training camps were set up in Eastern Europe for young Zionists going to Palestine; the Czech Communist party, which had recently seized power in

Prague, provided Skoda arms; and an airlift to Israel was set up in March, 1948, even before the new state was declared.[7] Like Soviet intervention in the Spanish Civil War, the Israeli operation was clandestine, but it was too large for complete concealment. Consequently, it represented a significant extension of Soviet commitments in a region subject, in the final analysis, to military interdiction by the Western powers.

In the upshot, Soviet military aid to Israel led neither to embroilment with major powers nor to substantial Soviet influence in Palestine, though it may have diverted Western attention from other areas of Soviet activity. From 1948 until 1955 Soviet strategy in the Middle East did not involve major moves in the Arab area, but reverted—between 1951 and 1953—to exploiting opportunities on the Iranian boulevard. Beginning in 1955, the U.S.S.R. resumed the strategy of leaping over the northern tier, but this time in much greater force. It is no concern of this paper to trace the dramatic and complicated events surrounding initiation of Soviet arms aid to Egypt and Syria, the Suez invasion, and subsequent crises. A few basic aspects of Soviet strategic involvement should be noted, however. While the arms aid is no secret, it has never been stressed in Soviet publications.[8] As in the case of the Zionists, the direct supplier at first was Czechoslovakia, a circumstance which appeared to dilute the U.S.S.R.'s formal commitment. When Great Britain and France attacked Egypt, the Soviet regime hastily withdrew its military technicians. Doubtless the withdrawal reflected Soviet awareness of the dangers of committing its forces in an area distant from the Soviet frontier, where they could be isolated by overwhelming Western air and sea power. A few days later, in connection with Soviet threats to send "volunteers" to aid Egypt, a *New York Times* editorial underscored this danger: "The time to stop the 'volunteers'—Russian, Chinese, Indonesian, Afghan or whatever they may be—is now, before they get in. Afterward it could mean war. We can stop them, for they have no right to be in the Middle East, and we have the power to stop them."[9] If the danger had materialized, the U.S.S.R. would have had to cut its losses or greatly escalate the conflict. It is unlikely that the Soviet regime was prepared to escalate in 1956, but its spokesmen exploited the new factor of long-range ballistic missiles to make ambiguous threats, then and in the so-called Turkish-Syrian crisis the following year. Later Soviet publications have quoted these threats, in all their ambiguity, as demonstrations of Soviet power in the Arab area.[10]

II

As was suggested at the start of this paper, the interest of the Soviet Union in enhancing its material power is by no means the only influence on its Middle Eastern policy. However important interstate relations may be in Soviet practice, Leninist theory regards social forces—classes—as the prime actors. Lenin taught, and all his successors have believed, that the social forces in "colonial and semicolonial" regions exploited by the "imperialism" of the advanced countries should be regarded in a special light. In contrast to "feudalists" (which, on rare occasions, the U.S.S.R. has favored on a purely tactical basis), the "national bourgeoisie" of the "exploited" countries represents a progressive force. It is struggling, even though in its own interests, to oppose exploitation by the advanced countries and is "objectively" weakening imperialism, and it is ushering in the "bourgeois democratic" stage which is a necessary precursor of "socialism." Since Soviet writers consider all Middle Eastern countries except Israel to be engaged in this struggle for "national liberation," their national bourgeoisies are key elements. Soviet policy, therefore, has nearly always been directed both at securing direct strategic objectives *and* at forming alliances with national bourgeois regimes. The exception that proves this rule, in the Middle East, is Stalin's complete reliance on force in dealing with Turkey in 1945–46. Stalin was scarcely entombed, however, before a Soviet note to Ankara renounced his demands for bases on the Straits. Subsequent Soviet statements blamed the pressure on the "cult of personality" and Molotov's direction of Soviet foreign policy.[11] Among all the criticisms of Stalin's policy, this admission of mistakes in trying to secure advantages from a noncommunist state is almost unique. It seems to indicate Soviet distaste for letting the threat of naked force against a national bourgeois regime remain on the record.

As indicated earlier, the Turkish nationalist movement under Mustafa Kemal (Atatürk) was the first major ally that Soviet Russia found in the Middle East. In fact, as Soviet sources tacitly admit, the pro-Soviet period of Turkish foreign policy ended by 1936, two years before Kemal's death. According to one close observer, a major source of friction between Turkey and the U.S.S.R. was Kemal's personal antipathy to Lev Karakhan, the Soviet ambassador between 1934 and 1937.[12] Despite their opposition to Kemal's later policies, Soviet spokesmen have found it convenient to extol him posthumously in order to paint his "reactionary" successors blacker; the tactic is a familiar one in Soviet foreign propaganda—as witness its contrasts of Roosevelt and Truman, Kennedy and Johnson. Yet, despite the very harsh criticism directed against later Turkish governments, Soviet sources have never ceased to describe them as "national bourgeois."

At first sight it seems somewhat curious, especially in the post-Stalinist period, that nearly all of the Middle Eastern "national bourgeois" regimes regarded most favorably by the U.S.S.R. have been dictatorships, or at least directed by charismatic leaders. One need not postulate an affinity between the Soviet regime and personal dictatorship, however, for it is fairly evident that only strong leaders could provide a symbol of national cohesion sufficient to maintain the struggle against Western influences while simultaneously implementing the drastic social transformations that the Soviet Union approved. Obviously, however, leaders strong enough to oust Western influence may also act as bulwarks against Soviet penetration. Since the U.S.S.R. has always regarded the national bourgeois regimes as transitional stages in the achievement of communist control, there has been a constant ambivalence in Soviet spokesmen's appraisals of even nationalist regimes that they regard as promising. Such was the case with Kemal and his contemporaries Reza Khan (later Shah Reza Palevi) in Iran and Emir Amanullah of Afghanistan.

During the fifteen years between the tacit break with Kemal and Dr. Mohammed Mossadegh's appearance as head of the Iranian government, no contemporary Middle Eastern national bourgeois leader was celebrated in Soviet publications. Mossadegh's case is particularly revealing of the ambivalence of the Soviet appraisal. As will appear subsequently, much of this ambivalence arose from his relation to an exceptionally strong communist-controlled party, the Tudeh. Even apart from this consideration, Soviet spokesmen were bound to have mixed feelings about Mossadegh's regime. His bitter opposition to Great Britain, in relation to nationalization of the Anglo-Iranian Oil Company, was completely in line with Soviet interests in denying strategic resources to the West. His *petit bourgeois* supporters were favorably contrasted with the "comprador bourgeois" servants of imperialism, but his National Front was criticized for including some of the latter. Even the Iranian national bourgeoisie was accused of serving its "narrow class interest" in ousting foreign competitors. Apart from its treatment of the Tudeh, for Soviet writers the main fault of the Mossadegh movement was its remaining a "prisoner of the myth of Soviet expansion." As a result, they wrote, Mossadegh tried to pit the United States against Great Britain instead of relying on the communist bloc.[13] It cost the U.S.S.R. little, of course, to attribute all these defects to Mossadegh once he was ousted and imprisoned. Nevertheless, Soviet writers continued on the whole to regard the National Front favorably and to write that the "spirit of struggle, or, as it is called in the East, the spirit of Mossadegh has not vanished."[14]

The Soviet authors just quoted wrote in 1961 that "after the defeat of Iran right up to the middle of 1958, Egypt played the main role in the national liberation movement in the Near East."[15] The terminal date suggests that Soviet appraisals of the Egyptian "national bourgeoisie" have been as ambivalent as the view of the Iranians. In fact, Soviet perceptions of the Egyptian situation have been so complex (over the long period between

1953 and 1967) that one can only outline them here without determining precise turning points or identifying all nuances. Basically, Soviet expectations for a favorable turn in Egypt began in the early 1950's with the increasing friction between Great Britain and Egypt over Suez and the Sudan. The Naguib-Nasser coup of 1952 heightened these expectations, but it was not until the arms deal of 1955 and the crescendo of events leading to the Suez invasion that Soviet commentators came to see the Egyptian regime as a major factor in the disruption of imperialism. From 1957 on, perceptions of Egypt were inextricably involved with concern for the Egyptian and Syrian Communist parties. From 1958 to about 1963 the Egyptian nationalists were sharply criticized by Soviet publications. Apart from the internal communist issue, Soviet spokesmen had always been suspicious of pan-movements in the Middle East and elsewhere, regarding them as barriers to Soviet expansion and communist penetration, or even—in the case of Pan-Turkism and Pan-Islam—as potential attractions for Soviet peoples.[16] Gamal Abdel Nasser's pre-eminence among Arab leaders made his United Arab Republic appear as a plausible first step toward Pan-Arab unity. At the same time, Nasser's relations with the West improved somewhat, lessening his utility as a force against "imperialism." Throughout the period, however, Soviet criticism—particularly of Nasser personally—was restrained.[17] Soviet economic and military assistance continued to flow to the U.A.R. Unlike the ousted octogenarian Mossadegh, Nasser could be useful again.

For a time after the Egyptian national bourgeoisie declined in Soviet favor, Abdel Karim al-Kassem's Iraqi regime took its place. Indeed, one ground for criticism of the Egyptian "big bourgeoisie" was its alleged effort (actually Nasser himself was strongly behind the scheme) to incorporate Iraq into the U.A.R. At first Kassem's violent overthrow of the Hashemite kingdom in Iraq in 1958 seemed the most spectacular windfall for Soviet policy in Middle Eastern history. Except for a brief period in 1940, Iraq had been closely linked to British policy. It provided the Western-oriented Middle East Treaty Organization with its headquarters and its only direct link with the Arab world. American and British response to the Iraqi coup was so extreme—involving the dispatch of troops to Lebanon and Jordan—that the successful perpetuation of Kassem's regime inevitably appeared to be a serious reversal for Western policy.

In 1958–60 Soviet publications praised Kassem's regime to a degree rarely if ever before equaled in their discussion of Middle Eastern national bourgeois governments. Most important was the emphasis on the role of "mass organizations" and the freedom of communist and "progressive" political activity. But Kassem's foreign policy was also unequivocally supported, and the emphasis given agrarian reform was acclaimed.[18] Much later a major Soviet work on Iraq contended that the Kassem regime itself developed reactionary tendencies as early as March, 1959, but the Soviet press appears not to have given vent to serious misgivings until late 1960. This criticism was directed to Kassem's suppression of communists, which posed a difficult problem for Soviet policy-makers. For months, however, more emphasis was given to U.A.R. anticommunism. Evidently friction was also developing between Soviet and specialists in Iraq and the local population.[19] In 1962 two of Kassem's policies apparently aroused more serious Soviet concern. The bitter campaign against the Kurds threatened a long-term Soviet interest. Kassem's efforts to take over Kuwait, while undoubtedly welcome as a threat to British oil interests, posed a new dilemma for Soviet policy. Nasser was adamantly opposed to Kuwait's incorporation into Iraq, which he regarded as a threat to the Arab League and hence to Egyptian influence. Probably by that time the U.S.S.R. was coming to realize that Nasser's regime was far stronger and more stable than Kassem's, while no more opposed to communist penetration. Consequently, continued Soviet preference for Kassem would have constituted a poor wager. Quite possibly the pro-Nasser revolution in Yemen in September, 1962, convinced Soviet policy-makers that, with all his defects, Nasser could do far more than Kassem to promote Soviet goals in both the Arab countries and in Africa. Kassem's overthrow and death at the beginning of the following year provided Soviet spokesmen with another "cheap" opportunity to downgrade an erstwhile national bourgeois hero. His policies in Kuwait and Kurdistan, his "personal dictatorship," and his antiprogressive measures were immediately denounced in strong terms—partly, perhaps, in an attempt to save Iraqi communists from the harsher measures that the new Baath regime justified by associating them with Kassem.[20] Still, his "good beginning" in anti-imperialism and land reform was noted, and a French evaluation of him as the victim of Western intrigues against the "greatest obstacle" to U.S. plans was cited.[21] In later years, however, as Baath elements moved closer to Soviet positions, Kassem was evaluated more harshly as "a "unitary leader" in whose hands was concentrated immoderate power. Being a limited, extremely ambitious man, Kassem did not understand the logic of revolution and did not see its perspectives. Most of all, he feared that some political forces would sweep out his personal dictatorship."[22]

Up to 1963, at least, while Soviet policy emphasized the "national bourgeois" movements, its experience with them had been too unsatisfactory to enable it to discard other sources of influence in the Middle East. As in other parts of the world, certain ethnic minorities, marginal or alienated in the larger society, appeared from time to time to present special opportunities for communist policy. As noted above, a major reason for Soviet disillusionment with Kassem was his bloody suppression of the Kurds, the Middle Eastern ethnic minority to which Soviet writers have devoted the most continuous attention. According to an American reporter, Kurd nationalists claim an enormous triangular territory reaching from Caucasia to the Mediterranean and the Persian Gulf.[23] Soviet ethnographic maps indicate a much more modest area of predominantly Kurdish territory, corresponding fairly closely to Western estimates.[24] Even so, "Kurdistan" forms a strategic wedge cutting directly across the most difficult mountain barriers to the heart of the Arab territories. It embraces a fourth of Turkey, as much—apart from desert regions—of Iraq, a substantial portion of northwestern Iran, and a corner of Syria. There is even a tiny Soviet Kurd minority of about 60,000 persons which has received disproportionate official recognition.

While the Red Army occupied northern Iran, the Kurds, as well as the larger Azerbaijani Turkish minority, were encouraged to seek autonomy; the "terror" unleashed against "democratic forces" there after Soviet withdrawal has continued to be a major Soviet complaint against the Iranian government.[25] However, Soviet policy-makers apparently have been wary about stirring up the Kurd issue in Iran and Turkey, though from time to time Soviet spokesmen refer to this potential weakness. Occasionally, Soviet sources indicate that they recognize that, precisely because the Kurd problem is so serious for Turkey, Iran, and Iraq, it may unite them in a way detrimental to Soviet interests.[26]

In its last years the royal government in Iraq seems to have had considerable success in incorporating the Kurdish population into the national community—even the Minister of the Interior was a Kurd.[27] Since Kassem was bitterly opposed to Turkey and Iran, the U.S.S.R. no longer needed to fear that encouragement of the Kurds would lead to Iraqi understanding with Iran and Turkey. At the same time, the Soviet policy-makers seemed to believe that the Kurds could bolster pro-communist forces in Iraq. For example, the Kurdistan Democratic party was described as more progressive in land reform than the Iraqi *petite bourgeoisie*.[28] As a result, the fierce repressive campaigns instigated by Kassem and his immediate successors aroused bitter protests in the Soviet press, which justified the Kurds' "fight for their rights."[29] Since the end of all-out hostilities in 1964, the Soviet press has dropped the Kurd issue—partly, no doubt, in recognition of the fact that Nasser played a significant role in mediating between the Iraqi government and the insurgents.

While Soviet spokesmen have been understandably cautious about exploiting the Kurd issue against potentially more useful nationalist governments in power, from the Marxist-Leninist point of view the Kurds, an exploited peasant nationality, may play as "progressive" a historical role as the national bourgeoisie of the dominant ethnic groups. The situation of the Diaspora minorities, the Jews and the Armenians, is fundamentally different. From the Leninist standpoint these groups, disproportionately engaged in commercial and manufacturing activities dependent on Western contacts, constitute a large part of the Middle Eastern "comprador bourgeoisie." Soviet sources rarely pursue this analysis to its conclusion. But one Soviet writer has pointed out that prior to 1913 the comprador bourgeoisie of Turkey was predominantly Greek, Armenian, and Jewish, and that as a result of the expulsion of the Armenians the Turkish national bourgeoisie was strengthened.[30] While the writer does not directly state that the expulsion (incidentally, the second most frightful example of genocide in modern times) was a "progressive" development, the conclusion inevitably follows from Marxist-Leninist analysis. In fact, the most pronouncedly nationalist elements among both Jews and Armenians have always been regarded by Soviet writers as extremely dangerous reactionaries. In 1920 Soviet Russia co-operated with Kemal to suppress the fervently nationalist Dashnak party's efforts to create an independent Armenian state. Soviet opposition to Zionism has been unremitting: recently, for example, the newspaper *Trud* contended that "the history of the Zionist movement shows that it has organic and permanent ties with imperialism.[31]

The very factors that have made the Armenian and the Jewish bourgeoisie "reactionary" from the Leninist standpoint have at times made them potentially useful in Soviet Middle Eastern policy. Their "cosmopolitan" or "comprador" relationships make them exceptionally well-informed, adaptable, and enterprising elements in a region where these qualities are in short supply. In addition, the fact that the groups' interests greatly transcend the Middle Eastern area has occasionally provided the U.S.S.R. with special leverage. Thus, Soviet encouragement of recruitment and training of Zionist forces in Eastern Europe was a significant element in creating a viable Israeli military force. Communist bloc military aid was kept strictly clandestine, but, as in the following passage from the speech of a leftist Israeli parliamentarian at the 1949 Congress of the Partisans of the Peace, hints of its importance were permitted while Soviet support of Israel in the United Nations was overtly emphasized:

The Jewish people will never forget Gromyko's historic speech in the United Nations and the support given it at Lake Success by representatives of Poland and Czechoslovakia, who demanded the right of the Jewish people to emigrate to Israel and the right to national independence, especially considering that during the years of the war our people had had to undergo such unbelievable suffering. . . . I want to emphasize that the immense majority of our patriots belonged to the progressive camp. They always understood that we are not fighting with the Arabs but are defending ourselves against imperialist aggression. . . . The sympathy shown us by the Soviet Union and the countries of people's democracy proves that we are not alone on the field of battle.[32]

As late as mid-1949, when Jewish cultural leaders in the U.S.S.R. itself were being denounced or murdered, the communist satellites continued measured support of Israel, as in the refusal of Poland and Czechoslovakia to attend the Beirut UNESCO conference because it was held in a "nation at war." As the passage quoted above suggests, however, pro-Soviet spokesmen were careful to stress their lack of opposition to the Arabs. Very quickly the Soviet regime discovered that the overwhelming majority of Israelis, far from supporting "progressive" organizations, was inclined toward the West. Internal considerations also made the Soviet regime more overtly anti-Semitic. Even though Soviet policy in the Arab world remained in low key until 1954, fierce denunciations of the Israeli "ruling circles" appeared in the U.S.S.R. from 1949 on. Consequently, after significant relations with the Arab national bourgeois leaders could be established, the Soviet leadership was prepared to sacrifice the Israeli position in order to give the Arabs all-out support. The fleeting wager on the Zionists had not paid off, and even the history of the 1948 events was revised to maintain that the United States was the chief supplier of munitions for the Israeli army and that "the ruling circles of the U.S.A. . . . placed decisive emphasis on the creation of a Zionist state in Palestine.

The Democratic party, which was in power in the U.S.A., also counted on this means to snare the Jewish voters for the Congressional elections and the forthcoming Presidential elections."[33]

Superficially the Soviet position on the Armenians has been quite different from the line on Zionism, but there are fundamental similarities. Since the Armenian "national homeland" is within the U.S.S.R., the Soviet regime has immensely greater leverage in its relations with Armenians in the Middle East. Even prior to the Revolution, Armenians played a disproportionate role in Russian studies and publications dealing with the Middle East.[34] The Diaspora in the Arab countries—consisting, to a large extent, of refugees from Turkey and their descendants—was important in the first stages of the development of local Communist parties. When Syria and Lebanon were under French mandate the Armenians played a major, if not dominant, role in forming the first significant Communist party in the Arab world.[35] Probably more important than actual enrollment in the Communist parties was the general influence of the Soviet Union among Middle Eastern Armenians, especially in Syria. While the Dashnaks remained bitterly opposed to the U.S.S.R., the other major factions, the Ramgavars and the Hunchaks, could be enlisted in "united fronts" with the communists. This susceptibility arose in part from the fact that most middle-class Armenians adhere to the division of the Armenian Gregorian church headed by the Catholicos of Echmiadzin, who reside in the U.S.S.R. But another potent factor was bitterness toward Turkey, which led Armenians in Syria to take a leading part, for example, in protests against Turkish annexation of the Alexandretta (Iskanderun) district in June, 1938.[36]

The case just mentioned, though of transitory significance, suggests that at times Armenian sentiment, even when directed by local communists, has escaped Soviet control. It is difficult to see how Soviet foreign policy, on the eve of Munich, could have profited from stirring up trouble for Turkey and France—despite the increasing coolness toward Turkey. More recently, it is said, manifestations of Armenian anti-Turkish feeling have threatened to disrupt delicate Soviet tentatives for rapprochement with Ankara.[37] In this case the Soviet regime did not hesitate to take action against the Soviet Armenian communists responsible—a small indication of the general Soviet tendency to assign priority to relations with the national bourgeoisie in control of states at the expense of marginal minorities. More significant has been the apparent Soviet co-operation in Nasser's liquidation of the flourishing Armenian community in Egypt. Even a Soviet Armenian source admits that many, especially youths, are inclined to leave the U.A.R.[38] Cutting its losses, the Soviet government has encouraged the departing Armenians to "return" to Soviet Armenia, where their skills no doubt make them useful, but where they cease to provide the network of influence which the U.S.S.R. formerly could manipulate.

IV

If both doctrinal and practical reasons have inclined Soviet policy-makers to treat the Middle Eastern Diaspora as expendable when it comes into conflict with a dominant national bourgeoisie, they face a deeper dilemma when the interests of local Communist parties are opposed to Soviet co-operation with a national bourgeois regime. The whole history of Soviet manipulation of foreign Communist parties shows, of course, that these are regarded as expendable if major U.S.S.R. interests are at stake. Conversely, there is no doubt that Soviet policy-makers have generally regarded communists as the most reliable supporters of Soviet interests and have envisaged communist dictatorships as the only sure means for permanently withdrawing countries from the "camp of imperialism." The question, therefore, has been whether a national bourgeois regime should be supported because of its short-run disruptive effect on imperialism, even though it may for an indefinite time act as a bulwark against communist penetration. We have already noticed that this question complicated Soviet relations with all of the major national bourgeois leaders in the Middle East; but a somewhat closer examination is required to illuminate the nature of the Soviet dilemma.

In many Middle Eastern countries communists have been so weak that there has been no reasonable prospect of their attaining power in the foreseeable future. Mustafa Kemal, for example, virtually wiped out the incipient Turkish communists, and they have never regained major importance. By far the most influential early communist development took place in Iran. Centuries-old Russo-Iranian commercial and cultural ties have greatly enhanced Soviet prestige in Iran. For example, whereas until recently the most highly regarded hospitals in major Arab cities have nearly always been American, British, or French, in Teheran the Russian hospital exerts great attraction. These pervasive ties undoubtedly facilitated—however indirectly—communist recruitment during the period of Red Army occupation of northern Iran in the early 1920's; the cadres secured then were available to expand communist influence during the occupation of 1941–46. In October, 1941, the Tudeh ("Masses") party, "the first party of a new type in Iranian history," was formed. The secretary general and "head of its Central Committee" (the formulas are completely Stalinist) was Dr. Reza Radmanesh, who had become a Communist party member in Gilan in 1921.[39] The Tudeh party and the front organizations rapidly developed a large following among intellectuals and urban workers and even had some success with the peasantry.[40] The real opportunity for Tudeh came with Mossadegh's ascendancy in 1951–53. After he broke with the Western powers his extremism alienated much of the Iranian elite, particularly the officer corps; for other reasons he lost the support of the more fanatical Muslim groups. Step by step his dependence on the Tudeh seemed to increase. Mossadegh, however, was from time to time sufficiently concerned about this growing dependence to act against the more extreme Tudeh-inspired demonstrations. After his defeat he was denounced as the premier who had acted "most brutally" against "democratic organizations."[41]

The Tudeh party as an organization maintained unquestioning loyalty to the U.S.S.R. It fervently supported the separatist movements in Iranian Azerbaijan and Kurdistan while the Red Army fostered them, and it acquiesced in their suppression when the "danger to world peace and international security" which the "imperialists wanted" became too acute to suit Moscow.[42] While pressing Mossadegh for more radical domestic measures, the Tudeh party supported him "without reserve" in foreign policy (even though he was later accused of being insufficiently friendly to the communist states) in order "not to isolate Mossadegh's *petit bourgeois* circles but to spread the slogan of a broad fighting front of all anti-imperialist forces."[43] At one time the Tudeh party is said to have supervised the Iraqi Communist party[44]—a regional headquarters function customarily assigned only to the most reliable national units of the world communist movement. Even this loyal party in the period of communist "monolithism" inspired some disquiet, however, because of its tendency toward intransigency: one of its leading officers reports that the "idea among some progressive forces" that a new world war was desirable to free the "oppressed" had to be combatted "in the interest of the world peace movement."[45]

The Iraqi communists caused the U.S.S.R. much more concern. While few at the time of Kassem's coup, they played some part in that bloody affair and developed rapidly during the first months of his regime. Soviet writers apparently believed the communist fronts had a real chance of becoming a dominant force: "a peculiarity of the political life of Iraq is the marked activity of mass popular organizations—trade unions, the movements of partisans of the peace, organizations of women, etc."[46] In at least apparent contradiction to the later Soviet evaluation noted in Section II above, Kassem's dependence on the communists seemed to increase for a short time after the mutiny of his forces in Mosul in March, 1959, but in May he rejected communist demands for participation in the government. In July the communists, in their turn, were implicated in an insurrection. The situation was greatly complicated by the fact that the Iraqi communists were divided between a cautious and an intransigent faction.[47] As a result, the Iraqi situation became a kind of test issue between Moscow and Peking, with the Soviet policy-makers anxious to demonstrate the superiority of their generally more prudent tactics, but at the same time fearful of laying themselves open to a Chinese charge of sacrificing foreign communists. After the unsuccessful insurrection, the cautious faction of the Iraqi leaders sought—with slight success—to appease Kassem. *Pravda* took the unusual step of publishing their apology.

As long as Kassem was in power, Soviet writers were cautious in criticizing him, but after his demise they made analyses of his shortcomings very similar—apart from apparently opportunistic invective against his personal dictatorship—to earlier critiques of Mossadegh. The discussions, published during 1959–62, as well as similar, though less trenchant critiques of the U.A.R. regime, provide a fairly good insight into the basic Soviet requirements for a satisfactory national bourgeois leader. The basic dilemma of reconciling national bourgeois stability and communist penetration is to be resolved by convincing the national bourgeois leader that the problem does not exist: "The recent events in Iraq have once more confirmed one of the most indisputable lessons of the liberation movements of peoples: a split of national unity, the suppression of democratic freedom and the persecution of progressive forces inevitably jeopardizes the newly attained national independence and are in irreconcilable contradiction with the vital interests of the young sovereign states."[48] Another obvious requirement, as noted earlier, is close adherence to the Soviet line in foreign policy; "neutralism" may be acceptable, real neutrality is not. Soviet criticisms of Iraqi internal measures point to the fundamental changes that Leninist analysis requires of the co-operative "national bourgeois" regime because they lay the foundation for eventual communist control. One of these measures was the reinstallation of "old bureaucrats trained by the English, who hated everything progressive" in place of the "democrats" Kassem had placed in important posts immediately after the coup.[49] Evidently Kassem had gone further than any other national bourgeois leader in following Lenin's basic prescription of "smashing the old state apparatus"; his reversal, therefore, was a source of chagrin for Soviet observers. The second basic measure was land reform, regarded as essential to eliminate the "feudal" order. Mossadegh was assailed for his alliance with landlords and for failing to enlist peasant support.[50] One of the main themes of early Soviet praise for Kassem, on the other hand, was his radical approach to the agrarian problem.[51] Even when he was posthumously vilified, his land-reform legislation, passed in 1960 after communist influence was on the wane, was carefully analyzed as a "progressive" measure designed to end landowner power. Blatantly contradicting the insistence on compatibility of bourgeois national and "progressive" interests in the national liberation, long-range communist interests were emphasized:

However, the Iraqi Communist party could not view the law solely in the light of the tasks of the antifeudal struggle, although these tasks were the principal ones at that stage. As the emphatically revolutionary party of the proletariat, it represented specifically proletarian interests in this struggle (just as the bourgeois represented its interests—but in that case reactionary ones). These interests included not only carrying out the bourgeois-democratic revolution to the end, but deepening it, as well as creating, in the course of revolutionary transformation, the prerequisites for the transition of the country to the path of noncapitalist development.[52]

When there is an inescapable choice between a national bourgeois regime introducing changes that Leninist analysis regards as "objectively progressive" and essential for eventual communist takeover, on the one hand, and immediate freedom of action for local communists, on the other, Soviet policymaking exhibits near-schizoid tendencies. While in recent years these tendencies have arisen in part from the strain of competing with Peking for world communist allegiance, it is significant that the most striking instance of uncertainty in choosing between the "objectively progressive" regime and the local communists occurred in Syria at the beginning of 1958, before competition with Peking was a major factor. To many contemporary observers, Syria in 1957 seemed to be drifting into the communist camp. Very probably this impression, engendered by the turbulence of Syrian politics and the bombastic propensities of Syrian politicians, was exaggerated. Nevertheless, the Soviet attitude toward the Syrian national bourgeois regime was highly favorable. Apart from supplying arms and other material assistance, the U.S.S.R. staged a spectacular confrontation with Turkey in order to appear as Syria's defender. In contrast to the other Middle Eastern national bourgeois regimes singled out for Soviet attention, the Syrian nationalist movement has never been dominated or even symbolized by an individual leader. In 1957 Colonel Abdel Hamid Serraj appeared most powerful, but he avoided publicity and overt exercise of authority. Indeed, though he was really a strong adherent of Nasser, many contemporary observers regarded Serraj as a procommunist. Soviet and communist analysts could hardly have been deceived on this point, but they may have considered the absence of a Syrian national bourgeois charismatic leader as extraordinarily propitious for communist penetration. Communists were free to organize, propagandize, and even participate in legislative action. While far from numerous, Syrian Communist party membership was well entrenched; and under Khalid Bagdash, the most prominent Arab communist (actually of Kurd origin), the party had apparently been assigned regional supervisory functions formerly exercised by the Tudeh party. Syrian politics, which represented essentially the interplay of rivalries between the merchants and land-owning notables of the Damascus and Aleppo areas, showed few "progressive" tendencies. There was no agrarian reform, industry was in private hands, and the bureaucracy was intact.

Under these circumstances, Nasser's positive response to a sudden appeal of the Syrian elite for unification of Egypt and Syria posed a critical problem for the U.S.S.R.[53] Apart from the importance of maintaining the friendship of both the Syrian and the Egyptian elites, Soviet policy-makers must have recognized that the union would introduce "objectively progressive" Egyptian measures in Syria. On the other hand, the Syrian communists would suffer. At the governmental level, the Soviet regime acquiesced in the formation of the U.A.R., but the Syrian Communist party—with at least subsequent sanction by the U.S.S.R.—protested violently. While Soviet competition with Peking for the allegiance of the world communist movement was scarcely a factor in the initial Soviet reaction, Bagdash's patronage by Peking, after he had been forced into exile by Nasser's police, undoubtedly influenced the increasingly anti-U.A.R. Soviet reaction.[54] In January, 1959, Khrushchev himself took the very unusual step of denouncing U.A.R. suppression of communists. In the next three years Soviet analyses continued to emphasize this criticism of the U.A.R. A union on the basis of maintaining the "bourgeois-democratic order" in Syria would have been acceptable, but the Syrian bourgeoisie and landowners, fearing electoral victory by communists and "democratic organizations co-operating with them," plotted with the Egyptian big bourgeoisie to install the Egyptian system, suppressing all parties except the National Union.[55] In mid-1961 the Central Committee of the Soviet Trade Unions went so far as to protest the "torture of Syrian patriots and imprisonment of working class activists."[56] In retrospect this protest looks like an authorization for communist co-operation later that year in the Syrian nationalist break with the U.A.R., which the Syrian Communist party then denounced for having "killed and tortured patriots."[57] At the same time, Soviet spokesmen (who, as noted earlier, had additional grounds for dissatisfaction with the U.A.R.) tended to solve their theoretical dilemma by claiming that the U.A.R. regime in Egypt as well as in Syria was not really carrying out basically progressive measures. The continued influence of the banks and other organs of the big bourgeoisie; the existence, despite an agrarian reform, of large land-holdings; the role of the National Union as "a broad organization whose program includes the idea of creating a so-called class harmony between the big bourgeoisie and the working class, between big landowners and fellahin," was criticized.[58]

Even at the time of the break between Syria and Egypt, however, the Soviet press quoted Nasser's explanations as well as the

Syrian communists' rejoicing. As the new Baath regime in Syria turned to repressing communists, Soviet publications pointed with nostalgia to reforms, such as the nationalization of Syrian industry, that the U.A.R. had carried out. Within a few years the picture of the 1961 break was completely revised: in Soviet analyses it became a conservative Syrian bourgeois plot to forestall the introduction of the progressive U.A.R. land reform.[59]

V

By that time the Soviet Union was undertaking a significant reappraisal of the Nasser regime. One reason, probably, was the final recognition of Nasser's charisma in the Arab world. With the death of Kassem and the petty squabbles of the Baath leaders in Syria and Iraq, Nasser had no personal rival who was even potentially acceptable to the U.S.S.R. At the same time, his expansionist policy in Yemen and Africa brought him into renewed conflict with the Western powers, without (as in the case of his earlier efforts to unify the Arab countries) threatening to pose a broader barrier to communist penetration. Indeed, the extension of Egyptian influence, backed by Soviet technical aid, promised to make the Red Sea area a new boulevard for the expansion of Soviet influence all the way to sub-Saharan Africa.

In addition to these particular strategic reasons, Soviet reappraisal of Nasser seems to have been part of a broader reconsideration of the desirability of encouraging regimes that did not follow the complete Leninist revolutionary model but that had taken the "noncapitalist path." In 1966 a major Soviet publication accepted the definitely non-Leninist category "developing [*razvivaiushchiesia*] countries" for the U.A.R. and other Middle Eastern states.[60] As we have seen, two prerequisites for acceptable national bourgeois regimes were sweeping land reform and replacing the old state apparatus. Whereas Soviet analysts were highly skeptical of earlier national bourgeois leaders' willingness to take these steps, by 1965 they were congratulating Nasser on fundamental reforms. The land reform was now regarded as fundamentally progressive. The U.A.R. had "liquidated feudalists and big capitalists as a class" and "deprived the bourgeoisie of its leading role in the economy when it attempted to sabotage reform measures."[61] In 1965 the Egyptian Communist party formally dissolved itself. Many former members or sympathizers were allowed to collaborate with Nasser's Arab Socialist Union but were treated with suspicion.

It would be impossible to follow the kaleidoscopic twists of Baath policy in Syria and Iraq, or Soviet efforts to reappraise these regimes. By 1966, however, the U.S.S.R. appeared to have established a relationship with Syria not very different from that of 1957. The Soviet government was supporting, if not encouraging, Damascus in its intransigency toward Israel and the Western powers and was providing extensive aid, while communist activity in an essentially unstable situation had resumed importance. Although Syria had not become a Soviet satellite, the potential for Soviet direction seemed strongest there. Soviet writers hailed Syria's entry onto the "noncapitalist path," along with the U.A.R.'s. On several occasions, indeed, Soviet statements used the term "socialism" to refer to Syrian measures, while Soviet spokesmen such as Premier Kosygin were careful, even in Nasser's presence, to refer to Egyptian measures as "profound socio-economic reforms."[62] Quite possibly these nuances reflected a Soviet desire to flatter the Syrian leaders and even to suggest the possibility of their admission to the "socialist camp." As in 1957, the relatively unsophisticated and unstable nature of the Syrian regime may have made that country seem a more promising candidate than Egypt for Soviet manipulation. Even before the reopening of Arab-Israeli warfare in June, 1967, however, the Soviet wager in the Middle East appears to have been placed on *both* the Syrian and the Egyptian nationalists. By 1966, reservations about the dominant "national bourgeois" character of these movements were no longer voiced publicly; instead, a more subtle analysis stressed the role of specific elements of the bourgeoisie, particularly the officer corps.

Simultaneously, Soviet publications paid unusual attention to Arab-Israeli disputes and to the alleged role of Israel as a spearhead of American and West German imperialism. In early 1967, in contrast to earlier Soviet handbooks on the Middle East, a major publication of the Institute of World Economics and International Relations devoted much of its space, including the last substantive chapter, to Israel's internal "reactionary bourgeois regime" and its "neoimperialist" policies abroad.[63] Significantly, the author insisted on the U.A.R.'s right to order the United Nations truce force out of Sinai: "if Egypt alone takes back her agreement, the U.N. force must be withdrawn."[64] This is hardly the place to discuss the week-long war between the Arab states and Israel, especially since many aspects of the Soviet role remain obscure. But some aspects are so intimately related to our general interpretation of Soviet Middle Eastern policy that summarizing them can serve to bring together the principal threads of this analysis.

1. As the last quotation indicates, the U.S.S.R. almost certainly encouraged a confrontation between the Egyptian and the Israeli forces. Undoubtedly one motive was to bolster Syria's position—and Soviet influence there—by increasing military pressure on Israel's southern frontier. Apparently Soviet military intelligence grossly overestimated the capacity of the Egyptian forces. As late as the second day of the war, the Soviet press ran in the face of all the evidence of an Egyptian debacle by referring to an imminent Egyptian counteroffensive. Nevertheless, it is doubtful that the U.S.S.R. desired actual hostilities or that it encouraged the dangerous step of closing the Straits of Tiran.

2. Apart from its amazing intelligence failure, the Soviet regime was deeply embarrased by its manifest inability, short of provoking an unpredictable widening of the conflict, to provide effective military succor to the Arab states. A Soviet naval squadron, reinforced by several warships that had passed through the Turkish straits, was a well-advertised presence in the eastern Mediterranean. But, lacking aircraft carriers or a significant amphibious landing force, the squadron had no

capacity for intervening effectively, even if Moscow had wished to take such a risky step. As a result the crisis threw into sharp relief the lack of flexibility in Soviet strategic power, as compared to that represented by the United States Sixth Fleet, which many observers were convinced would have intervened effectively if Israel had been threatened with annihilation. In their disappointment some Arab observers went so far as to assert that the United States alone could function as a great power in the Arab Middle East. Far from cutting its losses, however, the U.S.S.R. renewed its military and political efforts in the area. Hasty dispatch of large quantities of heavy arms by airlift and by sea—taking advantage of the port facilities that Yugoslavia made available—provided at least a token restoration of the military balance between the pro-Soviet Arab states and Israel. In the longer perspective, the U.S.S.R.'s strategic interest in using Egypt as a boulevard to the south probably was enhanced by the demonstration that Soviet military power could not be projected far from its bases. Given the impracticability of Soviet development of a self-contained amphibious force like the Sixth Fleet, the securing of a chain of bases from Rijeka via Alexandria and Suez to Yemen may well appear to be the only feasible means of establishing an effective Soviet military presence in East Africa as well as in the Arab Middle East.

3. To offset the prestige losses just described, the Soviet leadership could take satisfaction in the sharp heightening of Arab animosity toward the United States and Great Britain, and in the possibility that this animosity would spread to other Muslim areas. While the material losses were limited—partly because of the sharply reduced importance of Middle Eastern oil in the past decade—the debits to the West in prestige and in interruption of military communications were considerable.

4. While Soviet military intelligence was puerile, Soviet political analysis of the dominant role of charismatic leaders like Nasser was vindicated. Despite his extreme miscalculation, Nasser remained the dominant figure of the Arab world as well as the dictator of Egypt. The pro-Soviet regime in Syria appears equally unshaken by its military defeat, while King Hussein, the

closest ally of the United States and Great Britain in the Arab Middle East, is in a precarious position. Without depreciating the very large element of opportunism in Soviet Middle Eastern policy, one may conclude that in this area Leninist analysis of social forces has been more accurate than have purely pragmatic calculations.

5. As indicated above, during the middle 1960's Soviet analysis of Arab social forces had become somewhat more flexible and penetrating. The Egyptian catastrophe seemed to open up new vistas for implementing this analysis. Very soon after hostilities ended, Soviet commentators attributed the defeat to reactionary elements in the Egyptian officer corps: "Individual generals and senior officers . . . were out of sympathy with the chief line of the government's policy, aimed at carrying out profound social transformations in the country. Taking advantage of their official positions, many of them actively opposed any political work whatsoever among the soldiers and non-commissioned officers, which clearly reduced the army's fighting capacity."[65] The need for replacing these elements with "patriotic" younger officers, many of whom had been trained in the U.S.S.R., was linked to a need to purge the Egyptian bureaucracy. Since Nasser was not loath to put the blame for the debacle on the higher military officers, many of whom had in fact performed deplorably, Soviet advice had a good chance of being accepted. If carried far enough, this line would lead to that "smashing of the old state apparatus" which Soviet analysis has unswervingly regarded as the fundamental prerequisite for construction of a socialist system. That Nasser and his lesser counterparts in other Arab states will, even in their chagrin, risk delivering themselves into the almost irreversible course of adoption of the Leninist political model is far from certain.

For the moment, one can conclude that fifty years of Soviet Middle Eastern policy has resulted in very little strategic gain. But Soviet analysis of social evolution has been moderately successful and may, in the proximate future, lead to more significant gains.

NOTES

1. The present paper is intended only as a survey to suggest some of the possibilities of comparative analysis of a major aspect of Soviet policy over a considerable extent of time and space. I am particularly indebted to my students for the expert and detailed examination, in the various Middle Eastern countries, of specific aspects of the problems touched on here: to Dr. Monte Palmer for his study of inter-Arab politics; to John S. Swanson for his study of Soviet and communist policies in Syria and Lebanon; and to Arnold Krammer for notes on communist-bloc aid to Israel.

2. I use the term "Middle East" to refer to the territories that Soviet sources call "Near and Middle East": Egypt, and all of Southwest Asia up to the Soviet and the Pakistani borders.

3. Akademiia Nauk SSSR, Institut mirovoi ekonomiki i mezhdunarodnykh otnoshenii, *Mezhdunarodnye otnoshennia posle Vtoroi Mirovoi voiny* [International Relations after the Second World War] (Moscow: Izdatel'stvo politicheskoi literatury, 1962, 1963, 1965); hereafter referred to as *Mezhdunarodnye otnosheniia*.

4. Soviet sources continue to avow *this* arms aid frankly; see, for example, D. I. Vdovichenko, *Natsional'naia burzhuazia Turtsii* [The National Bourgeoisie of Turkey] (Moscow: Izdatel'stvo institut mezhdunarodnykh otnoshenii, 1962), p. 224. In speaking of "aid" or "assistance" I make no effort to distinguish between gifts and loans, on the assumption that the latter (however costly) provided items which could not have been obtained elsewhere.

5. The basic treatment is in the two volumes by Walter Z. Laqueur, *Communism and Nationalism in the Middle East* (New York: Frederick A. Praeger, 1956) and *The Soviet Union and the Middle East* (New York: Frederick A. Praeger, 1959).

6. Bozorg Alavi, *Kämpfendes Iran* (Berlin: Dietz Verlag, 1955), pp. 68, 78. Though published after Stalin's death, this account resembles the abject subservience to Moscow of East European communist writing between 1948 and 1953.

7. Apart from contemporary newspaper reports, the memoirs of Mordekhai Oren, *Prisonnier politique à Prague* (Paris: Réné Julliard, 1960), are most revealing because Oren was deeply engaged in negotiating communist-bloc aid for Israel in 1948. But I am especially indebted to Arnold Krammer for additional corroboration derived from his interviews in Israel and inspection of documentary sources there in 1966.

8. See, for example, Institut mezhdunarodnykh otnoshenii, Kafedra istorii mezhdunarodnykh otnoshenii i vneshnei politiki SSSR, *Istoriia mezhdunarodnykh otnoshenii i vneshnei politiki SSSR* [A History of International Relations and the Foreign Policy of the U.S.S.R.], vol. III (Moscow: Izdatel'stvo "Mezhdunarodnye otnosheniia," 1964), p. 495, which refers to the "barbarous activity of the interventionists against almost unarmed Egypt" (hereafter referred to as *Istoriia*).

9. *New York Times*, November 15, 1956.

10. *Istoriia*, pp. 495, 505.

11. *Mezhdunarodnye otnosheniia*, I, 255.

12. Hans W. Hartman, *Die auswärtige Politik der Türkei, 1923–1940* (Zurich: Verlag A. G. Gebr. Leemann & Co., 1941), p. 24. It is very doubtful, however, that Karakhan's failure in Turkey was the real ground for his execution.

13. *Mezhdunarodnye otnosheniia*, II, 169; A. V. Bashkirov, *Ekspansiia angliiskikh i amerikanskikh imperialistov v Irane (1941–1953 gg.)* [Expansion of English and American Imperialists in Iran] (Moscow: Gosudarstvennoe izdatel'stvo politicheskoi literatury, 1954), pp. 178, 186; P. N. Andreasian and A. Ia. El'ianov, *Blizhnyi Vostok: Neft' i nezavisimost'* [Near East: Oil and Independence] (Moscow: Izdatel'stvo vostochnoi literatury, 1961), pp. 206–7, 220.

14. Andreasian and El'ianov, *Blizhnyi Vostok*, p. 220; cf. *Izvestiia*, July 28, 1961 (translated in *Current Digest of the Soviet Press*, XIII, no. 30, p. 18; hereafter referred to as *Current Digest*).

15. Andreasian and El'ianov, *Blizhnyi Vostok*, p. 203.

16. G. A. von Stackelberg, "Changing Soviet Views on Arab Unification," *Bulletin of the Institute for the Study of the USSR*, VII, no. 3 (1960), pp. 5ff.

17. Cf. Hugh Seton-Watson, "Die 'Nationale Bourgeoisie' in Theorie und Praxis der Sowjets," *Osteuropa*, X (1960), p. 757.

18. See especially Akademiia Nauk SSSR, Institut mirovoi ekonomiki i mezhdunarodnykh otnoshenii, *Mezhdunarodnyi ezhegodnik* [International Yearbook] (Moscow: Gosudarstvennoe izdatel'stvo politicheskoi literatury, 1959), pp. 345–46; *ibid.*, 1960, pp. 176–80.

19. *New York Times*, April 25, 1960.

20. See especially the Soviet Communist Party Central Committee statement (an unusual step) published in *Pravda*, February 17, 1963, the World Federation of Trade Unions statement appearing in the same issue (both translated in *Current Digest*, XV, no. 7, pp. 18–19), and the article on Iraq in *Pravda*, February 23, 1963 (translated in *Current Digest*, XV, no. 8, p. 29).

21. *Ibid.; Pravda*, March 16, 1963 (translated in *Current Digest*, XV, no. 11, p. 24.

22. *Mezhdunarodnye otnosheniia*, III, 549.

23. *New York Times*, July 7, 1954.

24. Akademiia Nauk SSSR, Institut etnografii, *Atlas Narodov mira* [Atlas of the Peoples of the World] (Moscow, 1964), pp. 68, 70–72.

25. I. I. Korobeinikov, *Iran: Ekonomika i vneshniaia torgovlia* (Iran: Economy and Foreign Trade) (Moscow: Vneshtorgizdat, 1954), p. 129. Cf. Klaus Mehnert, "Iran und die Sowjetunion," *Osteuropa*, X (1960), 220.

26. See Vdovichenko, *Natsional'naia burzhuazia Turtsii*, p. 237, on the Kurd problem as a basis for Turkish-Iraqi alliances in 1946 and later.

27. *New York Times*, May 26, 1957.

28. S. N. Alitovskii, *Agrarnyi vopros v sovremennom Irake* [The Agrarian Question in Contemporary Iraq] (Moscow: Izdatel'stvo "Nauka," Glavnaia redaktsiia vostochnoi literatury, 1966), p. 146.

29. *Strany Blizhnego i Srednego Vostoka* [Countries of the Near and the Middle East] (Moscow: Izdatel'stvo politicheskoi literatury, 1964), p. 49.

30. Vdovichenko, *Natsional'naia burzhuazia Turtsii*, pp. 8–9. It would be interesting to compare the position of the Middle East and European Diasporas in soviet policy to the equally "comprador" overseas Chinese in Peking's policy to see whether the ethnic relation of the latter to the *dominant* nationality in the communist state overrode doctrinal reservations.

31. *Trud*, January 6, 1961 (translated in *Current Digest*, XIII, no. 7, p. 22).

32. *Pervyi v semirnyi kongress storonnikov mira, Parizh-Praga, 20–25 Aprelia 1949 goda: Materiali* [First World Congress of the Partisans of Peace, Paris-Prague, April 20–25, 1949: Materials] (Moscow: Gosudarstvennoe izdatel'stvo politicheskoi literatury, 1950), pp. 229–30. At the time of the Slansky trial (1952) Israeli officials were equally outspoken in recognizing earlier aid.

33. *Mezhdunarodnye otnosheniia*, I, 265. On the munitions see *Istoriia*, p. 128.

34. See Xenia J. Eudin and Robert C. North, *Soviet Russia and the East, 1920–1927: A Documentary Survey* (Stanford, Calif.: Stanford University Press, 1957). It is interesting that a major editorial office for publishing "Eastern" literaure is still located on Armenian Lane in Moscow.

35. See the list of early Syrian communist leaders—five out of six of whom have Armenian names—in Loretta Kh. Ter-Mkrtichian, *Armiane v stranakh arabskogo Vostoka na sovremennom etape: Nauchno-populiarnyi ocherk* [Armenians in the Countries of the Arab East in the Contemporary Stage: A Scientific-Popular Essay] (Moscow: Izdatel'stvo "Nauka," Glavnaia redaktsiia vostochnoi literatury, 1965), p. 40. The mere appearance of this pamphlet, which is virtually a guide to Armenian procommunist organizations, is interesting.

36. *Ibid.*, p. 42ff.

37. Hans-Eckardt Kannapin, "Die türkisch-sowjetischen Beziehungen seit 1960," *Osteuropa*, XVII (1967), 129.

38. Ter-Mkrtichian, *Armiane v stranakh arabskogo Vostoko na sovremennom etape*, pp. 29ff.

39. Alavi, *Kämpfendes Iran*, p. 103.

40. The basic treatment is George Lenczovski, *Russia and the West in Iran, 1918–1948* (Ithaca, N.Y.: Cornell University Press, 1949), and a 1952 supplement published separately; see also Sepehr Zabih, *The Communist Movement in Iran* (Berkeley: University of California Press, 1966).

41. Alavi, *Kämpfendes Iran*, p. 150.

42. *Ibid.*, p. 94.

43. *Ibid.*, p. 150.

44. *New York Times*, April 4, 1956 (based on an interview with the Iraqi Minister of the Interior).

45. Alavi, *Kämpfendes Iran*, pp. 165–66.

46. *Mezhdunarodnyi ezhegodnik* (1959), p. 346.

47. See especially Donald Z. Zagoria, *The Sino-Soviet Conflict, 1956–1961* (New York: Atheneum, 1964), pp. 258–60.

48. *Pravda*, February 23, 1963 (translated in *Current Digest*, XV, no. 8, p. 29).

49. *Mezhdunarodnye otnosheniia*, III, 549.

50. *Mezhdunarodnye otnosheniia*, II, 169; Andreasian and El'ianov, *Blizhnyi Vostok*, p. 207.

51. *Mezhdunarodnyi ezhegodnik* (1959), p. 159; *ibid.* (1960), p. 176.

52. Alitovskii, *Agrarnyi vopros*, p. 144. One may, of course, confront here the problem of audience discrimination in Soviet pronouncements. Alitovskii's book (published in 1,400 copies) is doubtless intended for Soviet specialists and perhaps for foreign communist cadres, while the statement quoted above emphasizing Iraqi national unity appeared in *Pravda*, which is routinely scrutinized in foreign capitals. In general, Soviet specialized publications on the Middle East are more revealing than the central press, though few actual contradictions have been encountered.

53. See especially Oles M. Smolenskii, "Moscow-Cairo Crisis, 1959," *Slavic Review*, XXII (1963), 715ff.

54. Zagoria, *The Sino-Soviet Conflict*, pp. 260–62.

55. V. I. Nikhanin, ed., *Mezhdunarodnye otnosheniia i vneshniaia politika Sovetskogo Soiuza, 1950–59* [International Relations and the Foreign Policy of the Soviet Union, 1950–59] (Moscow: Izdatel'stvo Instituta mezhdunarodnykh otnoshenii, 1960), pp. 230–31.

56. *Pravda*, June 3, 1961 (translated in *Current Digest*, XIII, no. 22, pp. 18–19).

57. *Pravda*, October 7, 1961 (translated in *Current* Digest, XIII, no. 40, p. 22).

58. *Mezhdunarodnyi ezhegodnik* (1960), p. 235.

59. *Mezhdunarodnye otnosheniia*, III, 552; *Izvestiia*, August 8, 1963 (translated in *Current Digest*, XV, no. 32, p. 21).

60. *Mezhdunarodnyi ezhegodnik* (1966 ed.), p. 78ff.; earlier editions had used the categories "semicolonial" or "newly sovereign."

61. *Mezhdunarodnye otnosheniia*, III, 553; cf. (on the broader implications of the U.A.R. example of the noncapitalist path) the Soviet party publication Akademiia Obshchestvennykh Nauk pri TsK KPSS, Kafedra istorii mezhdunarodnogo rabochego i kommunisticheskogo dvizheniia, *Natsional'no-osvoboditel'naia bor'ba narodov na sovremennom etape* [The National-Liberation Struggle in the Contemporary Stage] (Moscow: Izdatel'stvo "Mysl'," 1966), pp. 59ff.

62. *Pravda,* May 18, 1966 (translated in *Current Digest,* XVIII, no. 20, pp. 3–4). On Syria see *Izvestiia*, May 2, 1966 (translated in *Current Digest*, XVIII, no. 18, p. 27); and the statement of Soviet Communist party representatives on the program of the Arab Socialist Renaissance party (Syria) in *Pravda*, February 12, 1967 (translated in *Current Digest*, XIX, no. 6, p. 21).

63. O. Z. Tuganova, *Mezhdunarodnye otnosheniia na Blizhnem i Srednem Vostoke* [International Relations in the Near and Middle East] (Moscow: Izdatel'stvo "Mezhdunarodnye otnosheniia," 1967), p. 23.

64. *Ibid.*, p. 53.

65. Igor Beliaev and Evgenii Primakov, "When War Stands at the Threshold," *Za rubezhom*, no. 27 (June 30–July 6, 1967), pp. 7–8 (translated in *Current Digest*, XIX, no. 26, p. 7).

CHAPTER 9

Soviet Relations with Asia

A Half-Century of Soviet Policy in Asia

Harish Kapur

A Half-Century of Soviet Policy in Asia

Harish Kapur

From the voluminous Soviet literature that is available, it is evident that the Soviet leaders have displayed a continuous doctrinal interest in Asia since the Bolshevik Revolution. From an ideology applicable to the advanced European societies, they have, through the years, transformed Marxism into a revolutionary strategy relevant to countries far removed from the preliminary stage of industrialization. From a theoretical concept aimed at radical redistribution of the wealth already produced, it has been converted into a movement aiming at the creation of wealth through the coercive power of the state. And, from an ideology that was to inspire revolutions in Europe, it has gradually evolved into a concept that inextricably links the consummation of revolutions in Europe with their success in Asia.

But, despite the manifestation of deep doctrinal interest in Asia, Europe during the interwar years occupied the principal place in Soviet diplomacy. It was toward Europe that the Bolshevik leaders first turned in order to incite communist revolutions; and it was in this part of the world that they primarily concentrated their offensive and defensive diplomatic actions once it became apparent that revolutions had failed.

This concentration on the European continent was dictated by a number of objective factors: in the first place, the eyes of almost all the leading Bolsheviks were concentrated on Europe, where communist revolutions were believed to be around the corner. The Bolshevik Revolution was considered the prelude to a series of revolutions in the West which would culminate inevitably in the communization of Europe and eventually of the whole world. All this was in line with the original Marxist expectation that socialist movements would first come to power in the industrially developed countries of the West.[1]

Bolshevik Russia's geographic position was the second factor that contributed to Asia's being placed in the background. The area directly under Soviet influence at the time was separated from the Asian countries by independent governments or movements in Central Asia, trans-Caspia, trans-Caucasia, and Siberia. Thus, when the Soviet leaders talked about the East during this period, they usually referred to Baku, Batum, Tashkent, and Tbilisi rather than Peking, Teheran, or Ankara. However important Asia might have been, they could not do much about it in the early days while there was urgent work to be done closer to home.

Third, the civil war, foreign intervention, and foreign blockade had created so much confusion, suffering, violence, and privation that it was hardly possible for the Bolshevik leaders to take on additional tasks in Asia.

By 1920, however, the general situation in Soviet Russia, as well as in Europe, had undergone radical changes that encouraged the Soviet leadership to take an increasing interest in Asia. With the defeat of Kolchak and Denikin, it became possible for Soviet Russia to bring under her control the eastern borderlands, which had declared their independence from Moscow immediately after the October Revolution. Soviet Russia then found herself contiguous to such Asian countries as Iran, Turkey, Afghanistan, and China; it was no longer possible for the Bolsheviks to take only a theoretical interest in Asia, or simply to issue appeals to the Asian people to revolt against their internal and external oppressors. Obviously something more was needed to draw the revolutionary masses of the Asian nations into an alliance with the revolutionary workers and peasants of Soviet Russia.

In addition, the communist revolutions in Europe, in which so much hope had been placed, had not succeeded. The revolutionary uprising staged by the communists in Berlin in January, 1919, not only failed to touch off an October Revolution but it ended in disastrous defeat and in the physical elimination of Rosa Luxemburg and Liebknecht, the two outstanding leaders of German communism. The Munich Soviet collapsed after a few weeks, and the Hungarian soviet government quickly disintegrated under heavy internal and external pressure. Hope again flickered in the summer of 1920, when the Red Army stood at the gates of Warsaw; but, again, this did not last long, because the Poles launched a counterattack that led to the general retreat of the Red Army and, along with it, the virtual disappearance of all hope of successful revolutions in Europe.

By contrast, the Asian continent was seething with discontent in the early twenties; almost all the important countries there were undergoing profound revolutionary changes. Under Amanullah, Afghanistan had become independent; the Turkish nationalist movement under Kemal Atatürk had transformed itself into a government; and the Iranian regime was fast becoming independent of British control. In China, waves of mass protests against Japan had been launched by students; working-class movements had gained momentum in Shanghai, Hankow, and elsewhere. General unrest among workers and peasants in India culminated in a series of large-scale political and economic strikes. And, even more important for revolutionary Russia, the years 1920–21 witnessed the formation of Communist parties in Iran, Indonesia, and China.

All these momentous upheavals could not but impress the Bolshevik leaders. If Europe had failed them, Asia could revive their flagging spirits. Lenin, who immediately had grasped the importance of these events, did not hesitate to express his satisfaction over the manner in which Asia was changing. In almost all his communications and reports during the first few months of 1920, the Bolshevik leader made a point of referring to Asia. In his report to the All-Russian Central Executive Committee on February 2, 1920, he spoke confidently of the importance of "our relations with the peoples of the East."[2] In his interview with the *New York Evening Journal* on February 21 of the same year, he referred pointedly to the awakening of the Eastern people "to a new life, a life without exploitation, without landlords, without capitalists, without merchants."[3] In still another report, delivered to the All-Russian Congress of Toiling Cossacks on March 1, Lenin stressed that in every country of Asia there was "an awakening of political consciousness, and the revolutionary movements grow from day to day."[4]

Having made this initial shift, the question with which the Bolshevik leaders were then confronted was what policy they should formulate toward these countries—what concrete strategy they should follow in order to draw the Asian nations into an alliance with the workers and peasants of Russia. A simple statement that Asia had become significant obviously was not enough. A new policy was needed, a new strategy had to be worked out, and it was to these tasks that the Soviet leaders turned their attention.

The question was extensively discussed at the Second Congress of the Comintern in July-August, 1920,[5] and found its characteristic expression at the Baku Congress in September, 1920,[6] and at the First Congress of the Toilers of the Far East in January, 1921.[7]

The Leninist thesis on the national and colonial question was accepted at the Second Congress of the Comintern and, despite some opposition, was asserted at the Baku and the Far Eastern congresses. Proceeding from the basic assumption that the Asian countries were going through bourgeois democratic revolutions, Lenin expressed the view that it was the duty of the Communist parties to assist national revolutions and even enter into alliances with these movements. But this support and these alliances should be temporary and ought to be made on the condition that "the elements of future proletarian parties existing in all backward countries which are communist in everything but name should be grouped together and trained to appreciate their special tasks, viz., the task of fighting the bourgeois demo-

cratic movements within their own nations."[8] The clear implication in Lenin's thesis was that the bourgeoisie in the colonial
countries was essentially progressive.

SOVIET DIPLOMATIC AND REVOLUTIONARY ACTIONS

Having formulated a general strategy toward Asia, the Soviet
leaders were now faced with the difficult and delicate task of
applying it to the concrete reality of Asia. And the concrete
reality on that continent was far from uniform. The Asian
countries were at different stages of political development and
were led by nationalist leaders with varied backgrounds and
objectives. Some had gained political independence, but most
were still far removed from this goal.

The Soviets' policy throughout the interwar period was to
seek collaboration with the national governments of Asia and to
extend Soviet influence over them by gradual and unobtrusive
methods, without undermining the opportunities for profitable
economic relations with Western countries. Military assistance
was extended to Kemal Atatürk in his quest for full Turkish
independence; every possible support was extended to Amanullah in the effort to eliminate British influence in Afghanistan.
No stone was left unturned—including diplomatic and military
threats—to persuade the Iranian government to loosen its
political and economic ties with Great Britain.

Soviet policy toward the colonial world, however, was frankly
revolutionary. Despite many tactical fluctuations, Moscow's
basic and permanent objective was to extend open support, both
moral and material, to nationalistic forces seeking independence
of European control. This policy was unfettered by the con-
fines and trappings of classical diplomacy; there were no independent states in these regions with which diplomatic relations
could be developed, no national governments with which the
Soviet leadership could establish political or economic relations.
There was no question of signing treaties of friendship, alliance, or nonaggression with such countries. What the Soviets

had to deal with in the colonial area during this period was the rising opposition of political forces seeking power to establish governments that would be nationalistic in their objectives, policies, and outlooks.

In pursuing such policies, both in the independent and the colonial areas of Asia, the Soviet government was trespassing in Great Britain's sphere of influence and was thereby coming into conflict with the British. This was nothing new. It had happened during the time of imperial Russia. In fact, the entire history of the last century was, to a considerable degree, a history of Anglo-Russian conflicts. In the Crimean campaign, in the Russo-Turkish wars of 1822 and 1877, in the war with the Caucasus, and finally in all the Central Asian campaigns, Russia faced the Britain of Palmerston, Chamberlain, Kipling, and Curzon, either as an open or as a secret enemy. When the Bolsheviks came to power, this conflict became, if anything, more acute. Tsarist Russia had been a country the British could understand—a country that, while an enemy, had a social and political outlook similar to their own and that could be counted on to observe the norms of classical diplomacy. Tsarist Russia, in other words, had been a country with which the British could talk, negotiate, and even bargain. The Bolsheviks were different. Their revolutionary statements were totally incomprehensible to the empire-oriented British. They were in some ways a greater menace to Britain than were their predecessors, since they could not be forced or persuaded into bargaining for the future of Asia.

Thus, the first thirty years of Bolshevik history also were times of constant and continuous conflict with Great Britain. The Bolsheviks, like the pre-revolutionary Russians, were trying to dethrone Britain from the Straits, to oust her from Iran, to neutralize her influence in Afghanistan, and to knock at the very doors of India, where the situation had become ominous for British interests. But the similarity between Soviet and tsarist Russia ends here. The pre-revolutionary Russians were driven, by the very nature of their political and economic outlook, to aim at displacing British influence in order to pursue a policy more or less similar to that of the British. The Bolsheviks, on the other hand, by the very nature of their revolutionary outlook—at least during most of the interwar period—were driven to a policy of strengthening nationalist governments in independent countries and extending moral and material support to the nationalist movements in countries aspiring to independence. The first thirty years of Soviet history were filled with declarations, proclamations, and appeals, as well as revolutionary and diplomatic activities directed toward the complete isolation and eventual defeat of imperialism.

But, despite these efforts, imperialism was hardly defeated. Britain and France continued to exercise effective control over colonial areas under their domination. And the more vigorous nationalist forces, which were continuously expanding their influence under the impetus of the attractive force of their stated objectives, did not come under Soviet influence. Nor did Soviet influence increase significantly among the nationalist governments, though there is evidence that Soviet moral and material support may have played an important role in the decline of imperialism in these countries.

Immediately after World War II, Europe once again attracted the attention of Soviet leaders; for it was there that the aftermath of war had brought economic dislocation, political instability, and the consequent hope of revolutionary upheavals. Almost half of Europe had come under Soviet control, and the Communist parties of France and Italy had become powerful factors in the political lives of their countries, thereby generating new hopes of kindling revolutionary fires in the heart of Western Europe. But, within two or three years after the war, Soviet hopes of exercising significant influence in Western Europe were dispelled; despite the existence of mass Communist parties in France and Italy, Western Europe, with assistance from the United States, rapidly asserted its determination to remain noncommunist. Europe became stabilized in a brief period of time, irrevocably limiting the range of Soviet maneuvers to minor shifts of orientation in one country or another. A combination of factors had contributed to the stabilization process: the firm resistance of the Western world, the balance of mutual deterrence in the strategic weapons field, and the miraculous economic growth of Western countries.

SOVIET RUSSIA TURNS TO ASIA

The situation in Asia, by contrast, was far from stable. As a result of the stresses and strains engendered by World War II, almost all the countries in the region were undergoing profound revolutionary changes. The decolonization process, to which the Soviet leaders had been giving their continuous support since the Revolution, had set in irrevocably, bringing independence to some countries and assuring it to others.[9] Even more significant for Moscow were the events in China, where the Communist party, relying principally on its own strength, had finally consummated its revolution in 1949, after years of struggle.

The Soviet Union could hardly ignore these developments. To do so would have meant, in effect, to abdicate hegemony to the Communist party of China, which already had moved to arrogate to itself the leadership of the Asian revolutionary world[10] and which had demonstrated its bent toward independent thinking, much to Moscow's displeasure.[11] Moreover, the factors that had underlain the intensive growth of Soviet interest in Europe had undergone a significant evolution. Communist revolutions in the advanced countries of Europe were no longer considered indispensable to the success of communism in the Soviet Union. A succession of five-year plans had transformed the U.S.S.R. into an advanced industrial nation, making it possible for the Soviet leaders boldly to proclaim their entry into the stage of "building communism" within their national borders; the concept that the attainment of communism in the Soviet Union required revolutions in advanced European countries had gone by the board. The Soviet Union had emerged from the war with the undisputed status of a world power, while Britain, France, and Germany had been considerably weakened and had no hope of recovering their prewar status. Moreover, the Soviets no longer regarded Europe with the same fear as during the interwar years; they no longer dreaded an attack from Europe, having effectively brought Eastern Europe under their military and political influence. At the same time, hopes of communizing Western Europe—either through indigenous revolutions or through military pressure—had been dispelled, and the Soviet Union became a fervent advocate of the status quo in Europe.

Obviously, the Soviet Union could no longer assign Asia a secondary role. It could no longer permit its objectives in Europe to determine its policy in Asia. A new assessment of the Asian scene and of the Soviet response to it had become necessary. But the communization of China highly colored the generic Soviet view of the important political changes the rest of Asia was undergoing. The nationalist revolutions, not being of the same dimensions as the changes in China, were considered to be formalistic innovations of no major significance, the main purpose of which was subtly to disguise the continuous presence of the colonial powers.[12] The revolutionary developments in China were for the Soviet leaders convincing proof that communist revolutions were around the corner. Appeals were made, statements were issued from Moscow and through the Cominform, calling upon the Asian Communist parties to seize this opportunity to overthrow the newly independent governments of their countries.

If Moscow was impressed by the unexpected success of the Chinese revolution, it was also perhaps fearful of the important influence Communist China could exercise on the other Asian Communist parties. Such a possibility could not be excluded, in view of the apparent similarities existing among the Asian nations which made the Chinese experiment more relevant to Asian conditions than the one that was taking place in the Soviet Union. An effort was made, therefore, to stress the dangers of considering the Chinese revolution "as some kind of stereotype for people's democratic revolution,"[13] and pressure was exercised on some of the Communist parties to follow the Soviet revolutionary path.[14]

Responding to this militant line, the Asian Communist parties openly and blindly raised the flag of communist revolt without making a rational assessment of the political situations in their countries, and without seriously analyzing their chances for success.[15] The net result of all this revolutionary din was disaster. Many Communist parties in the area were crushed and isolated from the mainstream of political life. For the Soviet Union, this undoubtedly was a serious setback; not only had her capacity to exercise important influence over the continent diminished significantly, but her image as a great friend of Asian nationalism, so sedulously projected since the Bolshevik Revolution, was tarnished. The nationalist leaders, who in the past had looked favorably upon Moscow and had considered the Soviet leaders champions of nationalism, openly manifested their disappointment; some of them did not hesitate to condemn the Soviet policies publicly. Thus, the first time the Soviet Union seriously turned toward Asia, she found herself more isolated than ever; and, instead of obtaining a further diminution of Western influence in Asia, she was now confronted with the prospect of its increase and consolidation.

SHIFT TO MODERATION

Such a serious setback made it imperative for the Soviet leaders to re-examine their policy; and it must have become evident to them that their assessment of the Asian political scene had been influenced largely by the dichotomic situation in Europe rather than by the political reality existing in the area. In the first place, many nationalist leaders and their political parties apparently were too strong and too deeply rooted among the people of their countries to be overthrown by artificially created revolutionary upheavals. And the Communist parties, though sufficiently powerful to create confusion in their respective countries, were not effective enough to take over the reins of power. Second, many of the Asian leaders, having been impressed at some stage of their lives by the Soviet Revolution of 1917, had openly and firmly proclaimed their intention to introduce a much more far-reaching socialist pattern of society in their countries than had ever been intended by the noncommunist leaders of the West. Clearly, this was in many ways a unique situation, and the Soviet leaders' contemptuous identification of it with capitalism not only had demonstrated the extent of Soviet dogmatism but also had exposed a lack of political sophistication—an inability to understand new trends, new thoughts, and new movements.

As a consequence, a rapid change was introduced in Soviet ideological thinking and policy. Although evidence of such a change had begun to appear during the last few months of the Stalinist epoch, new trends became clearly evident after the Bandung Conference in 1955. Rather than strive for immediate control over these areas, Soviet diplomacy now limited its objectives to the task of detaching them from their ties to the "imperialist bloc" and slowly attaching them to the "camp of peace and socialism." The new trend in Soviet policy was defined as "working with the national bourgeoisie," and it was more concerned with influencing the orientation of these leaders in world affairs than with encouraging their overthrow by the local Communist parties.

The situation in Asia being what it was in the middle fifties, it obviously was not possible to pursue a uniform diplomatic action that would encourage the entire area of noncommunist Asia to simultaneously turn to Moscow; for the Asian countries were seriously disunited in their international outlooks. Some were nonaligned, while others had sought alignment with the West. In these circumstances, it was decided to adopt a policy of supporting nonaligned nations in their conflicts against the aligned Asian and Western nations. India was supported against Pakistan on Kashmir. Afghanistan was given unconditional support against Pakistan on the Pakhtoon question. The Arab world was encouraged against Israel; and Indonesia was given complete support against The Netherlands on West New Guinea. By jumping into the maelstrom of Asian politics, by supporting the nonaligned nations, and by morally and materially assisting those nations which had serious difficulties with the

West, Soviet Russia jettisoned the disdainful manner she had adopted toward Asian problems in the past.

Such a policy bore fruit for Soviet diplomacy. A fund of good will rapidly developed among Asian nations that only a few years earlier had viewed policies expounded by Moscow with great skepticism. For instance, the Khrushchev-Bulganin visit to India in 1955, during which the Soviet leaders categorically supported India on the Kashmir question, furbished the Soviet image in that country.[16] Similarly, the Soviet decision to side with the Arab world against Israel and to extend support to Nasser during the Suez Crisis of 1956 was a major breakthrough for the expansion of Soviet influence in the Middle East.[17] By throwing her diplomatic and political weight on the side of one nation against the other, Moscow may have been aggravating international tensions, but this was an important means of establishing effective footholds in Asia.

Such diplomatic actions, however, while effective in ameliorating the Soviet image among the nonaligned nations, were not enough to bring about their orientation toward Moscow. These nations had been inhibited in their efforts at disengagement from the West by their excessive economic dependence on the former colonial powers. Practically all their aid came from the West, and almost all their trade was geared to Western markets. Many nations regarded this as a serious disadvantage but could take no effective action to remedy it, because of the communist world's total lack of interest in developing significant economic relations with Asia. After the death of Stalin, however, and with the inauguration of a friendly policy toward the nonaligned countries, the development of economic relations with them became a key lever of Soviet foreign policy. Important credits were given to these countries, trade was encouraged, and technical assistance was offered. For example, Soviet credits to India, the U.A.R., and Afghanistan constituted 35 per cent of all investments for economic development of these countries between 1956 and 1961.[18] Trade between these countries and the Soviet Union also took a great leap forward. For example, in 1961 one-third of Egyptian exports and slightly under one-twelfth of Indian exports were geared to socialist countries.[19]

In contrast to this policy of moderation toward the non-aligned countries, the Soviet Union continued her militant line against those that were aligned. This apparently was done with the firm conviction that the decision-makers in such countries—unlike those in the nonaligned nations—were holding the reins of power by force and would inevitably tumble under continuous Soviet pressure. Thus military threats were made against these countries, warnings were issued, and opposition elements were encouraged to stage uprisings. All this was of no avail, for such a policy did not lead any of these countries to forsake their relations with the West. If anything, the Soviet threats only emboldened them to turn more and more toward their Western allies to seek even firmer ties with them than before.

THE SINO-SOVIET DISPUTE AND ASIA

With the eruption of the Sino-Soviet dispute in the early sixties, the situation underwent an important change. The international communist movement, which had managed to maintain—despite Yugoslavia's defection—a façade of monolithic unity under Moscow's leadership, was seriously disrupted. Communist China violently criticized Soviet policy on questions of international relations, defiantly challenged Moscow's claim to leadership of the international communist movement, and read the Soviet Union out of the "anti-imperialist front."[20] The differences between the two countries rapidly escalated into a dispute of major proportions. The ferocity with which the two communist giants are today striving to undermine each other's position is as striking as the enthusiasm with which they had once indulged in fulsome praise of each other.

Against this background the Soviet Union had once again to re-examine her over-all policy toward the Asian countries. While the original Soviet objective of seeking a diminution of Western influence in Asia continued to be an aim of Soviet diplomacy, it was no longer the only one. The containment of

Chinese communism was added as a goal. This was clearly a difficult task, for the Soviet Union now had to frame a strategy that would take into account the containment of "right-wing" America and "left-wing" China—a task by no means easy for a country which had been accustomed to formulating a strategy directed solely against the West. Soviet diplomacy responded to the new situation by forging a policy which was more varied, more dexterous, and more far-reaching than the one that had been launched at the Twentieth Congress of the Soviet Communist Party; and it appeared to react very effectively to the diverse political situations that obtained in Asia at the time.

First, the Soviet policy of extending moral and material support to the nonaligned countries was intensified. Economic and military assistance was increased considerably, cultural exchanges were strengthened, and every effort was made by political means to bring these countries closer to Moscow in their diplomatic alignments. The rapidity with which Soviet diplomacy adjusted itself to the rising economic demands of the nonaligned countries is striking—the more so when one considers its marked indifference in this sphere only a few years earlier. Equally striking was the relatively prompt Soviet agreement to participate in major economic projects refused by the West. Assistance in building the first stage of the Aswân Dam was undertaken by Moscow after the United States had decided to withdraw its promise of 56 million dollars to finance the project.[21] Technical and financial assistance was provided for the construction of the Bokaro steel project in India after Washington had reneged on its promise to finance the construction of this plant in the public sector.[22]

If the intensification of economic assistance was a significant development in Soviet diplomacy, the U.S.S.R.'s decision to extricate herself from an immoderate involvement in many conflicting issues faced by some of the nonaligned countries was more notable. In the Pakistani-Afghan dispute on the Pakhtoon question, the Soviet Union ceased to side openly with Afghanistan.[23] On the Cyprus issue, the previous Soviet position of open and unconditional support to the Cypriot government against Turkey was slowly abandoned;[24] and on the Indo-Pakistani dispute over Kashmir, a posture of subtle neutrality was now adopted.[25] In fact, during the Indo-Pakistani conflict of September, 1965, the Soviet leaders went even further: rather than limit their efforts to improve relations with India and Pakistan, they began to display concern over the manner in which the relations between the two countries continued to deteriorate; they began to consider that the advancement of Soviet interest in the subcontinent, as well as in Asia, was closely linked with an improvement of relations between the two countries. Such an attitude led finally to the opening of an important diplomatic offensive to bring the two countries together, to discuss and resolve the issues that divided them. These efforts resulted in the meeting of Ayub Khan and Shastri in Tashkent. The Soviet contribution here was undoubtedly significant; it would be no exaggeration to suggest that without Kosygin's active intervention the formal agreement never would have been reached.

The changed Soviet attitude on such controversial issues is undoubtedly a significant development in Soviet diplomatic practice; this was apparently the first time the Soviet leaders had neither manifested disdain for neutrality on such issues nor taken sides in favor of one nation against the other. The adoption of such a policy not only reflects the growing sophistication in Soviet diplomatic behavior but is perhaps also an important sign of Soviet consensus that this is the only effective way, in the existing circumstances, to aggrandize Soviet diplomatic influence.

Perhaps the most significant change—and one that is likely to have a lasting effect on Soviet diplomatic behavior—is in the realm of Soviet ideology. A decade of post-Stalinist experiences appears to have led the Soviet leadership to adopt a more tolerant attitude toward noncommunist varieties of socialist doctrines. The vital structural changes in many of the nonaligned countries are no longer identified with capitalism; rather, an increasing effort is being made to study them, to ascertain their impact on developing societies, and to determine the extent to which they are different from capitalistic societies. These investigations are colored, of course, by the Marxist proclivities of the Soviet leaders. But the fact that a relatively sober and sophisticated examination of these societies is under way is an indication of the extent of change in Soviet thinking. Ideological innovations included the suggestion that a few Afro-Asian countries, having initially embarked on the "noncapitalist" path of development, were moving toward the more positive and precise goal of "national democracy" and that it was now permissible for Communist parties to co-operate with "revolutionary democrats" under the latter's leadership.[26]

Is it possible that Soviet Marxism might evolve further in the direction of liberal change, responding even more effectively to the realities of the nonaligned world? Is it possible that the radical structural changes that many Afro-Asian leaders are forcefully introducing in their societies may one day be as acceptable as socialism to the Soviet leaders? And is it possible to conceive of Soviet theory evolving to a point where the introduction of socialism is no longer considered as the exclusive responsibility of the Communist parties? Although the Soviet leadership at present would hesitate to accept such prognostications, the possibility of such developments cannot be excluded, considering the magnitude of the changes that have already occurred and the serious discussions that have begun on the whole question among the Marxists.[27]

Important changes also evolved in the Soviet attitude toward some of the aligned nations that were either contiguous to the Soviet Union or not far removed from Soviet territory. Despite considerable Soviet pressure in the past, the leaders of these countries had acquired a certain political stability and had shown surprising immunity from revolutionary upheavals. Therefore, rather than obdurately pursuing the militant line, the Soviets turned to a policy of moderation. Pressure on Iran, for example, was reduced; the long-standing border problem was resolved, and important economic initiatives were taken.[28] The propaganda offensive against Turkey was abandoned; stress was laid on the close relations that had existed between the U.S.S.R. and

Turkey during the time of Kemal Atatürk, and some recognition was extended to Ankara's view on the Cyprus question.[29] Pakistan's disengagement from the West was encouraged; economic relations were developed, and a neutralist attitude was adopted on the Kashmir question.[30] Japan was tempted by important economic contracts.[31] Such a policy resulted in the considerable improvement of relations between Moscow and these countries. With all of them, important economic agreements were concluded, and, with Iran and Pakistan, even the question of military assistance was broached.[32]

It would be an oversimplification to attribute the improvement of Soviet relations with these countries exclusively to the expression of moderation in Soviet policy or to the adeptness with which the Soviet leaders acted; for it is most unlikely that a small nation would be induced to change its attitude toward a big power simply because the latter had become more friendly and more flexible than it had been in the past. Changes in a country's policy stem generally from changes in the international situation. Pakistan had begun to show signs of disengaging from the West because of the apparent reluctance on the part of the United States and Great Britain to give her unconditional and complete support on the Kashmir question.[33] Admittedly, there is evidence to suggest that the West perhaps was more sympathetic to Pakistan's point of view than to India's, but it would nonetheless be difficult to produce evidence of complete support of all that Pakistan did to attain her objectives in Kashmir. Turkey, too, had become disenchanted with the Western countries on the question that concerned her directly: the Western posture of neutrality on the dispute over Cyprus and the United States' decision to withdraw outdated intermediate missiles from Turkish territory were two important factors that led Ankara to disengage to some extent from the West.[34] Iran had begun to see advantages in being less dependent on the West.[35] And Japan had once again become a major power eager to play an independent role in international affairs.[36]

The Soviet Union, there is no doubt, had made great strides among the nonaligned and, to some extent, the aligned nations of Asia. But this relative success was possible only after she had moderated her policies and had softened Leninist formulas in order to adapt them to the changing realities of Asia. Soviet diplomacy thus did not try to outdo the Chinese in revolutionary militancy; on the contrary, Moscow's diplomatic behavior attested to a judgment that moderation was a more effective means of extending Soviet influence and a more efficacious weapon with which to contain both Communist China and the United States.

But what of areas where limited military conflicts have broken out or where the "national liberation struggles" against governments openly allied with the West have been initiated by political forces known for their pro-Soviet proclivities? Is it possible, in such instances, for the Soviet leaders to adopt policies similar to the ones that have been formulated toward the type of developing countries mentioned above? Obviously the line must be drawn here, as the pursuit of such a policy would be tantamount to the virtual abdication of Soviet influence in the violently explosive areas and consequently an exposure of Soviet inability to accept the role of world power for which she has been so sedulously striving since World War II. Furthermore, the U.S.S.R.'s influence among the revolutionary forces would inevitably diminish, and she would become even more vulnerable to the Chinese Communist charge of indifference toward revolutionary wars. In such cases, therefore, the Soviet leaders are obliged to give a military inflection to their policies—particularly where the Chinese Communists are directly active in their revolutionary endeavors. But the military inflection that so far has been given to Soviet policy either has taken the form of militant verbal declarations or, alternatively, has manifested itself in the extension of military aid. The Soviet leaders have been careful to avoid direct embroilment of their armed forces in such conflicts. During the Korean war, the Soviet Union, while willingly extending material support to Communist China and North Korea, was careful to avoid a direct conflict with the United States. Yet, when one examines the history of the period, one is struck by Soviet complicity in the origination of the war. At the time of the Suez Crisis in 1956, the Soviet leaders supported Nasser but publicly threatened to send "volunteers" to the Middle East only after the crisis was virtually over.[37] In the Congo the Soviet Union preferred to operate through the United Nations, despite direct appeals from Patrice Lumumba.[38] Even in Vietnam, which evidently has become a major bone of contention between Peking and Moscow, Soviet involvement is limited to economic and military assistance. It might appear from the language of the declarations emanating from Moscow that the Soviet leaders are resolved to go much further than they permitted themselves to go in the preceding wars of such nature.[39] But this appears unlikely, considering the physical distance that separates the two countries and the serious logistic problem such an intervention would create for the Soviet armed forces. And in past instances, even when the Soviet Union created situations of formal confrontation with the United States, a policy of retreat was invariably adopted once U.S. determination to resist became apparent. In the attempt to drive the Western powers out of Berlin in 1948–49, Stalin created the Berlin blockade; but, in the face of Western determination to airlift food, fuel, and other necessities of life to Berlin, the Soviet leaders gave in and transferred the dispute to the conference table. Unquestionably this was one of the greatest tactical defeats suffered by Soviet foreign policy since World War II. The Soviet retreat from Cuba in 1962 was even more dramatic. The Soviet leaders, faced by American determination, rapidly withdrew the missiles they had installed on Cuban territory—testimony to Soviet cautiousness where direct military involvement is concerned. Thus the Soviet Union so far has avoided direct military confrontation with the United States. If the past is any guide to future Soviet actions, one might suggest that circumspection will continue to govern Soviet military policy.

CONCLUSION

During the interwar period, Europe occupied the principal place in Soviet diplomacy despite the manifestation of considerable doctrinal interest in Asia. But since World War II—particularly after Stalin's death—Soviet interest in Asia has increased steadily. Every year since 1953 the world has witnessed a growing Soviet involvement in the Asian game of politics. Today there is no doubt that the continent of Asia has come to occupy a central place in Soviet diplomacy. Most Soviet aid, technical assistance, and political endeavors appear to be directed toward that continent; and most Soviet speeches and declarations on foreign policy appear to be concerned with Asia and other areas of the Third World.

The shift from Europe to Asia is understandable. In Europe it is no longer possible for the Soviet Union to make diplomatic headway, to increase her influence or break some of the diplomatic deadlocks that continue to haunt that continent. Despite France's disengagement from the United States, despite the remarkable defreezing of economic and cultural barriers between the two blocs, Europe remains partitioned politically and militarily, with no scope for the Soviet Union to advance her political cause on the other side of the barrier. Furthermore, it is hardly possible for Moscow to attract noncommunist Europe by her economic development and social advancement. If anything, it is the European countries of the West which are today inspiring some of the economic and political changes in the socialist countries.

In Asia, on the other hand, it is still possible for Moscow to make headway. The political lines are not sharply drawn, and the Asian countries do not have reason to believe they have nothing to learn from the socialist experiment that has been carried out in the Soviet Union.

This manifestation of deep interest in Asia has resulted in the considerable increase of Soviet influence on that continent—so much so that one might even say that Soviet influence in Asia is as great as that of the United States. But this was achieved only after the Soviet leaders had softened Leninist formulas and had, to some extent, accepted noncommunist varieties of socialist doctrines forcefully expounded by Asian leaders. Asia, in fact, has become such an important factor in Soviet diplomacy that it is deeply influencing Soviet policy toward the West. In light of the unrelenting Chinese criticism of Soviet leadership as insufficiently militant, possibilities of substantive settlements with the West in Europe appear to have diminished. Any Soviet dealings with the "imperialists" are immediately exploited by the Chinese as "capitulationism," thereby effectively impeding the Soviet leadership's quest for détente with the West.

While the conflict in Southeast Asia has made it difficult for the Soviet Union to take steps to improve relations with the West, it has not deterred Moscow from continuing a moderate policy toward the majority of noncommunist countries of Asia. Soviet relations with these countries continue to develop on an even keel precisely because of Soviet moderation. However, in those areas where conflict exists—for instance, in Vietnam—the Soviet Union has given more militant meaning to her ambiguous doctrine of support for "wars of national liberation," which sanctions Soviet military assistance. Although the Sino-Soviet dispute and the attendant Chinese charge that Moscow lacks enthusiasm for local revolutionary initiatives have led the Soviet Union to intensify her military assistance in Vietnam, Moscow continues to practice restraint in its diplomatic policy. Nonetheless, it must be admitted that the revolutionary upheavals, now complicated by Peking's rampageous hostility, have brought many risks that the Soviet leaders could not have imagined when they thrust themselves on the Asian scene after 1953.

NOTES

1. For details, see M. T. Florinsky, *World Revolution and the USSR* (New York: Macmillan, 1933), *passim*.

2. V. I. Lenin, *The National Liberation Movement in the East* (Moscow: Foreign Languages Publishing House, 1957), p. 238.

3. *Ibid.*, p. 240.

4. *Ibid.*, p. 244.

5. For an interesting account of the national-colonial question discussed at the Second Congress see G. D. Parikh, in *M. N. Roy's Memoirs* (Bombay: Allied Publishers, 1964), pp. 368–82.

6. For details see *Pervyi s'ezd narodov Vostoka: Baku 1–8 sentiabria 1920. Stenograficheskie otchety* (Moscow, 1920), *passim*.

7. For details see *The First Congress of the Toilers of the Far East held in Moscow January 21–February 1, 1922: Closing Session in Petrograd, February 2, 1922* (Petrograd: *The Communist International,* 1922), *passim.*

8. V. I. Lenin, "Preliminary Thesis on the National-Colonial Question," *Selected Works,* vol. X (London: Lawrence and Wishart, Ltd., 1938), p. 237.

9. E. M. Zhukov, who emerged as the principal spokesman on colonial affairs after the war, viewed the revolutions in the colonies as of major consequence. For a detailed view see "Velikaia Oktiabr'skaia Sotsialisticheskaia Revoliutsiia i kolonialnyi Vostok," *Bolshevik* (Moscow), October, 1946.

10. In a speech to the Trade Union Conference of Asian and Australasian representatives on November 16, 1948, Liu Shao-chi predicted that revolutions in Asia would follow "the path of the Chinese people" (*New China News Agency,* November 23, 1949).

11. Following the communist-Kuomintang split in 1927, the Communist party of China, thrown largely on its own resources, developed an indigenous strategy of armed revolution organized from rural bases which was not acceptable to the Soviet leadership. For a detailed theoretical review of this strategy, see Benjamin Schwartz, *Chinese Communism and the Rise of Mao* (Cambridge, Mass.: Harvard University Press, 1951), *passim.*

12. Soviet attitudes toward the newly independent countries were extensively discussed at the Orientalist Conference in June, 1949. Summaries of the reports read at the conference are found in *Colonial People's Struggle for Liberation: Reports to the Institute of Economics and Pacific Institute of the Academy of Sciences* (Bombay: People's Publishing House Ltd., 1949), *passim.*

13. Questioning the universal application of the Chinese model to all new nations, E. Zhukov said at the conference of Orientalists in November, 1951: "It is risky to regard the Chinese revolution as some kind of 'stereotype' for People's Democratic Revolution in other countries of Asia." The summary of the speech is translated in *Current Digest of the Soviet Press,* IV, no. 20 (1952), pp. 3–7.

14. The Communist party of India was pressed in 1948 to follow the Soviet path of revolution.

15. For details see Frank N. Trager, ed., *Marxism in Southeast Asia* (Stanford, Calif.: Stanford University Press, 1959), *passim.*

16. G. D. Overstreet and M. Windmiller, *Communism in India* (Berkeley and Los Angeles: University of California Press, 1959), p. 460.

17. For the rise of Soviet influence in the Middle East see Ivar Spector, *The Soviet Union and the Muslim World, 1917–1958* (Seattle: University of Washington Press, 1959), pp. 222–38.

18. V. Rymalov, *La Collaboration économique de L'URSS avec les sous- developpés* (Moscow: Editions en Langues Etrangères, 1961), p. 47.

19. For details concerning the U.A.R.'s economic relations with Soviet Russia and other socialist countries see Baard Richard Stokke, *Soviet and East European Trade and Aid in Africa* (New York: Frederick A.

Praeger, 1967), pp. 103–42. For India's economic relations with the U.S.S.R. see *East European Trade,* no. 22 (January, 1965), published every month in New Delhi.

20. For details see *The Polemic on the General Line of the International Communist Movement* (Peking: Foreign Languages Press, 1965), *passim.*

21. I. Komzin, *The High Aswân Dam* (Moscow: Foreign Languages Publishing House, n.d.), pp. 6–7.

22. *East European Trade,* no. 22 (January, 1965), p. 43.

23. Though it would be difficult to produce an exact text indicating changes in Soviet policy, it is evident that the Soviet leaders extricated themselves from an immoderate involvement on the Pakhtoon question by giving less and less importance to the whole question in Soviet declarations and publications.

24. *Le Monde* (Paris), December 25–26, 1966.

25. Harish Kapur, "The Soviet Union and Indo-Pakistani Relations," *International Studies* (New Delhi), July-October, 1966.

26. *World Marxist Review* (Prague), February, 1963, p. 41.

27. See Uri Ra'anan, "Moscow and the Third World," *Problems of Communism* (Washington, D.C.), January-February, 1965.

28. On January 16, 1966, agreements on economic and technical cooperation were signed; *Soviet News* (London), March 3, 1966.

29. During his visit to Turkey in December, 1966, Kosygin stated that any solution of the Cypriot question must "respect the legal rights of the two communities, the Turks and Greeks in Cyprus," *Le Monde,* December 25-26, 1966.

30. The *Novosty Press Agency* (Moscow) is reported to have released a statement on November 12, 1965, through the Soviet Embassy in Pakistan, which concluded with the following significant paragraph: "The only thing desired by the Soviet Government is the establishment of stable peace between Pakistan and India, and as far as this basic desire is concerned, the Soviet Government equally appeals to the leaders of Pakistan as well as India to display wisdom restraint and patience. The Soviet people are convinced that only under these conditions, not on the battlefield, but at the round table of peaceful negotiations can and should a final and stable agreement be reached between Pakistan and India on the Kashmir question." For the complete text see *Thought* (New Delhi), November 27, 1965.

31. In January, 1966, when a Japanese trade delegation was in Moscow, the Soviet government is reported to have stated that it does not exclude the co-operation of the two countries in exploiting the vast resources in Siberia. In fact, Tass (Moscow), the Soviet News Agency, published a statement in which it said that the "participation of Japanese firms in Soviet plans of development would be profitable to both countries" (see *Le Monde,* March 12, 1966).

32. Although a military agreement with Pakistan has not been reached, an important military agreement with Iran was concluded in February, 1967; see *New York Times,* February 20, 1967.

INDEX

Designed by Gerard A. Valerio

Composed in Times Roman text
by Baltimore Type and Composition Corporation

Printed offset by The Murray Printing Company
on Clearspring Book Offset

Bound by Moore & Company, Inc.